PLANNING AND URBAN GROWTH:
AN ANGLO-AMERICAN COMPARISON

Planning and Urban Growth:

an anglo-american comparison

Marion Clawson and Peter Hall

Published for
Resources for the Future, Inc.
by
The Johns Hopkins University Press, Baltimore and London

Copyright © 1973 by The Johns Hopkins University Press
All rights reserved
Manufactured in the United States of America

The Johns Hopkins University Press, Baltimore, Maryland 21218
The Johns Hopkins University Press Ltd., London

Library of Congress Catalog Card Number 72-12364
ISBN 8018-1496-0

Library of Congress Cataloging in Publication data will be found on the last printed page of this book.

preface

This book is the capstone to two major research efforts of the past five or six years. Political and Economic Planning (PEP), a nonprofit research and planning organization in Britain, has made a comprehensive study of urban growth, including planning, in Britain; particular attention has been focused on the developments of the period since the end of World War II and more particularly on the working of the 1947 Town and Country Planning Act. The results of that study are being published by Allen and Unwin in two volumes in 1973, under the overall title *The Containment of Urban England*, by Peter Hall, Harry Gracey, Roy Drewett, and Ray Thomas; Volume One, *Urban and Metropolitan Growth Processes, or Megalopolis Denied*, and Volume Two, *The Planning System: Objectives, Operations, and Impacts*. As this study progressed, three reports by Ray Thomas were published by PEP: Broadsheet 504, *Journeys to Work*, November 1968; Broadsheet 510, *London's New Towns: A Study of Self-Contained and Balanced Communities*, April 1969; and Broadsheet 516, *Aycliffe to Cumbernauld: A Study of Seven New Towns in Their Regions*, December 1969.

Concurrently, Resources for the Future (RFF), a nonprofit American research organization concerned with the economic and social aspects of natural resource use, has conducted a study of urbanization, and more particularly of suburbanization, in the United States during approximately the same time period. The results of its research were published in 1971 by The Johns Hopkins University Press in the book *Suburban Land Conversion in the United States: An Economic and Governmental Process*. Throughout the conduct of the British and American studies, the respective research teams conferred at intervals. This cooperative relationship has been beneficial to each book and especially to this capstone book, which had been planned from the beginning. The necessity to explain to one another the many aspects of the domestic scene that differ from those prevailing in the other country has been salutary for all persons connected with the project.

The books mentioned above are moderately detailed and technical; they marshal data, examine critically the meaning of these data, and draw conclusions about urban development in each country. Each includes many references to relevant professional literature, especially in the subject country but to some extent in other countries as well. Because the evidence has been presented as carefully as possible in those books, the present book can be rather different. It draws heavily on the parent books, it states general relationships and conclusions and, except where necessary to provide basic information as underpinning for more general discussion, it keeps detailed analysis to the minimum. The interested reader, particularly specialists of various kinds, may find it desirable to consult the other books if he wishes to know more about how certain data were obtained or analyzed, or if he wishes to know about other professional literature on the subject.

At the same time, the present book is more than a mere summarization of the parent books. Researchers always learn more than they are able to include in their basic research reports; the authors feel they have acquired an understanding of urban growth and related problems in each country that goes somewhat beyond what is written in the basic books resulting from the related projects. The current book includes many judgments and interpretations which flow from the earlier research but which previously may not have been stated explicitly. In addition, when it seemed that a comparative analysis called for it, we have introduced some new materials. Where our discussion flows rather directly from the earlier books, we have not generally cited the sources. Where we have used new materials, we have more commonly given their sources. Since one of our objectives was to restrict the length of the present book and to keep the style as simple and direct as possible, we have omitted some footnote citations and discussions that would have been included in a more technical treatment.

The basic research on which the parent books rest was carried out before 1970; hence the 1970 Census data for the United States and the 1971 Census data for Britain could not be used in them. Instead, those books were based upon the 1960 Census for the United States and the 1961 and 1966 Censuses for Britain, as well as upon many other sources of information in each country. Without substantially delaying the present book and investing substantial additional research time in its preparation, it was not possible to make a new analysis in each country using the latest censuses. Consequently, our basic analysis here rests on data for 1960 and 1961, with such updating as is readily possible from the 1970 and 1971 censuses.

* * * *

The authors wish to acknowledge the help they have had from numerous persons, in particular from Ray Thomas, Roy Drewett, and Harry L. Gracey, senior members of the PEP research team; George A. McBride, J. B. Wyckoff, Gerald L. Cole, and Gerald F. Vaughn of the RFF research team; John Delafons, David Donnison, Frederick Gutheim, Lord Holford, Maynard M. Hufschmidt, Max Nicholson, Wilfred Owen, Lloyd Rodwin, Gerald Smart, and Melvin M. Webber, who read a draft manuscript and offered us useful and trenchant comments; Anne Whalley and Bob Peacock, who provided invaluable research assistance on the British side; Diantha Stevenson, who typed numerous drafts with care and competence in the RFF offices; and Vera W. Dodds, to whose editing this book owes much of the clarity we have sought and the style we have hoped for. To all of these, our deepest thanks; we alone, of course, are responsible for any errors or inaccuracies that may remain.

The PEP study, on which this book is partly based, was financed in large part by a grant from the Leverhulme Trust.

Washington and London
August 1972

MARION CLAWSON AND PETER HALL

contents

LIST OF TABLES

LIST OF FIGURES

LIST OF PLATES

Photographs of United States scenes by Louis B. Schlivek, Regional Plan Association. Photographs of British scenes, except No. 6, by Aerofilms Ltd.

PLANNING AND URBAN GROWTH:
AN ANGLO-AMERICAN COMPARISON

introduction

Over the centuries cities have grown as economic output rose, as transport improved, and as sanitation and other measures made it possible for larger numbers of people to live in close proximity to one another. But large-scale urbanization is a relatively recent phenomenon in world history. Homer Hoyt has estimated that in 1800 only slightly more than 1 percent of the world's population lived in cities of 100,000 or more population, but that by 1960 the proportion had grown to 20 percent of the total.[1] In that year, 42 percent of the people of the Americas lived in these large cities, but in Asia the proportion similarly urbanized was only 12 percent and in Africa it was only 8 percent. At whatever date, if the urban cutoff point were lower than Hoyt's 100,000—at the 2,500 level which defines "urban" in the United States, for instance—the percentages would be much larger.

The pace of urbanization has picked up sharply in the past decade or two, especially in the economically less-developed countries. There, improvement in health conditions has lowered deathrates while birthrates have remained unchanged, thus leading to rapid increases in total population. Economic and social opportunities in the rural areas have been, or have seemed, less attractive than in the cities, and rural people have flocked to the cities. Man, as a species, is congregating himself into urban complexes at a rate and on a scale that leaves the ultimate result much in doubt today. Within many of these complexes decentralization, or movement toward the suburbs, is going on simultaneously, especially in the higher-income countries.

One aspect of this worldwide urbanization is the emergence of "world cities."[2] Such cities are usually centers of political power, both national and international; this attracts a host of institutions whose business is dealing with government; they are typically centers of trade, often are seaports, and today possess great international airports as well. Such cities have also typically become centers for professional talents in medicine, law, science, arts, and literature. They are centers of wealth and power, a position that gives them influence beyond that of the size of their population alone. Hall identifies twenty-four metropolitan centers in the world with 3 million or more population in 1960 (or in the nearest year for which data were available), but he considers only seven of these large metropolitan centers as truly "world cities." He shows that not only have these cities grown in total

---

[1] Homer Hoyt, "The Growth of Cities from 1800 to 1960 and Forecasts to Year 2000," *Land Economics*, vol. XXXIX, no. 2 (May 1963).
[2] Peter Hall, *The World Cities* (New York: McGraw-Hill, World University Library, and London: Weidenfeld & Nicolson, 1966).

population since about 1800, but they have grown greatly as a percentage of their respective national populations. For instance, between 1800 and 1961 London grew from less than a million to 11½ million, or from 8 percent of the national population to 22 percent; Moscow grew from less than half a million to nearly 8 million, or from 0.5 percent to nearly 4 percent; and New York grew from only 60,000 to nearly 15 million, or from about 1 percent to over 8 percent of the national population. Hall concludes that these large world cities will absorb increasingly large proportions of national population in the future, and that other smaller but still very large world metropolises will develop, so that, desirable or not, an increasing proportion of the world's population will be found in very large groupings of people.

The urbanization of Western Europe, North America, and a few other rapidly developing parts of the world in the nineteenth and early twentieth centuries was a part of the industrialization then going on. Industries could often best develop in cities; a labor supply, sufficiently close under the transportation conditions of the day, was one essential; so were raw materials and markets. Industries either developed in established cities, or provided the impetus for the creation of cities. Thus, in 1801 Birmingham (England) was a small city of only 71,000 people, but the industrialization based upon nearby deposits of coal and iron made the center into a major agglomeration of nearly 3 million by 1961. Many forces have drawn people to the growing cities, but availability of jobs has surely been one major attraction. Throughout this period of the Industrial Revolution, up to perhaps World War I, industry provided a substantial proportion of the new jobs, and services to industrial workers provided many of the other jobs.

The current massive urbanization, especially in the economically less-developed countries, is different. Such countries are having great difficulty in developing viable industries; the economies of scale in manufacturing and marketing make it most difficult for new industry to compete with long-established industries in older industrial countries. But, even in the latter, employment within industry is not rising much, if at all; in the United States, for instance, total employment in industry seems to have hit a plateau in recent years at a level well under double what it was as long ago as World War I. In Britain during the 1950s and 1960s, manufacturing has employed a declining proportion of the labor force. New technologies often require more capital but employ less labor, while total value of output mounts. The largest rise in employment in economically advanced countries has been in business (such as banking, insurance, and the like) and in services of many kinds; but the lower-income countries do not have the mass purchasing power to support extensive development of such employments.

In highly urbanized countries like Britain and the United States, migration is no longer a major force in city-building simply because the nonurban areas lack enough people to provide the kinds of migrant streams they provided in the past— their large cities must increasingly grow of their own demographic processes. But the city growth of the less economically advanced countries, which is both so impressive and so appalling, is largely a matter of migration from non-city areas. Migration is always a net resultant of both push and pull—push away from the areas of origin, pull into areas of destination. However difficult it is to measure these forces of push and pull, it seems that the earlier city-building of the presently economically advanced countries was primarily a matter of pull—the attraction of jobs, often in industry, and an attraction that existed in spite of some highly undesirable living conditions in cities of that day; and it seems that much migration to the rapidly growing cities of the presently economically less-developed countries today is more a matter of push. Living conditions in the nonurban areas are, in total, worse than living conditions in the cities, however unattractive the latter may appear to many of us.

Urbanization and the migration upon which early urban growth was based are complex economic, social, cultural, and political processes. Differences in money income or in real income are one factor, but only one; differences in living style may far outweigh economic factors. Moreover, while the average of all the migrants to a city may be no better off than they would have been had they stayed in the nonurban area, yet some may achieve a degree of relative affluence that would have been impossible without migration—the prospect of the big gain outweighs the average probabilities. And poor people around the world have learned that they have political power in the cities to wring concessions from their governments, which they could never attain in rural areas. Even in such economically developed countries as Britain and the United States, migration from rural to urban areas, or continued residence in the latter for those born there, depends on far more than a simple comparison of incomes at each location.

The modern city is the scene of complex interrelationships, both of an economic and physical kind. Cities are, above all, places where specialization in employment occurs. Various persons perform tasks for a substantial clientele—tasks that are highly specialized and hence would be valueless in a country that was not economically advanced. Consumers obtain goods and services from a large number of suppliers. Often these goods and services represent only a small part of their total consumption, and their purchases in turn may be only a small proportion of the sales of their suppliers, yet without this kind of specialized economic interchange the modern city would have little rationale for existence. It is noteworthy that when a city is largely destroyed by war or by some natural disaster such as a flood or earthquake, the city rebuilds in the same location, often to the same pattern. The economic web of actions and interactions among groups and persons is as nearly invisible as are the subterranean structures that serve the city, yet it is extremely powerful.

The social structure of the modern city is equally complex. Social relations may take many forms involving many interests. They may range from the most friendly, as among the members of an extended family, to outright warfare, as between rival gangs. All major cities of the world have organized crime, including drug traffic and prostitution. The social strength of the city lies in its cultural diversity, in its variety of life styles. The individual may have many choices as well as many constraints.

The modern city also has a complex political structure, regardless of the country, state, or province in which it lies. Many of the services of the city must be provided by government in some form—water supply, waste disposal, fire fighting, police protection, education, and many others indispensable to any modern functioning city. The city officials may be elected by the citizenry, or they may receive their power from some higher level of government. Political contests among parties or groups with divergent interests, or among rivals intent on personal power and position, may or may not lead to better government. Alliances among interest groups may be open or concealed, and may be directed toward winning of elections and good government or toward defrauding others in some way. It is far from unknown, for instance, for police to be in effective collaboration with criminals.

Physically, economically, socially, and politically, a modern functioning city has been built incrementally. Land was converted from some rural to some urban land use, parcel by parcel or area by area; buildings were constructed, one at a time, each conditioned by as well as conditioning the buildings on surrounding land; economic ties have been developed over the years as customers have been won, sources of supply discovered, and accommodations of sorts reached with rivals; social ties of all kinds evolve, often slowly; and the political line-up today may reflect political history as much as it does today's interest relationships. This is not to deny the influence of city planning, at least in some cases. But the planning must start with the city as it has grown over the past and as it now exists; and new developments must be added to this existing structure. Both positively and negatively, the heritage of the past is very great: past investments have created values, not only for the object of the investment but for other properties and other people as well, and the economic and social life has inherent strength and value. This heritage may be ill-adapted to present needs, yet difficult to change.

Scope, Content, and Orientation of the Book

This book does not attempt to deal with the modern city in all its complexity; perhaps that is too large a task for any single book. Here we are concerned primarily with urban land use in two countries, and more particularly with land use changes whereby cities grow and expand. This focus, however, necessitates some consideration of a number of closely related matters, among them population growth and movement, employment and work force, housing, and the land market. These matters have been included to the extent that they are relevant to the central theme of land use change. Since the region of greatest land use change is the suburb, particular attention is given to that area. Extensive study and analysis are given to the processes whereby some one person or combination of persons arrives at a decision and is able to implement that decision—for instance, to build dwellings or other structures on certain land while passing up other land.

The study is concerned primarily with Britain and the United States. However, as will be shown in chapter 3, two very similar and largely urbanized areas in each country can be identified for special analysis. In the United States, an area along the Atlantic Coast has exactly the same acreage and very nearly the same population as does England and Wales; the overall man-land ratios are closely similar for the two areas. American law, systems of land tenure, and systems of government owe much to their British origin, although there are differences, particularly in government. A direct comparison of urban planning, land use controls, urban growth and development, and related matters reveals much that is of interest and value to the people of both countries.

Several reasons underlie this emphasis on land use. For one thing, urban land is valuable and scarce; there is no overall scarcity of land for urban development in either country, but choicely located land is scarce and always will be—it is a valuable resource, to be conserved and used wisely. But a great many other aspects of the modern city are closely related to land use. Almost all city planning in each country has started with current land use and includes some plan or prescription for future land use; other aspects of future urban growth are then related to the expected pattern of land use or are factors molding it. If one wishes to control the form of the future city, then perhaps control over land use is one of the more promising methods. The struggles between interest groups within cities, or between the city and the surrounding countryside, have frequently focused on land use or on proposed changes in land use.

This book is not the place for an extended analysis of the future of the city as a form of human settlement pattern. Nevertheless, an evaluation of past urban growth, including an evaluation of planning for such growth, must implicitly, if not explicitly, be based upon some notion of the future of the city. Mankind seems to be moving toward ever greater concentration in cities, especially in large cities; so that within a generation urban concentrations of 10 million or more persons, unknown until a few decades ago and still relatively uncommon, may mushroom in many areas of the world. All sober projections of future population numbers and distribution contemplate vastly more rapid growth rates in urban than in total population. Many of the economically developed countries today have urbanization ratios (measured somewhat differently and not always precisely) around the general order of 80 percent. Though far less urban today, the economically less-developed countries are moving up rapidly. Will the whole world become about 80 percent urban? How much of this projected urban growth will be in relatively large cities, and how much in smaller ones? These are questions for which no one has final answers, nor need we be concerned here with quantitative projections. Suffice it to say that every indication today is for a vastly increased urban population in the world of tomorrow.

There has been much interest in both Britain and the United States in the potentialities of "new towns," or cities developed where there were none before, or of larger cities developed from smaller ones or villages. However, based on the evidence in chapter 6, it appears extremely unlikely that new towns, even if pushed at a rate not now probable, can absorb a major part of the anticipated urban population growth in either economically developed or less-developed countries. While rebuilding of older city centers is urgently needed in Britain and the United States —as well as elsewhere in the world—the rebuilding may not accommodate many more people and often will accommodate fewer than at present. The projected growth in urban population, therefore, must be accompanied by a large increase in urban acreage. Whether the latter should be proportional to the increase in population, or more, or less, is an important issue in itself. But areal expansion of cities as a whole seems inevitable, thus focusing attention on the processes by which such expansion is decided, the mechanisms by which it is brought about, and the results of alternative approaches. That is what this book is all about.

In the course of the following chapters one theme will clearly emerge: the conventional picture of British and U.S. urban development is generally correct. In spite of many similarities of geography, economics, and government, Britain and the United States have greatly different—even fully opposite—attitudes toward the form of desirable urban growth. While the United States has permitted and even encouraged low-density, discontiguous urban growth that leapfrogs into the countryside around the cities, Britain since World War II has operated a quite strict and notably successful policy of urban containment. The contrast is particularly striking, because in many other respects both countries have experienced similar social and economic trends, and both have shared some common policies; thus both have had rising populations and more households, rising affluence, and higher car ownership, and both have in effect encouraged mass owner occupancy of single-family homes. Many of the forces working for rapid urban spread, in other words, have been present in both countries; but in Britain they have been countered by a strong and effective system of physical planning, which has not been present in the United States.

This feature necessarily makes the treatment of the historical record slightly different for the two countries. Whereas in the United States planning has had only a slight impact on urban growth, in Britain it has been crucial. Consequently, in discussing the background to urban growth in the next two chapters, a special feature will be made of the planning system that was set up in Britain after World War II; for the United States, no such extended treatment will be necessary.

Our purpose is to present, so far as it is possible in a book of modest length, a comprehensive view of the urbanization and suburbanization processes of Britain and the United States. The ubiquitous growth of large urban centers has proceeded rapidly in these two countries in the past generation and longer; it has been the subject of much legislation and public action in each country. How much, and where, have cities grown; what is their form and use of land; by what processes are decisions made to expand and to convert some land from rural to urban uses? These are the questions to which this book is directed.

In general, the book is directed to the informed and interested person concerned with urbanization and the attendant range of economic and social problems. In particular, it is directed to a variety of professional groups, including economists, urban planners, geographers, political scientists, and others. The style has been chosen to communicate with the expected varied audience; professional jargon and complicated analytical techniques have been kept to a minimum, and the treatment has been broad. The book has been written in the hope that it will be read with equal interest in both countries, as well as in others; terms or words common in one country have been, as far as possible, translated into terms and words fully understood in the other. Each of the authors has tried to keep in mind the fact that he was writing, in part, for the reader who does not fully share his terminology, his understanding of common economic and social conditions in his country, or his knowledge of governmental processes in his country.

Country Definitions

This book is primarily a comparison of planning and urban growth in two countries; hence it is essential at the beginning to define and briefly to describe the two countries, especially their governmental structure.

American readers should be informed that *England and Wales* is the smallest unit of central government in the other country. Some national legislation applies only to England and Wales together or to each separately. For some statistical, planning, or other purposes, certain regional divisions of England and Wales are recognized (e.g., West Midlands, North West, etc.), but these do not have separate elected governmental bodies or otherwise exercise governmental powers.[3] The next larger national area is *Great Britain*; in addition to England and Wales, it includes Scotland. Some legislation applies only to Scotland, and some governmental powers reside in Scotland separately from England and Wales. A still larger national unit is *United Kingdom*; in addition to the foregoing areas, it includes Northern Ireland. (There are also the dependencies of the Isle of Man and the Channel Islands of Jersey, Guernsey, and others; but these are not included in any of the data or the discussions in this book.)

The situation as to local government in Great Britain is confusing to an American, in part because there are ancient cities and counties, now rendered largely obsolete by newer administrative counties and by county boroughs, which are (de facto if not de jure) really cities; and in part because local government in Britain is in a stage of conversion which by 1974 will establish metropolitan and nonmetropolitan counties. The relationship between the administrative counties, which have extensive planning authority but usually include no large city even though they may include a great deal of suburban land and population, and the county boroughs, which are in effect the larger cities, is spelled out in some detail in some of the chapters of this book. A useful oversimplification is to say that the county boroughs have the people and the administrative counties have the land, and therein lie most of the conflicts of land planning as well as some of the results. The above terminology and description applies particularly to England and Wales; the terminology in Scotland is somewhat different, though the practice is rather similar.

The foregoing is a description of the British local government system in the period 1945–72—the period studied in this book. In April 1974 a new system will take its place. Within England, the major urban agglomerations will be administered by metropolitan counties responsible for broad land use and transportation planning, and metropolitan districts for most other purposes. Outside these there will be nonmetropolitan counties, usually but not invariably following the lines of the former administrative counties, plus nonmetropolitan county districts. In both metropolitan and nonmetropolitan counties the county authority will be responsible only for drawing up broad structure plans; detailed local plans within the framework of the structure plans, as well as control over new development in conformity with both sets of plans, will normally become the responsibility of the district authorities. Thus everywhere planning responsibilities will be shared between two tiers of local government; the independent county boroughs will be abolished. With allowances for local geography, the reform in Wales will be similar to that in England. That in Scotland will be a bit different: broad regional authorities will

---

[3] They have advisory Regional Economic Planning Councils reporting to central government, serviced by Regional Economic Planning Boards of officials. Each region also has a standing conference, or similar body of constituent local planning authorities—an informal, non-statutory body—to discuss regional planning matters.

cover wide areas around the major urban agglomerations, and there will be bigger districts at the second-tier level than in England.

In this book our standard term is *Britain*, an abbreviation for Great Britain. We use it when describing legislation, governmental procedures, housing conditions, or other facts or relationships that apply generally to Great Britain as contrasted with the United States. We also use the term *Britain* for statistics or situations that apply specifically to Great Britain. In some instances, data are available only for England and Wales or only for the United Kingdom. In others, data for one of these national areas seemed more appropriate than others for the comparisons we were making. In each case, we have used the term specifically applicable to the data or situation.

British readers should realize that the United States is a federal system of government. The U.S. government has specific legal powers stated or clearly implied in the Constitution; all other legal and governmental powers "are reserved to the States or respectively to the people," as the Constitution states it. The interpretation of the Constitution has changed over the decades and it has been amended; nevertheless, at any moment in time the Constitution, as interpreted by the Supreme Court, establishes the range of legal power of the federal government. There are now fifty states, but Alaska and Hawaii were admitted as states only in 1959; statistical data prior to that year generally do not include them, unless adjustments are made; there are special situations in each of these states, particularly the immense area of land in Alaska that is unique in its location and physical characteristics. As a result, some data and comparisons in the following chapters are for the older forty-eight contiguous states only.

In this book we use the terms *United States, U.S.,* and *American* more or less interchangeably, either to describe the U.S. situation in general and as contrasted with the British situation, or specifically to mean the fifty states. When our data or discussions relate only to the older contiguous forty-eight states, we have so indicated. The United States has some dependencies—Puerto Rico, the Virgin Islands, and some Trust Territories in the Pacific—but these are generally excluded from the statistical data and from consideration in our discussions.

States in the United States have many legal or governmental powers, most or all of which are spelled out in their respective constitutions. State laws differ substantially in important respects, and they cover a large part of the total governmental structure in the nation. Some legal powers have been delegated by the states to cities and counties or to other units of local government (e.g., school districts). For the purposes of this book, the most important delegation of power from states to local governments has been that of land use regulation and control; with some exceptions, such powers are available to and exercised by local government, although the extent of such power differs considerably from state to state, and sometimes according to county or city size and type within a state. These land use control powers are exercised by local governments with little or no effective control or supervision from either state or federal government. We use the rather cumbersome term *local government* to mean either cities or counties or both.

chapter **1**

The setting for urbanization
in the United States

In the quarter century since the close of World War II
there has been a massive urbanization or, more properly, a suburbanization, of the
United States. The national rate of population growth has been moderately high
during this period—of the general magnitude of 1.5 to 1.8 percent annually until
the later years, when it declined to not much more than 1.0 percent. This was a
sharp reversal of the trend to lower rates of population increase that had prevailed
prior to the war. Nearly all the increase has taken place in cities, or in urban
groupings of population some of which lie outside the legal boundaries of any city.
Much of rural America has lost population; in each of the three decades of the
1940s, 1950s, and 1960s, about half of all counties in the United States lost population, and many others had lesser rates of net migration outward. In chapter 4,
we shall show that similar changes have been under way in Britain.

But within the cities or urban groupings the movement of population has been
outward, toward the suburbs. Since the mid-1940s many cities, both large and
small, have failed to gain significantly within their borders, and some have actually
lost population. The movement to the suburbs has racial, social, and economic
aspects, which will be explored later in this chapter. But the significant point here
is that the population concentration apparent at the national scale becomes a population dispersion at the local or metropolitan scale.

These postwar changes in settlement pattern are the intensification of trends long
under way. During the nineteenth century, settlement in the present United States
spread from a strip perhaps 200 miles wide along the eastern coast, to the entire
midcontinent. Forests were cleared, prairies plowed, farms developed, railroads
built, and towns and cities developed. Even in the earliest pioneer years in each
region there were cities—small by modern standards, yet highly significant in their
trade, social, and political aspects, and sometimes containing a substantial proportion of the small population of rather large regions. And throughout this long
period there had been migration of young men and women from the farms to

the cities; during the early decades, in fact, the cities grew only because of this migration, their own birthrates being inadequate for much net growth.

In the United States, the term *urban* was long defined to mean that persons lived in towns and cities with 2,500 or more people. By this standard, urbanization has advanced steadily throughout American history. In 1850, about a sixth of the population was thus urban; by the time of World War I, half was urban and half rural (figure 1). By 1950, the old definition was no longer appropriate; substantial numbers of people outside the legal boundaries of cities were nevertheless living in clearly urban settlement patterns. Accordingly, the definition was revised to reflect actual settlement pattern rather than legal boundaries, and the proportion of the population that was urbanized was raised by about 4 percent in the process. On this basis, by 1970 almost three-fourths of the total population was urban.

The definition of "urban" is different in England and Wales, where an administrative ruling determines that certain areas are "urban" regardless of how many of their inhabitants are located in an urban settlement pattern. In general, all conurbations (large urbanized areas), county boroughs (cities), municipal boroughs (smaller cities), and urban districts and Greater London are classified as urban. All the rest of the country is nonurban, although it may contain substantial settlements of an essentially urban form. Urbanization in England and Wales, by this definition, greatly preceded urbanization in the United States. In 1851, for example, England and Wales were half urbanized, a situation that did not exist in the United

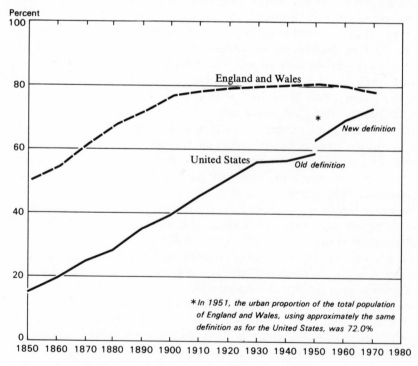

FIGURE 1. Proportion of total population that is urban—England and Wales and the United States, 1850–1970.

States until more than sixty years later at the time of World War I. But urbanization in England and Wales reached a plateau by 1920; recent changes suggest some slight decline, rather than further increase. One must be hesitant to draw close comparisons between the two countries as far as level of urbanization is concerned, because of the definitional differences. An attempt in 1951 to estimate urbanization in England and Wales on the same basis as in the United States produced a figure several percentage points below the usual British definition. One may tentatively conclude that at present the two countries are about equally urbanized, and at a level unlikely to increase much further in the future, in part because there is relatively little population not now urbanized.

A flag of warning should be raised here: much data about urban population is based upon changing definitions of the cities themselves. Because most American cities have expanded their boundaries, data on their populations do not relate to the same land area over a long period of time. This process has been more common and on a larger scale than is generally appreciated, even by students of urban development. For instance, there were eighteen cities in the United States in 1950 with 500,000 or more inhabitants; their total populations rose about threefold from 1890 to 1960, but their total land area increased nearly two and a half times, thus density (on the basis of total population and total area) rose only about 25 percent. There were seventy-three other cities, inhabited by more than 100,000 but less than 500,000 people in 1950, where the record was similar—a fourfold increase in population, a nearly threefold increase in total area, with an overall increase in density of only about 20 percent. Had the boundaries of cities remained constant, the shift of population from older city to outer suburbs, so noticeable in the past quarter century, would be seen to have been occurring for a long time. Cities are still expanding their boundaries at irregular intervals and by varying amounts but in recent years expansion has become more difficult in many states. Not only have laws changed but in many circumstances the boundaries of one city now touch those of another city. Increasingly, metropolitan areas are emerging, with one or sometimes two major central cities, some satellite cities, and some population in unincorporated surrounding territory.

Because the old legal *city* no longer means a readily definable area of land more or less fully used for urban purposes, it has been necessary to develop some new concepts. The *Standard Metropolitan Statistical Area*, or *SMSA*, is an urban grouping that includes one city with a population of at least 50,000 (or, in some cases, twin cities closely interrelated, either or both of which have 50,000 inhabitants or which together have this population), and surrounding territory closely integrated economically with the central city. The boundaries of the SMSAs follow political jurisdictions—*counties* in most of the country, *towns* in New England. As such, in 1960 they included extensive areas of forest, desert, and farmland, especially in some regions—the Duluth SMSA in Minnesota, for example, reached more than 100 miles to the Canadian border to include some canoe wilderness, the San Bernardino–Riverside–Ontario SMSA in California included thousands of square miles of the Mohave Desert, etc. In 1970 there were 243 SMSAs in the whole country, which included 68 percent of the national population (table 1).

Another new concept has been the *urbanized area*. Basically, this seeks to de-

TABLE 1

NUMBER, POPULATION, AND AREA OF STANDARD METROPOLITAN STATISTICAL AREAS,
AND OF URBANIZED AREAS, IN THE UNITED STATES, 1950, 1960, AND 1970

Item	1950	1960	1970
Standard Metropolitan Statistical Areas			
Number of SMSAs	168	212	243
Total population (million)	89.2	112.9	139.4
Total area (square miles)	207,583	310,233	387,616
Population as percent of national population	59	63	68
Urbanized Areas			
Number of urbanized areas	157	213	248
Total population (million)	69.2	95.8	118.4
Total area (square miles)	12,805	24,978	35,081
Population as percent of national population	46	54	58

lineate areas actually built up and in essentially urban uses. The difficulty here arises from the fact that much urban development is not contiguous. A residential subdivision, which may contain from a few hundred to a few thousand residents, may lie several miles distant from the nearest similar development. Generally speaking, an urbanized area is the built-up part of an SMSA. In 1970 the 248 urbanized areas contained more than 80 percent of the population of the SMSAs but on less than 10 percent of the SMSAs' area. Both SMSAs and urbanized areas have increased in area and population in each decade since 1950 at roughly similar rates.

Increasingly, data on urbanized areas and SMSAs are being used for economic and social analysis instead of data for cities as such. These data are reasonably inclusive of population, labor force, and employment of an economically significant city-like area; they do, however, include a great deal of land not urban in use, and this difference has confused many unwary persons who use such data. We are aware of criticisms of both concepts, but both are established statistical measures of considerable value and use.

URBANIZATION FROM THE 1920s TO THE END OF WORLD WAR II

If the urbanization of the United States since World War II is to be understood, it must be considered in light of the history of the previous quarter century. In the 1920s an active house-building industry existed wholly under private auspices (figure 2). About three-quarters of a million new dwelling units (houses and apartments) were built each year, the number of new households formed annually was almost equally high, employment was high, and in general it was a period of prosperity. While some of the new housing was in the suburbs or on the periphery of cities, some was well within them; while automobile ownership was moderately high and rising rapidly, the kind of commuting so common in recent years had not yet been experienced. Most building in those years was done by quite small builders; even middle-sized builders constructed only a dozen or two houses a year; and often the house was built on the lot owned by the prospective occupant, frequently to his plans and specifications.

This period ended abruptly at the end of the 1920s and the early years of the 1930s, with the coming of the Great Depression—an economic depression of length, depth, and severity without parallel in U.S. economic history, before or since. Formation of new households fell off drastically as marriages were postponed or the young couples lived with parents, and as younger or older adults, alone or in small combinations, were unable to afford separate households. Construction of new dwelling units plunged to less than 100,000 in 1933. Unemployment rose sharply to a fourth of the total labor force. The normal migration of young men and women from farms and rural areas to cities slowed down or reversed, with the result that many counties losing population both in earlier and later decades gained in the 1930s—the farm and rural areas were less unattractive than unemployment in the cities.

Substantial recovery slowly took place throughout the 1930s under the New Deal. Unemployment gradually fell, both by increase in private employment and by means of various public works, yet it remained relatively high throughout the decade. New households were formed, but the rate was still low in relation to the population and in view of the backlog. Dwelling unit construction moved upward and by the end of the decade was at a moderately high but not record level. Various federal programs stimulated and aided dwelling construction and home purchase.

World War II brought still another set of sudden and dramatic changes; all the indexes shown on figure 2 turned down sharply. Unemployment nearly vanished as men and women were taken into the Armed Forces and as military programs demanded vast quantities of materials of all kinds. Indeed, the situation was much more dramatic than these figures suggest, for many thousands of persons were drawn into the labor force who, statistically, had been considered not as unem-

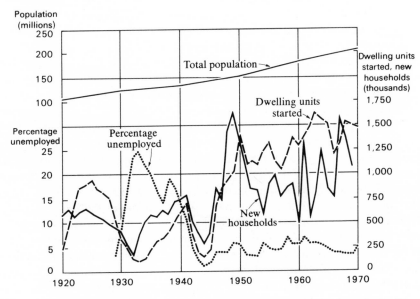

FIGURE 2. U.S. total population at census dates, net new households formed, dwelling units started, and percentage of labor force unemployed, by years, 1920–1970.

ployed but as unemployable. Dwelling construction fell sharply and nearly vanished, except in areas of intensive war effort, as building materials were reserved
for priority purposes and were generally unavailable for private building. Likewise,
new household formation fell off sharply in spite of a rising marriage rate;
with the man off to war, the girl moved in with her parents or with other women
in a situation similar to her own. The war period was one kind of prosperity—
plenty of jobs, plenty of money in the hands of consumers, but a marked shortage
of goods to buy.

When World War II ended in 1945 there was an immense backlog of pent-up
demand for housing and for consumer goods generally. Demobilization of the
armed forces proceeded rapidly. The returning men and their wives sought a living
place of their own, furniture for it, an automobile, and other consumer goods. And,
by and large, they had money to pay for what they wanted. Liquid funds in the
hands of consumers were at a high point. The stage was set for a great expansion
of housing and associated economic output.

Urbanization Since World War II

By and large, the quarter century since the end of World War II has been a
period of economic prosperity and advance in the United States, and this has had
its effect on housing development. Gross national product in 1947 was $234 bil-
lion[1] in current prices; by 1971, it had exceeded $1,000 billion, also in current
prices. Some of this apparent increase was eaten up by rising prices, and the larger
current total is shared by more people than previously; nevertheless, disposable
personal income per capita, measured in terms of 1960 prices, rose from about
$1,500 or $1,600 in the immediate postwar years to over $3,000 in 1970—a more
than doubling in real terms. In 1946 the Employment Act was passed, stating as
a national objective the promotion of full employment and of advancing economic
welfare. Perhaps, in retrospect, no one would contend that U.S. economic policy
in the intervening years was as good as it might have been; particularly during the
later 1950s there were periods of relative stagnation. Yet the economic advances
have been great and have been largely sustained.

National policy favored housing development, especially in the early postwar
years. In general, a policy of easy money was adopted; loans were readily available and interest rates were kept low. The Federal Housing Administration (FHA)
had been established during the New Deal days; one of its programs was to insure
mortgages on homes. Buyers were enabled to purchase homes on a modest down
payment, often on the order of 10 percent, and to amortize the remainder of the
loan over twenty years or more, with the lender paying real estate taxes and fire
insurance out of amounts included in the monthly payments. Lenders were guaranteed by FHA against losses of more than very modest amounts; an additional
monthly charge, usually half of 1 percent, was laid on the purchaser to finance
this guarantee. This program, of a kind previously almost unknown in the United

[1] In U.S. terms, a billion is a thousand million; in British terms, a billion is a million million.
In this book the U.S. definition is used throughout.

States, greatly facilitated home purchase by regularly employed persons of moderate income. FHA obviously had to exercise some controls over both building and lending if its guarantees were not to become burdensome; construction, appraisal, and lending standards were established, which became, to a large extent, the standards of the building and financing industries.

In the immediate postwar years FHA guarantees on lending were stepped up, and in addition special programs for home purchase by war veterans were initiated by the Veterans Administration. Down payments were reduced, sometimes to zero, and the easy money policy ensured a flow of funds into mortgage lending. Some states also initiated special housing programs for their veterans. Federal income tax laws have always favored home purchase; the rental value of the owned home is not considered income, and the real estate taxes and interest paid are deductible from income before tax is calculated. These measures have provided substantial financial inducement to home ownership under the federal income tax rates prevalent in recent decades. In 1946 a series of steps was taken to accelerate the rate at which apartments and other rental property could be depreciated, to provide the owner with a tax-free cash flow; however, these steps did not directly aid the renter (tenant) of apartments.

Much housing in the United States was old, lacked modern facilities, or was badly dilapidated at the end of World War II. At least 10 percent of the houses had been built before 1890 and at least an equal number had been built during the 1890s. With some exceptions, this older housing was substandard; some, indeed, had been substandard when built—rooms too small, lacking in windows, without plumbing, or without electric wiring; on some structures many of these deficiencies had been remedied by remodeling, but remodeling in the United States has generally been costly in terms of the gains achieved. Some housing built after 1900 was also substandard. While some housing in this category was to be found in rural areas and in smaller cities, it was most noticeable in the larger cities. Consequently, replacement of substandard housing was an additional factor leading to a housing boom after World War II, particularly as many people could afford better housing.

The government programs favoring house building and home buying, on top of the accumulated backlog of demand for housing and the accumulated cash reserves of many potential purchasers, resulted in a level of building of housing units previously unknown in the United States. Reference to figure 2 will show that more than a million new units were built in 1949 and in every year of the 1950s. Under these conditions of high demand, the house-building industry boomed; thousands of new builders entered the market; much rather shoddy housing was constructed as well as some that was good; it was a seller's market; and almost anything habitable could be sold. The rate of new household formation shot up, as the figure shows; married couples who had previously doubled up with parents or others established their own homes, and many thousands of single persons, especially the young and the old, established their own households.

In this expansionary process, sites for new building in the cities, especially in the older parts of cities, were either difficult or impossible to find on the scale required. There was, generally, insufficient vacant land available for building sites; land assembly was often time-consuming; and clearance of old housing, however dilapidated it might be, reduced the supply of habitable space at a time when every effort was being made to extend the supply. The builders turned to the suburbs, to which buyers were also attracted for various reasons explained below. Moreover, the builders were in a hurry—the seller's market might not last, and one should get one's share while the getting was good. As one result, buyers did not quibble over land prices that were not too seriously out of line with the general market; a quick transaction was preferable to a better but slower bargain, even if it meant moving on to a more distant parcel. Suburban development quickly took on the discontiguous or sprawled nature that characterizes American suburbs today. Discontiguity had been present prior to this time, but it now became more pronounced. The private automobile freed the suburbanite from dependence on public transportation, and the septic tank freed him (or seemed to do so) from connection to the public sewer. On lots ranging from one acre upward a sewer line could be built from house to tank and a spreading ground used to assimilate the wastes. Serious health problems might arise later, but initially the septic tank seemed a satisfactory solution. A builder could buy a tract of land hundreds of yards, or even some miles, beyond any neighboring suburban development, erect houses, and sell them—and thousands of such houses were built.

A major reinforcing development was the racial change going on in most larger cities. The American Negro was rural and largely farm in residence up to 1930 or even up to 1940. At that date, more than half of all Negroes were living in rural areas, although their exodus from agriculture (often at the option of their white landlord, not of their own choice) had already begun. In one generation they have become dominantly urban, and largely big-city urban. The movement of Negroes to cities took place not only in the South, but in the North and West as well, and many cities that previously had included only a small black colony began to acquire large black districts. Some cities, such as Washington within the District of Columbia, became more than half black in a few years. Many of the immigrants to these cities were illiterate, lacking in skills that made them easily employable, and often with a life-style that grated upon older city residents, black as well as white. No small part of the white migration to the suburbs was motivated by a desire to escape the racial situation of the city, especially as it was reflected in schools.

A number of factors combined to induce or force whites, especially young couples with children, to move to the suburbs in the decade after the war. As noted, there simply was not enough vacant land within the cities to accommodate the new housing needed. The new house in the suburb was fresh and clean, even if shoddily built. It typically was equipped with at least some of the gadgets of modern living, such as stove, electric dishwasher, refrigerator, and sometimes carpets, which were included in its purchase price, and the buyer could quickly bring in his own television and other gadgets. The suburb offered escape from the older city, both from its dinginess and from its new racial mix. The new suburbanite was attracted by a community composed of other people in his age, income, and social class; he generally expected better public services and lower taxes, though he was sometimes disappointed on both scores.

These general inducements were reinforced by some very powerful economic incentives. The low down payment was a major help; the monthly payments were often less than rent of similar quarters. These were years of persistent inflation in the United States. The rate of price advance was very great at the end of World War II; after a levelling off, it spurted again as a result of the Korean War; was slow but persistent throughout the 1950s and early 1960s; and mounted again toward the end of the 1960s. For the whole period from 1948 through 1968, the average of annual rises in the index of consumer prices slightly exceeded 2 percent. The precise rate of price rises was less important, perhaps, than their persistence, which led to the expectation of continued price rises. And once the general public or an industry group comes to expect higher prices and to act upon such expectation, it goes far toward guaranteeing the continuance of price increases. One could buy a house or vacant land in the expectation of a rise in its price, with fairly high assurance that one would be right.

Chapter 2 will point out that Britain has also experienced a steady and even more rapid rise in prices over the same period, with generally similar consequences. In both countries, the purchase of a house was a magnificent hedge against inflation, not merely for the purchaser's small investment but for the whole cost of the house. Neither principal nor interest rates in the United States were subject to adjustment during the period of the loan. In many situations a family could buy a house, live in it five years, and abandon it without economic loss. In fact, few abandoned their loans unless the house was impossibly shoddy, but chose to sell the house often at a price which, in current dollars, meant that their occupancy had been costless. Given these circumstances, the wonder is not that a movement to suburbs ensued and reached large proportions, but that it was not greater. The fact that many families have emotional and other ties to old homes has been one major factor affecting the rate of adjustment of housing to current economic and social conditions.

The housing boom of the 1950s was dominantly in the building of detached single-family homes, each on its own plot of land. Although some inducements were available to builders and owners of apartment houses, the individual could not obtain the same advantages from renting an apartment that he could from buying a house—his hedge against inflation was missing, and his rent could not be deducted from his income in figuring taxes as his interest and real estate taxes could be deducted in his owned home. Later, builders began constructing apartments for a wider range of family sizes and tastes, as well as sometimes providing open space and other amenities for their apartment structures. The result was that apartment house building began to boom in the early 1960s; through the 1950s more than 80 percent of all new housing units were single-family dwellings, whereas in the early 1970s the proportions are more nearly equal. Moreover, the suburban apartment house has become common. Sometimes surrounded by open land under the ownership and management of the apartment owners, it provides a life-style that has many desirable features of suburban living without the cares and responsibilities of house and yard (garden) maintenance.

Although the need for housing was the major force affecting land use in the suburbs, other concurrent developments were important. Many industries have moved to the suburbs in the past quarter century; older central city locations often involved antiquated structures, were too small, or presented problems of slow, costly transportation. Major highways have been built into, near, and around many large cities; the Interstate Highway system, which often includes a circumferential or belt highway around large cities, has been a major new locational force. The scale of such highway building has been greater in the United States than in Britain. The new highways have led to relocation of economic activity in a manner reminiscent of the changes brought about by the coming of the railroads more than a century ago. And as jobs and workers moved to suburbs, retail and wholesale trade followed them. The suburban shopping center—occupying several acres of land, with huge parking lots to accommodate customers' cars, and with numerous one- or two-level stores—has become a dominant part of the American urban scene. As a result, older downtown shopping districts are almost invariably in decline, relatively if not absolutely so. The type of personal transportation that enables suburbanites to visit one shopping district applies equally well to another if they prefer it, and as a result competition among shopping districts is perhaps keener than among stores within one district.

In thus briefly summarizing the suburbanization trend of postwar years in the United States, one should not leave the impression that all has been well. The new suburbs have been closed, effectively if not in theory, to the lower half of the income structure; and considering what they have provided for their residents, they have been unnecessarily costly. Although a vast upgrading of housing has occurred in the United States in the past quarter century—both in the construction of new housing and in some improvement of old housing—there are still some millions of substandard, dilapidated, outdated, or deficient housing units, primarily in the older city centers and in the more remote rural areas. Sheer abandonment of housing units on farms no longer operated as separate units, in rural areas experiencing outmigration, and in city slums has become common. Still standing in many large cities today are hundreds or thousands of derelict housing structures, unoccupied and physically going to pieces, but not yet torn down.

Dispersed Decision Making

The dominant fact about U.S. urban expansion is the extreme dispersion of its decision making; in a particular subdivision or group of houses there may well be a score or more of major actors—individuals, corporations, and public agencies. To some extent their work is cooperative, inasmuch as each must play some minimal favorable role if the whole enterprise is to succeed. In other respects the efforts of the various groups are competitive; not only does each strive to secure for himself the largest possible slice of the pie being cooked by all, but some work to offset others. No individual, group, or agency takes or must be charged with responsibility for the final result; perhaps no one would have chosen it had the full responsibility been his. There is interplay and feedback among the groups; whenever one starts in the complex process of transforming a bare tract of land into a group of suburban houses, one comes back in the end to one's starting point (figure 3). Since land and building materials, as physical inputs, are needed if houses are to be built, we may well start with them. The land involved in suburban growth

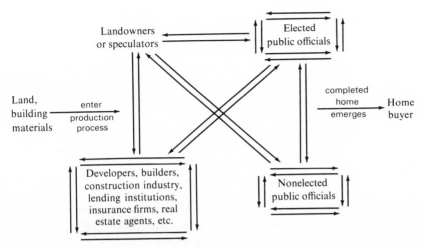

FIGURE 3. In the United States interactions abound among various actors and interest groups in the suburbanization process.

is nearly all privately owned at the time of its development; only rarely will it be in public ownership. However, all land in the United States was once the property, in the proprietary sense, of one or another unit of government, from which it was transferred to private owners. Land along the Atlantic Seaboard, as well as a few tracts elsewhere, was once the property of some European power, which granted it to an individual, colony, or landed proprietor. About two-thirds of all land in the United States was once the property of the federal government and was transferred to private individuals (either directly, or through the states or a recipient of a land grant, such as a railroad). A full legal history of any land title in the United States always must begin with this original transfer from public to private ownership.

Lands were transferred from public to private ownership for a variety of purposes—agriculture, forestry, land speculation, and townsites, among others—and by a variety of laws. During its history some of this land has been included in actively operating farms, but this is not invariably the case. Some land has never been wholly cleared of forests or otherwise prepared for cropping. In the Northeastern Urban Complex discussed in chapter 3, for example, more than half of all land today is neither in farms nor in any form of urban use. The essential point about the complex land history is that the original alienation of land from public to private ownership and the subsequent land transfers were in sizes of holdings as well as in land uses unrelated to urban land use—at least until the most recent of such land transfers. Sizes of ownership parcels in potential suburban development areas vary greatly from less than an acre at one extreme to several hundred acres at the other; only rarely will the size of parcels be optimum for suburban development by the particular developer.

As development proceeds, a little land may go directly from farms to residential, industrial, or trade uses. In most cases, however, the genuine operating farmer sold out long ago. There are numerous incompatibilities between farming and suburban residential living, even when they are separated by considerable distances. Dairy, poultry, and other livestock produce odors and their manure provides breeding ground for flies; crop dusting with insecticides is likely to annoy suburbanites; so may dust from field crop operations. But the farmer may suffer thefts, vandalism, and interference with normal farm operations; and, as some farmers quit, those who try to remain may suffer a lack of supply stores and marketing outlets because the volume of business has declined to unprofitable levels. Some farmers may cease operations and hold their land for later sale to suburban developers. More likely, they will sell to a professional land dealer, who looks upon the land as a commodity to be traded in, rather than as a factor of production to be used in a production process. To a considerable degree information is lacking about the number of ownerships that typically intervene between the last operating farmer and the actual builder; not even a good terminology exists to describe such landowners. They are often called *speculators*, but anyone who owns land in expectation or hope of a price rise is a speculator. Sometimes owners of land in the intermediary stages are called *dealers,* or simply *landholders,* or *investors.*

Whatever their most appropriate name, there are apparently great differences among these intermediate landholders as far as their personal situations, tax liability, willingness to hold for future gain, and other factors are concerned. The initial purchaser from the farmer may often have to wait some years for actual development of the land; some, at least, seem to prefer to buy land at or near agricultural value, and to hold for the long pull. When the suburban land market is very active because a suburb is expanding rapidly, groups of individuals may be formed to buy land and promote its early development. Interested in a quick turnover, they are willing to take some risks and pay more for the land, in order to put together a "deal" whereby their land is brought into actual development.

The land dealer's real asset is his superior knowledge or his superior judgment. If everyone had the same expectations of the future date of development of raw land and the same expectations of its price at that date, there would be no room for differences of opinion about its present value. (Different persons might have different interest rates on which they would be willing to hold land, but this would be a personal rather than a land matter.) The dealer who knows more than others or thinks he does, or who has a different judgment about the future than others can pay his price for land and hope to make a profit from its later sale. It is precisely because his real commodity is knowledge, not land, that land dealers as a class are so reluctant to give information about their operations. Not infrequently, they conceal their personal identity behind corporate names, or trust arrangements, or get other individuals to act for them; to reveal their identity might well spoil the operation.

The initiative for suburban development, whether for residential or for other purposes, often begins with a "developer." Such a man may obtain options on land, or he may have a less formal arrangement with some landowners; he may make some improvements on the land, such as building roads within the tract and subdividing the large tract into building lots; he may, in extreme cases, even build a few houses. However, developers generally try to keep actual operations and investments to a minimum; they are entrepreneurs, or arrangers, or promoters, however one wishes to describe them. Sometimes they may obtain new zoning for a tract of land, if this is required, or they may seek to have public services, such as sewers, extended to the land.

If a developer proposes or arranges a suburban development, he usually turns to a builder or builders, either to construct houses by arrangement with the developer or to buy the land from him. Where the pace of suburban development is slow, the builder may be his own developer; he may arrange with a real estate dealer to find a suitable tract of land and then do the (limited) promotional work himself. Builders vary greatly. Some are skilled workmen with business sense. Such men are likely to build relatively few houses annually, often less than twenty-five; they work on the job themselves besides supervising a limited number of workers. They are usually dependent on a real estate agent or land dealer for building sites, and on a real estate agent to sell their houses; they cannot buy materials in quantities, nor can they adopt labor-saving mass production techniques. Nevertheless, their own skill as workmen and their close supervision of workers often enable them to compete successfully with larger-scale operations. The National Association of Home Builders, the trade organization for builders, found that 65 percent of all its members returning a questionnaire in 1969 built fewer than twenty-five single-family houses annually, although such small builders accounted for only 17 percent of all houses built.

The more successful of the small builders often become medium-size builders, who construct from twenty-five to a hundred houses annually. The largest builders, those who construct more than a hundred houses annually, are a minority of all the firms, yet build half or more of all the houses. They can utilize more specialized help: a land man to find good building sites and acquire land, an architect to design the houses they build, and a sales unit. They can buy materials in larger lots and at lower prices, as well as conduct something like assembly-line production, with crews moving from house to house, carrying out a few specialized tasks in an ordered sequence.

But house builders of all sizes tend to have other business interests—often serving as real estate brokers, building commercial and industrial buildings as well as homes, and engaging in other activities. When home building booms, small builders enter the business; when competition is tight or the market is slow, many, especially the smaller ones, are shaken out. In the past decade or so, very much larger builders, capable of building several hundred houses a year, and sometimes with economic integration back to the sources of raw materials, have entered the house-building field. These largest builders are capable of building a large subdivision of several hundred homes, planning and developing it as a unit, including shopping districts.

Almost all builders in the United States operate on a low equity. They borrow funds to buy materials or obtain them on credit from the supplier, and borrow to meet wage bills. They require credit for the building process. The houses they build are sold as quickly as possible—ideally, sold before they are finished to a buyer who sees a sample house, likes the neighborhood, and has the house finished to his order in such matters as paint color. The builder is rarely in a position to finance the buyer, who must find his credit elsewhere. When the house is sold, the builder has gotten his money out. Builders have preferred, possibly rightly, to use whatever equity capital they had or could accumulate to expand the scale of their operations, rather than to increase their percentage equity in the structures they did build. Operating on a high debt structure is called "leverage." If the deal goes well, the builder makes a very high return on his limited capital; if it goes sour, he can lose all he has, and quickly.

The size of the decision-making unit for builders is appropriate to their scale of operations. For the smallest builders it may still be a single house, as it generally was for house builders a few decades ago. But, increasingly, it is the subdivision—a tract of land, varying from a few acres at the smallest to some hundreds at the largest—within which the builder or the developer plans such elements as internal layout, street locations, and lot sizes, constructs the needed internal improvements, and also builds all the houses to a style or in a group of styles. Increasingly, home buyers are interested in "neighborhood"—those intangibles that help to create the local atmosphere, including the kinds of people who will buy the other houses. The larger builders and developers all tend to emphasize "neighborhood" in their advertising.

The subdivision may lie close to existing developed suburban areas, or it may lie relatively distant from them. In some cases, where infilling brings development to previously bypassed land, it may be surrounded by previous development. The small builder can play a special role here, for he may be able to use relatively small bypassed areas that larger builders would not wish to develop. The builder acquires a tract of land which, while not necessarily the best tract, is tolerably satisfactory to him given its price and location. This is the process known in economics as "satisficing," or meeting satisfactory standards, rather than "optimizing," or securing the best possible deal. Savings in time, and perhaps in effort, are more important than any likely gains in terms of a better price.

A housing development requires a range of public services to at least a minimum degree of acceptability. Among them are roads and highways within the project and leading to major arterials outside from which the entire urban or metropolitan area is accessible; some source of domestic water supply (piped water from the public water system preferably, but private wells if groundwater is readily available and promises to be of acceptable quality); a means of disposing of domestic sewage (connection to the public sewer system preferably, but the individual septic tank or cesspool if the lots are large and the soil type permits this method of waste disposal); and schools, for the typical house buyer in a suburb is interested in moving there precisely because he has children. Also needed are such utilities as electricity, gas (if this is generally available in the area), and telephone, all of which in the United States are usually provided by privately owned utilities (although there are some cooperatives). These utilities are so ubiquitous in the United States, and their providers are generally so eager for new business, that any suburban development of more than a few houses would have no difficulty in getting such services.

By and large, in the United States public and private services of the types just described are charged on a "postage stamp" basis. The charges for central sewer service, for example, are likely to be no greater for the distant than for the close-in subdivision. There is no penalty for distant location and no saving for a closer one, as far as either builder or house buyer is concerned. Typically, the builder is responsible for these services within the limits of his subdivision, and the costs are naturally added to the price the buyer pays. In general, the capital costs of building new sewer lines, new schools, and other relatively costly public improvements are not charged against the new subdivisions, but against all taxpayers in the county or other unit of local government providing the services. The older residents thus help to pay the costs of such services to new residents, while the latter in their turn will help to pay the costs of yet another and newer group of settlers. In the end, the suburbanite may pay the full costs of all public services he receives, but he is unlikely to do so at the time of his house purchase. Indeed, he may be unaware of the costs his location is causing to the local government, or even of the costs he will be required to pay in the end.

The land that the builder wishes to develop may be zoned for the use he intends to make of it—not only for residential use, for instance, but for lot size and thus for land cost and dwelling type as well. If so zoned, there is no problem. If existing zoning will not permit the type of construction proposed, then the zoning must be changed. Many land deals are contingent on a change in zoning, which is likely to be the task of the developer and his lawyer. Many lawyers specialize in this type of practice; they acquire expertise and connections that enable them to get most zoning applications approved.

Many suburbs have some sort of a general plan. (The planning process is considered in more detail in chapter 5.) There is likely to be a planning board, typically of part-time members who have business or professional interests, and, at least for the larger areas, a planning staff. Zoning of land and planning are two separate steps. The zones established may rest on the plan and be the legal mechanism for implementing it, but much zoning has been carried out without written or formal plan—though it may be argued that the zoning body must have had some implicit plan in their minds when acting on specific cases. The planning board may or may not also be the zoning board; in either case there is provision only for local appeals from the decisions of the zoning authority. The general governing board of the unit of local government—the county commissioners or the city councilmen or whatever either may be called—is often the appeal board for actions of the zoning authority.

The nominal planning agency may not be the real one. That is, a special planning board or agency may exist, with or without staff, and may nominally be responsible for preparing plans for developing a suburban county or area. But its plans generally lack legal status or binding power over the decisions of the general governing board of the county or area and also over other specialized units of local government. Where public sewers are necessary for development (because soil and other conditions prohibit private septic tanks), the sewer agency may be the real planning body; where public sewers are built, private housing development will almost surely follow, regardless of what the general plan says; and where public sewers are lacking, private development will be blocked, again regardless of the general plan. Although sewer builders are often the most powerful of such specialized agencies because their services are practically indispensable, some of the same relationships exist for the highway builders, and to a lesser extent for the agencies that provide other local services. While schools are extremely important, generally speaking the building of schools follows the need for them. The general governing board of a county or city may, and often does, ignore the plans developed by its general planning agency; indeed, it may endorse a general plan and then proceed to take specific actions in contradiction to the plan—and sometimes, apparently, without realizing what it is doing. Specialized agencies, such as sewer builders and general governing boards, acquire clientele or political support within their own area; the actions they take in contradiction to the general plan may win them substantial support from various special interest groups.

With general planning agencies so frequently ineffective, why do counties and cities insist on having them? In the first place, these agencies are not totally ineffective; they often can help the general governing board with some specific and difficult problem, even when their role and the results they achieve are far different from what the usual professional planner would choose. Also, there is a widespread belief in the United States that local planning is a "good thing," that such planning leads to a more effective use of public funds. Relatively few elected officials of general (but local) government would denounce planning as a process or planning agencies as a general accoutrement, nor would they press for their abolition. Moreover, federal grants-in-aid are based increasingly on general or overall local plans; to get the desired federal grant, the local government must have a plan—however little it actually uses this plan.

Zoning of undeveloped suburban land is seldom firm: when a market develops, the zoning can often, perhaps usually, be changed to accommodate the new use. Contrarily, merely zoning or rezoning land for a use does not guarantee that it will be used in this way if there is no market for that use. Some local zoning bodies have zoned far more land for industrial use, for example, than is likely to be needed for decades, if ever. The private market for land gives small credence to zoning, because it is assumed that the zoning can be changed if the demand is great enough. Thus the local tax assessor also gives little credence to zoning, because under law he is required to assess land at its full market value (though often he does not). If zoning is so flexible, why bother with it? In the first place, it does sometimes have effect; it is not always changed as requested. In the second place, there are costs involved in getting zoning changed—costs to be measured in terms of time perhaps more than in terms of money. And thus development is likely to proceed in accord with a plan if no significant economic advantages are to be seen in the rezoning of a tract that is already appropriately zoned.

The credit institutions often play a critical role in the suburban development process. Credit is required by the builder and also in most cases by the home purchaser. The credit institutions in the United States have always emphasized that they make "sound loans" and do not have social objectives in mind in making or in refusing loans. What they really mean is that they operate in about the same way as other credit institutions—none likes to get far out of line with the "market." In times of prosperity and easy money they are far more expansive than in times of financial stringency. And, at least until very recent years, they have operated to reinforce racial and social segregation as well as to discriminate against lower-income areas. They have been much concerned with the "quality of the neighborhood," because they felt—rightly—that this would affect the resale price of property if they found it necessary to foreclose on a mortgage.

Almost all cities and suburban areas have building codes, which prescribe acceptable and inacceptable standards of building construction. The general purpose of these codes is to prevent substandard or dangerous building practices, which often the purchaser could not readily detect. Defective electric wiring might otherwise be covered up, for instance, and thus constitute a fire hazard. But this noble purpose has been soiled in application. Building codes are frequently attacked by public commissions and prestigious engineers as unnecessarily restrictive; they are generally couched in terms not of planning practice but of final performance of the resultant buildings; and they tend to sanctify some building practices of a bygone time, thus inhibiting or preventing use of new methods that may be superior in terms of safety, convenience, and cost. Moreover, they have helped to establish or maintain local monopolies in building; the newcomer is repelled by a system of building codes he does not understand. In this, the public officials responsible for the building codes, the builders, and the local labor unions have frequently joined forces to build or preserve their local monopoly.

The developers, the builders, and the others grouped in the lower left corner of figure 3 must deal with the various public agencies. Their first contacts are usually with the agencies' nonelected officials—the employees. The latter differ considerably in training and in personal backgrounds. They ordinarily seek to serve the public of the area of local government within which they operate, yet often their personal attitudes tend to align them with some interests rather than others. The proclivity of local governments to discourage low-income and/or racial minorities may be fully accepted by many nonelected public officials, for instance. Or they may be fully in sympathy with building codes or other devices that tend to prevent outsiders from competing with local builders, even though this causes higher-cost housing for local citizens. The employee of local government who continues in the same location over a long period of years, as many do, must have reached some sort of accommodation with enough local political support to guarantee his retention. Often he lacks the protection of any form of civil service; even one who is so protected must still live with his constituency.

But the nonelected employees of local government also have professional standards by which they live and work. If the local situation is too unsatisfactory they can seek employment elsewhere, though this usually involves personal costs in selling a home, moving, and getting reestablished. The fact that they can, and under some circumstances will, move away from an unsatisfactory situation imposes some degree of discipline upon the local government body. Too much should not be made of this discipline through moving; where outright fraud or bribery or blatant political favoritism has been practiced (and perhaps proven by court cases), some nonelected local officials have nevertheless continued to work there—whether genuinely unaware of what was going on, or able to shut their eyes to what was not their direct responsibility, or willing to tolerate a bad situation in the hope that it would be temporary, one does not know. But undoubtedly some discipline for honesty, competence, and good government is imposed by the professional standards of nonelected public officials, and it would appear that such standards have risen over the decades.

Both nonelected public officials and the various private interest groups must deal with the elected officials of local government, and these in turn depend upon the local electorate. Local government varies enormously within the United States. There are slightly more than 3,000 counties: these vary in area from a few score to more than 15,000 square miles, and in population from less than 1,000 to over 5 million people; their powers of government vary from few and weak (as in New England) to many and powerful. There are about 5,000 legally incorporated cities of less than 50,000 population in the United States. Moreover, there are special districts of many kinds—school districts, sewerage districts, drainage districts, and others, to the tune of about 90,000 in total. Virtually all units of local government have some sort of governing board with (perhaps limited) legislative powers and often but not invariably with administrative powers as well—councils or selectmen for cities, and commissioners or councils or supervisors for counties. Most cities have a mayor, who is elected by the voters or occasionally by the council from its membership; many also have elected officials.

In recent years a few counties have experimented with an elected administrator. Most counties will have an elected sheriff, a tax assessor, a registrar of deeds, and various other elected officials. Many counties have an independently elected school board.

More important than the formal structure is the politics of local government. In a county or town first undergoing suburbanization the elected officials are likely to represent the established and often politically conservative rural or small-town electorate and to be generally hostile to suburbanization, planning, and zoning. As suburbanization proceeds, the land speculator and the developer are likely to play an increasing and often dominant role in local government—they quickly see how their economic interests may be forwarded by ensuring a local government friendly to their wheeling and dealing, and they devote the time and energy needed to get elected. They often find allies in old rural landowning families: at this stage, they, too, wish to capitalize on booming land sales. Planning is often weak and limited; zoning officials are often compliant. Later, as the county or town acquires a larger population of established and permanent suburbanites who develop political relationships among themselves, planning is likely to be strengthened, zoning acquires more stability and authority, and the wheeler-dealer may be replaced by a steadier developer who is more likely to have real capital to invest and to be more interested in real building.

Most elected officials of county, suburban city, and other local government are nominally part-time, and their salaries are fixed accordingly. In practice, such positions often require so much time and attention as to be virtually full-time. They are demanding in terms of personal qualities, and expose their holders to public criticism of private actions—surely an unattractive feature to many persons. Given their demands in terms of time, ability, and loss of privacy, and given their low pay, one may well question why anyone should seek office. Yet it is a fact that often several candidates compete for each office, and it is not uncommon for a candidate to spend far more (some of which may be contributed by others) on his campaign than his total salary for his term of office.

There are several explanations for this willingness to serve as a local elected official. In the first place, it would be a serious mistake to underestimate the genuine dedication to public service motivating many such men and women; as residents of an area, interested in the quality of life there, they feel an obligation to help govern in a manner to achieve their goals. In many instances they are members, and in a sense representatives, of organized or unorganized groups with similar ideals and objectives; their service as elected officials is as much a service to their group as to the general electorate. In other cases, service as an elected official of local government is a step toward later election to a more rewarding state or national office; the tradition of politics in many areas is for service locally and a moving upward in a political hierarchy. Their local service is thus a form of investment in a political future. Often, however, service as a local elected official has more immediate and more tangible personal rewards. A local lawyer may seek a reputation and a practice as a zoning lawyer; a tour of duty as an elected official may be very helpful to him in this regard. Or his partner may practice such cases while he occupies the local office. Indeed, in many instances he may continue to accept such cases himself, sometimes but not always disqualifying himself should a case come before his group. What is true of lawyers is more or less equally true of insurance men, or even engineers, or real estate agents, or land dealers, or developers. With complete propriety, such men may serve as elected public officials while at the same time adding to their personal income in the future if not currently; and, regrettably, many such local officials have acted in improper or even illegal ways, sometimes getting caught, sometimes not.

The elected local official is nominally the superior and the supervisor of the nonelected official. In practice, he is highly dependent on the latter for specialized knowledge, including the history of various issues. The nonelected official can help to make the elected official look informed, intelligent, and alert; or he can frustrate and obfuscate him to the opposite end. One device is to "buck up" so much detail to the elected officials that they are overwhelmed, with no time or energy to deal with more basic issues. Some elected officials, it is true, want details and specific cases to come to them for decision, believing that in this way they can serve their electorate in a manner that will make the latter appreciative of their help. A symbiotic relationship among elected officials, nonelected public officials, and powerful interest groups within the county or local area may well arise; each helps the others in return for support and tangible rewards. And those who seek to oppose or reform or confront the local power structure can be opposed, evaded, or diverted in numerous ways.

In the end, the suburban development process produces houses that can be, and nearly always are, sold promptly. At this stage the house buyer is king; it is his money or his credit that fuels the whole process. If house sales are slow or if price concessions must be made, this may well be ruinous to the builder—his leverage now works against him. House buyers can obviously only react to what is offered to them; at a period such as that immediately following World War II, when housing in general was scarce, a family often felt lucky to get any house. In more normal times, potential house buyers can pick and choose. Their choices at any date will have more influence on the kind of houses developers and builders will offer next time around than they can possibly have on houses already built or partially completed. Since buyers require credit and various public services, this brings them in contact with the business groups and public agencies already described—and the ring is closed.

THE SUBURBAN LAND MARKET

The suburban land market in the United States has characteristics that go far toward explaining the kind of suburbs commonly built. The market is a private one, but one that operates within a framework of public laws and actions. Relatively little is known about the way this private land market operates, and even less in terms of statistical data on numbers of sales, acreage, prices paid, and the like. A federal tax, which is proportionate to the sum paid, must be paid on all transactions in land. Revenue stamps must be affixed to documents for each such sale, from which one can calculate the price paid. To be legal, land transactions must ultimately be recorded at the designated county office. Thus, the basic sources exist for data on the suburban land market in roughly the same way that data are available about the stock market or the grain exchanges. In practice, however, such land data are not compiled and published, and it becomes a major research job to ascertain the activities in a suburban land market. One must often trace transactions through county registry journals—a time-consuming and tedious process. And one can never be sure that the reported transactions are bona fide, or that they are arm's length. A piece of land may be reported as sold from the ABC corporation to the XYZ company—but is John Smith the owner of each, the sale being only part of his effort to create the appearance of an active market or a part of some complicated financial deal he was arranging? In the detailed studies on which this book rests some of these local land records were studied; while a great deal of information can be assembled from them, much time and effort is required to do so and, even so, one can never be certain that the full story has been uncovered.

The present price for undeveloped suburban land is a consensus among buyers and sellers (weighted by their respective abilities and willingness to put money on the line) as to the future date of development and the price that will then be paid for the land, such future price being discounted back to the present, including a risk factor as to both development date and price. All land, as all fixed investment, includes both current income and expected future changes in income as part of its price-determining formula. But in the case of suburban land current income is frequently zero—the land is idle, and intentionally so, to facilitate development when conditions are ripe. With rare exceptions, undeveloped suburban land that conceivably could be developed within twenty years has a price far above its price for any alternative use. There are exceptions: good citrus-growing land in California and Florida, where the agricultural value may be several thousand dollars an acre; or land bearing mineral deposits, where values are also very high. But the vast majority of undeveloped suburban land with any prospect for development within two decades is held at prices ranging upward from ten times its agricultural income.

The owner of undeveloped suburban land has to appraise his prospects for sale at different future dates, perhaps to an actual developer, perhaps to a land dealer or speculator; he must judge the kinds of uses most likely to develop when or if it is brought into some form of urban use, and the price likely to be paid for it then. He faces some holding costs for this land, the most important of which is likely to be not a cash cost, but the interest and/or dividends he could earn from selling the land and investing the proceeds somewhere else. He also must pay some real estate taxes on the land, whether it has improvements or not. In this respect, U.S. practice differs from British practice: there, no rates (taxes) are assessed against land as such, but only on improvements. In all states, real estate taxes are based on the full market price of the land or some fraction thereof, unless special tax laws have been passed to favor "farmers." Undeveloped suburban land is supposed to pay taxes on the same basis as other real property, with this exception. In practice, however, farm and unimproved suburban land is typically underassessed, sometimes at far less than half of its true value. In part this is due to the difficulty of determining its probable sale value, and in part it is due to the rapid upward movement of land prices in an actively developing suburb and the lag in reassessment; but in no small degree it is due to cozy relations between tax assessors and land speculators and dealers. There may be other holding costs, but they are generally minor.

The landowner who makes a judgment about future prices, and thus about discounted present prices, has established a reservation price, above which he will sell, below which he will not. Most such landowners take the position that if they cannot get "their price" this year, they can probably get it next year. As one looks at the postwar history of land prices in the United States, this expectation is a reasonable one. Since 1954, farm real estate prices have advanced 4 percent or more in almost every year, in spite of a generally depressed situation within agriculture; prices paid for recreation land by public and private buyers (as nearly as one can tell from imperfect and scanty data) have moved up more in the order of 8 to 10 percent annually; and suburban land as a whole (also on the basis of imperfect data) seems to have moved up in the range of 12 to 15 percent annually. General inflation and tender income tax treatment of capital gains from dealing in land have undoubtedly been two major forces behind this sustained rise in land prices.

The suburban landowner's expectation that he can get a higher price for his land in the future than he can now has been realized in many instances, but far from universally. Some have bought land only to see its value remain constant, or even decline. But, assuming that the price does go up, has holding such land been profitable? Much depends on the interest rate at which the individual landowner is willing to speculate in land, and on the taxes he must pay upon it. But even at low holding costs he must receive much more from the land than he paid for it if the transaction is to be truly profitable; at high holding costs, his margin must be still greater (figure 4). Most owners of undeveloped suburban land are in a strong personal financial position; if the market for their land is weak, they are not forced to sell. Their asking prices will come down little or not at all; the volume of land sales may decline to zero, but the price is little affected. There are exceptions, of course—people who speculate in such land largely with borrowed money may be forced to liquidate to meet their creditors. But loans are often hard to get on undeveloped land, partly because it is illiquid and turnover may be slow, hence most such land is owned by persons with adequate capital.

The builder faces a different situation. He must have land to build on if he is to operate at all. He is under many compulsions to keep up his volume of building; the larger builders over the years have developed organizations that must be kept busy; small builders face the need to earn a personal living. Given the low equity of each, buying land far in advance of actual building would be difficult or costly. In many situations a builder would rather pay a little more for a good building site than run the risk of being unable to operate at his capacity. If he pays more than he would like for raw land, he may be at little disadvantage with his competitors because they may have paid much the same for their land. As long as he stays about in line with the "market" and the industry generally, the price he pays

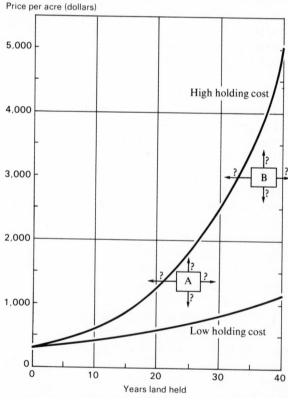

FIGURE 4. Shown above are two ranges of landowners' holding costs of undeveloped suburban land in the United States. Also shown are average prices received by farmers (A) and paid by developers (B).

for land is not crucial. Lot prices have doubled as a percentage of the price of finished house and lot in the past twenty years, and have increased far more in absolute terms. Generally, the higher land prices have been passed on to the house buyers. One way this can be done is to build more expensive houses on the more costly land so that the price of land is not high in proportion to the price of the finished house. But this, in turn, reduces the volume of houses that can be sold and operates to restrict the suburbs even more to families of above average income.

This structure of the suburban land market has two major consequences:

1. Given the disproportionate bargaining positions of the landowner or seller and the builder or land buyer, land prices have inevitably ratcheted upward since World War II both in terms of dollars per square foot and as a percentage of price of finished house. The pressures have nearly all been upward; there have been few pressures downward. Consequently, it has been difficult or impossible to build new houses at prices that families of average and lower incomes can pay. As long as the market is structured as it is now, it would take another economic depression of the type of the 1930s to affect these pressures significantly. Such a depression seems unlikely to be endured because the national cost would be too high. The market might, of course, be restructured to make land speculation less profitable.

2. Builders buy land where they can get it, within a wide geographical range. Frequently the tracts they can get quickly and at what is to them a tolerable price are not contiguous to already developed suburban tracts. Typically, discontiguity of subdivisions results—the sprawl so typical of American suburbs today. The pricing of public services does not discourage this type of sprawl, and may be said to encourage it.

chapter **2**

The setting for urbanization
in Britain

The distinctive themes of Britain's experience of urban growth in the quarter century from 1945 to 1970 have been two. First, there has been a deliberate attempt to set up a complex and effective system of land use planning that would give public authorities real control over the urban growth process. And second, this attempt has been made during conditions of quite unprecedented and unexpected growth and change. Growth in Britain has, perhaps, been modest in comparison with that of many of its neighbors on the European mainland and other parts of the advanced western world; but in many important respects—especially the rate of economic growth and the rate of population growth—it has notably exceeded the record of the interwar years. This is important because the planning system itself was set up between 1945 and 1952 in a remarkably short but intensive burst of legislation based on experience in interwar Britain and even, in some respects, experience dating back before World War I. A system designed in the light of one set of conditions has had to cope with very different circumstances.

THE PREWAR ANTECEDENTS

For this reason, before considering the actual postwar experience it is critical to understand the antecedents. In the nineteenth century Britain was the first country to experience mass industrialization and mass urbanization. Britain by 1891 was already a largely urban nation: 72 percent of the population lived in areas defined by the census as urban. No other country in the world at that time could muster a similar figure. But this very speed of urban growth, without benefit of any comparative experience and at a time when resources were very limited, had been paid for dearly. The great Victorian parliamentary reports and books like Engels's *Condition of the Working Class in England* tell the story. By the century's end, the worst excesses of uncontrolled urban growth had been curbed; elementary public health legislation had laid down basic rules for residential construction, which guaranteed minimal standards of air, light, drainage (sewerage), and water supply. But the great cities in the last decade of the century were still grim places, as major early works of social investigation like Booth's *Life and Labour of the People in London,* or Rowntree's study of poverty in York, amply testify. Controversy will doubtless continue to rage concerning the root causes of these conditions. Basic poverty of a large section of the population was undoubtedly a principal cause; the question is whether conditions were exacerbated by the lack of effective planning. But contemporaries, at any rate, were in no doubt that here was a physical evil, with a physical solution.

This was the message of the most important single contribution to British planning thought. Ebenezer Howard's slim volume, which emerged in 1898 under the title *Tomorrow* and was republished in 1902 under the more familiar *Garden Cities of Tomorrow,* argued that neither the late Victorian city nor the late Victorian countryside offered adequate living conditions to their inhabitants. The city was essentially the place of opportunities, both economic and social. But these were paid for by foul air, smoke-laden skies, unemployment, high rents, crime, and alcoholism. The countryside, on the other hand, offered a much superior physical environment. But writing at a time when rural England was in the depths of an agrarian depression caused by unlimited imports of cheap food from the New World, Howard clearly saw the other side of the coin: economic decline, a narrowing of social and economic horizons, a lack of opportunity.

The dilemma, Howard argued, could be resolved by a new type of community: Garden City, or Town-Country. New towns would be created in open countryside, well away from the existing urban slums. They would be comprehensively planned by agencies—Howard saw private enterprise as leading the way—which would buy not merely the land for the town, but also a wide surrounding tract of agricultural land that would remain as a perpetual greenbelt for it. People and jobs would be moved together from the old congested cities to the new garden cities, so as to create self-contained communities offering both homes and work in easy proximity. The size of each Garden City should be limited to preserve easy access to open countryside. But as population grew, further Garden Cities would be added close by. A multi-centered Social City would thus come into being, with each part within easy access of all others. Such social cities, or planned agglomerations, would offer all the advantages of town and country without the attendant disadvantages: accessibility to social and economic opportunities, coupled with a high level of natural environment.

Howard's is the most important single influence on the philosophy of the British planning movement, which was instrumental in bringing the postwar planning system into being. So it is important to realize that his ideas were developed in response to the conditions of Victorian England. Apart from two experimental Garden Cities at Letchworth and Welwyn in Hertfordshire, which Howard got started with private capital, his ideas lay fallow for nearly half a century until they were taken up dramatically in the official new towns policy that was so distinctive a part of the post-1945 planning package. His message was that the evils of the large city could and should be solved by a physical policy: constraint on the growth of existing cities, and decentralization of their surplus slum populations to new self-contained communities that would receive both people and jobs.

But even while Howard was writing it was becoming evident that the problems of the Victorian city might resolve themselves in a different way. As early as the 1860s and 1870s, new forms of transport—first the horse tram, the horse bus, the suburban steam railway (railroad) and then, around the turn of the century, the electric railway, the electric tramcar (streetcar) and finally the motor bus—were starting to change fundamentally the shape of British cities. The very high densities of population, which had been characteristic of the inner areas of early Victorian cities, began to thin out as the middle class sought suburban homes. Between the two world wars, as the municipalities went into the mass production of public housing projects, the manual working class began to follow.

The paradox of this interwar period is that it did produce such rapid urban growth, since it was a period of sluggish economic growth and of declining rates of population growth. Expectations of the future, except for some boom years in the 1920s, were generally poor; for much of the period Britain had a million or more unemployed. But there were a number of forces working for urban growth. Though, overall, both economic growth and population growth were slow, there was a considerable internal redistribution, so that some large urban areas in the Midlands and the South, such as London and Birmingham, grew rapidly by internal migration. Transport technology had a fundamental role: within a few years the motor bus became ubiquitous, allowing formerly inaccessible rural areas to be brought within easy reach of the cities, while around London electrification of railways (or even new construction of electric lines) had a powerful influence.

Both private and public housing could be built easily and cheaply. Land, which was not yet subject to the comprehensive powers over development introduced after World War II, was easily obtained and its costs of acquisition represented only a small fraction—less than 10 percent—of total development costs. Building materials such as timber were cheap because of the depression in the prices of primary products. Construction labor was readily hired at low rates. Credit was never more easily or more cheaply obtained; interest rates were low throughout the 1930s at between 4 and 5 percent. As a result, it seems certain that the real cost of housing in relation to incomes was lower during the 1930s than at any time between 1850 and 1970. Private builders sold houses at £400 or £500, with 95 percent mortgages, requiring deposits of as little as £20. Municipal housing was similarly completed at low cost even though Keynesian notions of corrective public spending had not yet gained credence, so that after World War II many large British cities found themselves in the fortunate position of having big stocks of good housing, built at low historic cost, which could be rented very cheaply.

As a result, and in sharp contrast to the situation in the United States (described in chapter 1), the annual total of housing completed in the 1930s reached a peak never exceeded after 1945 until the boom years of the late 1960s; though the rate of new household formation was low compared with postwar years, over 350,000 houses a year were being finished during the period 1935–39 (figure 5). These houses were provided by two main agencies, almost to the exclusion of all others. Overwhelmingly the more important of the two were the speculative private house

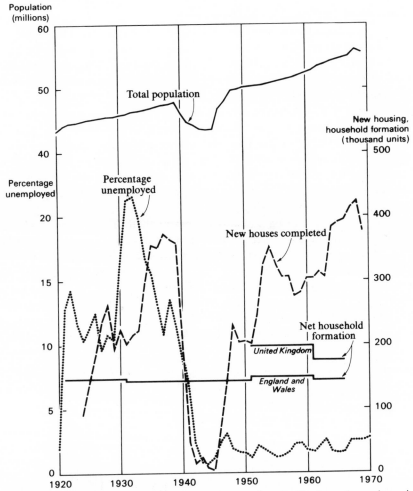

FIGURE 5. Total home population at census dates, net new households formed per decennium, and percentage of labor force unemployed by years—United Kingdom, 1920–1970.

builders, often working on a small scale with 100 houses or less a year. They built freehold housing for sale on mortgage, aided by the easy credit available from building societies. Their houses were built to extremely standardized designs without much imagination or, in many cases, much taste. But they did provide basic housing, suitable for family life, of a quality never before available to the great mass of the population. Characteristically, these houses were detached, or more usually semidetached, built at a density of about ten or twelve to the acre of residential land—which in terms of the average family size at that time, meant about fifty persons to the acre. They had one—or more commonly, two—living rooms, two or three bedrooms, with separate kitchens and bathrooms. By the standards of the 1970s they had crude heating (coal fires), inadequate electrical fittings, and poor insulation against winter weather. But some, if not all, of these deficiencies were capable of being remedied without too much difficulty by later remodelling.

The houses had small or medium-sized gardens (yards), adequate for family use and even capable of vegetable or small fruit production. They were developed in residential areas, which were usually segregated from factory or commercial zones but which contained provision for local shopping. They were invariably connected to public services, including main sewerage, water supply, and public transport systems; because the people who lived here worked in the cities, the new residential areas were built in the form of simple peripheral extensions to those cities. Even in the biggest city of all, London, building in the 1930s took place generally at not more than fifteen miles from the center; in big provincial cities such as Manchester or Birmingham, at not more than seven or eight miles from the center; and in smaller cities, at not more than three or four miles from the center. Though planners condemned much of the resulting development as urban sprawl, that term has to be interpreted in a relative sense.

Public municipal housing was less important than private house building during the whole of the interwar period, accounting for between one-third and one-half of all dwellings completed; yet during the late 1930s it was producing more than 100,000 dwellings a year (figure 6). This program produced homes for rent, with the aid of subsidies from the central government and, often, with local city tax (rate) subsidy also. Many of the homes were occupied by people displaced by the extensive slum clearance operations in the big cities during these years. Though there was some replacement in situ by blocks of apartments, generally the municipal

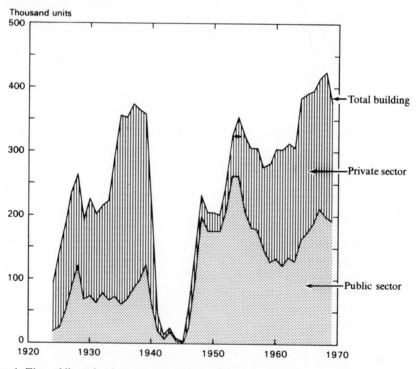

FIGURE 6. The public and private sectors of house building completions in the United Kingdom, 1924–1970.

programs consisted of estates of single-family houses built on previously undeveloped land. Such estates might be very large; outside the biggest cities, developments like Dagenham for London or Wythenshawe for Manchester might house 100,000 people on completion, forming virtual satellite towns. Yet these were not full garden cities in the Ebenezer Howard sense; physically, they were extensions of the city, and functionally, too, they remained part of the city, since most of their employed population had to commute back into the city for work. The densities were generally similar to the private estates, averaging about twelve houses to the acre; the houses might be a little smaller, with one living room rather than two, and with planning in rows rather than detached or semidetached form. As with the private estates, the municipal housing was served by an efficient and cheap public transport system—electric railways in London, usually streetcars or buses in other cities—which gave easy access over the short distances back into the cities for work.

As a result of these trends, especially around the faster-growing urban areas such as London and Birmingham and Manchester, there was relatively rapid consumption of land for urban development during the 1920s and 1930s. Between 1934 and 1939, the loss of agricultural land to urban uses averaged 60,000 acres a year—a rate never again reached after World War II, when the average loss varied between 36,000 and 38,000 acres a year[1] for a housing program which, at its peak in the late 1960s, equalled that of the 1930s. The result is clearly shown in maps at different dates for major English cities. London for instance grew in population from 6½ million to 8½ million between the two world wars, but the physical extent of the agglomeration approximately doubled.

Since there was no effective system of land use planning, there was no way of steering this growth into areas that planning theory suggested were desirable and away from places that seemed undesirable. West of London, the suburban spread engulfed large tracts of some of the most fertile market gardening (truck farming) land in all Britain. Unless purchased by public authorities (as happened in the Lickey Hills south of Birmingham or in Epping Forest and Burnham Beeches near London), or by the National Trust (a private charity), areas of rare scenic value might also be threatened. Farmers and conservationists saw common cause and in 1925 founded the Council for the Preservation of Rural England. By the 1930s conservation of land had become an active policy for many thinking people. The movement gained further support from the great survey of land utilization conducted in the early 1930s by the geographer L. Dudley Stamp, which at last produced accurate figures about the losses. In the circumstances, it was natural that people should turn back to the ideas of Ebenezer Howard for channelling urban growth into planned communities.

But the experiences of the 1930s brought yet another distinctive strain into British thinking about urban growth. As the country began to climb painfully from the trough of the Great Depression, it became clear that the cyclical downturn of

---

[1] This calculation is from Robin H. Best in "Recent Changes and Future Prospects of Land Use in England and Wales," *Geographical Journal*, 131 (1965), table 1, p. 3; and "Extent of Urban Growth and Agricultural Displacement in Post-War Britain," *Urban Studies*, 5 (1968), table 1, pp. 4–5.

1929–32 had merely overlain a deeper and perhaps less tractable secular trend: the continuing and deepening structural decline of many of the older industrial regions of northern and western Britain whose fortunes had been too narrowly based on the staple nineteenth century industries of coal, steel, and heavy engineering. While Greater London and the Birmingham area suffered relatively little even in the depths of the depression, areas like South Wales, North East England, West Cumberland and Central Scotland never seemed to recover from it. In American terms, of course, such peripheral zones were truly not very far from the areas of relative affluence: only 150 miles separated London from South Wales or Birmingham from County Durham. But to contemporaries they indeed appeared like two nations. The paradox was one of mushrooming urban growth in the South and the Midlands, coupled with complete stagnation or decline in the North. It appeared like an evident case of economic waste, which planning might prevent.

The Birth of the Postwar Planning System

Thus, in the late 1930s two strains of thought became intertwined. The idea of containing urban growth and of creating new communities was fused with the idea of correcting regional economic imbalances by positive government action on industrial location policy. This fusion was the contribution of an official commission of inquiry, appointed in 1937, which reported early in 1940—shortly after the outbreak of war in Europe. The Royal Commission on the Distribution of the Industrial Population, under the chairmanship of Sir Anderson Montague Barlow, pointed out that the continued growth of large urban areas represented an economic, social, and strategic problem demanding remedial action.[2] In particular, the commissioners agreed that the growth of London demanded immediate intervention. A minority went further and called for effective government control over industrial location throughout the country. Containment of urban growth and the creation of new planned communities were welcomed in principle; further inquiries were recommended into problems of rural land use and into land values.

One of these inquiries—the Scott committee on rural land use—which reported two years after Barlow in 1942, contributed yet another element to the evolving philosophy.[3] Underlying its many detailed recommendations was the basic notion that agriculture should occupy a specially privileged place in the national economy: it was not to be regarded as any other industry, subject to the hard rules of economic competition and possibly long-term decline, but was to be protected against competition for the land it used. Where it occupied first-class land, the system of land use planning should guarantee that it would never be displaced; elsewhere, it should always have first claim, and the onus of proof should be on the intending developer to show that a change of land use was in the national interest. These recommendations have to be understood in the conditions of 1942, when British

---

[2] *Report of the Royal Commission on the Distribution of the Industrial Population,* Cmd. 6153 (London: His Majesty's Stationery Office, 1940).

[3] *Report of the Royal Commission on Land Utilization in Rural Areas,* Cmd. 6378 (London: His Majesty's Stationery Office, 1942).

farmers had made a remarkable effort to increase home food supplies and thus overcome the wartime blockade. After the war, in the very different peacetime conditions, the recommendations were never carried out to the letter. But the feeling they represented was important in shaping day-to-day postwar planning policies.

Other official reports, which stemmed directly or indirectly from Barlow, also made significant contributions to the philosophy. The Uthwatt report on compensation and betterment, in 1942, recommended that the problems of land value in planning should be resolved by a very radical set of solutions: development rights on rural land should be nationalized, and the state should buy the land when it was needed for development; to this end there should be a central national planning authority to take decisions about land development; within the existing built-up areas, urban renewal should take place through municipal compulsory purchase (eminent domain); and there should be a levy on gains in land value, periodically reassessed and collected.[4] This bundle of solutions was not adopted, but in the 1947 Planning Act an equally radical solution was. Yet another important contribution came in 1945–46 from the committee on new towns under Lord Reith; it recommended that garden cities, on Ebenezer Howard lines, should be built by public corporations drawing finance direct from the central government Treasury, and were to be remarkably free from the existing structure of local government.[5] This prescription for the almost autonomous public corporation—responsible to the public only through an annual report to Parliament—was also used in the British Broadcasting Corporation and in the boards of nationalized industries such as coal, railways, and public utilities; it has been Britain's very distinctive contribution to thinking about management of public enterprises so as to combine entrepreneurial freedom and public responsibility.

At the same time, the wartime government took the lead in encouraging the preparation of ambitious regional plans—of which the best known, Sir Patrick Abercrombie's Greater London Plan, was actually produced and finished before war's end.[6] Abercrombie, a signatory of the Barlow minority report, which called for comprehensive controls over industrial location, produced a plan which was the embodiment of the Barlow ideals in practice. The continued economic growth of London was to be curbed by stringent industrial location controls; its physical growth, equally, was to be limited by a greenbelt, some five miles wide, around the existing built-up agglomeration; beyond that, new towns were to be built according to the Ebenezer Howard prescription, to take the overspill population that had to be rehoused from London's slums and congested inner areas; beyond that, again, expansions of existing small market towns were to take the rest of the overspill, at distances up to 100 miles from London. It was an ambitious, even a grandiose, plan which had an immediate emotional appeal. At war's end or shortly afterwards similar plans, equally ambitious and imaginative, were prepared either

---

[4] *Final Report of the Expert Committee on Compensation and Betterment,* Cmd. 6386 (London: His Majesty's Stationery Office, 1942).

[5] *Final Report of the New Towns Committee,* Cmd. 6876 (London: His Majesty's Stationery Office, 1945).

[6] Patrick Abercrombie, *Greater London Plan 1944* (London: His Majesty's Stationery Office, 1945).

by the central government or by local committees for the other great urban agglomerations of Britain. Everywhere, the themes were the familiar ones taken from
the Barlow report: containment, conservation of land, creation of self-contained
new planned communities.

The whole complex of ideas, then, came into being within a very short period
during the Second World War as a direct response to the conditions of the 1930s
—and even, in the case of the rediscovery of Howard, beyond that. They amounted
to a demand for radical interventionism on the part of government—interventionism
that would probably have been inconceivable before the war. Thus the government
should not merely give incentives to industry to locate in depressed areas, but
should if necessary prohibit it from locating in other areas, especially areas that
were deemed to be congested or suffering from urban sprawl. Again, the government should create a land use planning system with effective negative powers to
stop developers building on valuable farmland or on areas of scenic or historic
importance. The government should effectively nationalize development rights on
all land that was not already built upon. And the government itself should take
the lead in building new communities on a large scale, through the medium of
public development corporations.

The means were radical enough. But—and perhaps this is the reason for their
general acceptance at the end of World War II—the ends were basically conservative: to try to maintain the existing distribution of population by preventing the
drift of population from the peripheral industrial districts of the North and West
to London, the South East, and the Midlands; to try to contain the invasion of
unspoiled natural countryside and agricultural land by speculative housing; and to
create planned communities in carefully chosen locations, where the social problems
of great urban agglomerations could be ameliorated. All this made a profound
appeal to conservatives and radicals alike. Such a coalition could hardly fail to win
the day.

As a result, a remarkably concentrated burst of thinking between 1940 and 1946
was followed by an equally concentrated burst of effective legislative action between
1945 and 1952. There is an important lesson here: once the collective mind of the
British establishment is made up, politicians and officials can cooperate to drive
through even quite radical legislation without much interference. But undoubtedly,
the particular emotional climate of the immediate postwar period allowed the legislation to go through more speedily than would have been conceivable before World
War II; the nation was determined on radical changes in the social and economic
order, as the landslide Labour party victory in the 1945 election demonstrated.
Though town and country planning was not a major issue for the ordinary voter,
the new Labour government placed town and country planning in the forefront
of its legislative program.

This is not the place to describe the program and the resulting system of planning in detail; that is done in chapter 5. Only the broad outlines need be mentioned here. Basically, the system consisted of an interrelated set of new regulatory
powers and agencies. At the broad regional level, the Distribution of Industry Act
of 1945 gave the central government the power to control new industrial location
by a system of licensing plus inducements to private industrialists to move into

regions in need of development.[7] The New Towns Act of 1946 provided for the construction of new towns by public development corporations, as suggested in the Reith reports.

The Town and Country Planning Act of 1947, the cornerstone of the entire system, took the bold step of nationalizing development rights in land—not merely those on undeveloped land, as the 1942 Uthwatt report had suggested—so that they could be transferred to local planning authorities that would then have absolute and effective power over new development and redevelopment. Accordingly, it provided that these authorities should prepare and regularly revise development plans for their areas, and should then control all development in accordance with the plan. It provided further that all subsequent increases in land values due to development should revert to the state through the mechanism of a charge on development and through compulsory purchase (eminent domain) by public authorities at existing use values.

Following the 1947 Act, in 1949 the National Parks and Access to the Countryside Act at last provided for National Parks to be run by local planning authorities or by joint boards of those authorities, with advice and coordination from a National Parks Commission. Lastly, the Town Development Act of 1952[8] provided for an alternative way of building new communities in addition to the new towns machinery: voluntary agreements between local authorities in the great urban agglomerations and other authorities representing country towns, with central government funding for the provision of costly public services.

The intervention of this system into the urban growth process is the central theme of the British experience described in this book; there is nothing like it in the American experience already outlined in chapter 1. Throughout this book, we shall be concerned to ask what the effects of this intervention have been, and how far they can be regarded as beneficial. So it is important even at this stage to stress that both the objectives of the system and the machinery of implementation are distinctive and important.

On objectives, from the Barlow report onward, it seems to have been assumed that all men of good will were agreed. The continued growth of large urban agglomerations was bad on economic, social, and strategic grounds; the employer suffered as much as the employee from congestion, long commuter journeys, and inflated housing costs, and the best interests of both would be served by a policy of urban containment coupled with the building of new communities. Similarly, building on good agricultural land was an economic and strategic disaster for the whole nation, since it rendered Britain vulnerable to changes in world agricultural conditions or wartime blockade. Again, the continued decline of the older industrial areas was an economic drain on the whole nation, not just to those areas themselves. Such a style of argument suits a centralized decision-making structure, where a well-defined establishment of officials and politicians share common values. It tends to ignore the possibility that there may be losers as well as gainers from instituting a system of controls.

[7] This act was actually passed by the wartime Coalition government in its last days.
[8] Prepared by a Labour government but passed by the succeeding Conservative government after the election of 1951.

The machinery, too, had a distinctive stamp. It was mainly regulatory in character and it worked through classification of land use. This particularly applied to the very large element of physical planning in the entire system, where control was to be exerted through a detailed plan giving a blueprint of the desired future end-state of the system. The assumption was that the environment had an influence on society, and that this influence could be predicted. This, in turn, reflected an underlying belief that the pace of social, economic, and physical change would be slow enough to monitor and control. Furthermore, it was assumed specifically that a basic objective of the plan was to limit and to control change; for uncontrolled change was felt to be an inherently unstable and unhealthy condition of society, rather like a piece of machinery outside anyone's control. This belief, in which the British anticipated an important strand of American thought of the early 1970s, of course came in conflict with the reality of the postwar period.

The Postwar Pattern of Change

In the event, the underlying dynamics of the British economy and of British society have been greater than could ever have been imagined by those who created the postwar planning system. The rate of economic growth has been modest by international standards; yet it has produced a growth in gross national product of about 60 percent (in constant terms) between 1945 and 1970. Because it came about at the stage when mass consumption became the rule, it has had notable effects on the ownership of consumer durables, especially the private automobile. And this trend has been imposed on a rapidly rising population—the product of a birthrate that has oscillated as unpredictably as in any other western advanced country during the 1950s and 1960s but that has tended to be consistently higher than in the interwar period. Coming together, these trends have resulted in pressure for urban living space much greater than was imagined by professionals at the end of World War II. And naturally, they have run up against the philosophy of conservation and containment that was the basis of the planning system set up at war's end.

The dynamic of population growth, analyzed in more detail in chapter 4, is the most striking and least expected feature. It has resulted in annual additions to the British population considerably higher than were ever recorded in the 1930s. While the population of the United Kingdom between 1919 and 1939 rose only by 4½ million (from about 43½ million to about 48 million), from 1949 to 1969 the increase was 5½ million (from 50 million to 55½ million)—an absolute increase of about one-quarter greater (figure 5). Furthermore, this additional population has been dividing itself into more and smaller households as a result of demographic changes—increases in the numbers of young adults and old people—and of social changes such as earlier marriage and the tendency for young people to leave home for education or employment. The net rate of household formation was 198,000 a year in the 1950s, very little above the interwar levels; by the early 1960s it had fallen to 175,000 a year.

For a considerable time after 1945 these demographic and social changes were not fully reflected in the rate of new home construction. Whereas the late 1930s had seen an average of over 350,000 completed new homes a year, it was not until 1952 (apart from a momentary peak in 1948) that the industry achieved an annual total of even 200,000 new permanent homes. Up to this point, the postwar building program had been achieved almost wholly by public agencies including the local authorities and the new town development corporations—a remarkable reversal of the prewar pattern, reflecting the policies of the 1945–51 Labour government. Thereafter, the public sector never again achieved the totals of the early 1950s. But there was a rapid increase in private house building to compensate. Total completions rose sharply to 350,000 in 1954, recalling the levels of the 1930s. Thereafter they fell back to 300,000 and under in the late 1950s and early 1960s, rising sharply again after 1963 to levels that finally overtook the records of the late 1930s. In 1968, the record year, over 425,000 homes were completed in the United Kingdom: 226,000 of them by private house builders, just under 200,000 of them by all forms of public agency.

The remarkable fact is that this program has been accommodated with a smaller annual land take than was ever recorded in the 1930s. While there was an average loss of more than 60,000 acres every year to urban development in the 1930s, since World War II the rate of loss has tended to average about 40,000 acres a year.[9] This is the result of the policies of urban containment, which have been operated by the local planning authorities set up under the 1947 Planning Act. In later chapters we shall analyze the operation of these policies in detail. But the mere statistical achievement is remarkable enough when set against the background of rapid urban change.

The growth of the population and the house-building program to accommodate it have necessarily occurred for the most part on previously undeveloped land— however jealously the policies of conservation and containment have operated to restrict the process. It is not surprising, therefore, that some of the same trends are observable in British urban growth as have already been observed for the American process since World War II: growth has naturally been accompanied by outward spread of people, and more latterly of jobs. For purposes of analysis, the conventional statistical tabulations in the British Census are no longer very useful. They are based on a quite artificial distinction between urban and rural, which depends on whether an area happens to be described as rural for purely administrative purposes. Too often, this represents the reality of the 1890s rather than the reality of the 1970s; and it is not surprising that during the 1950s and the 1960s the rural districts have been experiencing rapid aggregate rises in population. In fact, many of the so-called rural districts showing the most dramatic growth contain parishes on the fringes of towns and urban agglomerations that happen to have received heavy suburban growth since World War II; functionally, these areas are no longer rural at all. We need a more meaningful and a more consistent definition, and the concept of the Standard Metropolitan Statistical Area—long familiar from analyses of urban growth in the United States and already used in

9 Calculations by Robin H. Best, summarized in A. M. Edwards and G. P. Wibberley, *An Agricultural Land Budget for England and Wales 1965–2000* (Wye, England: Wye College. 1971).

chapter 1 of this book—provides it. The SMSA has come under heavy criticism in recent years on various statistical grounds, and in trying to design a British equivalent we have taken note of the criticisms as far as we can. Our "Standard Metropolitan Labour Areas" are based on major centers of employment, in terms of a fixed minimum density of employment or (in certain problem cases) a minimum fixed total of employment. They take in all those administrative areas around this labor center, or core, which contribute 15 percent or more of their resident labor force to it. (In those few cases where two cores claim more than 15 percent, the one receiving most commuters, of course, wins.) The definition is deliberately as similar as possible to that of the American SMSA, save that the central employment mass is more rigorously defined—an important refinement in Britain, where so much of the population lives and works in big, rather amorphous agglomerations.

Using this concept, exactly 100 Standard Metropolitan Labour Areas could be defined in England and Wales at the Census of 1961. Over the forty-year period 1931 to 1971, these 100 SMLAs have contained consistently 76 to 78 percent of the total population of England and Wales; or in other words, with some slight slippage after 1961 they have retained a constant share of the total population growth. Overall, between 1931 and 1961 they added some 6½ million to their populations—3⅓ million in the twenty years 1951–71 alone. This growth, however, has been by no means evenly spread across the country. During the 1950s about two-thirds of the total growth of population in the 100 SMLAs was concentrated either in and around London or in the Midlands; during the 1960s the proportion was just over one-half. Seventeen out of twenty of the fastest growing SMLAs in the decade 1951–61, and fourteen out of twenty in the decade 1961–71, were in the South East. Conversely, the SMLAs with the poorest growth records in both periods were mainly in the North West and in Yorkshire. Though the main factor here was a regional one, size also was important: the biggest metropolitan areas tended to have poor growth rates, and by the early 1960s some of them were recording actual declines.

The use of the SMLA framework illustrates the fact that as the urban areas have grown, they have decentralized. Their growth has been disproportionately outside their central cores; in some cases these cores have experienced absolute decline of population—and, in a few cases, employment. Whereas, in 1931, 55 percent of the entire population of England and Wales lived in the SMLA cores, the proportion fell to 50 percent in 1951, to 48 percent in 1961, to 46 percent in 1966, and to 45 percent in 1971. In most cases the process here was one of relative decentralization: both core and ring added to their population totals, but growth was more rapid in the ring. Absolute decentralization—with actual loss in core population—tended to be restricted to the bigger SMLAs of northern England, where big urban renewal programs were displacing people in the late 1950s and 1960s. With employment, significantly, the history has been different.[10] Up to the 1961 Census, of those SMLAs that were gaining employment—the big majority—

---

[10] For employment, 1971 data were not available as this book went to press.

most were experiencing centralization of employment, and many of these were experiencing absolute centralization in the sense that employment was actually declining in the suburbs. The early 1960s witnessed a profound change: by then, the great majority of SMLAs recording growth in employment were decentralizing jobs, as they were decentralizing people. One can therefore generalize and say that while the tendency to decentralize people was already general in British metropolitan areas by the 1950s, the parallel tendency to decentralize employment only became general between 1961 and 1966. From the detailed records, it is clear that the biggest SMLAs were among the first to decentralize employment. And significantly, by the 1960s these were again leading the way in experiencing absolute loss of population and, in some cases, employment. The largest metropolitan area of all, London, was manifesting another trend by the early 1960s: its losses in population and in jobs were being balanced by rapid gains in a ring of separate peripheral SMLAs contiguous to London in an almost unbroken ring around the capital.

These trends seem to show clearly that, with a fairly short time lag, urban England and Wales are following the tendencies already so clearly manifested and so well documented in the urban United States. Rapid growth is accompanied by an outward push, both of people and of jobs. Partly, indeed, the decentralization of jobs is a lagged response to the decentralization of people; in any affluent society, the suburban residential population will generate a demand for local suburban service jobs, which will be tied with varying degrees of closeness to the residential population.

Other tendencies must increasingly reinforce these trends. As affluence increases, it is likely that people will wish to use more of their wealth to acquire bulky possessions that will demand more storage space. They will also demand more private space in and around the house; the census evidence shows clearly that space standards in the home, in terms of the rooms-to-people ratio, have increased greatly since the 1930s. Because of changes in life-cycle patterns—children going away for university or college education for part of the year for instance—families find that they need a generous surplus of house room, at least for part of the time. By the 1966 Census, car ownership in many suburban areas had risen to 70 percent and more of all households, compared with a national average of only about 45 percent. In general, detailed analysis does not clearly show a tendency to use the car for commuting to suburban jobs as compared with the commuting to the central cores —at least up to the time of the 1966 Census. But even then, the trend was fairly evident in the larger metropolitan areas such as Manchester, Liverpool, or Birmingham. The detailed land use–transportation studies, which were carried out in these larger agglomerations in the middle and late 1960s, clearly show how the use of the car is going to increase, not only for suburb-to-suburb work journeys but also for nonwork journeys of all kinds during the 1970s and 1980s. There seems to be no way of stopping the average English suburbanite from becoming almost as dependent on the car as his American counterpart. But this, if it happens, will add another turn to the wheel, encouraging further development of the dispersed living and working patterns that the car makes possible.

PLANNING AND THE ADAPTATION TO CHANGE

The planning system that was brought into being between 1946 and 1952, as we have seen, was designed for a very different set of circumstances: it assumed that change would be slow and controllable, and that the task was to restrict the rate of change in the interests of the community. In particular, it was committed to the task of urban containment in an era when social and economic forces contributed to unprecedented pressures for decentralization of urban areas. There has clearly been a conflict, and it has had two effects. First, growth has been controlled and limited; but secondly, the emphases of the planning system have been profoundly changed.

The intentions of those who campaigned for the creation of the postwar planning system and those who actually brought it into being are not always clear from the record of their writings or their legislation. But overall, it seems evident that they assumed a very different balance between private enterprise and public control from anything that had obtained before the Second World War. Decisions that had previously been taken by individual entrepreneurs, having only imperfect knowledge of each other's actions, would henceforth be taken by planners who could impose a coherent and consistent set of policies. Instead of individual industrialists taking a host of separate locational decisions, the consequences of which would later be felt by individuals who decided to migrate to seek work or by private house builders who decided how and where to provide homes for these workers, all the critical decisions—the location of new industry and the provision of new homes—would be taken by planners either in central or in local government; and by a dovetailing of national, regional, and local plans covering various aspects of activity, the decisions would be properly coordinated.

This did not amount to a demand for complete omnipotence (or omniscience) on the part of the planners. Private industrialists would remain in business and would be free to take locational decisions. Private house builders would continue to build and exercise their judgments as to where this was profitable. Above all, people would still be free to move into jobs or out of them, where and when they pleased, without direction. But all these decisions would be taken only within a framework of policies laid down in the national interest by officials in national and local government. The policies would be applied so effectively that, for instance, there would be no further growth of industry in the London area. And the great majority of people moving each year into new homes would do so in comprehensively planned communities away from existing urban areas; they would, therefore, be housed by public agencies of one sort or another, rather than by private speculative builders. This, at any rate, seems to have been the intention. And this was what was achieved in the earliest postwar years of the Labour government from 1945 to 1951. During that time, the great majority of all new houses built were provided by public agencies. The private developer, so important an agent of urban development in the 1930s, was reduced to a shadow.

Very rapidly after the census of 1951, all this changed. It was not merely a result of the arrival of a Conservative government in the election of that year, committed to a policy of private enterprise; it was the conjunction of the political factor and the sudden upsurge of the birthrate coupled with the beginnings of the mass consumer society, around 1955, which secured the transformation. For even a government committed wholeheartedly to comprehensively planned, publicly constructed new communities might have been hard pressed in the late 1950s to meet the combined demands of rising population, rising affluence, and the effects of the slum clearance program that began in earnest after 1955. As a result, as figure 6 shows, by the end of the 1950s the private developer was again responsible for a majority of all new housing; and urban growth in postwar Britain became a particularly good example of the mixed economy, in which private and public actors interact in complex ways to reach critical decisions about the pattern of development.

THE ACTORS: (I) THE PLANNERS

The "planner"—that bureaucratic figure who features so prominently in the political mythology both of the right and left—is, of course, still a key figure in this process. But in fact there is not one species of planner, but several, with different roles and even divergent interests. To the layman, the planner is the local authority planner who can give or deny permission for development at any scale, from knocking in a new window to the building of a new community. Professional local authority planners have a common educational background and a common career structure. They have usually received (or are working towards) a professional qualification of the Royal Town Planning Institute, which depends on a combination of taught courses (increasingly at a university or a polytechnic) and practical experience, and they naturally share many of the basic objectives of the postwar planning system, which have become almost articles of faith of the profession; after all, the planning profession as it has emerged in postwar England is largely a result of the career structure provided by the 1947 Act. Most planners have paid at least lip service to the ideals of urban containment, conservation of land, and the creation of self-contained communities. Most of them, for obvious reasons, have subscribed to the view that physical environment has a demonstrable effect on the performance of the economy or the quality of social life. They therefore naturally believed in making physical plans for the future shape of the built environment.

By the 1970s there were signs that these values were shifting; in the more progressive planning authorities younger planners tended to be more concerned with social objectives, but as a description of overall objectives over the 1947–70 period the above account is fair. The planners of the 1950s and 1960s therefore shared some common objectives, but they were also divided. Despite intense debate at the time, the 1947 Town and Country Planning Act was not accompanied by fundamental local government reform. The act gave planning responsibilities and powers to the largest local government units that were available—the counties and county boroughs. But this pattern of local government, dating as it did from the last twenty years of the nineteenth century, did not accord with the realities of planning in postwar Britain. Cities were divided from their own suburbs, which were in the territory of the neighboring county. And the bigger urban agglomerations might typically be fragmented for planning purposes, with separate planning offices in half a dozen county boroughs (cities) and three or four counties. There was no overall provision for coordination, and each authority tended to go its own way.

In this situation, whatever their training or their basic value systems, local authority professional planners naturally came over time to identify themselves with the political interests—using that term in a broad sense—of the local authority they served. Those planners who worked for authorities in the economically less-developed parts of the country, such as the declining coalfield areas of the North, would stress the objective of economic development and accompanying physical development, which would involve partnership between planners and developers; while those planners who served authorities in the more dynamic parts of the country, such as the Midlands and the South, would be more inclined to stress their role as regulators of private interests. But, especially in those more dynamic parts of the heavily urbanized belt that has been called Megalopolis England, there was an obvious clash of interest between city and county, in which the professional planner took part.

Planners in the cities would chiefly be involved in schemes for development or redevelopment of the urban fabric—including commercial city center schemes and extensive public housing schemes originated by the city housing department. The latter obviously involved a need for more land; in the 1930s land was usually easy to find at the periphery of the city, and the municipal housing agencies had developed large programs. But in the postwar period they found themselves confronted by another set of professionals, whose interests and values were opposed to theirs—the county planning departments, set up from scratch after passage of the 1947 Planning Act, and staffed by planners who tended to be deeply committed to the principles of urban containment. Though they might not be opposed to development as such, they were likely to oppose peripheral development of the cities on the model of the 1930s. Here, therefore, was a recipe for conflict between two sets of professional planners with different political interests and associated value systems. The comfortable notion of the pioneers who created the 1947 system—that professionals who shared a common education and a common set of values could agree on the best solution for the whole community—had in fact been replaced by a system of dispersed decision making, in which professional interests often clashed.

By the late 1960s and early 1970s, there were distinct signs that this situation might be changing. In the South East and North West, central and local government planners—including city and county officials—cooperated in producing overall regional strategies; in fast-growing urban areas such as Leicester, Nottingham-Derby, Coventry-Solihull, and South Hampshire, special subregional planning teams were set up jointly by city and county authorities; the new settlement structure plans, stipulated by an act of 1968, were similarly prepared by joint action; and the prospect of local government reform, abolishing the city-county division in most areas, encouraged cooperation. But the 1972 Local Government Act allowed county districts to prepare their own local plans with their own planning staffs, and may go a long way to restore the old attitudes.

In a conflict situation, planners and political leaders within any given local authority tend to share the same values and objectives. This is perhaps natural:

though independent minded, professional planners will tend to be loyal to the authority they work for, and will come to identify with it. The political leaders, for the most part, take up predictable attitudes; and in most cases these seem to have represented the views of those members of the public—often an interested but vocal minority—who elected them. In the county boroughs, whatever the political complexion of the ruling party, the first task of the elected representative has been to guard the interests of the city and its inhabitants. This, in the circumstances of the 1950s and 1960s, would be interpreted to mean a number of key objectives: redevelopment and expansion of the central business district, which supplies an important part of the city's vital tax base; renewal of the slum areas, which often occupied a wide belt around this central area; and the preservation and further development of the city's manufacturing industry, which again contributed notably to the tax base, and which was typically found at the periphery of the city.

In the postwar period, the first of these objectives has proved only too easy to achieve, but there have been resulting problems. The rapid increase in mass spending after 1955 has brought an unparalleled opportunity for large-scale city center development on the basis of partnership between the city and private developers; such an opportunity has appealed to politicians and planners alike. But given the rapid increase in ownership of private automobiles during the same period, the result must be congestion and a demand from the city for more funds to pay for parking garages, inner distributor roads of ever-increasing scale and complexity, and finally expensive connections to the national motorway system—which, like the equivalent American Interstate system, had not originally been designed as an urban network. Commercial renewal therefore makes the cities supplicants for subsidies from the central government—especially for highway funds. And because even these could provide no permanent answer to the dilemma of trying to fit cars into the urban fabric, the requests for subsidies are likely to be unending.

At the same time, slum clearance in the inner ring around the center—encouraged and financially aided by the central government in a big drive after 1955—has caused acute pressure for more housing land, which fortuitously has happened at just the point when the natural increase of the population began to rise. In these circumstances, the interests of the city are to retain as many as possible of its residents: if possible through new peripheral housing estates built on extensions of the city area—as was the model of the 1930s—or, failing that, in high-rise schemes built within the city boundaries. If, therefore, city officials are faced with county planners determined to enforce a policy of containment, and backed by government policies, they will tend to fall back on the high-rise, high-density solution—especially if special government subsidies are available to support the high costs involved. Thus, in many cases, all the agents in the process of development— city governments, county governments, and central government—found themselves locked together in supporting the high-rise solution, despite considerable evidence that it was both expensive and unpopular. And, though the high-rise solution was quite discredited by the late 1960s, other variants of the high-density pattern were not.

The strength of political feeling in the counties partly explains this; for here, the ideology of the planner and the values of the politician find common cause. In some of the more rural counties, an influential type of elected county representative might be one of the older residents—perhaps a member of an old county family, with landowning interests that go back perhaps centuries and with a name that is known and honored in the county. He feels intensely about the rural way of life and its preservation—especially if he is a landowner himself. Those who elect him are unlikely to own much land themselves, for typical English country dwellers have long ceased to be farmers; they are more likely to be retired people or to have professional jobs in the small county market towns, or even to be prosperous long-distance commuters to the city. Most of them have voluntarily chosen the rural way of life in preference to the city, and their aim is to retain it against all inroads. True, winds of change are blowing; and in the early 1970s there are signs that both the electorate and the elected representatives contain people who recognize the facts of urban growth. But, overall, both groups have tended to be stalwart defenders of the status quo. They are unlikely to look kindly upon rapid and large-scale change, such as would be entailed by the development of a new town or a satellite estate for the city or a new motorway or airport; and all such developments they will fight, often with a very professional organization and a great deal of subscription money. Their great fear is of the distant bureaucrat from the city or from London, who rides roughshod over their interests. "R. E. Mote," the goose-stepping, briefcase-carrying bureaucrat, who was invented by the Rural District Councils Association in their fight against proposals to abolish them, is the archtype of this figure; their constant vigilance is needed to frustrate him.

Local government reform has therefore been a politically tendentious issue in England, despite the fact that by the late 1960s almost all interests were agreed on the need for some change. The Royal Commission report of 1969, which was endorsed in broad outlines by the Labour government, would have shifted power decisively to the urban interests; over much of the country it would have resulted in single-tier, all-purpose government dominated by the major city, while in and around the conurbations would have been metropolitan governments operating at two tiers, and extending far out into the controversial greenbelt areas. It was no surprise that after the Conservative victory in the 1970 election, the new government should have replaced this measure of reform with a quite different one more favorable to rural interests. In the Local Government Act passed by Parliament in 1972, the boundaries of the so-called metropolitan counties are cut sharply back to the strict physical limits of the conurbations; and even outside these areas there is a two-tier system whereby the county prepares a broad outline plan, but the local districts are responsible both for drawing up detailed local plans and for the granting of planning permission. In effect, this means that the rural areas are given even more power than formerly to determine their own character; and it seems likely that they will use this, in many cases, to defend the status quo.

There are thus seeds of conflict in the situation. Whether these bear fruit in the ritual confrontation of a public inquiry or not, the system demands that conflict be resolved—if anywhere—by the central government. The Whitehall machine contains planners—some with the professional qualifications of the Royal Town Planning Institute, some without. They include the administrators—some London-based, some in provincial offices—who operate the Industrial Development Certificate and Office Development Permit schemes.[11] These exercise a most important power, denied to the local planner: the location of at any rate part of the basic employment that in turn generates the demand for new homes, new shops, new schools, and other services. They operate on a set of flexible but well-defined criteria that put national considerations before purely local ones. Thus they may deny a firm the right to move from a congested location in a conurbation to a neighboring overspill scheme, because they want it to move to a Development Area. They may also choose to deny the firm permission to expand in situ, on the grounds that it would create congestion or labor-supply difficulties. And here their views may not at all accord with those of the local politician or the local official, anxious to keep industry within the city limits. The industrialist finds himself playing an elaborate game with both, sometimes trading one off against the other; he will work to get an Industrial Development Certificate, so as to strengthen him in his negotiations with the local planners.

Another important group of central planners is the professional inspectorate of the Department of the Environment, which holds inquiries into objections against the development plans of the local planning authorities, and also hears appeals against planning refusals—including that significant category where one authority (a city for instance) appeals against the decision of another (a county) not to allow development within the latter's boundaries. The inspectors follow no set legal rules; their function is quasi-judicial, and they work on their own interpretation of good planning practice; they may even, in a minority of cases, be overruled by the Minister to whom they make their recommendations. But the influence of the Minister and his Whitehall officials is more pervasive than this. The inspectors' task is to apply good current planning practice to their decisions, and they are naturally guided by policy statements and guidelines. Thus, after 1955 they followed the guideline that greenbelts around cities were desirable to prevent further growth of large urban areas; after 1962 they followed the guideline that densities of new single-family house developments should be modestly increased in order to save land.

This, however, is only the formal way in which the central government tries to resolve conflicts. It may also operate through a series of more informal influences —such as the use of critical power to grant or refuse loan sanction for the infrastructure to support urban development (above all, sewerage); the power, similarly, to grant or deny central government subsidies for highway or school construction; and finally, the behind-the-scenes influence of the Minister or his officials on local leaders or planners.

It might be thought that planning, as a subject that affected many people intimately, would be an intensely political issue on which major reversals of policy would occur after both general and local elections. But in practice, generally that has not been the case. There have been some national party political controversies concerned with the interlinked questions of land acquisition and the taxation of

---

[11] These schemes, which provide for central government control over the location of a substantial proportion of new employment, are explained in chapter 5.

increases in land values. Locally, party political attitudes on the scale of public housing programs might affect the amount of overspill to be accommodated outside city limits, or housed expensively in high-rise structures within them. But generally, the controversies have not divided politicians on party lines. Major swings of policy —on national issues such as the need for regional planning guidelines, which came to be recognized after 1961, or the need to reform local government after 1965— came to be accepted almost simultaneously by politicians of all complexions, even if they might differ on details of policy. Clearly, Ministers allow themselves to be affected by the general drift of professional and informed opinion among their senior advisers. The future lines of policy change, at least over half a decade or so, could well be divined by anyone who cared to read carefully the professional journals or listen to pronouncements at professional meetings. Here, as elsewhere, the cohesion and flexibility of the British governing establishment is the key: an idea that gains general acceptance among professionals, officials, and politicians alike will soon after be implemented in legislation or in the general direction of day-to-day policy decisions.

THE ACTORS: (II) THE DEVELOPERS

The intention of the pioneers who created the 1947 planning system seems to have been that in future the private developer would play a minor part in the total process of urban growth and change. But ever since 1951, at any rate, that belief has not been realistic. Private development agencies take the real initiative in the development process, since they finally decide whether or not to build in a particular location; once their development plans are made, the planning agencies, either at central or local government level, are restricted to the negative role of refusal or acceptance of the proposals put up to them.

In practice, the interrelationships of private and public agencies are complex and difficult to analyze. Both know that they do not possess complete power; they work through a combination of bluff and counter-bluff, bargaining, and accommodation. Private industrialists, for instance, may find all sorts of loopholes in the Department of Trade and Industry's industrial location control mechanisms: they move to sites such as disused airfields, for instance, where no certificate is necessary because the buildings are classified as suitable for industrial use. Or they may prove to the official's satisfaction that they cannot reasonably operate anywhere but in their present location, so that permission for expansion is granted. Or they may threaten to go overseas. Or they may agree to a suggestion to move some operations to a Development Area, in order to have a better prospect of approval for a more important operation in a non-Development Area. Or they may play elaborate games of "space chess," moving different functions around in order to make the best use of what they have. Fundamental in all this is the fact that the private industrialist is usually quicker to respond to changing conditions than is the official who works within a set of guiding rules—flexible as these may be in practice.

Residential developers, too, tend to play elaborate games with local planning officials. They exist on a narrow financial margin between success and failure and are far from being free agents. They must find land that can be built on—which means land provided (or providable) with public services. If they are small developers, they must find land to which planning permission attaches; if they are big developers, they must usually find land to which permission does not attach but can be made to attach; in either case, the price must be low enough to develop at a profit, to secure detailed planning permission on matters like house styles and layout, to carry out the development process, and then to sell.

In practice, the developer is faced with a critical decision in which he has to balance the price he pays for the land, the number of houses he puts on this land, the time taken to get permission and build (which determines his carrying charges), and the price he will receive for the houses when he has succeeded in selling them. In all these elements, he is only one of a number of agents: others include the owner of the land, the planner, and the eventual buyer (together with the agency which supplies the credit). Land with outline planning permission and with servicing, ready for early development, tends to be scarce and expensive—at least within reasonably easy reach of the major urban areas. Land without such permission, or without necessary services, will be much cheaper, but its usefulness is highly speculative, and in any event is likely to be long-term. Bigger developers may afford such a gamble; the smaller man almost certainly cannot. Given the rising cost of credit, which has typified much of the postwar period, his only chance is to buy land with the necessary permission, agree on details with the planning authority as soon as possible, and start building.

It is not surprising, then, that many developers—especially the smaller, local ones —seek some sort of working accommodation with the planning office. They acquire a knowledge of what will be acceptable and what will not, while on the other hand the planning officer acquires a knowledge of the constraints affecting them. The working relationships between developer and planner, over time, tend to become fairly straightforward if not always smooth. Only in one of ten cases will refusals be taken to appeal; and then, commonly, they are in the nature of test cases brought by bigger outside developers, who want to see whether the time has come to establish a new policy line from the Department of the Environment on the release of a particular area, or a particular category, of land. Thus, in general, the local authorities have been able successfully to enforce their policies of containment and steering growth outside the major urban areas; developers have been willing to go along with them, provided they could get the necessary building land to stay in business, because the system reduced risk and gave them more predictable profits by maintaining the scarcity value of the land.

But here another constraint enters. The final product must be sellable. It must be soundly built to satisfy the demands of the building society or insurance society surveyor who will help determine the mortgage that can be given to the buyer. In addition, by the end of the 1960s, the mortgage agencies were demanding possession of a guarantee of fitness through the National House Builders' Registration scheme, which further raised minimum standards and thus costs. (In the United States the standards of the Federal Housing Administration, which insures private mortgages, have tended to be the standards of the building industry.) At the same time, especially in the fringes at the outer periphery of the metropolitan area, the builder is acutely conscious that he is likely to be selling to a marginal buyer: a buyer who, because of the rigid rules relating mortgage loans to income, will be unable to afford more than a certain price ceiling. The developer finds that land costs particularly, but also construction costs, are rising; and land costs at any rate are rising faster than the general price and income level, which will determine the selling price he can fix for his completed house. The most obvious way he can avoid the dilemma is to economize on land by raising the densities of his housing, as will be discussed in chapters 4 and 5. And in doing this, he is likely to find at least tacit approval from the local planning authority, which feels that it is implementing Department policy guidelines.

The Actors: (III) The Buyers

The third set of agents in the process of urban development is, of course, the people who will live in the new houses being developed for the first time; for overwhelmingly the great bulk of the developed land is for residential use and for certain necessary ancillary uses such as schools, shops, and parks. The pattern of urban development must obviously be shaped by the wants and the needs of these new residents; for whatever professional planners or politicians or developers may determine, houses have to be built in some reasonable relation to the pattern of existing population distribution and to the location of employment and services.

New homes on previously undeveloped land, by definition, are sold or rented to migrants. And here it should be noted that though mobility in Britain may be increasing—as a result of population growth, a higher rate of household formation, the increasing proportion of the labor force in managerial and professional occupations, and the growth of large-scale organizations whose members expect to migrate as part of their career structure—the British still seem markedly less mobile than the Americans. From the evidence in the 1966 Census, it appears that at that date two-thirds of all the people in England and Wales were still living at the same address where they had lived five years before; and of those who had moved house, one-half were still living in the same local authority area as five years before. In other words, during this five-year period, only one-sixth of the population had moved across local authority boundaries. And an analysis of the 1961 Census data indicates that in any one year less than one in one hundred of the population moved more than forty miles. Americans were more mobile: in the 1950–60 period, only half were in the same house at the end as at the beginning; of those who moved at all, two-thirds were in the same county (these included many who moved from city to suburb); but of the one-fifth who moved outside the county, many moved to another state.

There are a number of possible explanations for this relative immobility in Britain: a more settled career structure; smaller proportions of people with higher education and with professional qualifications; lower car ownership and hence a lower propensity to commute over long distances across country. But the pattern of housing tenure in Britain provides one good explanation in itself. Since World War II, about half the housing completions in Britain have been in the public sector. And apart from a small number built by new town development corporations and the Scottish Special Housing Association, the vast majority of this public housing has been built by local authorities. Again, a very small proportion of this local authority building has been outside city boundaries, in so-called town development schemes under the 1952 Act. But by far the larger part has been built by local authorities within their own boundaries. And once council tenants find low-cost, secure housing of reasonable quality in this way, they are not very likely to endure the problems and uncertainties of a long-distance move to another authority. The local authority housing program has been a factor working to restrict long-distance mobility among a large sector of manual workers in Britain.

Movement into new homes at some distance from the cities, we can surmise, is virtually restricted to a relatively small number of new town tenants and a much larger number of owner-occupiers buying their own homes from speculative developers, generally on mortgage. These latter people tend to move either because of a change of job, or because of a desire to change house, or both. In their selection of a new home, the qualities of the house and its accessibility to the place of work are again uppermost. The people moving into these homes are suburbanites and they recognize the fact; they expect to live, and they do live for the most part, in single-family detached or semidetached houses; the great majority of these new home buyers travel by car to work. They are not too dissatisfied with their move, mainly because they had quite concrete specifications that have been met; most expect to move again, and the majority want to move farther out toward the country, rather than inward toward the city.

These buyers of privately built houses in the suburbs form an increasing number —a majority, by the 1970s—of the population in England and Wales. (In Scotland the proportion of owner-occupiers is distinctly lower—a reflection of historic housing traditions and policies that have been very different from those in England.) This proportion rose rapidly between 1918 and 1945, and even more rapidly since then. Before World War I, owner-occupiers were a small part of the total housing market, accounting for not more than 10 percent of the total. Even at the end of World War II, after the great burst of private building for sale during the 1920s and 1930s, not more than about a quarter of all households owned their home. The proportion has risen from a quarter to a half in a quarter-century.

It is not difficult to see why. In a period of continuing and even accelerating inflation, property ownership has proved a magnificent buttress in Britain as in the United States; in effect, people have often been able to sell their houses after a period of years at an increased price, which meant that they had been living rent-free. And in addition—again, just as in the United States—public policy has provided the owner-occupier with a generous subsidy in the form of relief on income tax payments. This relief, which applies to the interest on the mortgage, has two paradoxical effects: it cushions the buyer against the rising interest rates typical of the postwar period, and it is of increasing benefit as the buyer's income rises. Tax relief policies in postwar Britain have positively encouraged millions of people to become mortgagees; anyone who did not, and remained in the declining private rented sector, was in effect sacrificing a government subsidy. And such has become the popular pressure for the extension of owner occupancy that in 1967 the Labour government introduced its option mortgage scheme to extend the benefits to those whose incomes were below the line where they would enjoy tax relief, by giving them an option to enjoy a rebate on their mortgage payments as if they had been liable to tax at standard rate.

Nevertheless, barriers to purchase remain. By and large, building societies or insurance associations work on the hallowed principle that mortgage commitments should not extend to more than about 25 percent of income; many building societies will not even take the wife's income into account, but concentrate solely on the main breadwinner. It was calculated in 1961 that only about 10 percent of households could afford to buy out of income, and it is doubtful whether any substantial change had occurred in this position by the early 1970s; many of the owner-occupiers of Britain, therefore, rely on possession of capital to some degree. Precisely how large is the barrier to owner-occupancy may be judged from income distribution figures. In 1968 the average price of all dwellings bought on mortgage by owner-occupiers in the United Kingdom was £4,344 and the average income of borrowers was £1,618, a ratio of 2.68. But at this date, one-quarter of the families with young children living in privately rented accommodation had incomes of less than £1,018. With an income of £1,018, on the basis of the ratio above, it would be possible to buy a house costing £2,728. Yet the proportion of all houses sold at this price or less in 1968 was well below 10 percent. In other words, such families were effectively excluded from the owner-occupier market, except through the option mortgage scheme that had been introduced only the year before. And in addition to the income barrier, there was an age barrier; it became difficult to obtain a first-time mortgage after the age of 40.

On the other hand, for any family that can get a toehold into the owner-occupier market, especially if this is done early in life, subsequently the whole process should be relatively painless; this family will be able to trade up the market, regularly selling its house at an inflated price, and buying a better one for the same mortgage payments, or enjoying increased tax relief if it goes for a higher rate of payment. Such a progression well suits the better-paid white-collar worker with the prospect of regular salary increments and promotions; it is not so easy for the blue-collar worker, particularly the lower-income unskilled worker, who may reach an income ceiling fairly early in life.

The typical new buyer on mortgage, then, is middle class, in a secure position, with a regularly rising income. His main concern will be to find housing within easy reach of his job, and so the location of new employment must be the key to the location of new suburban development, in Britain as anywhere else. Earlier in this chapter it was shown that in the 1950s and 1960s people and their homes have been decentralizing earlier and faster from the cities to the suburbs than have jobs; new houses have been built at steadily greater distances from jobs, on average, and commuter distances have been lengthening. Our own survey showed that new house buyers found that they had longer commuter journeys, both in miles and in minutes, after the move than before it. But public policies have helped to ensure that this burden has not been too great, either physically or financially. New and improved highways—particularly the national motorway program that developed many new radial and orbital links during the 1960s and 1970s—together with improved rail services and a falling real cost of motoring or longer-distance rail commuting in relation to income, have all contributed to a widening of the effective commuting radius around the major concentrations of employment in the cores of the metropolitan areas. It is no surprise, then, that many buyers of suburban homes are determined that their next move will be even farther into the countryside: they have recognized the advantages enjoyed by the existing rural residents in an age of universal public services and high car ownership; they realize that with improved transportation it is easy to live in rural surroundings and work in the city; and they want to join in. But here, again, are the seeds of further potential conflict.

The Actors in Interaction: The Land Market

Perhaps the supreme paradox of the postwar history of the British planning system is that the different actors still interact so vigorously in the land market. For the intention of the pioneers who set up the system seems to have been that in future the market should be unnecessary; the decisions of planners should largely replace it, and profits from land transactions for development should be eliminated by one means or another. This simple and logical view, however, depended on concentrating all real power in the hands of planners; the postwar reality has been very different, amounting to a modified version of that dispersed decision making that has been characteristic of the United States. Instead of replacing the market, therefore, the decisions of planners have become an element in it, powerfully modifying the way it works.

The precise details of the system as it was originally intended, and as it was subsequently modified, need not concern us at this stage; we shall look at them closely in chapter 5. Central to all the details is the fact that in 1947 the British effectively nationalized the right to develop land, with provision for compensation to individuals for their lost rights. Logically, thenceforth, the profit from development also belonged to the state. Either the state could take over the process of land development itself, buying all the land through the exercise of compulsory purchase (eminent domain) when it was needed for development, or it could effectively capture any profit from development. Both schemes were canvassed: an attempt to capture all or much of the profit from development has been tried twice in different forms, but in both cases, save for general capital gains tax, has been later abandoned.[12]

Yet the logic of the legislation remains: the whole system of control over land use depends on the nationalization of development rights, and it is clear that the pattern of development values increasingly reflects the decisions of the planner. A stroke of the pen on a development plan can make a difference of hundreds or thousands of pounds an acre in the value of land. Britain should perhaps count itself fortunate that its public officials, with very few exceptions both at central and local level, appear to be incorruptible. But the whole process puts a great strain

[12] Details are given in chapter 5.

on the planning system, and in turn distorts the pattern of land prices. For, especially in the inflationary conditions prevailing since World War II, any reasonably firm plan is—to quote the words of an official West Australian report—a speculator's guide.

As a result, the land market is almost the reverse of a free one. The secular trends in land prices reflect continuing inflation; local variations are a function of planning permission or the lack of it; and any speculative gains are truly the gift of the planner. The owner of land with planning permission has every interest in holding on to it as long as possible because inflation and shortage of development land will surely cause the price to rise faster than the general level of prices and incomes; the owner of land without such permission has every interest in getting its permitted use changed, since the result could be a windfall gain of huge proportions. But because agricultural land is not subject to local taxation in Britain, neither landowner will pay any cost penalty for holding on to the land.

Even were the state to remedy the situation by introducing yet another version of the tax on development profits, the outcome is uncertain; for on both previous occasions when this has been tried there is good evidence that the effect was directly inflationary. In conditions of land shortage, buyers may be prepared to pay a premium for land with development permission, especially as the value is rising so fast anyway. Thus they may be willing to pay the cost of the tax to the owner of land, passing it on in turn to the developer and thence to the buyer of the housing. Though the increase in urban land prices seems to be a well-developed feature of the postwar western world, occurring in situations as diverse as the United States, Israel, Japan, and Australia, it seems clear that an effective planning system—one that can limit and control the pace and direction of development—must automatically drive up the value of that land where development is possible; and that no amount of compensatory taxation is likely to prove effective in limiting the process. This is a theme that is important to students of urbanization and planning in all countries, and we shall need to return to it more than once in later chapters.

chapter **3**

Some British–U.S. comparisons

Every schoolboy knows that Britain is a "tight little isle," densely settled, using its limited land area intensively, and highly dependent upon foreign trade for its economic prosperity; and that the United States is a huge country, sprawling, extending 3,000 miles from east to west and 1,500 or more miles from north to south, with plenty of land, no great pressures of land scarcity, with a largely self-contained economy. This degree of knowledge (or of ignorance) is unfortunately not confined to schoolboys, and it leads to wholly erroneous conclusions as to the nature of urban land use in the two countries.

In fact, the highly urbanized area of the northeastern United States is remarkably similar to the major urbanized area of Britain. There are some important differences in the pattern and structure of urban areas in the two countries, but the similarities are far more striking than are the differences. This chapter will explore both similarities and differences.

SOME CONCEPTUAL MATTERS

First, however, it is necessary to define some terms if meaningful comparisons are to be made. While complete comparability cannot be attained, reasonable comparability both in concepts and in terms is possible, and necessary. The mere definition of cities, metropolitan areas, urbanized areas, and other similar terms has become difficult in recent years, as new patterns of settlement have come about under the impact of new transportation technology and new life-styles.

Once, it was fairly easy to define a city; almost everyone would have had the same definition in mind. The city was neatly bounded in a physical sense—by an actual wall if an old city, or by the limited distance from which workers could walk from their homes to their place of employment in the city center. There was a fairly clear and sharp break between the city and the country. While the city traded with its hinterland and with other cities, much of its economy was contained within the same bounds as its physical structures. Such cities were typically self-governing, and in both Britain and the United States the city of a century ago—or even to a large extent the city of half a century ago—had a political sphere which matched its physical extent and its major economic territory.

The historic picture is no longer accurate. Many older cities have spread into the countryside, often unevenly, especially in the United States where outliers and disconnected bits float like moons about a planet. In spite of some extensions of city boundaries, typically the legal city no longer includes all the physical city; and the economic city may be equally or more dispersed. Faced with this situation, statisticians, city planners, economists, demographers, and others have invented new terms and concepts in an effort to describe what actually exists, as contrasted with the old city. Every urban agglomeration or grouping of settlement in both countries includes three dimensions or ways in which it may be measured.

First, there is the functional or the economic city or city-like area. Its characteristics are described in terms of labor force, economic output, regional and personal income, internal transport, and even cultural and social activities and structures. In this day of extensive commuting from suburb or countryside to city, the functional or economic city may be rather inclusive; such matters as percentage of labor force commuting to or toward the city center may be a good measure of its boundaries, which may extend to include satellite cities or urban-like areas lying outside the boundaries of the city as a legal or political entity. No urban agglomeration is economically self-sufficient; those that are larger may trade extensively with other relatively distant cities in the same country or beyond it. It is extremely difficult to measure the outer limits of the economic influence of huge functional cities such as London and New York.

Second, there is the physical city, or the land the city-like form of settlement actually occupies. But, in this connection, what does "occupy" or "use" mean? Must land actually have structures on it, or be paved or otherwise dedicated to transportation? What about land formally dedicated to parks or other open-space uses? What about idle land within or adjacent to the used land? Small tracts of idle land may be a normal part of the growth process, but larger areas are harder to defend as part of land "use." This problem is particularly acute in the United States.

Finally, there is the legal or political city, the area within which the governing body of the city has jurisdiction. Even this is not as unequivocal as it might seem, at least in Britain, where cities, with the consent of the satellite city or borough, may undertake public housing or other activities generally possible in the United States only within the legal boundary of the city.

In the case of larger urban agglomerations in both countries, it is not easy to define the agglomeration or city by any of these definitions, or to do so in a way that will satisfy every student of urban development. In particular, the "grain" of the definition may affect the results; the definition is likely to follow boundaries of local governmental units, because data are usually tabulated according to such units. In the United States these are likely to be county boundaries (towns in New England); and a county economically and functionally related to a city may yet include a great deal of land that is not urban in its settlement pattern. The same applies in Britain, where the definitions are based on local authority areas (county or municipal boroughs, urban and rural districts). The problem is further complicated as cities or city-like areas grow toward one another, perhaps merging at their peripheries. Is a particularly urban-like area a metropolis in its own right, or is it a subsidiary part of a larger and relatively nearby metropolis?

In both Britain and the United States (and, we judge, in most other countries as well) it is possible to identify a number of "layers" or rings about a city center. Beginning at the outside and proceeding inward, the following major districts or layers are identifiable:

1. *A back country or hinterland.* This is the region from which at least some of the agricultural products consumed by the city residents will originate. Its citizens typically trade in the city, at least for some goods and services; although not urban in its general settlement pattern, yet the hinterland may be the dwelling place for some commuters to the city, and it may serve an important role as a recreation area for the city residents. The outer boundaries of a hinterland are highly indefinite; they may overlap those of other hinterlands serving other cities. On the inner side, the boundaries of the hinterland coincide with the outer boundaries of the metropolis.

2. *A metropolis, as a whole.* This term has variable definitions, depending in part upon the kinds of data available and the areas for which such data are summarized. By and large, the definition emphasizes the functional aspects of the metropolis, and more particularly the labor force and its employment. In the United States, the definition of a Standard Metropolitan Statistical Area (SMSA) involves two considerations: a city or twin cities (of 50,000 or more inhabitants) to constitute a central city; and economic and social relationships between contiguous surrounding counties and the central city, particularly as to labor force employment and density of population. In Britain, labor force is a major determinant of metropolitan area, so that in fact such areas have been defined in the PEP research study (see page v) as Standard Metropolitan Labour Areas (SMLAs).

The metropolis is invariably divided into a core and a ring, and in some instances is divided further into:

a) an outer ring of cities and counties least closely identified with the metropolitan center, often least densely settled as well;

b) an inner ring of cities and counties more closely identified with the center, likely to be more heavily populated and more densely settled;

c) and a core.

The boundaries between these are somewhat arbitrary, since there is normally a continuum of settlement and degree of economic development; the actual placing of the lines is likely to depend on political boundaries, such as county lines, since data are often available for such local governmental units. The core is likely to be the historic city—the city center as it once existed but which now may be somewhat overshadowed by economic and social developments farther out. "Suburb" is a more popular and perhaps more a social than an economic term; in general, the inner and outer rings would be suburbs, but not the core.

3. *Urbanized area.* This is less a different inner layer than it is the physically occupied area of the metropolitan area. The purpose of the urbanized area is to

identify the land actually "used" for urban purposes. In so doing, it invariably encounters the problem of idle or undeveloped land, especially in the United States. Although the concept of urbanized area is a useful one, and although the areas so delineated do begin to approach land actually used for urban purposes in the United States, yet a close reading of the definition will reveal how a great deal of essentially open land can be included as urbanized. On the periphery of an urbanized area, half or more of the land may be open; it seems likely that as much as 30 percent of the entire urbanized area is open. As has been noted, in Britain the PEP study adopted the American definition of urbanized area as a basic unit of analysis. This was done primarily for reasons of easy comparison with American works; but it was found that at least one of the factors governing the definition—the critical population density of 1,000 persons per square mile—was a significant one for Britain too, in that it defined areas where a high proportion of land was developed for urban purposes.

4. *Cities.* Within the metropolitan and urbanized areas lie the cities, as legal or political units. Although there may be much idle land within them, the foregoing definitions include their entire areas as urbanized and as part of the SMSAs (or the SMLAs). Because they are units of government, cities have important functions. They raise revenue by various taxes, and they carry out various public programs; consequently, data on their area, population, income, and other aspects of modern life are a necessary part of our analysis.

Some Overall Comparisons

The forty-eight contiguous states of the United States, with their nearly 2,000 million acres of land, are thirty-two times the size of the United Kingdom with its less than 60 million acres; the U.S. population is more than three and a half times that of the United Kingdom; and the latter had an overall national population density of 595 persons per square mile in 1971, or more nearly nine times the U.S. density of 68 per square mile in 1970 (table 2). To this extent, the stereotype of the big, thinly settled United States and the small, heavily settled British Isles is reasonably correct.

However, along the urbanized eastern seaboard of the United States one can easily delineate a region that is of exactly the same area as England and Wales (figures 7 and 8). By beginning in southern Maine and running into northern Virginia, and extending from the Atlantic Coast to the west one tier or more of counties beyond the major SMSAs, the area within the United States region exactly coincides with that of England and Wales. This region is closely similar to Gottmann's Megalopolis;[1] ours includes some counties his does not, and his includes others we omit; ours totals about 11 percent more than his. This U.S. area is less than half what Jerome Pickard has called the "Atlantic Region."[2]

[1] Jean Gottmann, *Megalopolis: The Urbanized Northeastern Seaboard of the United States* (New York: Twentieth Century Fund, 1961).

[2] Jerome P. Pickard, *Dimensions of Metropolitanism* (Washington: Urban Land Institute, 1967).

TABLE 2

AREA AND POPULATION, COMPARABLE U.K. AND U.S. AREAS, 1960 AND 1961

| | United Kingdom, 1961 | | | | United States, 1960 | | | |
| | Area | | Popu-lation (mil.) | Density[1] | Area | | Popu-lation (mil.) | Density[1] |
	1,000 sq mi	Mil. acres			1,000 sq mi	Mil. acres		
1. United Kingdom and United States (48 contiguous states)	93.0	59.5	52.7	566	2,974.7	1,904	180.7	61
2. England and Wales and equal area in United States (see figures 7 and 8)	58.3	37.3	46.1	791	58.2	37.2	37.6	646
As percent of nation	63%	63%	88%	–	2%	2%	19%	–
3. Megalopolis England and Northeastern Urban Complex	19.5	12.5	32.2	1,651	31.6	20.2	34.2	1,084
As percent of nation	21%	21%	61%	–	1%	1%	17%	–
4. SMSAs (U.S.) and SMLAs (Britain), within Northeastern Urban Complex and Megalopolis England	12.0	7.7	28.3	2,356	21.6	13.8	31.7	1,470
As percent of Megalopolis England and of Northeastern Urban Complex	62%	62%	88%	–	68%	68%	93%	–
5. Urbanized areas of the immediately foregoing	5.0	3.3	25.7	4,942	5.4	3.5	28.5	5,290
As percent of Megalopolis England and of Northeastern Urban Complex	27%	26%	80%	–	17%	17%	83%	–
6. 1970–71 population comparable to:								
line 1	–	–	55.3	595	–	–	202.1	68
line 2	–	–	48.6	834	–	–	42.6	732
line 3	–	–	33.8	1,733	–	–	38.9	1,231
line 4	–	–	29.2	2,433	–	–	35.7	1,653

[1] Number of persons per square mile, total population/total area.

Each of the larger regions shown in figures 7 and 8 covers slightly more than 37 million acres. The significant differences are these: England and Wales occupy 63 percent of the area of the United Kingdom, and include 88 percent of the U.K. population, whereas our selected region of the United States represents only 2 percent of the forty-eight contiguous states and only 19 percent of the total population; in England and Wales in 1961 there lived slightly more than 46 million people, whereas in the comparable U.S. region in 1960 the population numbered some 38 million. Since gross areas were, by definition, equal, the overall densities were about 22 percent higher in England and Wales than in the equivalent U.S. region—a vastly closer comparison than when national densities are used.

Within the larger areas delineated in figures 7 and 8, smaller areas contain most of the metropolitan population. These are Megalopolis England, with 12½ million acres and about 32 million people in 1961; and the Northeastern Urban Complex of the United States with about 20 million acres and 34 million people in 1960. (By 1970–71, the respective populations were 34 and 39 million; the U.S. area grew faster in the 1960s than did the comparable British area.) Some differences are observable: the British area is smaller overall (about 62 percent as large), has slightly fewer people, and has an overall density about 52 percent higher. But the general similarities are evident and the conclusion seems clear: the most urban-

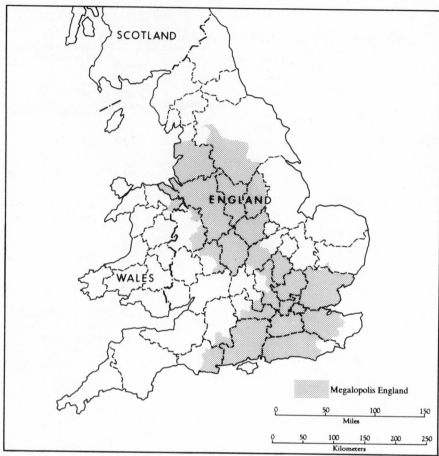

FIGURE 7. The heavily urbanized area of Megalopolis England shown in relation to the total
area of England and Wales, 1961.

ized areas of the two nations are closely similar in total area, total population, and
overall average density. One may, therefore, logically expect that they have faced
somewhat similar problems of urban growth and urban land use.

In each country, it is possible to delineate an urbanized area within the metropolitan areas—the land more or less actually "used" for urban purposes. In spite
of some problems and perhaps of some imprecisions in such delineation, as far
as circumstances would permit the definitions used in the countries have been the
same.[3] The urbanized areas of these two major urban regions are remarkably close

[3] In the United States, data on population, employment, land area, and other matters for both
the urbanized areas described in this paragraph and for SMSAs discussed in the following paragraph are collected, tabulated, and published by the U.S. Bureau of the Census, and thus are
readily available to any interested person. In Britain, neither concept finds expression in published Census reports; the latter do, however, include data for relatively small areas. The British
data had to be built up by the PEP research team from published Census data; as far as available data would permit, the definitions are the same as for the United States. For the SMSAs,
the two basic characteristics of the definition are a core city of 50,000 or more and close integration.

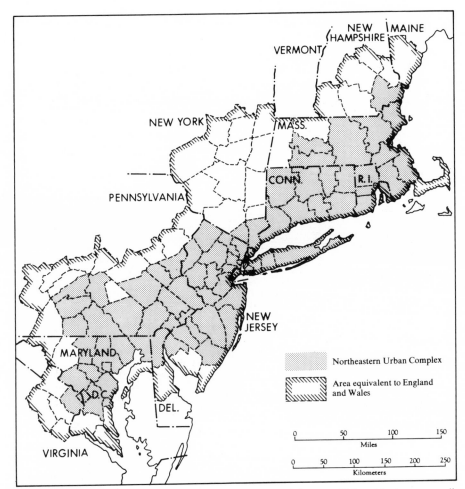

FIGURE 8. The Northeastern Urban Complex in the United States which, with the surrounding area shown, is equal in area to England and Wales, 1960.

in total area—the U.S. area is only 6 percent larger than the British one. The urbanized area is about a fourth of Megalopolis England and about a sixth of the larger Northeastern Urban Complex. Curiously enough, the U.S. area has an 11 percent larger total population, as well as a slightly larger proportion of the total population of the megalopolitan regional population, with the unexpected result that the overall density of population is about 7 percent higher in the United States

of adjoining territory. For the British SMLAs, the latter was measured by 15 percent or more of the labor force commuting to the core. Since there is a continuum in both core city sizes and in degree of commuting or other economic ties of hinterland to core, these or any other cutoff points are arbitrary. However, the U.S. definition has been widely used in the United States and the concept has gained acceptance elsewhere, so it seemed equally defensible and much easier to stay with it than to devise a new one. In spite of some arbitrariness and in spite of some odd examples in each country, the concepts, definitions, and results are believed to be rather closely comparable.

than in the British urbanized area. It would be still higher if all the idle land were excluded from the regions in each country; idle land is much more common in urbanized areas in the United States (where it may run to 30 percent of the total) than in Britain; hence, the difference in density for the urbanized areas in actual use would be greater than shown in table 2.

Each of the two major urban regions contains several metropolitan areas, and these may be compared (figure 9 and table 3). There is a single huge metropolis in each country—London in Megalopolis England and New York in the Northeastern Urban Complex—and then a succession of smaller metropolises. When

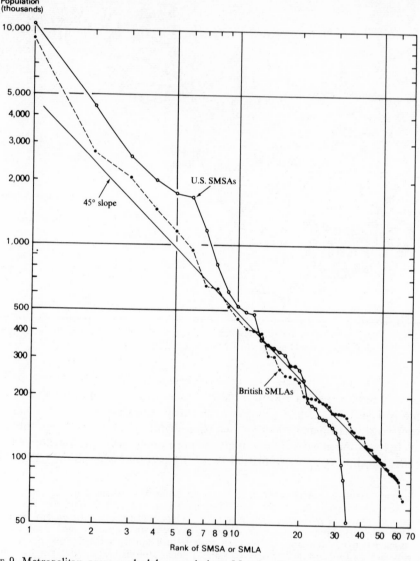

FIGURE 9. Metropolitan areas ranked by population—Megalopolis England, 1961, and the U.S. Northeastern Urban Complex, 1960.

ranked by size, the U.S. group includes thirty-four in 1960, ending with Meriden, Connecticut, which barely included the 50,000 minimum for an SMSA; the British group includes sixty-three, ending with Stafford which had 66,000 in 1961.

Numerous students of urban problems have long employed a technique of analysis which consists of ranking cities (or, in this case, metropolitan areas) by size, and plotting rank on the horizontal axis and population on the vertical rank, on double-log paper. The conclusion emerging from some of these studies—designated as a "law" by some students—is that doubling the rank means cutting the population size in half, and so on, proportionately; a line connecting the ranked cities or metropolitan areas thus becomes, on double-log paper, a downward sloping line at 45 degrees to the horizontal. For the range of metropolitan areas between tenth and twentieth in rank, this rule holds very closely for the urban regions in these two countries, and their respective lines almost coincide. Each country has somewhat more people in larger metropolises than this rule would indicate—the Northeastern Urban Complex much more so than Megalopolis England. If one adopts this rule and takes the tenth-twentieth range as the base relationship, then New York should have 5 million people instead of the 10.7 million it actually had in 1960; and similarly, the other SMSAs down to Jersey City would each have fewer people than actually reported. On the same basis, London would also have had 5 million instead of the 9.2 million actually reported for 1961, and similarly for the SMLAs down through Nottingham.

A marked contrast develops between the two countries for metropolitan areas below the rank of twentieth. In Megalopolis England, the relationship falls almost precisely on the 45 degree line; the differences are minor indeed. For the Northeastern Urban Complex, on the other hand, there is a notable deficiency in size of SMSAs below 250,000. An SMSA such as New Britain, in thirty-first place, should have had 160,000 people but had only 129,000 in 1960; Meriden, in thirty-fourth place, should have had about 150,000 but in fact had only 52,000; and there is a total lack of SMSAs from the thirty-fourth to the sixty-third ranks.

Each country has somewhat more concentration in large metropolitan areas, and thus somewhat fewer people in smaller metropolitan areas, than the generalized rank-size rule would indicate. There is nothing sacred about the latter, of course; it is merely an empirical generalization.

In the course of this study, the overall density data in table 3 were related to the total population of the respective metropolitan areas, but there is virtually no correlation between metropolitan population and metropolitan overall density; the latter ranges from a low of 262 (in York, Pennsylvania, which is a moderate-size city in a big county, all of which constitutes the SMSA) to a high of 13,580 (in Jersey City, which has a moderately large population concentrated on a relatively small area, and which is hemmed in on all sides by other SMSAs). Although both of these extremes are in the United States, the situation in Britain is not much better; extreme diversity characterizes each country. The U.S. metropolitan areas tend to have lower densities than the British areas of the same size, but there is overlap and, above all, wide scatter for each. One could easily conclude that much of this diversity in overall density arises because of the rather arbitrary character of the metropolitan area boundaries.

TABLE 3

Comparison of Metropolitan Areas Ranked by Size, Northeastern Urban Complex, 1960, with Megalopolis England, 1961

		U.S. Northeastern Urban Complex, 1960				Megalopolis England, 1961				
		Area		Population			Area		Population	
Rank	Metropolitan area[1]	Square miles	1,000 acres	Total (1,000)	Per sq mi²	Metropolitan area[1]	Square miles	1,000 acres	Total (1,000)	Per sq mi²
1	New York	2,149	1,377	10,695	4,964	London	1,496	959.3	9,157	6,120
2	Philadelphia	3,549	2,270	4,343	1,225	Birmingham	905	578.1	2,693	2,975
3	Boston	969	620	2,589	2,675	Manchester	457	291.5	2,042	4,475
4	Washington	1,485	952	2,002	1,347	Liverpool	270	172.8	1,481	5,485
5	Baltimore	1,807	1,155	1,727	956	Leeds	480	273.6	1,163	2,715
6	Newark	698	447	1,689	2,415	Sheffield	371	243.7	950	2,455
7	Paterson-Clifton	427	274	1,187	2,780	Coventry	640	409.9	644	1,008
8	Providence	634	405	816	1,287	Nottingham	288	184.4	635	2,205
9	Jersey City	45	29	611	13,580	Stoke	452	289.1	519	1,147
10	Hartford	514	329	525	1,023	Leicester	422	269.7	457	1,083
11	Allentown-Bethlehem	1,082	693	492	455	Portsmouth	74	47.5	410	5,550
12	Springfield	429	275	479	1,116	Southampton	485	310.1	402	829
13	Wilmington	787	504	366	466	Brighton	151	96.7	338	2,570
14	Harrisburg	1,075	688	345	321	Derby	267	170.3	315	1,181
15	Bridgeport	161	103	335	2,080	Bournemouth	177	113.5	305	1,725
16	Worcester	428	274	323	755	Luton	271	167.1	267	985
17	New Haven	200	128	312	1,560	Bolton	71	45.5	250	3,520
18	Lancaster	944	603	278	295	Southend	91	58.5	247	2,720
19	Reading	864	552	275	318	Reading	251	161.0	242	966
20	Trenton	228	146	266	1,166	Slough	121	77.3	231	1,910
21	York	911	583	238	262	Chatham	102	65.2	201	1,970
22	Lawrence	163	104	189	1,160	Preston	32	20.2	197	6,160
23	Waterbury	182	117	182	1,000	Doncaster	152	97.6	196	1,290
24	Stamford	120	77	178	1,482	Huddersfield	106	67.6	194	1,830
25	Atlantic City	575	368	161	280	St. Helens	72	46.4	190	2,640
26	Lowell	123	79	158	1,284	Blackpool	22	14.2	187	8,500
27	New London	286	183	157	548	High Wycombe	211	135.0	184	873
28	Brockton	164	105	149	910	Wigan	62	39.5	180	2,905

68

#										
29	New Bedford	142	91	143	1,006	Watford	52	33.2	169	3,250
30	Fall River	144	92	138	958	Warrington	118	75.5	168	1,425
31	New Britain	84	54	129	1,535	Blackburn	65	41.3	168	2,590
32	Norwalk	72	46	97	1,345	Halifax	64	41.2	167	2,610
33	Fitchburg	99	63	82	828	Barnsley	96	61.4	165	1,715
34	Meriden	24	15	52	2,168	Guildford	215	137.5	159	740
35						Northampton	218	139.2	151	693
36						Wakefield	62	39.7	140	2,255
37						Maidstone	224	143.1	138	617
38						Aldershot	46	29.5	132	2,870
39						Mansfield	215	137.6	131	608
40						Bury	52	33.0	130	2,500
41						Thurrock	70	45.0	130	1,857
42						Worthing	183	117.0	119	650
43						Rochdale	47	30.3	116	2,465
44						Burnley	72	46.3	114	1,582
45						Dewsbury	24	15.3	113	4,710
46						Bedford	186	118.9	106	570
47						Stevenage	192	122.8	106	552
48						Eastbourne	165	105.6	103	624
49						Chester	174	111.4	102	586
50						Colchester	134	85.6	99	737
51						Chelmsford	210	134.3	98	467
52						Tunbridge Wells	85	54.1	97	1,141
53						Leigh	28	18.2	93	3,320
54						Crewe	166	106.4	91	548
55						St. Albans	58	36.9	89	1,533
56						Basildon	42	27.1	89	2,115
57						Hemel Hempstead	73	47.0	88	1,205
58						Burton	62	39.7	88	1,419
59						Walton & Weybridge	30	19.0	86	2,865
60						Woking	50	31.9	84	1,680
61						Southport	15	9.7	82	5,470
62						Kidderminster	76	48.4	70	923
63						Stafford	133	85.3	66	496

[1] Where names are abbreviated the first name in complex is used.
[2] Total population divided by total area.

A further analysis was made, based on urbanized areas. The U.S. Bureau of the Census groups several metropolitan areas around New York City into a single New York–New Jersey Consolidated Area, hence there are only twenty-nine urbanized areas compared with the thirty-four metropolitan areas in the Northeastern Urban Complex. Overall densities are much higher for urbanized areas than for metropolitan areas; large areas of land not used for urban purposes have been excluded from the former. However, the relationship between overall density and total population is now not much closer in absolute terms. Since the variability is now around a higher mean density, it is somewhat less in relative terms, but is still large. How far do these differences in overall density of urbanized areas measure actual differences in the form of land use in each, and how far may they still be a reflection of somewhat varying definitions?

The range in overall densities for each country for both metropolitan and urbanized areas is evident in table 4; the most common frequencies are much higher for urbanized areas than for metropolitan areas; and, in spite of considerable overlap, there is some tendency for overall densities to run higher in Britain than in the United States.

The data presented in table 2 show that the average overall density of settlement in all urbanized areas of the Northeastern Urban Complex was higher than for all urbanized areas of Megalopolis England; yet in table 4 it appears that densities tend to run higher in Britain than in the United States. How can this apparent contradiction be explained? The answer lies in the fact that very large urban agglomerations (New York and all its environs included in the New York–New Jersey Consolidated Area, in particular) have both relatively high overall densities and such a large proportion of all the people that they dominate the results in table 2. When comparisons are made on the basis of numbers of urbanized areas, instead of a comparison weighted by numbers of people, the British areas show up with higher overall densities.

TABLE 4

NUMBER OF METROPOLITAN AREAS AND OF URBANIZED AREAS IN NORTHEASTERN URBAN COMPLEX, 1960, AND IN MEGALOPOLIS ENGLAND, 1961, WITH DIFFERENT OVERALL LAND USE DENSITIES

Overall density[1] (1,000)	Number of metropolitan areas in		Number of urbanized areas in	
	United States	Britain	United States	Britain
Less than 1	13	18	0	0
1–2	14	18	3	0
2–3	5	16	8	7
3–4	0	3	8	14
4–5	1	2	6	15
5–6	0	3	1	17
6–8	0	2	3	5
Over 8	1	1	0	5
Total	34	63	29	63

[1] Total population/total area; persons per square mile.

New York–London Comparisons

The foregoing section is based upon metropolitan areas according to one system of definition in each country; but, as has been noted, the definition of a metropolis is far from easy, nor are the results of different workers always the same. It thus seems desirable to move one step further into the analysis by taking the two largest metropolises of each country, and examining what lies behind the figures presented in the foregoing section.

London and New York are great cities on the world scale—no list of world cities, wherever compiled, is likely to omit either. The cities have some similarities: each is a great port, with trade to and from most major parts of the world, each is a great financial center, each has a vast range of business activities, and each has some manufacturing, although less today than at an earlier date. London is the seat of national government, a role carried by Washington rather than New York in the United States. London is a very much older city; it was an important place in Roman times and earlier, whereas New York began only about 350 years ago as a tiny settlement on a then-unknown continent. Each has grown enormously over the past century or more. Especially in recent times each has had its critics, primarily people who think both cities have already outgrown some optimum size.

The term *New York* has many different meanings (table 5 and figure 10). The island of Manhattan includes the older part of the metropolis, where Broadway, Wall Street, the United Nations, and the other internationally known parts of the metropolis are crowded onto some 22 square miles of land. In spite of the fact that the greater part of this island is used for commercial, transportation, and related land uses, the average density of residential use for the entire island is very high—over 77,000 persons per square mile. Such a density is achievable only by reason of the high apartment houses that characterize so much of Manhattan.

The next larger area to which the term *New York* might be applied is the legal city—the five boroughs of Bronx, Kings, New York (Manhattan), Queens, and Richmond. It is more than fourteen times as large in extent and has nearly five times as many people as Manhattan; it includes considerable undeveloped area in Richmond, as well as highly developed areas elsewhere. The New York SMSA, as defined by the U.S. government agencies, does not include adjoining SMSAs in New Jersey and in Connecticut, but still is nearly seven times the area and about 50 percent greater in population than the legal city of New York. The urbanized area, as defined by the Bureau of the Census, is actually smaller than the New York SMSA, omitting some of the more remote parts of Long Island and of Westchester County particularly, but including the developed areas of nearby New Jersey; it includes considerably more people than does the New York SMSA. The Bureau of the Census has also defined a "standard consolidated area" which is twice as large as the urbanized area but includes only a comparatively few more people.

But these are not the only definitions of New York. New York's Regional Plan Association is one of the oldest and most competent urban regional planning groups in the United States. A private organization, it has nevertheless received some financial support from government at various levels, as well as from numerous

TABLE 5

TOTAL AREA AND POPULATION, 1960, FOR DIFFERENT
DEFINITIONS OF "NEW YORK"

Source of information and definition of area	Population (1,000)	Total area		Overall density per sq mi[1]
		Square miles	1,000 acres	
1. Bureau of the Census:				
a. Manhattan	1,698	22.0	14.1	77,200
b. City of New York (5 boroughs)	7,782	315.1	201.7	24,700
c. New York SMSA (boroughs plus Nassau, Rockland, Suffolk, and Westchester counties)	10,695	2,149	1,375.4	4,975
d. New York urbanized area (includes northeastern New Jersey)	14,115	1,891.5	1,210.6	7,450
e. New York–Northeastern New Jersey Standard Consolidated Area	14,759	3,748	2,398.7	3,960
2. New York Regional Plan Association:[2]				
a. 1922 definition of region	15,822	5,528	3,537.9	2,960
b. 1947 region (22 counties)	16,139	6,907	4,420.5	2,340
c. 1965 region (31 counties)	17,624	12,748	8,158.7	1,381
3. Tri-State Transportation Commission:[3]				
a. intensively developed area	16,300	3,663.2	2,344.4	4,445
b. entire region	18,100	7,886.5	5,047.4	2,295

[1] Total population/total area; persons per square mile.

[2] Basic data from *The Region's Growth* (New York: Regional Plan Association, May 1967), pp. 81, 82.

[3] *Measure of a Region* (New York: Tri-State Transportation Commission, May 1967), p. 5 for population data, p. 9 for area data. Slightly different population data are used in other reports of the commission. These population data relate to 1963, hence are not fully comparable with 1960 data from other sources.

private sources. Its emphasis on an urban region began with its 1922 study, and probably was influential in the later establishment of SMSAs as general statistical areas. In 1922 the current extent of economic integration led to one definition of the New York region; this was expanded in 1947, and again in 1965. Each expansion increased area far more than it increased population. The 1965 definition begins to impinge upon other large metropolitan regions; for instance, the Philadelphia region includes Trenton, New Jersey, which the New York region (as here defined) also includes.

More recently, the Tri-State Transportation Commission (an agency involving the three states of Connecticut, New York, and New Jersey) in 1965 established still a different region, whose total and whose "intensively developed area" conform to neither of the two foregoing sources of definition.

We cite these differences in definition, not to suggest that agencies or organizations may be in error or are inconsistent one with another, but rather to illustrate the inherent difficulty of defining a meaningful region. The differences in population, between the various current definitions of the whole region, are not very great; the differences in total area are very large. This arises because of the inclusion or exclusion of different relatively thinly populated areas on the periphery;

some part of the latter may derive from difference in practice in following boundary lines of local units of government.

The foregoing deals with populations resident in the various regions or districts;
the distribution of employment is different (table 6). For the region as a whole,
slightly more than 40 percent of the people are employed. But employment exceeds
population by four times in the central business district of Manhattan and is greater
for Manhattan as a whole. Conversely, employment is low, relative to population,
in the outer parts of the metropolis. One would expect this general relationship,
of course; perhaps the notable fact is that for the decade 1956–65 there was no
significant shift in this relationship. The data obviously imply a degree of commuting from suburban home to city center; they understate this commuting to
the degree that reverse commuting also occurs. In the past quarter century, factory
employment has increasingly moved out of central New York to the suburbs, while
office employment in the city center has increased to roughly offset the decline in

TABLE 6

POPULATION AND JOBS, BY AREAS OF NEW YORK REGION, 1956 AND 1965

Area[1]	1956[2]			1965[3]		
	People (1,000)	Jobs (1,000)	Ratio of jobs to people	People (1,000)	Jobs (1,000)	Ratio of jobs to people
Manhattan, CBD	620	2,475	4.00			
Manhattan, all	1,811	2,718	1.50	1,565	2,406	1.54
Core	8,236	4,302	.52	8,757	4,453	.51
Inner Ring	4,573	1,572	.34	4,655	1,568	.34
Intermediate Ring⎱	2,566	826	.32	4,280	1,339	.31
Outer Ring ⎰				1,290	407	.32
Total Metropolitan Area	15,375	6,700	.43	18,981	7,796	.41

[1] These areas are not strictly comparable for the two sources and time periods; their definitions
are as follows:

	1956	1965
Core	Manhattan, Hudson, Brooklyn, Queens, Bronx	Manhattan, Hudson, Brooklyn, Queens, Bronx, City of Newark
Inner Ring	Richmond, Essex, Bergen, Passaic, Westchester, Union, Nassau	Richmond, Essex West, Bergen, Passaic South, Westchester South, Union, Nassau
Intermediate Ring⎱	Middlesex, Rockland, Morris, Monmouth, Somerset, Fairfield, Suffolk, Orange, Putnam, Dutchess	Fairfield South, Middlesex, Suffolk West, Mercer, New Haven, Rockland, Monmouth, Morris, Westchester North, Somerset, Passaic North
Outer Ring ⎰		Fairfield North, Suffolk East, Dutchess, Ocean, Warren, Putnam, Hunterdon, Litchfield, Orange, Ulster, Sussex, Sullivan

[2] Edgar M. Hoover and Raymond Vernon, *Anatomy of a Metropolis* (Cambridge: Harvard
University Press, 1959).

[3] *The Region's Growth* (New York: Regional Plan Association, May 1967).

manufacturing employment. Any increasing inward commuting of white-collar office workers has thus been balanced against an outward commuting of factory workers, many of whom live either in the city center or closer to it than to the location of their jobs.

A generally similar analysis can be made for the London metropolitan area (table 7). The conurbation center, as defined officially by the British Census, is very small—only half the size of Manhattan—and its resident population is only about 15 percent of Manhattan's. This is because its limits are deliberately defined to include only the central business district, including the associated cultural and educational functions; it is thus more strictly comparable with Manhattan's central business district, though its population amounts to only about half of the latter's. The Manhattan business district has retained a considerable residential population living at a high density in areas like the Lower East Side or Greenwich Village; the corresponding residential areas in Central London, such as Pimlico and Bloomsbury, are relatively much smaller and their populations are not nearly as dense. Surrounding the central area is Inner London, now consisting of the City of London plus twelve of the London boroughs—the area of the old London County Council before the government reform of 1963, now administered for school purposes by the Inner London Education Authority. It has more than ten times the area of the center for far more than ten times the population; interestingly, the overall density of population rises as this layer is added, principally because the center is so largely occupied by offices and other nonresidential land uses. Inner London compares quite closely with Manhattan as the city's high-density inner residential area; it has almost twice Manhattan's population, living on an area over five times as great, and its density is thus only a little over one-third that of Manhattan. In fact, the density of residential population in Inner London is closer

TABLE 7

TOTAL AREA, POPULATION, EMPLOYMENT, AND OVERALL DENSITY, 1961,
FOR DIFFERENT DEFINITIONS OF LONDON

	Area		Population	Employment	Overall density (persons per sq mi)
	1,000 acres	Square miles			
1. Conurbation Center	6.7	10.4	270,395	1,414,730	25,990
2. Inner London Education Authority Area	74.9	117.0	3,200,484	2,590,440	27,350
3. Greater London Council Area (Conurbation)	394.5	616.4	7,997,234	4,487,830	12,970
4. London Transportation Study (LTS) External Cordon Line	602.2	941.0	8,826,000[1]	4,773,000[1]	9,380
5. Standard Metropolitan Labour Area (SMLA)	959.3	1,498.9	9,156,700	4,413,700	6,108
6. "Metropolitan Area" (official definition)	2,823.7	4,412.0	12,453,000	6,098,000[2]	2,820

[1] 1962.
[2] 1960.

TABLE 8

POPULATION AND JOBS, BY CONCENTRIC RINGS OF THE LONDON REGION, 1961

	Density of population per sq mi	Density of employment per sq mi	Ratio of employment to population
Conurbation Center	25,990	136,000	5.23
Remainder Inner London	27,480	11,020	.40
Remainder GLC Area	9,600	3,790	.39
Remainder London Metropolitan Area (official definition)	1,170	420	.36
Total Metropolitan Area	2,820	1,380	.49

to that of the whole of New York City—an area nearly three times as great in area and in population.

The next largest definition is the Greater London Council (GLC) area—more than five times the area and more than double the population of Inner London, and with an overall density half as large. (Each of these progressively larger areas includes the whole of the smaller one, as in most of the New York comparisons.) As the administrative area of London, the GLC area is closely comparable with the five boroughs of New York City: the populations are very similar, but the area of Greater London is only about 30 percent that of New York City, so the overall density of population is over two and a half times as great. Since the density in Inner London is much lower than in Manhattan, this indicates that the population density in the outer areas of Greater London is much higher than in the corresponding areas (the four outer boroughs) of New York City (table 5). In both cities, these outer areas were to a large extent developed between the two world wars. (The maps on pages 76 and 77 illustrate these changes in definition.)

Slightly more extensive than the GLC area is the External Cordon Line of the London Transportation Study; this has been much more restrictively designed than the intensively developed area in the Tri-State Transportation Study for New York, as a comparison of the density figures indicates. Still larger is the Standard Metropolitan Labour Area (SMLA), which should be compared with the New York–Northeastern New Jersey Standard Consolidated Metropolitan Area; it is less than half the New York area in size, and has about 60 percent of its population, so that the overall density of population is over half again as great. Lastly, and most extensively of all, the official British government definition of its "metropolitan area" should be compared with the most generous definitions of the New York region, the 1965 New York Regional Plan Association area, or the entire region of the Tri-State Transportation Commission area. Covering over 4,000 square miles, the area of this London region is nevertheless only a little over half that of the Tri-State region, and about one-third that of the Regional Plan Association region; its population is rather over two-thirds as great as either of these two New York regions, so that here again the overall density is higher: about one-quarter higher than the Tri-State area density, and more than double that of the Regional Plan Association area.

As in New York, so in London, employment is more concentrated than is population (table 8). In the small central area, where the population density is just

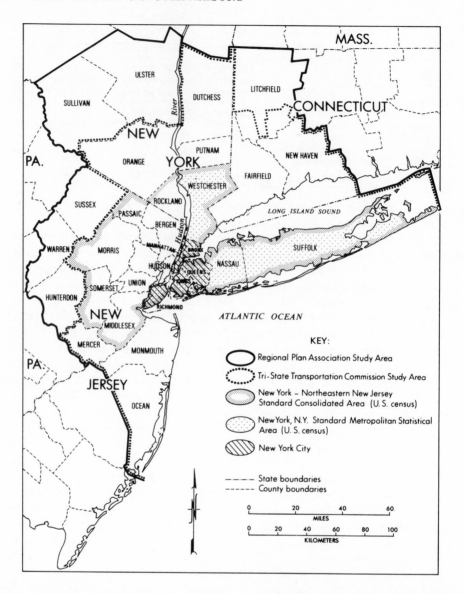

KEY:

Regional Plan Association Study Area

Tri-State Transportation Commission Study Area

New York – Northeastern New Jersey
Standard Consolidated Area (U.S. census)

New York, N.Y. Standard Metropolitan Statistical
Area (U.S. census)

New York City

—·—·— State boundaries
------- County boundaries

under 26,000 to the square mile, the density of employment is as high as 136,000 per square mile. But thereafter, employment density falls off much more rapidly than does population density. Even in the Inner London ring around the center, the density of employment is only about 40 percent that of population; and this broad relationship persists throughout the outer ring of the Greater London Council area and the remainder of the metropolitan area, with densities of population and employment falling in step. Thus the ratio of employment to population, which is as high as 5.23 in the central area, is almost constant at about 0.40 throughout the whole of the rest of the metropolitan area. This relationship is very similar to that observed for most of the New York area, though it is marginally greater;

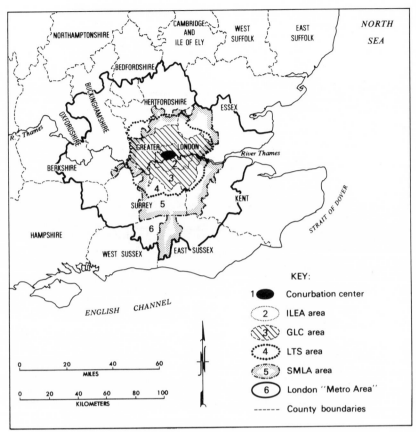

Figure 10. The maps on these two pages illustrate the varying ways in which an urban region may be defined. Both London and New York City have undergone many changes of definition over the years as they have spread in area.

what is different is the very high employment : population ratio in the center, which has no parallel in the Manhattan central business district.

On the basis of detailed information about resident population and land area by traffic origin zones (compiled as part of transportation studies), the New York and London metropolitan areas can be compared directly (figure 11). These data have been arranged in order of descending overall population density; a generally similar pattern of declining density is evident. Up to about 50 percent of their respective populations the overall density for New York averages higher than that for London by amounts ranging from a third to nearly double for the densest 20 percent of the population. The very large and high apartment buildings characterizing much of New York City do not have a counterpart in London. In the latter's more central residential areas, apartment buildings or houses divided into flats (apartments) may be closely grouped on the land, with relatively little open space on the lots but often with attractive neighborhood garden squares. Up to World War II, however, these areas were usually subject to regulations limiting their

Thousand persons per square mile

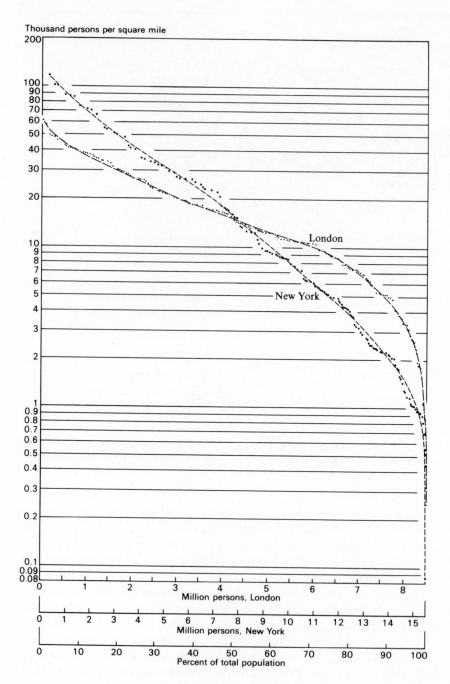

FIGURE 11. A comparison of overall population density per square mile, by traffic zone units—
New York in 1963 and London in 1962.

height to five or six stories. Since 1945 there has been greater freedom to develop high-rise blocks, to as much as forty stories in extreme cases; but still there has been an overall ceiling on the net residential density of 200 per acre in a small central area and 136 per acre in a wider inner zone around it, compared with densities as high as 1,000 per acre in new apartment building in Manhattan. In some areas of each metropolis overall densities of resident population may be moderate, or even low, because much of the land is used for nonresidential purposes. For the less dense half of the population, overall average densities in London are much higher than in New York, by as much as double in some deciles; nevertheless, marginal densities fall to almost exactly the same level in the two agglomerations. While there are clearly differences between these two great metropolitan areas, the similarities appear to be greater than the differences.

Philadelphia and Birmingham Metropolitan Areas

The foregoing type of analysis for the New York–London metropolises could be repeated for each pair of metropolises shown in table 3 and in figure 9; but the presentation of such an analysis would require a great deal of detail and space, and hence is not included. However, an abbreviated analysis for the Philadelphia and Birmingham metropolises will show that the general conclusions derived from the comparisons of New York and London apply here also.

Philadelphia is the second largest metropolis in the Northeastern Urban Complex, and Birmingham is the second largest metropolis in Megalopolis England; their metropolitan populations are about 40 percent and 29 percent, respectively, of the populations of the New York and London metropolises. While neither has the size, economic power, or international prestige of its larger brother, each is an important city. Philadelphia is relatively old by American standards; during much of the colonial period, it was the largest city, but by the time of the Revolutionary War it had given way to New York. Today it is the fourth largest city in the United States, trailing Chicago and Los Angeles, which lie outside the Complex we are examining. Birmingham, also a relatively old city, remained small until the Industrial Revolution. The coal and iron deposits nearby became the basis for industrialization, especially as it relates to engineering. For many years it has been the largest city of the industrial area of the Midlands, the "Black Country" of Britain. Philadelphia, too, is highly industrialized, but on a wide and rather diverse base. Like all large cities, each has important business and trade activities.

As with New York, so Philadelphia has various areas within its metropolis, or various areas that might be defined as the metropolis. At the center is the City of Philadelphia; surrounding the city and extending up the Delaware River to include Trenton is the Philadelphia urbanized area. In a series of studies begun in the early 1960s, a "Cordon Area" was established; it included not only the most heavily urbanized parts of the region but also those areas which the planners expected would be developed within a reasonably near future. The Cordon Area, roughly double the extent of the urbanized area, included only 12 percent more population; obviously, its outer parts must have been lightly used for urban purposes, if at all.

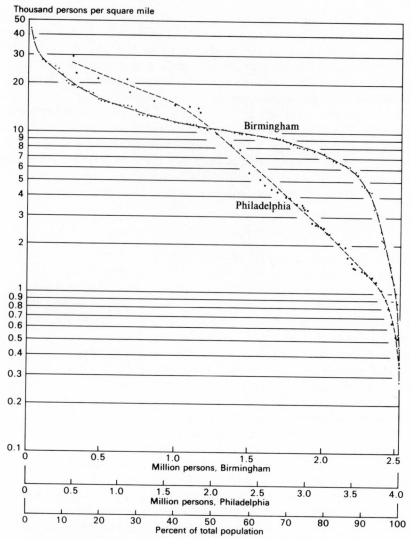

FIGURE 12. A comparison of overall population density per square mile, by traffic zone units—Philadelphia in 1960 and Birmingham in 1964.

The SMSAs for Philadelphia and Trenton are still larger—more than three times the acreage of the urbanized area but with only about 6 percent more population. In some respects, these SMSAs have peculiarly unfortunate boundaries for a study of urban land use. The Philadelphia SMSA includes Burlington, Camden, and Gloucester counties in New Jersey. Along their western edges, there is some modest urban development, whose residents often work in Philadelphia or otherwise have close economic relations with that city. But the greater part of the relatively extensive area of these rather large counties is not developed for urban purposes at all. These portions of the three counties add greatly to area but relatively little to population. There are also some very lightly settled parts of some of the Pennsylvania counties included in the Philadelphia SMSA.

TABLE 9

OVERALL POPULATION DENSITY, BY DECILES OF TOTAL POPULATION, NEW YORK, LONDON,
PHILADELPHIA, AND BIRMINGHAM, CIRCA 1960–1965

Percent of total population	Approximate density[1] at the point in array of zones by density			
	New York	London	Philadelphia	Birmingham
0	120,000	64,000	35,000	45,000
10	74,300	38,800	30,000	20,400
20	50,800	30,500	21,500	15,400
30	32,800	22,500	17,000	12,800
40	25,200	18,400	14,500	11,500
50	15,800	14,800	10,000	10,700
60	9,075	12,050	6,500	9,700
70	6,100	10,700	4,000	8,600
80	3,800	7,400	2,500	7,100
90	2,140	4,950	1,370	4,600
100	400	300	500	300

[1] Total persons/total area (in square miles).

A generally similar analysis may be made for the West Midlands (Birmingham) metropolitan area. There is a tiny core with a very small population—a central business district primarily. The City of Birmingham includes 40 percent of the metropolitan area's population; it seems reasonable to believe that there are differences in overall land use density within the city. The West Midlands conurbation is more than double the population of the City of Birmingham, with somewhat more than three times its area; these two points indicate a slowly declining overall density as one moves out from the city center. The areas included by the External Cordon line and the Standard Metropolitan Labour Area include relatively few more people but a substantially larger area, suggesting a very low overall density of land use at the edges.

By using population and area data for traffic origin zones (from transportation surveys), the zones may be arrayed in order of decreasing density in the Birmingham and Philadelphia metropolitan areas (figure 12). The results bear considerable similarity to the comparison of the New York and London areas. It will be recalled that the Philadelphia SMSA (including the Trenton SMSA) is about 70 percent larger in population than is the Birmingham SMLA; since overall population density is a function of city or metropolitan size (though only loosely so), one would expect somewhat higher densities in Philadelphia. The half of the population living in highest overall densities does indeed have higher densities in Philadelphia than in Birmingham. But the population living at the lower half of population densities has much higher densities in Birmingham, substantially so beginning at about the seventh quartile. This is simply another way of saying that the population–distance gradient is much steeper for Philadelphia than for Birmingham.

The data on overall population density, by deciles of population arranged in descending order of density, are summarized in table 9. Overall density for the most closely settled half of the population is a function of total metropolitan population. For instance, New York at its 50 percent density scale has more people per square mile than does London at the same relative point; but London has more than does Philadelphia. The same general relationship holds for the upper deciles of the density scale, although the coefficients of relation change. But at lower density deciles, this general relationship no longer holds. As the percentage of total population increases, the density falls much more sharply for the American than for the British cities. On the basis of these data, one would expect average density to rise in a metropolitan area as population increased; additions at the periphery would have relatively low densities, but the in-filling of previously bypassed areas and the conversion of strategic sites from single-family dwellings to apartment houses would raise overall density in older areas, sometimes substantially so.

AGRICULTURE IN THE AREAS EXAMINED

The most impressive differences between England and Wales on the one side and the equivalent area in the northeastern United States on the other side, or between Megalopolis England and the Northeastern Urban Complex, lie in their respective agricultures (table 10). There are approximately three times as many farms in the British area as in the American; they include twice as much land and about twice as high a proportion of the total land area; their area of cropland harvested is two and a half times greater, but it amounts to about the same percentage of total farm acreage. However, in England and Wales most of the land in farms but not in crops is permanent grazing land, much of which is of high productivity (by American standards), whereas in the United States much of the land in farms but not in crops is forest, generally badly degraded and cut over numerous times in the past. The British areas have several times as many cattle,

TABLE 10
AGRICULTURE IN COMPARATIVE AREAS OF NORTHEASTERN UNITED STATES
AND GREAT BRITAIN, CIRCA 1960

	United States		Great Britain	
Item	Area equivalent to England and Wales	Northeastern Urban Complex	England and Wales	Megalopolis England[1]
Number of farms	122,641	76,647	333,180	n.a.
Total land in farms (1,000 acres)	14,302	7,499	29,506	9,297
as percent of total land area	38%	37%	79%	74%
Cropland harvested (1,000 acres)	5,731	3,349	13,905	5,092
as percent of land in farms	40%	45%	46%	41%
Number of cattle, all ages (1,000)	2,049	1,122	9,028	3,225

Source: All U.S. data from Census of Agriculture, 1959; definitions of items given in source. England and Wales: number of farms from *FAO Production Yearbook, 1969;* land data for England and Wales from Robin H. Best and J. T. Coppock, *The Changing Use of Land in Britain* (London: Faber & Faber, 1962), p. 235; number of cattle and all data for Megalopolis England assembled for this study from Ministry of Agriculture annual June returns.

n.a.—Not available.

[1] Defined in terms of counties. This is a wider definition than that used elsewhere in this study, which is based on smaller civil divisions.

reflecting the larger area in grain and forage crops and the higher capacity of the permanent grazing lands.

There are several reasons why British agriculture should differ from that in the Northeastern Urban Complex. The physical endowment is different; in particular, the extensive permanent grasslands in Britain have no counterpart in the northeastern United States. The presence of a market presumably is much the same, since in both countries populations within the two regions are generally similar. British agriculture obviously has a much longer history, and Britain was once an agricultural nation, but the northeastern United States was also largely agricultural at one time. The fact that the northeastern United States is only one region within a large country, other parts of which are more generously endowed for agriculture, undoubtedly has a major effect upon agriculture within the Northeast. At one time, for instance, the Connecticut River Valley was the wheat breadbasket of the northern colonies; today, of course, wheat has moved a thousand miles and more to the west. Some part of the greater importance of agriculture in Britain is due to national policies in support of agriculture, including planning to reduce if not avoid urban encroachment on good agricultural land; and this in turn derives from the demonstrated vulnerability of British food supply in two world wars.

It remains rather ironic, however, that the country popularly considered to be the more highly urbanized turns out to have much the greater agriculture on a gross area of equal size to that in the northeastern United States.

INCOME AND CONSUMPTION COMPARISONS

In any discussion of social and economic conditions in two countries, comparisons of personal income and well-being have great interest; but they are also difficult to derive and are subject to misinterpretation. First of all, "income" is a term of many meanings and may be defined in several ways; although there is agreement among economists on different definitions, these do not always yield identical results for international comparisons. Then, too, the matter of income distribution among the citizens of each country is highly important: How far do averages conceal disparities, and is the extent of disparity, especially as to the very poor and the very rich, the same in each country? A lower average income in one country may be associated with lower average wages in that country; but how far does this reflect cheaper (and possibly better) services of all kinds? Changing life styles find expression in different combinations of goods and services in the consumption pattern of people in each country. If one is willing to consume more of those goods and services that are relatively cheap, and less of those goods and services that are relatively dear, one may live as well or better in a country of low average incomes than in one of higher average incomes. And, lastly, international comparisons are always plagued by exchange rate problems: Is the official rate the real one?

Despite these complexities, information (based on United Nations data, with as nearly identical definitions as possible) on average per capita incomes in the United States and the United Kingdom are helpful in making comparisons (figure 13).

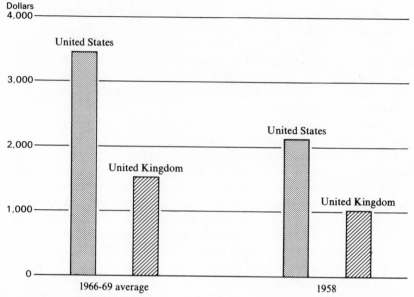

FIGURE 13. A comparison of per capita national income over an approximate ten-year span (at factor cost in current prices)—United States and United Kingdom.

On the average in recent years, the U.S. figure was somewhat more than double the U.K. one; in earlier years, the difference was not quite so large. During the 1950s national income in the United Kingdom moved upward rather more rapidly than it did in the United States: these were years of relative economic stagnation in the United States. In the 1960s the reverse is true: the U.S. national income moved upward faster than did that of the United Kingdom. These comparisons may give inadequate consideration to the greater availability of many public services at subsidized prices to the average consumer in the United Kingdom; they may also give inadequate consideration to the greater amounts and costs of travel in the United States, necessitated by the sprawled nature of its metropolises; and other corrections might be argued. But whatever may be the precise figures, and however much living styles may be adjusted to differences in cost of various consumption items, it appears fairly clear that *on the average* the American consumer is better off than his British cousin.

A major consumption item in each country is the personal car; not only is its purchase costly (in relation to annual income), but its operating costs are a significant item in the consumer's budget, and the provision of highways and streets is a major part of his tax load. Given the inadequacies of public transport in many areas, especially in the United States, a car may be essential to a job, hence an item of production; but a car also is always a consumption item, owned and operated in part for personal pleasure. Differences in car ownership, therefore, may serve as one index to differences in real consumer incomes.

Car ownership per 1,000 population in the United States rose rapidly during World War I and the 1920s, until by 1929 it had reached about 200 cars per 1,000 persons—about enough personal transport capacity to have moved the entire population by car at any given moment—and some cynic, observing the traffic jams of that day, wondered if the people were not out to demonstrate this capacity (figure 14). Severe depression in the early 1930s and restrictions on new car production during World War II meant that as late as 1946 car ownership per capita in the United States was not much above that of the 1929 peak. But since 1946, car ownership in the United States has more than doubled per 1,000 population and has risen still more in absolute terms. Today, car ownership in the United States is well over 430 per 1,000 population. Many families find that they require one car per adult as, over time, differences in job locations, life-styles, and other factors place stress on individual mobility. However, for a variety of reasons, including sheer cost considerations, many families are still without a car. There is every reason to expect that car ownership per 1,000 population will continue to rise in the United States, at least for some years; air pollution and other problems may force discontinuance of use in some cities and may also force major changes in car performance, but there is nothing on the immediate horizon to suggest a reduction in car numbers.

In 1950, still reflecting the slowdown in consumer goods production during World War II, Britain had 50 cars per 1,000 population, a figure exceeded by the United States in 1918; by 1960 it had nearly 110 cars, a figure exceeded by the United States in 1923. On this basis one might say that British car ownership, in

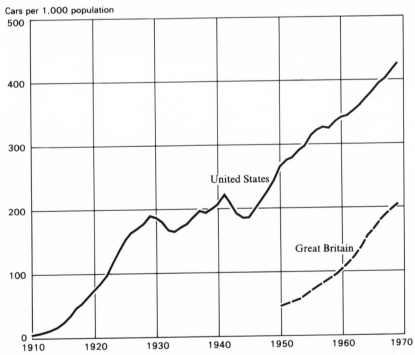

FIGURE 14. Differences in car ownership may serve as one index to differences in real consumer incomes between countries. By 1969 Britain had slightly more than 200 cars per 1,000 population, which was the U.S. figure in 1946. The British expect a continued rise of this dimension over the next twenty years.

relation to population, lagged about thirty-five years behind the United States. But by 1969 Britain had slightly more than 200 cars per 1,000 population, which was the U.S. figure in 1946; on this basis the lag is not much over twenty years. In the future, British car ownership may roughly parallel U.S. car ownership with a lag of perhaps twenty years. Estimates of car ownership in the year 2000, published by the Ministry of Transport, indicate a continued rise of this dimension. As per capita incomes rise, and as more families have sufficient discretionary income at their disposal, ownership of a car—and sometimes two or more—becomes increasingly common in Britain.

The experience in several Western European countries rather closely parallels, though does not exactly coincide with, the British experience. In relation to population France has somewhat more cars; West Germany, Belgium, and Switzerland, almost exactly the same number as Britain; and Italy, somewhat fewer. The upward trend in car ownership in each of these countries closely parallels the upward trend in the United Kingdom.

chapter **4**

Results of postwar urbanization in Britain and the United States

For many decades, but more specifically since the close of World War II in the mid-1940s, a major process of urban growth and development has been under way in Britain and in the United States. The process in more recent years may perhaps better be described as suburbanization, as contrasted with the urbanization of earlier decades. The purpose of this chapter is to describe some of the results of that process. As such, it builds upon chapters 1 and 2, wherein the general setting for urban growth and development in the two countries was described. With the general similarity of area and population in Megalopolis England and in the Northeastern Urban Complex, described in chapter 3, one would look naturally for some similarities, as well as some differences in results in the two countries. Urbanization and suburbanization in each country has been affected by their respective planning processes; hence the present chapter relates to the following one where the planning processes are considered in more detail.

DEMOGRAPHIC BACKGROUND IN THE UNITED STATES AS A WHOLE

Some of the demographic trends briefly considered in chapters 1 and 2 must now be considered in more detail. Implicit in this approach is the conviction that people, especially growing numbers of people, must be housed somewhere; that the trends of the past have been away from the open country and even away from the smaller towns and small cities, toward the larger urban agglomerations; and that the rate of population increase is only loosely related to economic and local environmental circumstances. While the record would suggest that the birthrate does indeed vary somewhat according to economic conditions of the moment, there are nevertheless demographic trends and forces largely independent of the business cycle or of the place of residence of the population concerned. In both Britain and the United States, as in most countries of the western world, a long downward trend in birthrates, greater than the downward trend in death rates, had resulted in lower rates of population growth by the time of World War II. Likewise, a long trend toward the cities, away from the countryside, had been apparent in each country, though there are notable differences between the countries in this respect.

In the United States, the crude birthrate had trended downward from 40 and 50 per 1,000 population in the early and middle nineteenth century (levels now experienced in much of the developing world) to slightly over 30 at the beginning of the twentieth century (figure 15). It continued to fall more or less steadily until the 1930s, when it ranged around 18 to 19. As a consequence, the net additions

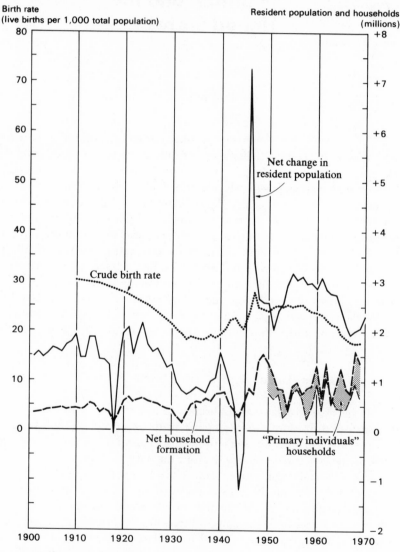

FIGURE 15. Crude birth rate, net changes in resident population, and net changes in households— United States, 1900–1970.

to resident population through the first three decades of the twentieth century ranged mostly from 1½ to 2 million annually. (Net additions to resident population may be negative, as in 1918, when large numbers of soldiers are abroad; but will be correspondingly higher in following years as these men are brought home. The process is most notable in 1943–45 and in 1946.) By the 1930s, the falling birthrate had reduced net additions to population to well under 1 million annually. This was the time when demographers, economists, and others were talking about reaching a constant population before now and at a level far below that of today. "Stability," not "growth," dominated thinking. Net household formation is loosely related to net additions to population; in periods of economic depression, of which the early 1930s were an extreme example, marriages are postponed, young married couples live with parents or with others of their age, and few persons establish single-person households.[1]

Although the crude birthrate had begun to rise by 1940, net additions to population and net households in the 1940s were dominated by World War II and its immediate aftermath. With many millions of men and women drawn into the armed services and many of them sent abroad, net additions to resident population declined and then became negative, and net formation of households fell off sharply. With the ending of the war, most of these men and women came back, sending net additions to resident population to a record 7¼ million in 1946; new households were formed as fast as housing would permit; and birthrate jumped a year later, as a deficit of child-bearing during the war was partially overcome. Net household formation reached what were until then record levels, of around 1½ million annually in the late 1940s and early 1950s.

All of the foregoing might have been dismissed as simply war-induced disturbances to more or less normal trends in birthrates, population change, and establishment of new households. What really gave the postwar period a unique character was the continued high birthrate; after a temporary peak in 1947, it remained on a plateau of 24 or higher per 1,000 population through 1959. Such a major reversal in the century-old downward trend was first greeted with disbelief by demographers, economists, planners, and public leaders; then, as it persisted, it was accepted as a permanent relationship, and population projections for a generation or more ahead were based on it. But it began to fall in the late 1950s, almost unnoticeably at first, then in larger measure, so that by the late 1960s it was below 18—lower than at any time in the 1930s. Net additions to resident population since the early 1950s have mirrored the changes in birthrate—around 3 million annually through most of the 1950s, now down to about 2 million annually. The outlook for future population change in the United States seems particularly unclear at the present: Will birthrates continue to decline, or will they stabilize, or even rise

[1] In 1960, the U.S. Bureau of the Census defined a household as follows: "A household consists of all the persons who occupy a housing unit. A house, an apartment or other group of rooms, or a single room is regarded as a housing unit when it is occupied or intended for occupancy as separate living quarters, that is, when the occupants do not live and eat with any other persons in the structure, and when there is either (1) direct access from the outside or through a common hall or (2) kitchen or cooking equipment for the exclusive use of the occupant." Although minor changes have been made, this is essentially the definition for the past several censuses.

again? The fertility rate (number of births per women of specified age) in the United States is nearing that which would ultimately produce a stationary population, but present age distribution of women in child-bearing ages ensures a rising population for another generation or two.

Net household formation through most of the 1950s and 1960s has shown some similarities, and some important differences from net additions to resident population. Year to year changes in net household formation are erratic, casting some doubt on the precision of these data. Smoothing out such fluctuations, the annual additions to households have averaged close to a million, exceeding that figure substantially in some years. The two postwar decades have thus seen new household formation at roughly double the rate of the two prewar decades. Two aspects of this are especially noteworthy. First is the large number of new households described as "primary individuals"—single-person households, for the most part; these have reached or exceeded half of the total in some years, if the data are accurate. Second, the net additions to resident population, when divided by the net additions to households, show a marginal rate of household size which has declined irregularly to well under two persons per household in the middle and late 1960s. The average size of all households has dropped greatly over the decades, from nearly five persons at the beginning of this century to only a trifle over three today. The upward trend toward more single-person households is likely to continue.

These statistics conceal the drama of a changing life style and a growing affluence. In an earlier day, young men, young women, and older persons of each sex typically lived in the homes of parents or of children. Today, the young man or woman who finishes formal schooling and gets a job (and many who do neither, if parents will supply the income) sets up his or her own household—typically, a small apartment, not a separate house. But the older person, whether widow or widower, or older married couple, whose children are grown and gone, maintains a separate household, sometimes in the house in which the family grew up (and which is often not well suited to the older person's needs but for which there is both a sentimental attachment and much inertia against change), and sometimes in apartments, some of which provide many special services for the elderly. These life styles, and the incomes underlying them, have rather obvious consequences for the kinds and locations of housing needed.

These changes in national totals of population and households had an important spatial dimension also. Two major flows of population have been evident: a movement away from most rural areas and small towns, toward the cities; and a movement away from the city center toward the suburbs.[2] Migration from rural areas and small towns to cities has been a feature of American life ever since independence. Farm population in the United States dropped from about 30 million at the beginning of World War II to about 10 million today, because of the agricultural revolution. As farm population dropped, the need for service population in small rural towns also declined. For both farm and small-town population, the changes have actually been greater than these data suggest, for it has been domi-

2 See chapter 1.

nantly the young people who have migrated; as the present aging population dies off, the population change in such areas is likely to be even swifter.

But the change within larger cities or metropolitan areas has been equally spatially oriented. By and large, the older city centers have either not increased in population or have reported rather small declines; all of the net increase has been on the periphery. These spatial shifts have had racial, age, and income aspects. Most cities have acquired a much larger black core population since World War II; in several large cities, blacks now outnumber whites, and in others there is a relatively large black core. Several million white families have relocated to the suburbs, or the newly formed white families have located there. The suburbs have particularly attracted the younger families, with small children; older whites have sometimes stayed in old locations, or have moved to apartments elsewhere in the older city, as well as locating in suburbs; and many of the new households of young people, often the single-person households, have located in apartments within the older city.

Demographic Background in the Northeastern Urban Complex

The foregoing has all concerned the United States as a whole; however, the same general relationships exist for the Northeastern Urban Complex (table 11). Since 1920, the population of the Complex (as defined on the basis of 1960 data) has never been as little as 19 percent nor as much as 20 percent of the national popu-

TABLE 11

Population by Component Parts of Northeastern Urban Complex, 1920–1970

	1920	1930	1940	1950	1960	1970
Total resident U.S. population (millions)	105.7	122.8	131.7	150.7	178.5	202.1
Population of Northeastern Urban Complex[1]						
millions	20.2	24.2	25.8	29.3	34.4	38.9
% of U.S. population	19.1	19.7	19.6	19.4	19.3	19.2
Population of SMSAs in N.E. Urban Complex[2]						
millions	–	–	23.7	26.9	31.7	36.0
% of Complex population	–	–	92	88	92	93
Population of urbanized areas in N.E. Urban Complex[3]						
millions	–	–	–	24.0	28.5	33.2
% of Complex population	–	–	–	82	83	85
Population of all cities with 25,000 or more population in 1960						
millions	–	–	18.2	19.5	19.4	19.3
% of Complex population	–	–	71	67	56	50

Source: 1970 Census for 1970 data; 1960 Census for other data.

[1] As defined on basis of data for 1960.

[2] For 1940 and 1950, as defined in 1950; for other years, current definition.

[3] Current definition in all years.

lation; the Complex has grown at the national rate. It has included no counties reporting persistent loss in population, except the larger city centers; and it has not experienced the extremely rapid growth rates that have characterized much of California, the Southwest, and parts of Florida. While it has gained somewhat in population from inmigration, particularly in its southern parts, it possesses a demographic momentum of its own, with a considerable surplus of births over deaths; in the absence of substantial outmigration, it will continue to grow. In 1960 the SMSAs of the Northeastern Urban Complex included 68 percent of the total area; hence it is not surprising that they included 92 percent of the population in that year. Some modest redefinitions of SMSAs from 1950 to 1960 and from 1960 to 1970 have kept the percentage of Complex population within SMSAs relatively constant.

The urbanized area included only 10 percent of the Complex area in 1950, 17 percent in 1960, and 21 percent in 1970; yet the urbanized area has included an approximately constant percentage of the Complex's population. In other words, the boundaries of the urbanized area have expanded at least as fast as the population has grown. Most of the population growth of the Complex has been within both SMSAs and urbanized areas.

In contrast, the population of cities with 25,000 or more people in 1960 has remained nearly constant from 1940 to 1970—an increase of somewhat more than a million between 1940 and 1950, and a very small net decrease in each of the two succeeding decades. As a consequence, the proportion of the population living in such cities has dropped steadily, from nearly three-fourths in 1940 to just half in 1970. Because the legal or political boundaries of cities do not conform closely to economic boundaries, it is not wholly accurate to say that the land outside of cities is "suburbs." The latter, in a popular sense of the term, sometimes lie within the legal or political boundaries of a city. By and large, however, areas outside of cities but within an urbanized area are "suburbs" both in a popular and a more technical sense. On this basis, suburban population has increased from perhaps 4 million in 1940 (we do not know exactly, because urbanized areas were defined only in 1950) to perhaps 13 million in 1970, or by threefold in thirty years—a period during which city population was essentially stable.

The Demographic Background in Britain

As in the United States, so in Britain, the demographic record in the twentieth century has been deeply disturbed by the extraordinary population movements attending both world wars. Figure 16 shows that at the onset of both wars net losses of well over a million home population per annum were recorded from the United Kingdom; for the most part these represented servicemen going on duty abroad, but in World War II they also included numbers of civilian evacuees moving to the Western Hemisphere and elsewhere. Conversely, the ends of both wars saw very large returning counter-movements, with over a million a year added to the home population after World War I and no less than 3 million after World War II. Clearly, in themselves these represent temporary migrations without much long-

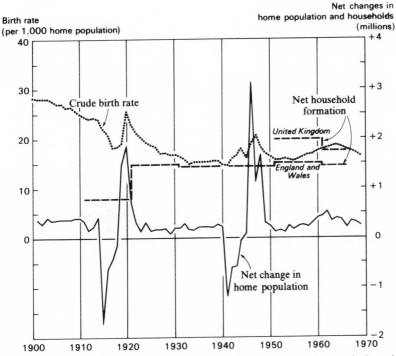

Figure 16. Crude birth rate, net changes in home population, and net changes in households—
United Kingdom, 1900–1970.

term significance for household formation or housing demand. But one effect
should be noted: the rise in the birthrate immediately after both wars, a product
of delayed marriages and delayed family building.

Apart from these perturbations, the long-term movements of the United Kingdom population appear clearly enough from the chart. Between the two world wars,
the birthrate continued to decline, as it had ever since the widespread dissemina-
tion of effective birth control techniques from the 1870s on. Having fallen from
28 per thousand in 1900 to less than 17 per thousand at the onset of the Great
Depression in 1930, it then appeared to reach a floor, falling more slowly to a low
point of just over 15 per thousand in the mid-1930s, with a slight recovery from
then to World War II. Throughout the forty years from 1900 to 1940, the trends
in British and American birthrates were remarkably similar, with the British rate
4 to 6 per thousand below the American rate in most years. The actual numbers of
births in the United Kingdom in most of these years remained fairly stable, at
between 700,000 and 800,000 per annum; and with a modest rate of net outmigration to the British possessions and elsewhere, coupled with a low deathrate which
declined slowly, the net additions to the United Kingdom population remained
remarkably steady during most of the interwar period, at between 100,000 and
200,000 each year.

As in every country affected by the conflict, World War II was responsible for
odd fluctuations in the birthrate, which at first fell even below its trough of the

mid-1930s, but then soon recovered to levels not known since the 1920s; indeed, the "baby boom" at the end of World War II was only the final phase of a process which had begun as early as 1942. This postwar rise in the birthrate was predicted by demographic experts, who just as confidently predicted that it would subside; and this duly happened. From a peak of 20.7 per thousand in 1947, the birthrate declined to as low as 15.4 in 1955—a level reminiscent of many years in the mid-1930s. During several years in the early 1950s, the absolute level of births fell below 800,000; and the net increase in home population was correspondingly low— between 100,000 and 200,000 a year. The Royal Commission on Population, reporting in 1949, confidently predicted that after a while the modest net increase of the population would turn into an actual decline; and few were heard to disagree.

What upset all these confident calculations was the unexpected birthrate from 1955 onwards. Coming some years after the corresponding American increase, it took the crude rate per thousand from a low point of 15.4 in 1955, to 17.5 in 1960 and to a peak of 18.7 in 1964—a level unknown since the 1920s, apart from the temporary surge to over 20 in 1947. After 1964, just as unpredictably, the birthrate turned down again; by 1971 it had fallen as low as 16.2, once again comparing with the low levels of the 1930s. The perturbations in the birthrate since 1950 have been small compared with the secular decline of the first thirty years of the century. The upsurge in birthrates in the late 1950s and early 1960s in Britain was not only later than the similar upsurge in the United States, but smaller as well—about 3 per thousand in Britain contrasted with 6 or 7 in the U.S. It appears unlikely in the foreseeable future that Britain will ever again achieve the birthrates typical before World War I. Nevertheless, coupled with very slowly declining deathrates and with comparatively high levels of immigration from the Commonwealth between 1958 and 1962, the rise in the birthrate took the annual net increase of the population to as high as 500,000 in 1962—a level never before reached, apart from postwar years, in the twentieth century. (In most postwar years, it should be noted, the net migration trend has been outward from Britain; and, by the standards of many West European nations, immigration to Britain has been very modest.) If this rapid increase had continued, it would have meant the addition of a city the size of Leeds to the British urban area every year. Even at the end of the 1960s the net increase of the population was still 300,000 a year— equivalent to the annual addition of a city the size of Bradford, and well above the levels of the 1930s or the early 1950s.

At the same time, this population was progressively dividing itself into more and smaller households.[3] During the period between the two world wars, and afterwards up to 1961, the net rate of household formation (which in Britain can only be recorded for intercensal periods, not for individual years) had remained remarkably constant at between 140,000 and 150,000 a year in England and Wales, or about 170,000 a year in the entire United Kingdom. This rate of household formation was far in excess of the growth of the population in households, as

---

[3] The definition of a "household" in the British Census has varied from year to year, but it is substantially similar to that used in the U.S. Census.

table 12 shows; the average size of household was declining sharply, due to social changes very similar to those occurring in the United States. As the average age of marriage fell, young people left the parental home earlier to set up households of their own; as people lived longer into old age, increasing numbers of them—the product of high birthrates before World War I—were forming small households consisting of a couple or a single widowed member. The significance of these changes was not fully appreciated at the time. Cullingworth in 1960 and Needleman in 1961 believed that this trend could be fully explained by changes in the demographic structure such as the greater numbers of old people. But even at the time this thesis did not apply to London, and it was later shown to lack much of its validity in other parts of the country too. Though the rate of new household formation slowed in the early 1960s—from an average of 198,000 a year in 1951–61 to an average of 175,000 a year in 1961–66—it remained more than double the population growth rate in both periods: certain groups in the population were apparently becoming more prone to set up their own households. Among the important factors was undoubtedly the greater mobility of the young, who tended to leave home to seek education. As in the United States, this trend toward greater fissioning of the population into more and smaller households will probably continue; for it must be remembered that in respect of certain social trends—above all, the increase in higher and further education—Britain is still some considerable way behind the United States.

In Britain as in the United States, the growth of population and the formation of households has an important spatial dimension. Here it is particularly important to use the right framework of analysis: the conventional treatment in the British Census, which divides population into urban and rural according to the accident

TABLE 12

Households, and Population in Households, United Kingdom, 1911–1966

	Households	Population in households	Average size of household
1911, England and Wales..........	7,943,000	34,606,000	4.36
1921, England and Wales..........	8,739,000	36,180,000	4.14
1931, England and Wales..........	10,223,000	38,042,000	3.72
1951, England and Wales..........	13,117,868	41,840,000	3.19
United Kingdom.............	14,891,374	48,030,731	3.23
1961, United Kingdom.............	16,871,520	50,923,448	3.01
1966, United Kingdom.............	17,747,119	52,189,599	2.94

	Percent growth in:		Ratio, growth in households: growth in population in households
	Households	Population in households	
	(decennial rates)		
1911–21, England and Wales..........	10.0	4.6	2.2
1921–31, England and Wales..........	17.1	5.2	3.3
1931–51, England and Wales..........	14.1	5.0	2.8
1951–61, United Kingdom.............	13.3	6.0	2.2
1961–66, United Kingdom.............	10.4	5.0	2.1

Source: British Censuses.

of whether the administrative areas they live in are so classified, actually obscures the true facts. During the 1950s and 1960s, according to these official statistics, the total rural population of Britain was growing faster than the total urban population. But this, of course, merely represents suburbanization; characteristically,

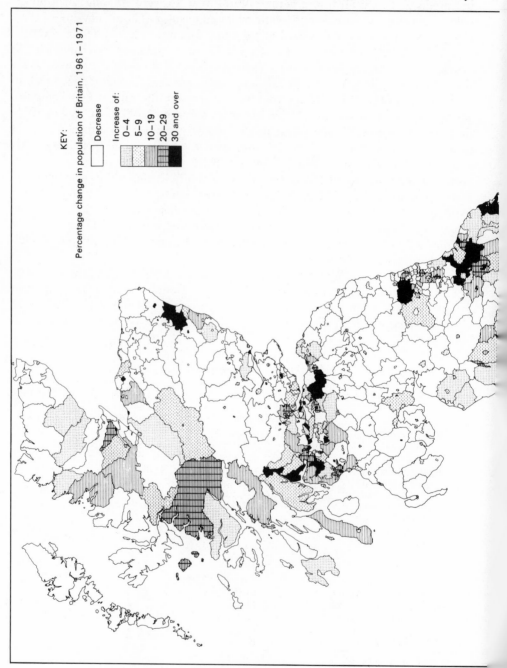

in the really remote rural areas far from urban influence populations were falling. Figure 17 shows the pattern of population decline and growth in Britain during the 1960s. It clearly demonstrates that the areas of decline have been concentrated in two sorts of place: first, the remoter rural areas such as Devon and Cornwall,

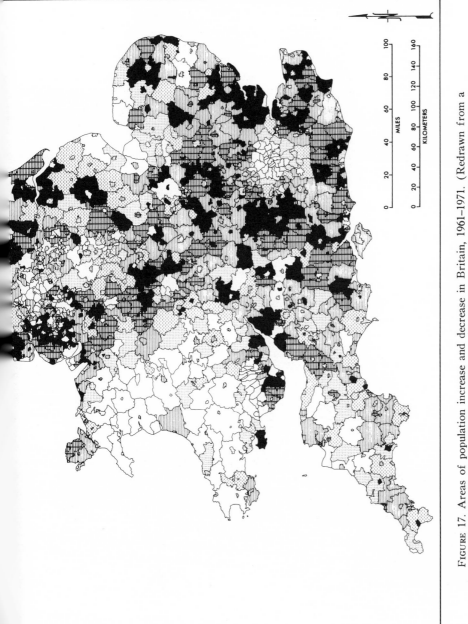

FIGURE 17. Areas of population increase and decrease in Britain, 1961–1971. (Redrawn from a map compiled by D. J. Sinclair, Department of Geography, London School of Economics.)

Mid and North Wales, the northern Pennine uplands of North England, and much of upland and highland Scotland; and second, the cores of the large urban agglomerations, which have been losing people due to slum clearance, urban redevelopment generally, and the suburban movement of the population. The areas of growth, conversely, have tended to concentrate in the heavily industrialized urban core of the country, particularly the area termed Megalopolis England; and there, they formed clearly marked rings of suburban growth around the major conurbations and larger freestanding cities.

In fact, Britain again resembles the United States in another important particular: that a substantial part of the total area has tended to lose population since World War I. For the whole United Kingdom, 25 percent of all administrative areas lost population in the 1931–51 intercensal period; this proportion rose to 39 percent during 1951–61, and since 1961 the trend has continued. Many of the areas undergoing losses in all periods were rural; the additions to the list in the 1950s and 1960s tended to be inner urban areas, especially in the major conurbations, in England. Since many of the rural areas recording persistent population loss were large and thinly populated, the actual percentage of the total area of the United Kingdom recording population loss is much larger than these percentages suggest.

In Britain as in the United States, then, the spatial pattern of population change is clear: losses from the rural margins and, increasingly, from the urban cores; gains, overwhelmingly concentrated in the suburban rings around the major urban agglomerations and freestanding cities; with this last trend most evident in Megalopolis England. With 21 percent of the land area of the United Kingdom, Megalopolis has accounted for a large, and almost constant, proportion of its population: around 61–62 percent of the whole. And just as with the Northeastern Urban Complex, with the exception of its urban cores Megalopolis has been outside the areas of persistent population decline during those decades.

TABLE 13

POPULATION BY COMPONENT PARTS OF MEGALOPOLIS ENGLAND, 1931–1971

	1931	1951	1961	1966	1971
Population of United Kingdom (thousands)	46,038.4	50,225.2	52,708.9	53,788.5	55,349.0
Population of Megalopolis England (thousands)	27,595.4	30,489.9	32,241.9	32,864.5	33,839.3
Percent of U.K. population	59.9	60.7	61.2	61.1	61.1
Population of SMLAs[1] in Megalopolis England (thousands)	24,446.2	26,919.8	28,320.4	28,724.0	29,190.8
Percent of Megalopolis population	88.6	88.3	87.4	87.4	86.3
Population of urbanized areas[2] in Megalopolis England (thousands)	21,701.0	24,128.6	25,715.2	n.a.	n.a.
Percent of Megalopolis population	78.6	79.1	79.8	n.a.	n.a.
Population of SMLAs cores in Megalopolis England (thousands)	17,652.6	17,577.2	17,588.8	17,151.6	17,008.8
Percent of Megalopolis population	64.0	57.6	54.6	52.2	50.3

n.a.—not available.
[1] Fixed definition.
[2] Shifting definitions.

TABLE 14
DECENTRALIZATION OF POPULATION AND EMPLOYMENT IN THE 63 SMLAs
OF MEGALOPOLIS ENGLAND, 1951–1971

	Data for				Changes[2] during		
	1951	1961	1966	1971[1]	1951–61	1961–66	1961–71
Population							
Megalopolis England (thousands)	30,499	32,242	32,864	33,839	1,743	623	1,597
Its SMLAs (thousands)	26,920	28,320	28,724	29,191	1,401	404	870
Percent of Megalopolis	88.3	87.8	87.4	86.3	−0.5	−0.4	−1.5
SMLA cores (thousands)	17,577	17,589	17,152	17,009	12	−437	−580
Percent of SMLA totals	65.3	62.1	59.7	58.3	−3.2	−2.4	−3.8
SMLA rings (thousands)	9,343	10,732	11,572	12,182	1,389	841	1,450
Percent of SMLA totals	34.7	37.9	40.3	41.7	3.2	2.4	3.8
Employment							
Megalopolis England (thousands)	14,263	15,104	15,781	n.a.	841	677	n.a.
Its SMLAs (thousands)	12,781	13,466	13,960	n.a.	684	494	n.a.
Percent of Megalopolis	89.6	89.2	88.5	n.a.	−0.4	−0.7	n.a.
SMLA cores (thousands)	9,527	9,952	10,014	n.a.	425	62	n.a.
Percent of SMLA totals	74.5	73.9	71.7	n.a.	−0.6	−2.2	n.a.
SMLA rings (thousands)	3,254	3,514	3,946	n.a.	260	433	n.a.
Percent of SMLA totals	25.5	26.1	28.3	n.a.	0.6	2.2	n.a.

n.a.—not available.
[1] Provisional figures.
[2] Changes in percentages refer to percentages shown in left half of table, not to changes in population and employment shown in right half of table.

A very high, though marginally decreasing, proportion of the population of Megalopolis is found in its sixty-three Standard Metropolitan Labour Areas: between 86 and 89 percent, living on some 62 percent of the area (compared with 92 percent, living on 68 percent of the area, for America's Northeastern Urban Complex in 1960) (table 13). During the period 1931–51 these SMLAs added some 2.5 million to their populations; during 1951–61, another 1.4 million; and during the decade 1961–71, yet another 0.9 million. Of course, since like the equivalent American SMSAs they are functionally and not physically defined, the British SMLAs include a good deal of fundamentally rural land with low population densities—the more so, because planning controls have operated to keep physical development off much of this land. But what is really significant is that the big additions to the metropolitan area populations have been wholly concentrated in the so-called urbanized areas outside the urban cores: that is, the contiguous zones around the cores with population densities of 1,000 and more per square mile. In fact, because new areas have been added to the urbanized areas from census to census, they have actually accounted for more than the net increase in the SMLAs considered as a whole. In other words, the growth of population in Megalopolis England has been wholly in its suburban areas—which is precisely what these zones are. These areas increased their population from 4.05 million in 1931 to 6.55 million in 1951 and then to 8.13 million in 1961: a doubling in thirty years at a time when the population of the urban cores was almost static at about 17.6 million. Were figures available for urbanized areas at the 1966 or 1971 Census, they would almost certainly show a marked continuation of this process.

Population, then, was decentralizing rapidly into the suburban rings of the metropolitan areas of Megalopolis. But employment was decentralizing much more slowly and more tardily. Table 14 shows that throughout the period 1951–71 for

total population and during the period 1951–66 for total employment, in Megalopolis between 86 and 90 percent were concentrated in its sixty-three Standard
Metropolitan Labour Areas. But the changes within these SMLAs were significant.
At the beginning of the fifteen-year period, 65 percent of population and nearly
75 percent of jobs were in the urban cores of the SMLAs; by 1966, these proportions had fallen to less than 60 percent and just over 71 percent, respectively, and
by 1971 population had fallen to 58 percent. The outward shift of population
between 1951 and 1966, thus measured, was a 5.6 drop in the core's percentage;
for employment the corresponding percentage was only 2.8. Furthermore, the table
makes it clear that in the early part of the period, during the 1950s, while the
outward shift of population was already marked, for employment it was barely
noticeable; only in the latter part, after 1961, did the outward movement of employment show signs of catching up. Figures 18 and 19 plot the results for the individual SMLAs for the period 1951–66, comparing the rates of decentralization

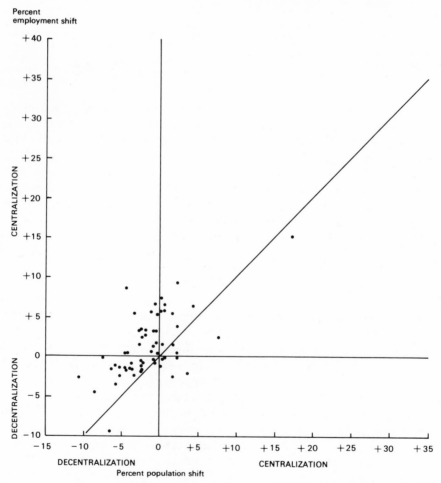

FIGURE 18. Population and employment shifts between 1951 and 1961 in Britain (63 SMLAs).

graphically. They make it clear that in the great majority of cases, population shifted earlier and more completely than employment. In the early period, indeed, there were many individual cases where decentralization of population (measured in the way described above) was accompanied by actual centralization of employment; and for some areas, this persisted even into the 1960s.

Of course, this gives no indication of how outward shifts of population related to outward shifts of employment in individual cases. But the commuting data, which are more plentiful and detailed in the British censuses than in the American ones, allow us to trace these relationships. They make it clear that in most cases the result was a marked increase in longer radial journeys, from the suburban ring of the metropolitan area to the core, or even outside the metropolitan area. For nine selected metropolitan areas from different parts of Megalopolis during the period 1951–66, the general tendency was for the proportion of all journeys that were wholly within the core to fall, and conversely for the proportion of journeys

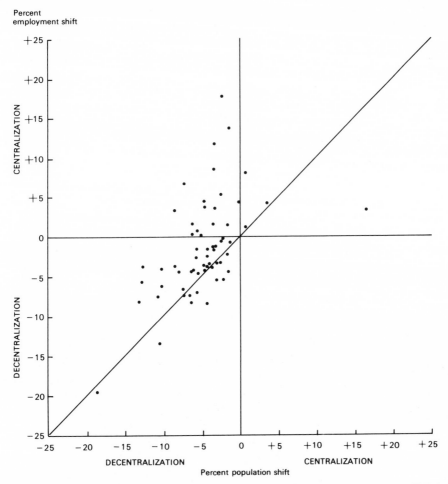

FIGURE 19. Population and employment shifts between 1961 and 1966 in Britain (63 SMLAs).

that took place from the ring to the core—or, in the case of areas near London, from the core or ring to other areas altogether—to rise. These last two categories of journey tended to be longer, in most cases, than journeys wholly within the core; in the case of journeys outside the metropolitan area in South East England, they were invariably very long journeys into Greater London, or thirty miles each way or more. One interesting exception to the rule was Stevenage, where the establishment of the new town caused a sharp increase in the proportion of local, short-distance journeys within the urban core. But, in general, the suburbanization of population coupled with the slower suburbanization of jobs seems to have caused an increase in the proportion of longer journeys—at any rate in the period 1951–61, after which the situation seems to have stabilized as the outward suburban movement of jobs speeded up.

It would be inadvisable to try to make an overall direct comparison, at any one census date, between the thirty-four SMSAs of the Northeastern Urban Complex and the sixty-three SMLAs of Megalopolis England with regard to their degree of decentralization of people and jobs; the rather different definition of the central core in the two cases, and in particular the more arbitrary character of the American definition, would preclude any firm conclusions. But a look at the commuting data, which is available for both sets of metropolitan areas at the 1960 and 1961 censuses, suggests that in a number of cases—above all, in the bigger metropolitan areas—decentralization of both people and jobs has gone much further in the U.S. examples. A high proportion of all recorded commuting trips—38 percent in Philadelphia against 16 percent in Birmingham (Britain), for instance—were ring-to-ring trips, made wholly within the suburbs. In smaller metropolitan areas this difference was often not so evident, and in some of these—above all the older textile SMSAs of New England and their equivalents in Lancashire or Yorkshire —it was hardly evident at all. But the commuting information and the indirect evidence about shopping patterns suggest that the American SMSA is usually more decentralized than its British equivalent. A higher proportion of work trips are made from suburban homes to suburban factories or offices, usually by private automobile. And a higher proportion of retail business of the durable or comparison goods type is done in suburban shopping centers, accessible by private car rather than by public transportation.

All this adds up to a considerably different urban or suburban life style in the two countries and to a different method of metropolitan functioning. It is difficult to describe such differences in life style accurately, and impossible to quantify them. Americans typically live in suburbs of lower density, more often in single-family homes with plots of land (yards, in America; gardens, in Britain) much larger than their British counterparts have, depend more on the private car (more families with two or more), shop more commonly (even for major luxury purchases) at suburban shopping centers, and otherwise geographically have more mobile and less tightly bounded lives. With the widespread ownership of cars, the American metropolis consists less of a series of rather closely defined neighborhoods or districts. The family shopping expedition, for instance, is far more likely to seek out a relatively distant suburban shopping center. The through motorways, and increasingly the circumferential belt highways, enable large numbers of cars to move at high speeds. Material possessions are likely to be more numerous, more expensive, and bulkier for the American family. In thus emphasizing the "more" aspect of the American metropolis, one must not overlook the situations in which "more" is worse—more crime, more air pollution from automobiles, perhaps more people alienated from society.

Housing Construction in the United States

In the climates of Britain and the United States permanent housing as a protection against the elements is a necessity, and in high-income countries housing involves comforts and luxuries, not merely shelter. The stock of housing at any date is relatively large; the annual additions to stock are relatively small—even the most active building year is unlikely to see an addition of more than 3 percent. Residential buildings tend to last for some decades, hence at any date much of the stock is relatively old. While some old housing survives in good condition, much is substandard by current standards.

The total housing supply is augmented annually in several ways: by new construction; by conversion of older houses into two or more apartments; and, usually in exceptional circumstances such as war or depression, by conversion of buildings originally designed for other purposes. It is diminished by demolitions—either privately, for new construction of housing or other structures, or publicly, for new highways or other purposes; by destruction through natural hazards such as fire, floods, or hurricanes; by degeneration, so that the structure is no longer fit for human habitation; and by merger of two or more units into one. In the short run, the supply of housing may rise or fall through changes in the vacancy rate, which can fall almost to zero at times of housing shortage; normally, to provide for the needs of a mobile society such as the United States, vacancies should run at 2 or 3 percent of the total stock.

All these forces, with the exception of the natural ones, are powerfully affected by economic conditions; if housing is scarce—absolutely, in time of war, or in relation to ability to pay, as in depression—structures are used for housing which would be scorned at other times; in prosperity, demolitions and abandonments and new building all increase. The following picture of average annual changes in the 1960–65 period can be calculated for the United States:[4]

Additions to supply:
new housing	1,525,000 units
net additions to mobile homes	90,000 units
Total additions, annually	1,615,000 units

Losses from supply, annually:
demolitions, about half of which are private and about half of which are public	295,000 units
conversions and mergers, resulting in a net loss of	40,000 units
natural causes	68,000 units
deterioration to the point where they are unfit for human habitation	83,000 units
change in use, net loss	94,000 units
net gain in vacancies	130,000 units
Total losses, annually	700,000 units

[4] Michael Sumichrast and Norman Farquhar, *Demolition and Other Factors in Housing Replacement Demand* (Washington: National Association of Home Builders), 1967.

This permitted the accommodation of about 900,000 new households annually; Sumichrast and Farquhar seem to regard household formation as the independent variable, with changes in housing units the consequence, but a reciprocal relationship may also exist, as noted elsewhere in this book.

In the United States, the relationships among these various forces of loss and of addition to housing supply vary considerably from year to year, as far as one can estimate from insufficient and perhaps not wholly accurate data. Although data on housing starts are available for many years, and presumably are accurate, yet data on demolitions, conversions, and other losses are less accurate and less detailed. Although data on numbers of households (and some data on types of households) have been available annually since 1900, one must calculate net formation of new households by difference between total numbers one year and the next; and the erratic year-to-year changes in the latter lead one to suspect the accuracy of annual estimates of total numbers of households. In general, there is a relation between net formation of new households and new building construction, but the relation is not a simple one. During 1960–65 there were about 1.7 new housing units built for each net addition to households; for the whole period 1910 to date, the relationship has been much nearer 1 to 1. But during both world wars and during the severe depression years of the 1930s, there were fewer new housing units built than there were net new households formed; the difference was made up by conversions, which added a third or more to the national housing supply in these periods. On the other hand, during the 1920s and during most of the 1950s and 1960s new housing construction considerably exceeded net new household formation; if the data are correct, in 1963–64 more than twice as many new units were built as net new households were formed. In periods of prosperity, not only does new building rise but abandonment of poor or substandard units increases, and demolitions rise to enable land conversion to other uses, as well as often a rise in vacancy rates.

Both houses and households go through aging cycles—not exact cycles, but general ones. Individual structures, however well maintained, tend to deteriorate; and neighborhoods, too, are more likely to go down than up as the housing stock ages. The deterioration, slow at first, accelerates with age. For the United States, it is estimated that 79 percent of housing units will still be habitable after fifty years; but by ninety years only 9 percent, and after a hundred years only 1 percent of the original housing units will be habitable.[5] It may well be that in the future, as standards of acceptable housing rise, this rate of obsolescence will be even higher.

At the end of World War II, the housing situation in the United States was very tight; there had been relatively little building or even maintenance during the war, and even during the preceding decade the rate of new building had been much lower than in the decade before that. A considerable part of the housing stock was old; a fourth or more had been built before 1900, some of it long before that date. Much was substandard by the accepted standards of the late 1940s; in 1950 only 64 percent was not dilapidated and contained private toilets, baths, and hot water. Much, indeed, had been substandard when built—total housing space too small,

---

[5] Marion Clawson, "Urban Renewal in 2000," *Journal of the American Institute of Planners,* vol. XXXIV, no. 3 (May 1968).

rooms too small for effective use, too few windows, no plumbing, no electricity, no central heating, etc. The situation was worst in rural areas but most cities had their miserable slums, worse for renters than for owners, and worse in the South than elsewhere. Many of these poor housing units were badly crowded as well, with 15 percent occupied by more persons than there were rooms.

What really distinguished the immediate postwar years from the earlier period was the high demand after the war, when several million men were demobilized from the armed forces in a period of little more than a year, many of them—and many workers in war plants also—with savings enough to make the down payment on a house. As Maisel said, ". . . it was a seller's market and the buyer took what he got . . . It may not have been much of a house, measured by some standards, since it was located on newly developed tract land and was meager in quality and detail; some critics thought it had atrocious design."[6] Poor as many of the new houses may have been, they were fresh and clean, and generally far above the alternatives of old housing available—or unavailable. Moreover, given the financial policies applicable to new housing, discussed in chapter 1, they may have been good bargains even when their quality was very low.

The rate of house building in the United States has exceeded one million units in every year since World War II; in no previous year had it been so high. It may well be argued that the rate of building has been far below national need—there is still a disgracefully large number of substandard housing units in use, as well as many derelict buildings. For the period 1945–70 inclusive, a total of 34½ million new housing units (including mobile homes) have been built; this compared with 38 million units in the housing stock at the beginning of this period, and with 68½ million units at the end of it. Before the war, about one-fifth of all new housing units built annually had been in structures housing two or more households—duplex (semi-detached) houses, row houses, and apartments. After the war, this declined sharply, to as low as a tenth in some years; these were the years when single-family detached houses claimed nearly all of housing construction. A good deal of popular and professional writing in those days talked of a new life-style, that of the suburbanite, as dominant, and of the single-family detached house as the universal form of housing. But in the early 1960s the percentage of apartments built began to rise, and for the 1960s as a whole multi-unit dwellings accounted for a substantially greater proportion of the total increase in dwelling units than did single-unit dwellings. The increase in multi-unit dwellings was particularly great in the suburbs.

There has been some modest renewal of decadent or slum areas since the close of World War II; some has been privately, some publicly, financed. In general, such renewal means the demolition of houses or apartments that are abandoned or substandard, or closely intermingled with buildings falling in these categories. Renewal should be distinguished from clearance of urban areas, often of low-quality housing, where the land is sought for transportation or other uses than housing. Where housing renewal takes place, whether privately or publicly, the new structures are normally of much higher quality than those they replace; they also

[6] Sherman J. Maisel, *Housebuilding in Transition* (Berkeley: University of California Press, 1963), p. 131.

cost more, and hence are usually unavailable to the previous occupants of the area. In many instances, particularly of public urban renewal, the cleared area has lain idle for many months before new building began. The public urban renewal programs have been subject to much criticism on these grounds.

The outlook for the next decade or two is for a relatively high level of dwelling construction in the United States. The relatively large numbers of young people born in the 1950s and early 1960s will mean the formation of many new households in the 1970s and 1980s; these, plus older and younger persons establishing single-person households, will create a substantial demand for new housing. Even a lowered birthrate during the next two decades will not much affect the *number* of new dwelling units demanded, although it might much affect the size and type of units needed. Much old, substandard housing will be replaced, especially if prosperity permits. The national administration has established a goal of 26 million new housing units to be built in the 1970s—substantially more than have previously been built in any decade in the United States, and more than six times the greatest rate of house building ever achieved in Britain. Many observers doubt that this goal will be reached, and some even question its desirability. But a high rate of building seems probable. The trend toward apartments is likely to continue; more marked may be the trend toward "mobile homes"—so large and heavy as to be mobile primarily in movement from factory to site. In spite of much talk about cheaper construction methods for houses, the mobile home offers the only possibility of a new house for several million families of modest to low incomes. Many suburbs and other areas have regulations making the siting of mobile homes difficult or impossible.

Throughout the postwar years, the cost of new houses to their first purchasers has risen steadily, for several reasons. First of all, prices of consumer goods, of raw materials, wages of all kinds, and most other items in the national accounts have gone up in price, so that it is not surprising that prices (or cost) of new houses have risen also. But some special features in the house-building industry have pushed up prices of new houses even more. There is some evidence that the wages of construction workers have moved up faster, even in relation to increases in the productivity of their labor, than has the general price level. The price of buildable suburban land has also risen more than the average of all prices.

Partly because of these differences in cost factors, and partly to meet the demands of at least some house buyers, the building industry in the United States has responded by building "more house per house"; that is, houses are larger, on larger lots of land, and have many features not previously included in typical new houses. Throughout the postwar years, in spite of rising real incomes of average families, the purchase of a new house has been beyond the capability of at least the lower half of the income scale. Lower-income people were restricted to buying older houses—usually equally difficult for them—or to renting; and often their choice was limited to the older, more rundown, and generally less desirable houses and apartments. The situation in this respect may well grow worse unless major breakthroughs for building lower-cost housing are made, or unless substantial subsidy in some form is extended to lower-income people to help them with their housing problems. A wholly private market in new housing is likely to serve not only the upper half of the income scale, but perhaps even less than that. In contrast to the situation in Britain, there has been little public subsidy to housing for low-income people in the United States. There have been a few public housing projects with subsidized rents, and in recent years a modest program of rent supplements (direct cash payments to low-income people); but the scale has been only a small fraction of that in Britain.

In the postwar period, some progress has been made in upgrading older housing that is still in use. But progress on such rehabilitation is slow and likely to remain so. First, the cost of a real modernization is often greater than the value of the modernized structure—even when the outside shell is sound, its value is often a third or less of the finished housing—and pulling out old wires and old pipes, and taking off old wall plaster, and replacing them with new, is often costly, particularly because the work often has to be done in cramped quarters. Second, credit for loans for rehabilitation is either unavailable or is not offered on as good terms as that for building new structures. Third, if the whole neighborhood has been drifting downhill, the value of rehabilitation for a single building may be relatively low. Lastly, if the decaying structure is a rental one, as it generally is, the landlord can usually make far more money by letting it decay and taking advantage of favorable income tax treatment, than he can from rehabilitation or rebuilding. Under U.S. income tax laws, the owner of such a structure may annually write off, as depreciation, a major part of the price he paid for it; this depreciation is tax free, so he gets a significant tax-free cash flow; after about eight years, it pays him to sell it, pay such capital gains tax as he has to pay, and let the next purchaser repeat the process.

However, there are some older parts of some cities where extensive rehabilitation of older houses has been undertaken privately. These are cases where the location of the properties concerned is highly advantageous; but such rehabilitation is moderately costly and does not produce housing for lower-income people.

Although the rehabilitation of housing has both progressed and lagged, depending on whether one looks at the achievements or at the task yet uncompleted, the purchase of appliances to put in housing units, even older ones, has moved much more rapidly. Many a substandard apartment is equipped with an electric refrigerator, an electric or a gas cookstove, a television set, and other appliances added in the past twenty-five years. There are several reasons why the addition of appliances has moved further than the rehabilitation of structures. Both tenants and landlords could add the appliances, while only the landlord could rehabilitate the structure, and he was generally not interested. The appliances would be added incrementally—one this year, another a few years in the future, whereas the structural rehabilitation was a much larger job, to be undertaken as a single unit. The appliances were movable; if the family succeeded in getting a better apartment or in buying a suburban home, the appliances would probably be usable there.

The Housing Construction Record in Britain

During the 1930s the annual rate of new house construction in Britain reached a peak never achieved previously—nor, indeed, subsequently until the late 1960s.

Many of the homes built in the 1930s were constructed by private builders for sale, and because of low costs of land and labor and materials they were remarkably cheap; it has been estimated that at that time it took only two and one-half man-years' labor to buy a new house in England and Wales, compared with over three years at the beginning of the 1960s. But at the same time there was a substantial municipal house-building program between the two world wars; and in the five years leading to the outbreak of World War II, no less than a quarter-million urban slums were demolished. These were the years when the birthrate in Britain reached its lowest level; and it might be thought that the result would have been a big improvement in housing standards. So there was; but some of the new construction was needed for additional household formation, which was running at a rate far greater than the additions to population.

World War II wiped out some of these gains, though the Luftwaffe attacks on British cities never achieved the scale of the destruction by the RAF or USAAF of the German urban fabric. Some 200,000 dwellings had been destroyed by war's end, together with another 250,000 houses so badly damaged as to be temporarily or permanently uninhabitable, and a further quarter-million severely damaged. A proportion of those houses destroyed, or damaged beyond repair, must have been slums in the big cities. But as compared with Germany, Britain, ironically, emerged from war's end with its remaining slum problem relatively untouched. When the time came to begin slum clearance again in 1955, the estimates then made by local authorities (which admittedly were separate and somewhat arbitrarily based) indicated that 850,000 slums remained in England and Wales alone. (These slums were mainly very small single-family terrace [row] houses, built before 1870, at rather high densities, without benefit of building regulations, and often lacking in elementary plumbing such as hot water, bathrooms, or inside toilets; they were highly concentrated in the bigger industrial cities.) In 1945 the house construction program had been virtually abandoned for six years, and government policies had to cope with millions of remaining servicemen, with the prospect of delayed marriages and births.

The response was a policy of building under tightly centralized control, using the local authorities as the main instrument; the great majority of new dwellings finished between 1945 and 1951 were in the public sector. Because of the shortages of essential building materials—shortages emphasized by repeated economic crises —it seemed essential to maintain the system of tight licensing of new building which allowed resources to be diverted to the public sector. But after 1951, with a change in government from Labour to Conservative and easier supplies of materials, this situation was rapidly reversed. Licensing of private building was ended; the proportion of private housing in the total program rose from less than 20 percent to about 60 percent during the 1950s; after 1955, local authority building was reduced in volume and was increasingly concentrated on slum clearance, together with some building for overspill from the major urban agglomerations and for old people. At the same time, in an effort to free privately rented housing from the controls that had effectively frozen it since 1945, a substantial measure of rent decontrol was enacted in 1957.

It was perhaps unfortunate that these changes, put through in good faith, occurred simultaneously with social and economic developments unforeseen or unappreciated at the time. From 1955, as we have seen, the birthrate began to rise, bringing with it a rising annual increment to the population; the rate of immigration rose sharply after 1958; the underlying trend of new household formation continued strong; and living standards began to rise rapidly. All these factors conspired together to create extra pressure on the housing markets—especially in the inner areas of the conurbations and cities, where so many new households are formed. Newly married couples, single students, or young professional workers who had left their parental homes to seek opportunities in the city, immigrants from the Commonwealth, and old residents all competed here for a shrinking total of privately rented housing. The only remedy for the situation would have been much easier access for many of these groups to new housing built on greenfield sites outside the cities. But at the same time policies were being forged to make this more difficult also.

Despite these limitations, the house construction record of the 1950s and 1960s is a fairly impressive one when viewed in historical context. From 1951 to 1961 an average of over 287,000 new dwellings a year was completed in Great Britain, with peaks in the early and late 1950s; from 1961 to 1965, an average of 332,000 a year; and from 1966 to 1970, an average of 385,000 a year. The net additions to the housing stock were of course reduced by the slum clearance program, which was accelerating throughout most of this long period, and by other causes such as demolitions for purposes other than slum clearance (for instance, for highway construction), conversions to commercial and other purposes, and increasing vacancy rates. The effect is set out in table 15. It shows that during 1951–60 there was probably a net gain in dwellings of about 230,000 a year; during 1961–65, above 235,000; and during 1966–70, about 270,000. In the two earlier periods these net additions were well in excess of net household formation (as recorded by the census), which was falling.

As the total housing stock grew, so it changed in tenure. Not only was the entire new building program, to all intents and purposes, concentrated in the private owner-occupied and public authority sectors; in addition, after the modification of Rent Control in 1957, increasing numbers of decontrolled private tenancies began to be sold off, sometimes to their former owners, sometimes to others,

TABLE 15

Net Household Formation, New Housing Completions, Conversions, and Clearances, Great Britain, 1951–1970

(Average per year, thousands)

	Net household formation	Housing gains		Housing losses		Net housing gains
		New construction	Other	Slum clearance	Other	
1951–60	194.5	286.9	10.5	49.2	18.0	230.2
1961–65	170.0	331.8	7.5	77.5	27.2	235.6
1966–70	n.a.	385.2	5.5	90.5	30.4	269.8

Source: U.K., Department of the Environment, *Housing Statistics.*
n.a.—not available.

thus further decreasing the numbers of private tenancies and swelling the ranks of the owner-occupiers. It has been estimated that during the 1950s and 1960s, in England and Wales, the owner-occupied sector gained an average of about 200,000–250,000 households a year (mainly through new construction, but also through sale of former private tenancies); council and other public tenancies gained an average of 80,000 a year, nearly all through new construction; while the private rented sector lost an average of 125,000 households a year.

Overwhelmingly, apart from a very limited amount of urban renewal in the form of luxury apartments or town houses in London, the private sector building program has involved the development of hitherto rural—and generally agricultural—land. This reflects the fact that the private program was principally geared to meet the needs arising from new household formation, especially through marriage and subsequent child rearing. Usually, it appears, new households forming for the first time—whether due to marriage, or to single persons splitting off from the parental household—would first move into privately rented accommodation, either furnished or unfurnished; this declining sector of the entire housing market thereby acted as a sort of waiting room for entry to the other sectors, with some then going into private ownership, some into public sector rented housing. But a proportion—probably an increasing proportion—of new households forming due to marriage might go directly into owner-occupancy, if they could afford the necessary deposit and meet the borrowing requirements of the building societies. The private sector seems to have been less well geared to meet the needs of other new households, particularly single persons who required small apartment accommodation; and conversions had to meet their needs. However, the important point here is that for the most part the private sector was not required to meet the needs arising from slum clearance; these were met by the local authorities, who in most cases had statutory obligations to rehouse most of the tenants they displaced.

The result was that while the private building program was chiefly directed to first-time, green-field development, much of the public program was concentrated on urban renewal of slum clearance sites. The slum clearance program indeed required that these sites be redeveloped for housing, though often the layouts were cramped and unsuitable for comprehensive redevelopment; cities having large areas of concentrated slums were paradoxically in a better position since they could proceed with comprehensive development area procedures. In the 1920s and the 1930s local authorities had usually redeveloped their slum clearance areas at fairly low densities, leaving an overspill population quite easily accommodated in peripheral public sector estates at the edge of the city not far away; this was the pattern of the developments at Dagenham in London, Wythenshawe in Manchester, and Speke in Liverpool. But because of boundary restrictions and tight planning controls exerted by neighboring counties, after World War II the cities were encouraged to redevelop at high densities—involving the use of high-rise apartment blocks rather than single-family homes—within their own boundaries, particularly since special central government subsidies were available for this purpose. Though high-rise blocks became very unpopular among residents and professional planners in the late 1960s, the high-density solution remained. In this way, the cities retained more of their populations, and thus the ratable value they brought through the real estate tax; while the counties guarded themselves against the intrusion of large numbers of low- or moderate-income residents, which they feared.

The slum clearance program reflected a large and growing backlog of old, poorly built, and poorly equipped housing—a backlog whose dimensions were not fully and accurately known until national surveys in the 1960s. Britain's housing stock is old by the standards of many of its European neighbors, with a high percentage of all housing built before World War I; different estimates, during the 1960s, all gave approximately the same results (table 16). Of this older housing, the oldest of all—that built before 1880—had been built in many cases without proper building controls, with small rooms, and without adequate sanitary provisions; it was likely to be exceptionally expensive to rehabilitate. Various estimates of the condition of the housing stock are compared in table 17; they broadly agree in showing that about 12 percent of the housing stock (1.8 million dwellings) is in very poor state, probably demanding demolition in the great majority of cases, while as much as a quarter more is in need of considerable renovation to bring it up to acceptable modern standards.

Two conclusions could be reasonably drawn from this evidence, as the government concluded in its White Paper, *Old Houses into New Homes*, in 1968. The first was that there was a need to shift housing programs progressively away from building for new household formation—since by the late 1960s there was no overall shortage of housing in the country, merely local shortages concentrated mainly in the inner areas of the conurbations—and towards redevelopment or rehabilitation of the obsolescent housing that remained. The second was that even though this new emphasis might mean an even bigger slum clearance program, there was a need to be selective: wherever possible, rehabilitation of the existing stock was preferable to demolition and rebuilding. To this end, in the 1969 Housing Act local

TABLE 16

ESTIMATES OF THE AGE OF THE BRITISH HOUSING STOCK

(*Percentage of all housing originally constructed*)

	Country	Pre-1880/81	1880/81–1918/20	1918/20–1940/44	After 1940/44
National Institute of Economic and Social Research (1964)	Great Britain	27	18	27	28
Government White Paper, *Housing in England and Wales* (1961)	England and Wales	26	21	30	23
Government Social Survey (1960)	England +Wales	19	29	30	22
Allen Report on Rating of Households (1963)	England +Wales	43		31	26
	Scotland	36		29	35
Government White Paper, *Old Houses into New Homes* (1968), quoting National House Condition Survey (1967)	England +Wales	38		27	35

TABLE 17

ESTIMATES OF THE CONDITION OF THE BRITISH HOUSING STOCK, 1964 AND 1967

Woolf, *The Housing Survey in England and Wales* (1964) England and Wales		National Institute of Economic and Social Research (1964) Great Britain		Government National Housing Condition Survey (1967) England and Wales	
Unfit	4%	Very poor and poor (some structural defects, in need of extensive repairs)	15%	Unfit	12%
Fit but with less than 15 years' life	8				
Fit and with 15–30 years' life	17	Fair–poor (structurally sound, in need of moderate repairs)	9	Fit but requiring repairs costing £125 or more, or lacking one or more of four basic amenities,[1] or both	29
Fit and with more than 30 years' life	71	Fair (structurally sound, in need of minor repairs)	41	Fit and requiring repairs costing less than £125, or no repairs; with four standard amenities	59
		Good (excellent state of repair)	35		

[1] Indoor lavatory, fixed bath, wash basin, hot and cold running water. Under 15% (over 2 million dwellings) lacked one or more of these amenities. The corresponding estimate for Great Britain, from the National Institute 1964 survey, is: lacking hot water 17%, lacking fixed bath 18%, lacking lavatory 5%. P. A. Stone, *Urban Development in Britain: Standards, Costs and Resources 1964–2004*, vol. I, *Population Trends and Housing* (Cambridge, England: University Press, 1970), p. 97.

authorities were given the power to declare General Improvement Areas, together with greater power to enforce repairs on reluctant landlords; improvement grants to owners of property, including local authorities, were greatly increased; and, to aid the clearance of the remaining hard core slums, the compensation provisions for owner-occupiers of slum houses were made more generous. To these provisions the Conservative government, in its 1971 White Paper, *Fair Deal for Housing*, added another: a simplified and speeded up improvement process for landlords in cases where the tenant might be reluctant to see the improvement go through because of the possible financial penalty he might have to pay. This in turn was linked to the other reforms in the 1971 document, which were implemented in the 1972 Housing Finance Act, and which will be discussed in a later section of this chapter.

COMPARISON OF BRITISH AND U.S. HOUSING

The foregoing two sections, dealing with U.S. and British housing, naturally suggest a direct comparison between housing in the two countries. But this is not easy to do; the data are neither perfect in concept nor in accuracy, in each country; and they differ in terms of classification and definition. It is necessary, therefore, in this section to explain a little about the data.

A contrast in the age distribution of housing is given in figure 20. In each country some housing is old, some middle-aged, and some relatively young. Because houses usually last for several decades and annual additions are small relative to the stocks, the ages of houses tend to vary over quite a wide span. The U.S. housing is somewhat younger than the British housing, both in having relatively more rather new houses and in having considerably fewer old ones. But the houses of both countries cover a wide span of age.

Age is, of course, only one factor of importance for description of housing. Condition, another prime factor, is much harder to define, being partly a subjective matter. Much depends on the personal attitudes of occupants toward their domicile and on social attitudes in the neighborhood. Some people may be attached to an old home, overlooking its faults and comfortable with its virtues, while a stranger would value the same structure less highly. However, on the average, age is one fairly good indicator of housing condition: old houses tend to be in poorer condition than do younger ones. But the extent of basic plumbing facilities, particularly indoor toilet and bathroom, is also important for itself and as a general indicator of housing condition. So is the degree of repair of the building, and similarly the degree of crowding.

There are no overall data on housing condition in Britain. But from the sample studies presented in table 17, it is possible to show in figure 21 a composite based on the data in the two right-hand columns of the table. There is a small fraction

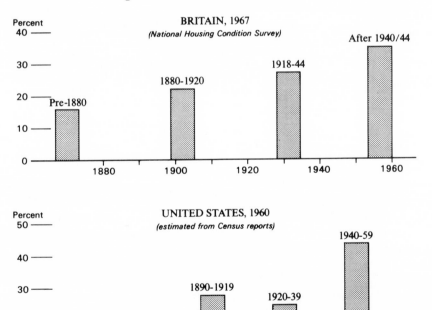

FIGURE 20. A comparison of the age distribution of all housing in Britain and the United States.

of very poor housing, called "unfit" in Britain and "substandard" in the United States, a term which in the United States applies to houses without basic plumbing facilities and/are dilapidated. There is also a small fraction of old and crowded housing, which nevertheless has basic plumbing features of flush toilet, bathtub or shower, and running hot and cold water. Perhaps comparable but, we would judge, averaging a somewhat better condition, is the relatively large number of housing units in Britain requiring major repairs; many of these are probably old, and some may be more crowded than their approximate American counterparts. In each country are relatively large numbers of reasonably good houses—middle-aged and standard or young and standard in the United States, and needing minor repairs only or simply classed as "good" in Britain. While there may be a rough approximation as to condition between the pairs of groups shown in figure 21, it would be a mistake to draw the comparisons too closely, for the British figures are synthesized and complete comparability is certainly not present in the data. Each country has a wide range in condition of housing, from very poor to very good.

The two countries might also be contrasted in their rates of building and of housing replacement. Unfortunately, no data exist that would enable us to present comprehensive balance sheets, by decades, for the two countries, showing additions to stock and losses from stock. Construction of new housing is only a part of such balance sheets, but it is a part upon which better data exist than for other parts.

TABLE 18

COMPARISON OF HOUSING CONSTRUCTION AND REMOVALS,
GREAT BRITAIN AND THE UNITED STATES, 1950–1970

	1951–61	1961–66
I. Great Britain		
Estimated population, beginning of period (1,000)	48,854	51,284
Estimated housing stock, beginning of period (1,000)	13,912	16,215
Total new housing units constructed during period (1,000)	2,869	1,659
Housing units lost, all causes, during period (1,000)	672	523
Housing units lost from slum clearance during period (1,000)	492	387
Annual rate of housing construction:		
per 1,000 population, beginning of period	5.8	6.5
per 1,000 housing units in stock, beginning of period	20.6	20.5
per 1,000 additional net households	1,475	1,952
	1950–60	1960–70
II. United States		
Estimated population, beginning of period (1,000)	150,697	178,464
Estimated housing stock, beginning of period (1,000)	46,137	58,326
Total new housing units constructed during period[1] (1,000)	15,003	14,487
Housing units lost, all causes, during period (1,000)	4,530	n.a.
Housing units lost from slum clearance during period (1,000)	n.a.	n.a.
Annual rate of housing construction:		
per 1,000 population, beginning of period	10.0	8.1
per 1,000 housing units in stock, beginning of period	32.5	24.8
per 1,000 additional net households	1,480	1,472

n.a.—not available.
[1] Including mobile homes, data for which for part of period were estimated.

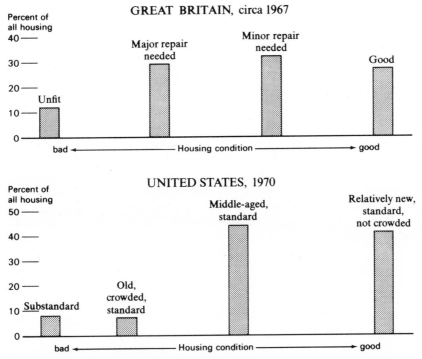

FIGURE 21. A comparison of the condition of housing stock in Britain and the United States.

The rate of housing construction in the United States, in relation both to the number of people and to the number of houses at the beginning of each decade, was significantly higher than the same rate in Britain (table 18). However, in comparison with the numbers of new households formed, the U.S. rate was the same as the British rate in the 1950s, and slightly lower in the 1960s. Net household formation and provision of additional housing are not unrelated phenomena; household formation stimulates housing, and housing availability makes possible new household formation, whereas lack of either inhibits the other. It would appear that each country had been about equally successful in meeting the needs of new households; for the United States, this required a much higher rate of construction, because birthrates were higher. In each country, far more new houses were built than new households were formed; this permitted replacement of older and generally unsatisfactory housing in each.

URBAN LAND UTILIZATION IN THE UNITED STATES IN THE POSTWAR ERA

Data about urban land use are seriously deficient in both Britain and the United States. Land *use* includes both the kind of activity carried out on the land and the intensity of that use—a two-dimensional matter; but in addition to these, reasonably complete data about land would include market phenomena such as prices and volume of transactions, and tenure information. Available data sources on urban land in both countries are deficient for all these types of information, but perhaps most markedly (except in Scotland) for prices; and data about urban land are less complete than data about some other land uses.

In both countries reasonably good information about agricultural land use began between about 1860 and 1880. It included data on total farm area and on acreages of various crops, and it has become steadily more accurate over the years. In both countries, too, there is independent information about forest cover. Estimates of urban land use, therefore, tend to have been produced as residuals from the rural land uses—an unsatisfactory procedure with an unknown margin of error and with lack of essential detail on the different land uses within the urban envelope. Since World War II, both countries have produced more detailed urban land use inventories as part of surveys for planning purposes. Those in the United States have suffered from lack of national standardization on critical matters of definition, and those in Britain, while benefitting from a standardized classification and map notation, nevertheless pose difficulties in use over wide areas. Finally, Britain has the benefit of two national land utilization surveys carried out under academic auspices: the first, organized in the 1930s by the late Sir Laurence Dudley Stamp, suffered from too great an emphasis on rural uses, which the second survey (organized by Dr. Alice Coleman in the 1960s) has partially remedied.

The nearest American equivalent is probably the study of land use carried out in connection with the Northeast Corridor Transportation Study, which assembled information for about the year 1960 in this broad area; but this was based on varied information sources, not on a new survey, and the differences of definition meant that the resulting classification of land uses was a very coarse one. The variety in these data was so great that it was possible to assemble data only on "residential," "commercial," "industrial," "public and semi-public" land uses (and the latter is more ownership than use), with a very large area in most counties estimated by difference from total land area and labeled as simply "other." Even these broad groupings of land use may not be comparable from county to county; the data seem to reveal some dubious differences, which probably spring more from the method of enumeration and classification of land use than from the actual situation on the ground.

In the United States, the figures resulting from a land utilization survey depend in large measure upon its "grain," or the size of the units of enumeration. For instance, an obviously residential area might be so classified; if the acreage is measured as a whole, one result may follow, but if each lot or parcel within the larger area is separately classified, a considerable acreage of idle land may be revealed. The typical pattern of suburban land use in the United States is one of sprawl, with substantial discontiguity between subdivisions; the way these presently idle lands are treated in any survey of urban land use will dominate the statistical result. There are many other problems too—whether to include factory parking lots as part of manufacturing or as part of transportation, whether to include factory offices as part of manufacturing or as business office, and countless others.

Briefly, an ideal system of urban land use information should include two major aspects: first, a recording in great detail of actual land use as observed on the ground, so that the basic data can later be grouped into any more inclusive system of categories that may be desired for any purpose; and recording of land use on each smallest recognizable parcel of land, so that spatial groupings can be built up on any desired basis. The urban planning studies made in recent years have usually included neither of these features, hence, new land use inventories frequently had to be made to collect essentially the same basic data when a different need arose. Moreover, almost none of these studies has included provision for current updating; when new needs arose, new surveys had to be made, even though a great deal of land use was unchanged.

The data on urban land prices in the United States are needlessly bad; in fact, they are nonexistent in a readily usable form, although the basic data from which statistics could be compiled do exist. The Federal Housing Administration does collect and publish figures on "market price of sites" for "new" and "used" sites, based primarily on figures in its appraisals for loans; while useful, these apply to only some urban land, which may not be representative of all urban land exchanges. On all real estate transactions in the United States it is necessary to pay a land transfer tax and to affix stamps to the papers, from which it is easily possible to estimate the prices paid. These are the declared values; one cannot be certain that these all represent bona fide sales, between willing seller and willing buyer, unrelated and independent; some may well be from one corporate entity to another, both controlled by the same individuals, for instance. But these data are not tabulated, summarized, and published by any agency—federal, state, or local. While considerable clerical work would be involved in doing so, and while the results would have to be tabulated by meaningful local areas, yet it would be perfectly possible to develop statistical series of urban land prices. This total lack of data on urban land transactions contrasts sharply with long-available data series on farm real estate transactions collected by the Department of Agriculture.

In 1950 the Bureau of the Census delineated urbanized areas for the first time; that census showed 8.2 million acres urbanized, nationally. Because of the way this definition was applied in practice, this acreage is too low by an unknown amount. In 1960 the urbanized area was calculated as 16.0 million acres; this figure is probably too high, again because of the method by which the definition was applied. This shows an apparent increase in urbanized area of 7.8 million acres; the population in the urbanized areas increased from 69.3 to 95.8 million, or by 26.5 million, over this decade. While this may be somewhat in error, the degree of error is probably less than for the acreages. Taken at face value, the figures suggest an overall population density of something less than 2,200 persons per square mile in the added urbanized area—we say "something less," because surely some or a large part of the added population settled on idle land in the previously defined urbanized area, thus reducing the actual numbers in the added urbanized area. This is a very low, even sparse, density for modern American suburbs; to the extent that the 1950 urbanized area is too low and the 1960 urbanized area too large, the difference between them is too large and the apparent density for the added area also too low, both perhaps by large percentages.

The 1970 urbanized area is reported as 22.5 million acres, or an increase of 6.5 million acres in the 1960s; this is an increase of 41 percent in this decade, compared with a near doubling in the 1950s. The population in urbanized areas grew by 22.6 million in the 1960s—less both absolutely and proportionately than in the preceding decade. The apparent density of the added area is only marginally above the comparable figure for the 1950s.

The urbanized area of the Northeastern Urban Complex was 2.10 million acres in 1950 and 3.45 million acres in 1960; the first is too low, and the second too high, and perhaps by an even greater percentage than was true nationally. In 1960 a number of New England "towns" were included as urbanized, when the larger part of the town land was not used for urban purposes; this did not affect population much, but it affected area considerably. And when the difference between 1950 and 1960 is calculated, this residual may be greatly in error, for it includes all errors in each component figure. The 1960 urbanized area represents a general "pushing out" of the 1950 urbanized area (figure 22). The urbanized areas of the Complex added 4.5 million people from 1950 to 1960; on the basis of 1.35 million added acres urbanized, this works out to about 3.3 persons per acre, or to about 2,100 per square mile. As with the national figure above, this is sparse density for American suburbs. It would require suburban house lots averaging two acres each—something that exists in only a few suburbs. And, to the degree that during the decade of the 1950s some people located within the 1950 urbanized areas, the density in the added area would be still less. Again, these comparisons based on reported changes may be greatly in error.

The 1970 urbanized area for the Complex is reported at 4.35 million acres, or a smaller increase, both absolutely and relatively, for the 1960s than for the 1950s. On the other hand, population increased more in absolute terms and only slightly less in relative terms in the 1960s. For the added area, the apparent density was about 3,300 persons per square mile—and, for reasons given earlier, the true density was probably less. While still low, this is more than 50 percent higher than in the 1950s.

These data, nationally and even more for the Complex, suggest that the 1960 urbanized boundary was pushed out too far, compared with the 1950 boundary; and that the 1970 boundary, while generous, was more nearly in line with the 1950 definition. At all three census dates the urbanized area included a lot of idle land, as previous discussions have made clear; but it is not clear that the extent of the idle land was constant from one date to another.

One measure of the probable densities of suburban residential land occupancy is shown in figure 23. This frequency distribution is calculated from available data for the counties of the Northeastern Urban Complex; it includes older residential areas as well as more recently developed ones, and is subject to the ambiguities of definition previously mentioned. The median density is in excess of ten persons per residential acre (however this was defined) and the mean density is about 13.6 persons per acre. Even if one excludes the high densities of the larger cities, the most frequent residential densities are between 5 and 10 persons per acre, or between 3,200 and 6,400 per square mile. It is by no means clear how much of the local street area is included in these areas. The reported densities are too high to the degree that no allowance is made for land uses other than residential, and too low to the degree that idle land may be included in the "residential" category.

The foregoing data, plus additional analyses of census data, plus some sample studies for various metropolitan areas, suggest that most suburban development of the past quarter century in the United States has had densities in the range of 3,000 to 6,000 persons per square mile of land actually included within development subdivisions. This would include local streets, local schools, and other local land uses, but not land used for various purposes lying outside of the suburban subdivision. One may hazard the guess that density, on this basis, must have averaged 5,000 persons per square mile. But many subdivisions have had far lower densities, when lot sizes were very large; and if idle land between subdivisions is included, many suburbs have far lower overall average densities.

The word "sprawl" is widely and loosely used to describe American suburbs. Actually, there seem to be three separable forms of dispersed settlement which, taken together, comprise sprawl:

1. There is discontiguity between subdivisions; one subdivision is developed by one developer, another by another, and so on, often with substantial areas of land between one and another. The discontinuity of development arises largely out of the suburban land market, described in chapter 1. In a search for buildable land, readily available, at prices not too exorbitant, the developer takes outlying tracts; neither he nor the house buyer is penalized by this discontiguity, in the form of higher charges for essential public services.

2. Large lot sizes have been common in many suburbs. Lot sizes may range from something under half an acre, upward to one, or two, or in extreme cases to five acres. This is land consumption on a relatively lavish scale. Many observers of the urban scene have argued that suburban settlers choose such large lots for the feelings of privacy and spaciousness which they convey; others have felt that these buyers chose the kind of house and neighborhood without much commitment to the land area involved.

3. Floor area ratio (FAR) measures the square feet of usable floor space in the structure as compared with the total land area; a one story structure which completely covered its lot would have a FAR of 1.0. In practice, few structures completely cover their lots; often the building codes would not permit this, even if home buyers should choose it. Many residential structures are more than one story in height. There are major differences between the ranch type house, without either basement or second story, and the older type houses with two full stories, basement and attic.

These three forms of sprawl often combine—a subdivision separated from its nearest neighbor by a considerable distance, with large lots, and ranch type houses, for instance.

During this past quarter century the overall (total population/total area) density of most larger cities in the United States as a whole and in the Northeastern Urban Complex has fallen. Such central city land has been used for purposes other than residential; exodus of whites to suburbs has, in general, been greater than inflow of previously rural and small town blacks to the center. While there is much variation in the relationship in the Complex, in general, cities with overall densities of 10,000 or more per square mile lost population in the decade of the 1960s, while most cities with a lower density gained. The idea of a "tipping point" has been

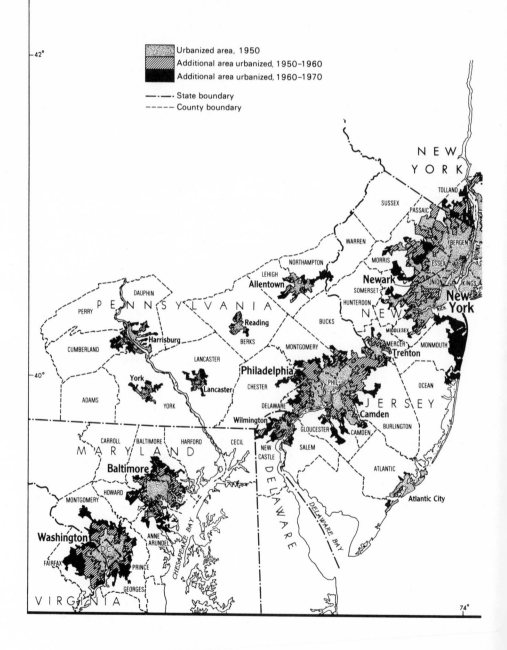

FIGURE 22. The U.S. Census reports the 1970 urbanized areas of the Northeastern Urban Complex to be 4.35 million acres, representing almost a doubling in area since 1950. But throughout the three reporting dates, the urbanized areas have included a great deal of idle land.

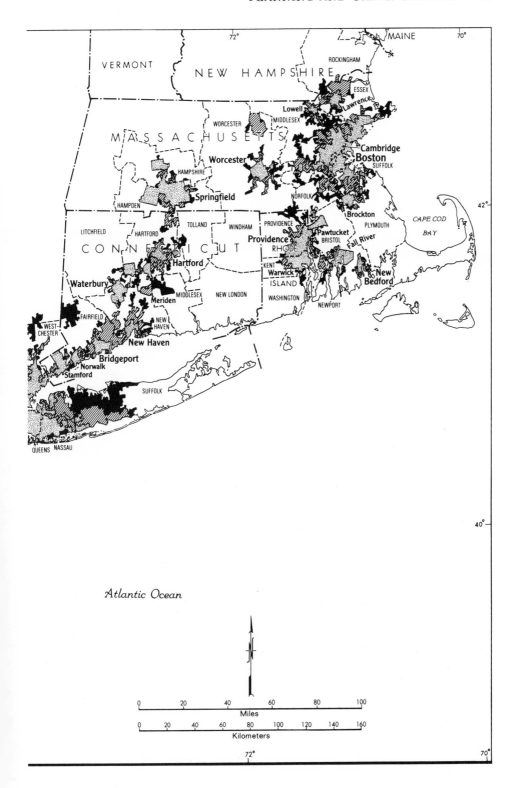

Atlantic Ocean

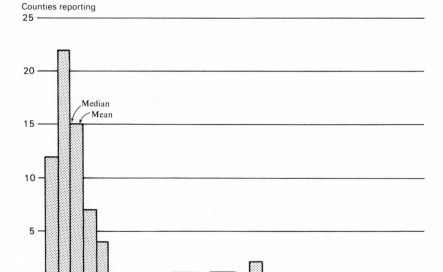

*One county in 270–275 interval.

FIGURE 23. Counties in the Northeastern Urban Complex reporting various densities of residential land use, circa 1960.

introduced by various writers, including Colin Clark. In the contemporary American scene, one can say that cities with average overall density of 10,000 or more per square mile are, in some sense, "full"; additional people are accommodated by spreading outward, rather than by building upward—with all that this implies in terms of travel.

LAND USE PATTERNS IN BRITAIN

The chief sources of land use information in Britain—the national land use surveys conducted on a voluntary, private basis in the 1930s and the 1960s, the local authority planning department estimates, and the agricultural returns—have been compared, refined, and analyzed in a major research program extending over several years by Dr. Robin Best, which at last has given a reliable and consistent picture of changing land use patterns in England and Wales. Though the most important output of this study has been an estimate of the extent of urban development on a national scale, Best has also produced a number of regional or local estimates which show variations in the extent of the urban cover from one part of the country to another.[7] They provide a necessary framework for more par-

[7] Throughout this section, "development" means broadly built development, including residential, commercial, industrial, all transport, and open space (parks). This is generally similar to the definition used earlier for analysis of land use in the United States.

ticular studies of local variations, such as were undertaken in the PEP study of urban development in postwar Britain.

The first important conclusion from Best's work is that urban development forms a much smaller part of the total land area of Britain than is popularly supposed. Even in England and Wales, which is clearly more urbanized than the whole of Britain, only about 12 percent of the land area was covered by various forms of urban development in 1970; this proportion had risen from about five percent at the start of the twentieth century, and was predicted by Best to rise to between 16 and 17 percent of the total area by the year 2000 (table 19). As already noted in chapter 2, Best found that the rate of consumption of agricultural and other rural land for urban purposes was much higher during the 1930s than at any time after World War II—a measure of the effectiveness of the urban containment policies practiced in Britain since the 1947 Planning Act (table 20).

In Britain, urban growth almost invariably involves the loss of productive farmland; idle land near to urban areas is a rare phenomenon and virtually all lowland areas outside the built-up zones, apart from some derelict land in industrial and mining areas and limited woodland areas, is in agriculture. In the United States, in contrast, about 40 percent of the Northeastern Urban Complex is not in urban use, or in public open space, or in farms. While some of this has tree cover, forestry in a purposeful sense is not practiced on it, and much of it is idle.

This overall picture in Britain, of course, conceals considerable localized pressures for urban growth in the major urban regions. Best's detailed analysis of urban growth in the period 1945–65, made in conjunction with A. G. Champion, shows that the greatest transfers have been in the main urban and industrial belt extending from London up through the Midlands to Lancashire and Yorkshire—the area we term Megalopolis England.[8] However, Best's analysis (and the subsequent work

[8] R. H. Best and A. G. Champion, "Regional Conversions of Agricultural Land to Urban Use in England and Wales, 1945–67," *Institute of British Geographers, Transactions*, 49 (1970), pp. 15–32.

TABLE 19

URBAN ACREAGE, ENGLAND AND WALES, 1900–1960,
WITH PROJECTIONS TO 1980 AND 2000

Year	Population (millions)	Urban area (million acres)	Urban land provision (acres per thousand population)	Urban area as percent of total land area
1900–1	32.5	2.0	61.5	5.4
1920–1	37.9	2.2	58.0	5.9
1930–1	40.0	2.6	65.0	7.0
1939	41.5	3.2	77.1	8.6
1950–1	43.8	3.6	82.2	9.7
1960–1	46.1	4.0	86.8	10.8
1970–1	50.1	4.4	87.8	11.9
1980–1	53.8	4.9	91.1	13.2
1990–1	58.2	5.4	92.8	14.5
2000–1	63.7	6.0	94.2	16.2

Source: Robin H. Best, "The Future Urban Acreage," *Town and Country Planning*, vol. 32 (1964), table 1, p. 352.

TABLE 20
Losses of Agricultural Land to Urban Areas, England and Wales, 1927–1965

	Average area transferred per year to:		
Period	Building and general construction development	Sports grounds	Total urban area
1927/28–1933/34	37,800	9,000	46,800
1934/35–1938/39	50,000	10,600	60,600
1950/51–1959/60	32,800	3,500	36,300
1960/61–1964/65	35,100	3,100	38,200

Sources: Robin H. Best, "Recent Changes and Future Prospects of Land Use in England and Wales," *Geographical Journal*, vol. 131 (March 1965), table 1, p. 3; Best, "Extent of Urban Growth and Agricultural Displacement in Post-War Britain," *Urban Studies*, vol. 5 (1968), table 1, p. 5.

at PEP) demonstrated that in a physical sense this is an incipient, not an actual, Megalopolis: the areas of rapid urban growth form two rather clearly separated zones. One of these is around London; the other embraces the West and East Midlands, Lancashire, and Yorkshire, and can be called the Central Urban Region; while between the two runs a clear divide formed by rather rural counties with rates of urban growth that are far below the national average. The analysis by Best and Champion shows that while conversion rates for the London area have actually slowed down over the twenty-year period 1945–65, those for the Central Urban Region have speeded up. This is due, the authors suggest, to the fact that in the latter region slum clearance and rising space standards added their influence to that of rising population and household formation.

Even though Megalopolis in a physical sense does not exist, it is clear that here is the belt within which the main pressures of urban growth are exerted. Megalopolis forms therefore a convenient unit for the more detailed study of urban growth patterns, which was undertaken as part of the PEP program (see the Preface to this book). In contrast to Best's work, this consisted of a series of detailed cross-sectional pictures of land use for dates when national survey data happened to be available: the early 1930s (the First Land Utilization Survey of Great Britain, conducted by L. Dudley Stamp), the late 1940s (the maps and compilations of land use by the Planning Authorities as part of their preparation of their original Development Plans), and the early 1960s (the Second Land Utilization Survey of Great Britain, conducted by Dr. Alice Coleman). Within Megalopolis England, the detailed land use maps resulting from these surveys were analyzed by a sampling technique to give a quantified picture of land use for uniform, small square zones, corresponding to the squares of the metric grid used on all official British maps.

Figure 24 shows the resulting picture of land use in Megalopolis England for the early 1960s. The basic unit of analysis is a square 10 km × 10 km, or about 40 square miles in extent. The immediate impression given by the map is that though this is the most heavily urbanized belt of England, remarkably little of

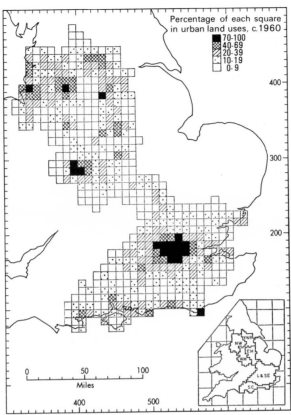

FIGURE 24. The map shows the degree of urban development in Megalopolis England, circa 1960.

the land is actually covered by urban development. Overall, according to the analysis, only 17.8 percent of the total area of Megalopolis was taken for all kinds of development in the early 1960s—as compared with a little under 12 percent, according to Best's analysis, for England and Wales as a whole. This should not be surprising, for Megalopolis is defined in terms of functional urban areas as indicated by commuting patterns, and these extend widely into comparatively sparsely populated countryside. In fact the degree of urban development does not vary much from one major division of Megalopolis to another (table 21). The North West part, comprising the Metropolitan Economic Areas in Lancashire and Cheshire, is the most heavily urbanized, with 22 percent developed; the area around London comes next, with a little over 20 percent; the other divisions have between 12 and 18 percent of their land area developed for all kinds of purposes.

By far the most important single use of land in the developed area of Megalopolis is residential land (including local streets, shops, schools, and associated land uses); it takes up about 51 percent of the developed area, or about 9 percent of the entire area of Megalopolis. But the proportion of residential area to total developed area varies considerably from one division of Megalopolis to another,

TABLE 21

THE DEVELOPED AREAS OF MEGALOPOLIS ENGLAND, CA. 1960–1965

(Areas in square miles)

Major division	Total area	Developed area	As % total area	Residential area	As % total area	As % developed area
London and the South East	7,413	1,515	20.4%	870	11.7%	57.4%
South Coast	2,741	374	13.6	229	8.4	61.3
West Midlands	2,973	450	15.1	164	5.5	36.4
East Midlands	2,239	262	11.7	111	5.0	42.4
North West	3,166	688	21.7	317	10.0	46.0
Yorkshire West Riding	2,317	429	18.5	205	8.8	47.8
Megalopolis	20,849	3,718	17.8	1,896	9.1	51.0

Source: Second Land Utilization Survey of Great Britain.

as table 21 shows. Perhaps the most striking fact to emerge from this analysis is that of a total area of some 20,000 square miles in Megalopolis, housing and immediately associated uses account for less than 2,000 square miles. Differences in density in future development, therefore, could have relatively little effect on the overall picture for a long time to come.

When the land use data are compared with population data—a process involving some degree of inaccuracy, since the land use is recorded by squares and the population by irregularly shaped areas—the picture that emerges is one of very economical use of land (table 22). Comparing total population and total area, the population of Megalopolis appears to have lived at a density of about 1,560 per square mile (2.4 per acre) in the early 1960s; taking into account just the developed area, the proportion rises to over 8,700 per square mile (14 per acre). And taking just the residential area, the population density rises to about 17,000

TABLE 22

POPULATION DENSITIES IN MEGALOPOLIS ENGLAND, CA. 1960–1965

	Population density					
	Persons per total area		Persons per developed area		Persons per residential area	
Major division	(per sq mile)	(per acre)	(per sq mile)	(per acre)	(per sq mile)	(per acre)
London and the South East	1,870	2.9	9,151	14.3	15,936	24.9
South Coast	765	1.2	5,608	8.8	9,159	14.3
West Midlands	1,462	2.3	9,661	15.1	26,507	41.4
East Midlands	953	1.5	8,149	12.7	19,234	30.1
North West	2,040	3.2	9,387	14.6	20,373	31.8
Yorkshire West Riding	1,561	2.4	8,429	13.1	17,639	27.6
Megalopolis	1,560	2.4	8,746	13.7	17,151	26.8

Source: U.K., Census 1961; Second Land Utilization Survey of Great Britain.

per square mile or about 27 to the acre. This last proportion shows considerable variation from one major division of Megalopolis to another. Of course, these overall proportions include all the land classed as residential areas within Mega-lopolis—including older, higher-density areas as well as newer, lower-density areas. In general, the population of Megalopolis England seems to have been remarkably economical in its use of land. (By way of contrast, the mean density—total popu-lation divided by total area—for the entire urbanized area of the United States was about 5.3 persons per acre—about 3,375 persons per square mile—in 1970; and the median density for residential land use in the counties of the Northeastern Urban Complex was about 10 persons per acre—about 6,400 per square mile— around 1960.)

The impact of urbanization on the rural countryside, it may be argued, is not merely a function of the percentage of the land that is developed, but also of the degree of compactness or scatter of that development; the 18 percent of the land area of Megalopolis that was developed in the early 1960s might be highly concen-trated in a few areas, or scattered in many. In fact, as the frequency distribution in table 23 shows, urban development in Megalopolis is not merely limited; it is quite highly concentrated. Of the 540 squares, each 100 square kilometers in ex-tent, which constitute Megalopolis, no less than 39 percent had less than 10 percent developed. Since virtually all the countryside, even in quite thinly populated areas, has some development in the form of isolated farms or hamlets, such areas can be regarded as completely rural. Additionally, another 31 percent of all squares had between 10 and 20 percent of their land area developed; such areas could be described as more thickly settled rural. In other words, no less than 70 percent of the total area of Megalopolis consisted of areas the casual observer would regard as rural. A further 19 percent were lightly influenced by urban development, with

TABLE 23

FREQUENCY DISTRIBUTION OF 100-SQUARE-KILOMETER SQUARES, BY DEGREE OF DEVELOPMENT, IN MEGALOPOLIS ENGLAND, CA. 1960–1965

Major division		Number and percentage of 100-square-kilometer squares with: percent of area developed					Total squares
		0–10	10–20	20–40	40–70	70–100	
London and the South East	No.	70	61	43	6	12	192
	%	36	32	22	3	6	100
South Coast	No.	27	29	10	4	1	71
	%	38	41	14	6	1	100
West Midlands	No.	36	24	10	4	3	77
	%	47	32	13	5	4	100
East Midlands	No.	35	13	6	4	–	58
	%	60	22	10	7	0	100
North West	No.	23	23	22	12	2	82
	%	28	28	27	15	2	100
Yorkshire (West Riding)	No.	21	20	13	5	1	60
	%	35	33	15	8	1	100
Megalopolis	No.	212	170	104	35	19	540
	%	39	31	19	6	4	100

Source: Second Land Utilization Survey of Great Britain.

between 20 and 40 percent of their areas developed; 6 percent were heavily influenced, with between 40 and 70 percent urbanized; and a mere 4 percent of all the squares were more or less completely urbanized, with 70 percent or more developed. What was most remarkable, perhaps, is that the proportions did not vary much from one major division of Megalopolis to another. The areas least influenced by urban development were the East and West Midlands and the South Coast, with between 79 and 82 percent of their constituent squares having less than 20 percent development; the most heavily influenced, the North West with only 56 percent. The South East, often quoted as the area most heavily threatened by rapid urban growth, was close to the average for all Megalopolis with 68 percent of its squares having 20 percent development or less.

Overall, therefore, Megalopolis is "urban" only in the sense that the great majority of its people do urban jobs in urban areas. The greater part of the land area is free of urban development, and is comparatively little influenced by such development nearby.

These results may also be compared with another independent method of estimation. In the PEP study (see page v), "urbanized areas" were defined for Britain on the same basis as in the U.S. Census; that is, they were aggregations of small zones with at least 1,000 residential population to the square mile at any given census date. Nationally—that is, in the whole of England and Wales—the urbanized area within Standard Metropolitan Labour Areas included 3.31 million acres at the Census of 1961, as compared with a total of 4.00 million urbanized acres for the whole country according to Best's calculations. Within the Standard Metropolitan Labour Areas of Megalopolis, the urbanized areas accounted for nearly 2.6 million acres or for just over 20 percent of the total area, as compared with 18 percent developed area in the detailed analysis of the Second Land Utilization Survey. The estimates for urbanized areas omit some areas reaching the necessary level of population density, but outside Standard Metropolitan Labour Areas.

SERVICES, PLANNING, LAND PRICES, AND DENSITIES

In both the United States and Britain, the availability and pricing of necessary public services and the rigor and direction of land use controls have had their effect upon land prices and upon density of residential settlement on the land. Services have generally been available in both countries; in the United States, the septic tanks have been an important device freeing suburbanites from dependence on central sewer systems—sometimes only temporarily, because the septic tanks later failed and sewer lines had to be installed, often at considerably added cost. The "postage stamp" pricing of American services such as water and sewers has also removed incentive from both developer and suburbanite for compact settlement. These, plus the typically loose planning controls in the United States, have inevitably led toward one form of suburban sprawl. In Britain, planning controls have been tighter and sprawl at the edge of cities has rarely occurred, but the same planning controls have pushed people (and, to a lesser extent, jobs) into suburban towns and villages.

The past quarter century has seen a general inflation or rise in prices in both the United States and Britain. As would be expected in such prolonged periods of price increases, the price of land has also risen. In the United States, farmland, land for recreation purposes, and suburban land suitable for building each has risen in price.[9] Manvel estimates that during the 1956–66 period the average rates of price increases were 7.6 percent annually for vacant lots in all cities, 6.5 percent for nonfarm residential property, and 5.5 percent for commercial and industrial property.[10] These differences in rates of rise may not seem large, but over a decade or longer they amount to substantial sums of money. The price of new lots, as reported by the Federal Housing Administration, rose by nearly five times from 1946 to 1967.[11] In a number of studies, annual rates of increase in suburban land values up to 14 percent or more have been reported.[12] All of these are to be contrasted with a rise of the general price level of about 2 percent annually over the same period.

The rising prices of residential site land, particularly in the suburbs, has had an effect on housing in both the United States and Britain, although the nature of that effect differs. In each case, a higher cost per acre has added to the cost of the finished house and lot, but this additional cost for land alone is less important than the effect of the adjustments made to these rising land costs. In the United States, the major adjustment to rising site costs has been to increase the size, quality, luxury, and cost of the house; in spite of this, the site cost has risen from about 12 percent of the total cost of site and house in the period around 1950 to over 20 percent today. In an effort (not wholly successful) to avoid site costs becoming too large a proportion of the total cost of the finished house, the size and cost of the latter have also been advanced substantially. The result has been further to price lower-income people out of the market for new housing.

Urban growth in Britain since World War II has assumed patterns characteristically different from those typical in the United States; in several important respects, indeed, they are almost diametrically opposite. Planning controls have operated quite deliberately to contain the growth of the larger urban areas and to reduce the physical impact of urban development generally. The individual residential estates constituting the new suburbs have been made contiguous at a local

---

[9] Marion Clawson, *Policy Directions for U.S. Agriculture: Long-Range Choices in Farming and Rural Living* (Baltimore: The Johns Hopkins University Press), 1968, pp. 233 ff.; and Bureau of Outdoor Recreation, *Recreation Land Price Escalation* (Washington: U.S. Department of the Interior), 1967.

[10] Allen D. Manvel, *Three Land Research Studies: Trends in the Value of Real Estate and Land, 1956 to 1966; Land Use in 106 Large Cities; and Estimating California Land Values from Independent Statistical Indicators* (by Robert H. Gustafson and Ronald B. Welch), prepared for consideration of the National Commission on Urban Problems, Research Report No. 12 (Washington: U.S. Government Printing Office), 1968.

[11] A. Allan Schmid, *Converting Land from Rural to Urban Uses* (Washington: Resources for the Future), 1968.

[12] Grace Milgram, *U.S. Land Prices—Directions and Dynamics*, prepared for the National Commission on Urban Problems, Research Report No. 13 (Washington: U.S. Government Printing Office), 1968; Curtis C. Harris, Jr. and David J. Allee, *Urbanization and Its Effects on Agriculture in Sacramento County, California: 2, Prices and Taxes of Agricultural Land*, Giannini Foundation Research Report No. 270, California Agricultural Experiment Station, University of California, 1963.

scale in a way that has not been true for the United States; but at a slightly larger scale of analysis they have been made completely noncontiguous in a way that also is uncharacteristic in North America. British planning has worked quite deliberately to impose its preference for medium-sized or small towns as opposed to peripheral suburban expansion of big cities or conurbations; therefore, it has pushed new suburban development away from the fringes of the bigger urban areas, and toward small towns or villages—especially the less attractive ones, which, in the planners' view, were not worth conserving. The characteristic development form of the postwar United States has been a series of separate subdivisions, with intervening tracts of open land, spreading away in all directions from the larger urban areas. The characteristic form in Britain consists of a smaller number of subdivisions at a few select places some distance away from the main urban mass, and separated from it by a much more clearly defined, and generally much wider, greenbelt (figure 25).

The form of suburban growth is quite different, also, if one considers the density of residential development. In the United States several factors—among the most important, lack of main sewerage and deliberate low-density zoning—have acted together to reduce residential densities in the postwar period. Whereas at the end of World War II seven or eight houses to the acre was still common, by the end of the 1960s four, or even two, houses to the acre was a usual norm. (There were signs, in a number of suburban developments within the Northeastern Complex at the beginning of the 1970s, that this trend might be reversed, first through the development of suburban apartment houses on a large scale, and secondly by a distinct swing toward suburban town house construction with quite small yard spaces and much higher densities overall.) But in Britain, public planning policies were urged by the central government and enthusiastically accepted by the county planning authorities, which had the effect of systematically raising the densities of typical suburban single-family housing. Whereas eight to ten houses to the residential acre had been characteristic in the 1930s, up to thirteen were being built in many areas by the 1960s.

To some extent, especially under the impact of rising land prices in the 1960s, this actually led to a reduction in the floorspace area of the house itself. But mainly, of course, the space had to be saved around the home, not in it. Yard (garden) space was reduced greatly, especially in the more modestly priced housing developments. This was all the more necessary, because at the same time planning authorities were beginning to insist on more and more provision for the private automobile—including not merely garage space per house, but additional carports for additional cars. In most cases, given the tight constraints of cost acting upon the private builder, this space could be found only by reducing the area of lawn around the house.

These reductions, whether in the size of the house or in the size of the space around it, were most serious at the lower end of the price scale for new owner-occupied housing, because it was here that the rising costs of land began to bite most severely in the 1960s. Ratcheting land prices seem to have been an unfortunate feature of urban development in most countries of the Western world since 1945; they reflect certain basic features of the postwar economic situation, especially the

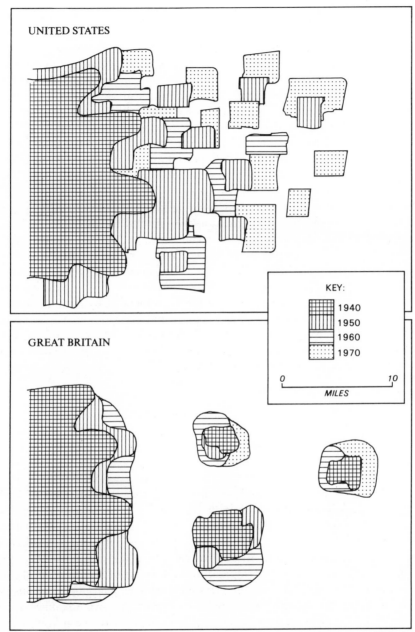

FIGURE 25. A schematic diagram of the form of urban development in postwar United States and Great Britain.

general inflationary pressures and the generally rapid growth of population and urban areas. But there can be no doubt that in Britain the problem has been severe. House prices have tended to rise faster than the general level of prices during the 1960s, reaching a level of about 10 percent appreciation per year towards the end of the decade. The Nationwide Building Society figures show that the price of new houses in Britain rose by 72 percent over the whole period mid-1967 through mid-1972 (in the South East by 86 percent); in the second half of 1971 alone, they rose by 12 percent, and in the first half of 1972, by 17 percent. Since construction costs rose only as fast as wages and prices generally, and since builders' profit margins were being squeezed, there can be no doubt that the rise in land prices was the basic cause. The PEP study shows that in a number of case studies in Megalopolis England, land prices approximately doubled during the 1960s, rising from between 4 and 12 percent of the total house price at the beginning of the decade to between 21 and 30 percent at its end—and this on a sharply rising price per house. Individual cases in South East England, indeed, showed even higher percentages.

The private builder, who must have building land if he is to avoid going bankrupt, has found himself in a dangerous position; he had to buy but the seller often had no need to sell. According to the county planning offices, enough land had been allocated for development to meet the needs of rising population; according to the builders, too much of this land was either unserviced or was already held by other developers. The developers responded in various ways. At the bottom end of the owner-occupied market, they necessarily responded by cutting space standards in and around the home, and even by cutting the quality of the house itself; but many switched into the higher end of the market, where the rising cost of land was less serious in relation to the final selling price of the product, or even transferred their main operations to building abroad.

Postwar Housing in Social Context: A Summary

At this point it may be helpful to summarize some of the implications that will be dealt with more fully in the closing chapters of this book.

In the United States and Great Britain, the postwar period has witnessed relatively rapid population growth and new household formation, coupled with rising incomes and greatly improved material living standards; these forces, working together, have produced an irresistible pressure towards urban growth. Partly because of the long tradition in both countries of the preference for single-family homes, partly because of general social forces that seem to make such homes the general norm in the affluent Western world, and partly because of technical developments such as the general availability of the private automobile, a large part of this urban growth has taken the form of individual homes built by private builders for sale, and intended for single-family occupancy. These homes have been built on previously undeveloped land beyond the existing physical boundary of the urban area; in both countries, they can fairly be described as suburbs. As a result, both in Britain and the United States there has been a marked decentralization, or outward movement, of populations within the metropolitan areas; the older developed areas, or urban cores, have failed to grow as rapidly as the new suburban rings, and in many cases they have experienced actual population loss. These net changes conceal much larger volumes of individual and family movements; characteristically, new immigrants to the metropolitan areas, from other parts of the country or in some cases from abroad, first form households in the metropolitan cores, only later joining the movement to the suburbs if they are able.

In both countries, these trends have been actively encouraged by public policies in the spheres of housing and transportation. Owner-occupiers, buying their homes on mortgage, have received remarkably similar income tax concessions in both countries. Coupled with the general progress of inflation, which has caused land and property prices to rise more sharply than the general price or income level, this has meant that owner-occupiers have enjoyed a very favorable position in relation to other members of the population; they could enjoy well-equipped new housing for a relatively modest cost, and trade upwards in the market from time to time if they wished, using their capital appreciation to provide a deposit on a bigger or better house. At the same time, certain types of transportation cost have fallen relative to the general income or price level, making suburban living more attractive. In particular, the costs of using the private automobile have risen far more slowly than the general price level; and in both countries, large-scale highway construction and improvement programs have made it easier and faster to commute over longer distances from more distant suburbs to jobs in the metropolitan cores.

In both countries, new houses for sale have been priced out of reach of a substantial proportion of the population; the lower-income fourth, third, half, or even more of the total population could rarely afford to buy a new house. Even purchase of an older house was out of reach of a large section of the population; in Britain, for instance, in 1968, only 7 percent of mortgagees had household incomes of less than £1,000 ($2,400) a year, compared with 31 percent of households in local authority tenancies and 42 percent of privately rented tenancies. Clearly, in both countries the bottom 25 percent of all households, in terms of income, was effectively excluded from owner occupation. This group, of course, was highly concentrated by age; it included younger workers at the start of their careers, and retired persons depending on pensions. But since many of the latter group had already paid off their mortgage before reaching retirement age, the real problem was concentrated among the low-wage families.

Table 24 shows median and lower quartile household incomes for a typical young family (with all children under 5 years of age) in different housing tenures in Great Britain in 1968. Among local authority tenants, one-quarter of families had incomes under £1,040; among privately renting families, one-quarter had incomes under £1,018; among mortgagees, the lower quartile point came much higher, at £1,287. Developing this point, it is possible to calculate what percentage of these tenants could afford houses in different price brackets on the assumption that they could reasonably buy a house valued at two and one-half times their income; this can be compared with the percentages of all houses bought on mortgage that were actually sold at these prices in the same year, 1968. The conclusion is strikingly simple. About two-thirds of all houses bought with mortgages were in the price range £3,000–£5,000; that is, they could be bought by families with incomes between £1,200 and £2,000 a year. But a substantial proportion of all families in rented accommodation had less than £1,200 a year. For fully 50 percent of both local authority and private tenants, there was no possibility of buying some 80 percent

TABLE 24

HOUSEHOLD INCOME DISTRIBUTION, BY HOUSEHOLD STRUCTURE AND TENURE,
GREAT BRITAIN, 1968

(*in* £)

	Local authority renters (tenants)	Private unfurnished renters (tenants)	Owner-occupiers (mortgagees)	Owner-occupiers (outright owners)
All households				
Upper quartile	1,828	1,656	2,364	1,890
Median	1,337	1,105	1,824	1,211
Lower quartile	854	598	1,416	669
Households with children under 5 only				
Upper quartile	1,537	1,625	1,955	(¹)
Median	1,252	1,296	1,562	(¹)
Lower quartile	1,040	1,018	1,287	(¹)
Households with elderly people only				
Upper quartile	595	626	(¹)	950
Median	438	408	(¹)	645
Lower quartile	352	315	(¹)	448

Source: Department of the Environment, Welsh Office, and Scottish Development Department, *Housing Statistics*, No. 20 (Her Majesty's Stationery Office, February 1971).
[1] Sample too small for analysis.

of the total available housing out of income. Such families must either rely on the public sector for housing or compete for a limited supply of privately rented housing—often poor in quality or expensive in terms of monthly outgoings, or both. They therefore are unable to achieve gains in equity in housing created by steadily rising prices, and hence are unable to trade upward. The same situation occurred in the United States, except that there the available public sector housing was much more limited; for the great majority, private renting was the only alternative to owner occupancy. This limitation, then, is one of the most important features of postwar policies in both countries. We shall return to it in detail in chapter 8.

Despite these broad similarities, there were very evident differences in the pattern of urban development in the two countries. One has just been noted: it is that the public sector has accounted for a much larger share of new construction in Britain than in the United States, and so has been able to provide a large amount of quite high standard, modern housing for that group which is excluded by income from the advantages of owner occupancy. Over the whole quarter century from 1945 through 1970, over 57 percent of the total output of new housing in the United Kingdom was provided by public agencies, the great majority of which was built by the local authorities. Virtually all this housing was subsidized by central government; much was also subsidized by local authorities from their own rate (real estate tax) funds. And virtually all of it was originally built for rent, even though subsequently some of it was sold off to tenants; the tenants received considerable subsidy from central or local funds. In the United States, in contrast, public housing accounted for less than 3 percent of all nonfarm housing starts in the period 1945–69, though, in addition, close to 27 percent of total housing starts were private building with special government financing through the Federal Housing Administration or Veterans Administration schemes, by means of which many people were enabled to buy houses who otherwise could not have done so.

It is clear, therefore, that in the United States a much narrower spectrum of the total population enjoys publicly subsidized rental housing. Curiously, at first sight the distribution of tenures in the two countries is not very different. In England and Wales in 1971, it was officially estimated that a little over one-half of all dwellings were owner-occupied; more than one-fourth were rented from local authorities; the remainder, one-fifth of the total, were rented from private landlords. In the United States in 1969, some 64 percent of all occupied dwelling units were owner-occupied and 36 percent rented. But the great bulk of the latter represented private renting; at the 1960 Census, only just over 1 percent of all dwellings were low-rent units supervised by the Housing Assistance Administration of the Department of Housing and Urban Development; and though the numbers of such units nearly doubled in the next decade, they still did not account for more than 2 percent of the total stock in 1970. Furthermore, save for some dwellings in New York City up to the summer of 1971, all the privately rented stock in the United States is free of any form of rent control or regulation. In England and Wales, in contrast, no less than 1.3 million tenancies were still controlled in 1971 and 1.2 million were subject to rent regulation. Together, they accounted for about three-quarters of the stock of privately rented dwellings.

These differences have had profound effects on urban development patterns. In Britain, new households characteristically tend to form in the privately rented sector. Some remain there; but a majority moves out in two directions. The larger wave moves into owner occupancy; the smaller into local authority housing. Thereafter, despite some sales to council tenants, there is not much transfer between the two streams. In the United States, apart from a very small percentage of poor families, there is only one route out of the privately rented sector: into the owner-occupied sector, together with nearly two-thirds of all American households. In Britain, too, the public sector has carried much of the statutory burden for rehousing under the large-scale slum clearance schemes which have been carried through since 1955. In the United States, it is clear that the public sector is far too small to undertake a similar role.

The British public sector has played a major role in urban renewal in postwar years. It has torn down one and one-quarter million slums and replaced them by municipally owned and managed dwellings, many of them on the slum clearance sites themselves, some of them on overspill schemes on green-field sites at the periphery of the city or beyond. Thirty percent or more of the total British public sector building program in the postwar period has been devoted to these needs; the rest has gone to meet the needs arising from new household formation, or to the relief of overcrowding. Though an exact estimate is impossible, it appears that in broad terms, when the slum clearance element is subtracted from the total public sector program, the remaining program of green-field development was almost equal in size to the corresponding private program. In other words, of the total urban growth of postwar Britain, about one-half was carried through by public and about one-half by private agencies; the first almost wholly for rent, the second almost wholly for sale. In the United States, in contrast, virtually the whole program of new development has been carried through by private agencies—mainly for sale, but for rent in a minority of cases.

The second major contrast concerns the operation of public planning controls upon public and private sector alike, but especially upon the operations of the private builder for sale. (These controls, and the associated plans, are the subject matter of chapter 5.) The effect has been to contain and channel urban growth in Britain in ways that have not been observable in the United States. They have produced greater contiguity of separate residential developments at the local scale, avoiding the leapfrogging and scatteration of subdivisions, which have been so characteristic of the United States; but at a larger scale they have deliberately prevented contiguity by restraining the growth of the larger urban areas and channeling development into the smaller towns and the villages at some distance away. At the same time, they have consciously worked to ensure greater density of development within the residential areas themselves; and this has been assisted by the generally rapid rise in land values, which has been an important result of the planning restrictions. In turn, this increase in density has been achieved in some limited degree by limiting the size of the house itself, but mainly by reducing the amount of private open space around it.

Curiously, however, one effect of the two very different patterns of development seems to have been similar. Greater contiguity at the local scale, but less at the larger scale, in Britain seems to have the same result as the reverse pattern in the United States: the new homes are separated from various opportunities, in the way of jobs or services or social interaction, by greater distances than if there had been more contiguous forms of development. It is difficult to measure this precisely, because in Britain the problem has been compounded by the fact that employment —and also services of all kinds—have so far decentralized less rapidly with population than in the United States. Planning controls, together with the perfectly natural pursuit of self-interest by the cities, have led to the retention by these cities of much of their employment, especially in the service industries but also in manufacturing; the great increases in retail turnover during the 1950s and 1960s have been disproportionately accommodated within the cities rather than in the suburbs where the new populations were being housed. As a result, particularly during the 1950s, one effect of the policy of urban containment was to increase the number and also the average length of journeys to work or to shop. This was almost the reverse of what the policy of containment was intended to achieve.

PLATES

1. Lower Middlesex County, New Jersey (left) and London Greenbelt, Elstree, Hertford-shire (right)

Lacking tight overall planning controls, American urban growth has typically leapfrogged, giving scattered development with intervening open land which often has no useful purpose: this example, between New York City and Philadelphia, shows single-family housing, light industry and research, garden apartments, and more single-family housing. British greenbelt policies, in contrast, have contained urban development, compacting different urban uses together in the interest of preserving a rigid line against open countryside, which is still well farmed.

2. MIDTOWN MANHATTAN (left) and THE WEST END OF LONDON (right)

Both these are areas of relatively recent (post-1920) office and retail development, which has replaced former high-class housing. The development in New York City is, however, at a higher density; though new high-rise office blocks have transformed London's skyline since World War II, they do not compete with Manhattan's skyscrapers. In both pictures, the background is composed of the older office area: Manhattan's Downtown (on horizon), and the City of London (right background).

3. CENTRAL PHILADELPHIA (left) and CENTRAL BIRMINGHAM, ENGLAND (right)

After New York City and London, these are the two greatest cities in the respective urban regions compared and contrasted in this book. Despite extensive redevelopment during the 1960s, Birmingham's center has few really high-rise buildings compared with Philadelphia, and it is altogether a relatively small employment center with only about one-tenth the employment in London's central business district (in 1961). The impact of new highways on central Birmingham is much greater than in central London, befitting a major center of Britain's automobile industry.

4. LEVITTOWN–FAIRLESS HILLS, PENNSYLVANIA (left) and WOODLEY, READING, ENGLAND (right)

In both countries, a majority of new housing on previously undeveloped land has been constructed by private developers and builders for sale. But in the United States the large developer became important soon after World War II, building extensive developments that took on the character of new communities, as in this Levitt development of the 1950s, in Pennsylvania. The small builder has remained more significant in England, so that new suburban areas appear less homogeneous in style. Generally speaking, English densities are higher (ten to twelve per net acre in this example) as against about seven in Levittown and even lower in later developments.

5. MILFORD CENTER, MILFORD, CONNECTICUT (left) and CENTRAL READING, ENGLAND (right)

In the Northeastern Urban Complex, jobs and services have followed homes in dispersing widely throughout the new suburbia. This cluster, developed around the interchange between the Connecticut Turnpike and the old U.S. Highway 1 in Connecticut, contains a shopping center, movie theater, three motels, four factories and a trailer park. In England, in sharp contrast, new out-of-town development of services has been severely restricted by planning controls, and the main emphasis has been on redevelopment of the older central commercial cores, often involving costly highway access.

6. SUBURBIA—AMERICAN (left) and BRITISH STYLE (right)

Typical American suburbia of the 1960s takes the form of ranch-style, detached houses (bunga-lows in English terminology) at a density of two to four houses per acre. British suburbia of the same period is built at a generally higher density (eight to twelve houses per acre) with a much higher proportion of row (terrace) housing and semi-detached forms. This example is built on the semi-Radburn principle; garages for the row houses (foreground) are at their rear.

7. WOODBRIDGE, NEW JERSEY (left) and HULME, MANCHESTER, ENGLAND (right)

The 1960s have seen extensive construction of apartment blocks in the suburban tracts of the American Northeastern Urban Complex; they account for a substantial proportion of all new home construction. This has not occurred on any scale in Britain; apartment block construction there is invariably associated with renewal of inner urban areas by public (municipal) agencies, as in this view of a slum clearance area in Manchester.

chapter 5

Planning and land use controls in the United States and Britain

In the modern world, planning by the individual, the corporation, or any unit of government not only is essential but unavoidable. The making of an investment, whether in manufacturing plant, public service facilities, or in one's own education makes sense, if at all, only in the context of some assumptions or some plans for the future. Denying an interest in planning or criticizing the planning efforts of others does not free one from a dependence on the future.

For units of government, the significant questions are: Who does the planning? by what rules? to what ends? by what processes? The answers to these questions throw some light on the kinds of plans made; the process affects the results, if it does not determine them. Earlier chapters have dealt implicitly with urban planning in Britain and in the United States, or have presented some of the background or some of the results of such planning. In the present chapter we look at the planning process in each country explicitly, trying to answer the general questions raised above.

Most advanced industrial countries have found it necessary to institute some degree of control over land use in the interests of economic efficiency or (more commonly) of the well-being of their citizens. Ever since the reaction against the unplanned nineteenth-century industrial city, local administrations have sought to ensure that building takes place where it can be minimally serviced by what are regarded as essential public services (though the definition of these may vary from place to place); to provide minimum standards of light, air, and protection against flood or fire hazard; to separate different land uses, especially where some of these may prove noxious or hazardous or simply unpleasant in varying degrees; to protect exceptionally fine landscapes, historical sites, or recreational areas; and to reserve land for essential public uses, such as reservoirs or highways. But different advanced countries—and even different regions or cities within advanced countries —have tended to differ both in the importance they have attached to some of these objectives and in the means they have used to pursue them. Again, the important questions are: Who enforces the controls? by what rules? to what ends? by what processes?

At first sight, it might appear that planning—as generally understood by the lay public—is inevitably connected with the control of land use. Planning, in common parlance, is concerned with the making of physical plans showing the location of different investments and the different uses of land. In any society where there are varying agents of development—which includes any society except perhaps a pure Maoist one—the plan will only become meaningful if it can be enforced by some system of controls over the actions of these various agents. Otherwise, it will remain a purely academic paper plan; and as it comes to be widely ignored, then the planning process itself may come into disrespect. Despite this obvious fact, experience in many advanced countries in the twentieth century shows that many physical plans have proved ineffectual in varying degrees, simply because they were not accompanied by any means of implementation, or because the apparatus of implementation that did exist was not sufficiently concerned to defend the plan.

This in turn reflects a fact of modern organization. The kinds of plans we have been describing in the last paragraph—the kinds the general public instinctively think of when they hear the words *plan* or *planning*—characteristically have been made by one kind of public planner. This is the professional planner, whose chief job has traditionally been physical planning; he may be called a *general physical planner*, since he is concerned to integrate in a spatial sense many or all programs of modern government, which in practice means many or all aspects of modern life. His central concern is to impose some sort of order on the programs of development made by other public agencies and also by private agencies. But the people who make these programs are, in effect, another sort of planner. They can be called the *specialist functional planners*: the men who design programs for development in a particular area. Within the public sector there are highway engineers who make highway plans, medical men who make plans for hospitals, educational planners who make plans for schools, and so on. Within the private sector, there are supermarket chain planners who make plans for new retail stores or central warehouse facilities, residential developers who plan programs of real estate building, and industrialists who plan extensions of their plant capacity or completely new plants. Whether labelled private or public—and in many spheres the boundary between the two sectors is different from country to country—these planners are usually concerned with a single function, or a closely related group of functions. Although as part of their working environment they necessarily take account of the plans and programs of other public and private agencies and groups, they are not required to, and frequently do not, concern themselves with the implications of their plans for those of others. Such men are "specialized" in the sense that they are specialized in certain functions, but their specialty is not planning. They are likely to have somewhat different training, different professional histories, and, above all, differences in interest and objective as compared with the general physical planner. Though they may agree that they all gain by accepting the rules of the general planner, very often they will find themselves wanting to bend those rules.

In fact, the position is complicated still further by the fact that the general physical planners do not speak with a single voice. Normally, for obvious practical reasons, general physical planning is a function of local government—albeit with some degree of central coordination from above in certain cases. Many of the specialist planners, on the other hand, work in agencies that are centralized to a considerable degree. The supermarket planner or the national planner works either in a national office or in a regional office of a national organization, with a good deal of close coordination from the center. Just as specialist agencies may have different interests —even within the same field, as when one supermarket or motel chain has interests different from those of its rival—so, very often, local administrations may have different and even opposed interests from those of their neighbors. The solution of one authority's slum problem may involve decanting surplus residents on a neighboring authority. One authority, trying to clean up its river system, may involve its neighbor in costs of treatment. One authority, trying to attract valuable commercial or retail development, may throw an unwanted traffic load onto the highway system of the neighboring authority. And the physical plans of these different authorities—comprehensive as they may be within the boundaries of their respective interests—will simply reflect the sum of all these potential conflicts.

To overcome some of these difficulties, two related solutions have been suggested and, to varying degrees in different places, implemented. The first is to create multifunctional units of local government—"all-purpose" or "multipurpose" authorities —so that the planning of the different functions can be integrated in a single organization. The second is to improve this integration by creating a new top-level planning function—variously called *general comprehensive* or *public corporate* or *urban management* planning—within the organization. Such planning units have been concerned with the total scope of government activities in their area. There has been division of opinion as to whether this function should be performed by the general physical planner or by some other person. But these steps are far from complete implementation in either of the two countries we are discussing, and they still fail to deal with the problem of integrating the work of the functional planners in private organizations.

In this chapter, our chief interest lies in the first group—the general physical planners; we shall focus on their programs for plan making and for implementation. But one cannot ignore the second group—the limited function planners—for sometimes they prove far more influential.

The Historical Basis of Planning and Land Use Control in the Two Countries

Comprehensive general planning and effective land use control are relatively recent activities in both Britain and the United States. They have evolved in slightly different ways in the two countries; and these divergent origins express themselves in one basic difference in the ways in which the two systems now operate. Despite many similarities in the planning and control processes in both countries, and in the training and outlook of those who operate the processes, this basic difference is so important that it needs to be stressed at the outset. It is this: In Britain, since the Town and Country Planning Act of 1947, plan making and development control (or control over land use) have been statutorily exercised by the same agencies as part and parcel of the same system. The act of drawing up the plan, and the process of controlling land use in accordance with the plan, cannot be meaningfully considered apart. But in the United States, though there may be some association between plan making and land use control, it is far weaker and less formalized. There are plans, drawn up by planners—general physical planners, in the sense we have defined. And there is a system of land use control, or zoning. But each can perfectly well exist without the other. And there is no necessary connection between the two.

To explain this difference, it is necessary to go back to the historic origins of planning and control in the two countries. In both, planning as a profession is relatively recent. The Town Planning Institute in Britain (which became the Royal Town Planning Institute in 1971) was founded in 1914; the American Institute of Planners was founded in 1917. For several decades after their foundation both institutes were small and their practitioners, by definition, were people who had received their training in other fields—most commonly, as architects or as engineers, or as chartered surveyors in Britain. These last represent the profession of land management in Britain. The interest of those groups in planning, therefore, was a by-product of their original professional concern: architects saw planning as a larger-scale problem of civic design; engineers saw it as the design of a set of standards to achieve fairly mundane though important objectives such as the provision of adequate light, air, or public services; and chartered surveyors saw it as a problem of the wise management of land in the interests of the public authority they served. Planning in a wider, more comprehensive sense—the coordination of different programs, as we have defined it—was slow to develop.

In Britain, there had been concern over the effects of unplanned urban growth as early as the 1840s, as was indicated in chapter 2. The immediate effect was to create the important profession of public health engineering, concerned with the provision of pure water supplies and adequate sewerage to the growing industrial cities, and with the imposition of minimal standards of daylighting and density through local bylaws. From the time of the earliest model communities, like Bournville (1879) and Port Sunlight (1887), architects also became involved in this process. It was essentially the union of these two groups that produced the Town Planning Institute; by definition, from its inception it was a body of professionals actively involved in practical work, stressing the achievement of professional qualifications and the maintenance of professional standards, rather than an intellectual organization concerned to discuss objectives or pursue research. These latter functions were pursued by different people—often not professional planners at all—working in different organizations. Outstanding among the individuals were Ebenezer Howard, the creator of the Garden Cities program for the planned decentralization of urban populations and employments to new planned communities, and Patrick Geddes, with his call for the planning of whole regions as a coordinated whole. Together, their ideas made a strong case for a regional planning that took in cities or urban agglomerations and their whole hinterlands in opposition to the narrower town planning that was the chief concern of the working professionals. They and their followers found a natural forum for debate and propaganda in the Town and Country Planning Association, which Ebenezer Howard himself founded and which fought a powerful campaign for the establishment of a national new town program in the period between the two world wars.

Although there were some limited extensions of town planning in practice during this period in Britain, in no wise did they correspond to the very radical program of regional planning and urban decentralization advocated by the Town and Country Planning Association. It was in fact the establishment of a series of Royal Commissions and official Committees of Inquiry in the late 1930s and early 1940s —Barlow on Industrial Location, Scott on Rural Land Use, Uthwatt on Compensation and Betterment, Reith on New Towns—that led directly, in a very short period during and immediately after the war, to the creation of the British planning system. And it is important that the definitive 1947 Act borrowed the name of the advocacy organization: it was called the Town and Country Planning Act, stressing that meaningful planning could be carried on only on a regional scale, so that conurbations and cities could be planned together with their rural hinterlands. In the event, the aspiration toward regional planning was not accompanied by the setting up of adequate regional machinery. But one most important aspect of the 1947 system in practice was the setting up of quite new county planning offices for the mainly rural areas outside the major cities. These, by definition, had to be staffed by quite new professional planners, many of whom had no other professional qualification; at this point an effective planning profession was born in Britain. In the cities, on the other hand, the new statutory obligation of planning was usually attached to the Borough Engineer's office, where historically it had always belonged.

In the United States, also, city planning was a weakly staffed and poorly recognized activity until about World War II. As in Britain before 1947, its development as a profession was limited for a long time by lack of effective power over land use. As a matter of historic fact, such powers materialized in the United States more than twenty years before they did in Britain. Land use zoning began in a major way in New York City before and during World War I, and spread to several hundred additional cities by the mid-1920s. The legal issue of zoning power was largely resolved, or at least a resolution was begun, with the Supreme Court decision in the case of *Village of Euclid* v. *Ambler Realty Co.*, 272 U.S. 365, 1926. This established the legality of zoning—i.e., the freedom of a local jurisdiction to make and enforce restrictions on the use of land within its area. A model zoning law was prepared by the Department of Commerce, under the personal leadership of the then Secretary, Herbert Hoover. During the Great Depression of the 1930s, too, planning at the federal level was instituted under the National Resources Planning Board and reached a degree of comprehensiveness and activity never attained before or since. During those days, with acts like the establishment of the Tennessee Valley Authority, the United States appeared far ahead of Britain in implementing the ideas of regional planning embodied in the writings of men like Geddes. The Board was abolished in 1942, and since then the federal government and various other agencies (some of them private) have inched their way back into planning over the space of three decades, mostly on a more limited or more specialized scale. But most public planning of those days was done by men not trained as planners, in the sense we have used in this chapter.

Since World War II, urban planning has emerged on a larger scale in the United States. The training of a body of men as planners has been, to a great extent, a postwar phenomenon. Urban planning in the United States still relies to a considerable extent on citizen bodies or boards, with full-time trained staff in the larger cities but without it in small towns. In 1968 planning boards or similar organizations were functioning in over 10,000 units of local government. About a fifth of them were in New England-type townships, many without professional planning staff; nearly a sixth were in counties, and of these some were large and well-staffed while others were small and poorly staffed; and some of the rest, in small cities, were also poorly staffed.

While comprehensive or general planning was developing in each country, specialized or functional planning was also developing in each. In the United States, highway planning became highly important in the postwar years, especially as major throughways were pushed into the larger cities, inevitably displacing people, often poor people, in the process. Many a city or metropolitan area undertook a "comprehensive" planning effort—often confined, in practice, to highways and other public works—with highway planning funds. In 1962 amendments to the Federal-Aid Highway Act required that, after July 1, 1965, no federal highway funds could be spent in any metropolitan area that did not have a comprehensive transportation planning process. But federal funds were also available to finance a large part of the cost of urban and metropolitan planning—the "701" funds, so named because they were provided by Section 701 of the 1954 Housing Act. Likewise, federal grants for sewer construction, for open space, for educational purposes, for urban renewal, and for other purposes all put stress on comprehensive plans for the metropolitan areas concerned. These latter plans were often developed by what we have called limited function planners.

But limited function planning has also developed in Britain in recent decades. The Board of Trade (now the Department of Trade and Industry), under the Distribution of Industry Act of 1945, has exerted a powerful influence, not to say control, over the location of industrial jobs. It is a striking anomaly that this power was never given to the government department responsible for physical planning. The Electricity Boards, both in the provision of new electrical generating capacity and in the location of power lines, have exerted some influence over industrial and other location. River Authorities, with only indirect and partial local authority control, and the Water Resources Board have been responsible for major reservoir schemes (projects). The planning of the national parks and the reservation of outstanding areas in the countryside have exerted some influence on where people live, work, and play, as have similar activities in the United States. And the transportation planners have obviously played a role. All these organizations have had their limited function planning staffs, by whatever name they were known.

As a result of all this, in each country in the early 1970s there exists a body of trained planners, or men trained primarily in some other profession who nevertheless today talk the jargon and know the procedures of the planning profession—

a body of men whose numbers greatly exceed those found one generation ago, and who were nearly unknown two generations ago. In each country some private business firms now employ planners—men whose duty it is to assemble data, make analyses, and provide plans or suggestions to guide the future development of their firms, especially in urban areas. Some of the larger firms have larger and far better trained staffs than do some of the smaller cities and counties. And, at least in the United States, there is developing a new kind of planning, "advocacy planning," by means of which various interest groups (racial minorities, conservationists, or other) employ specialized planners to develop plans to meet their interests. This latter group of planners is anathema to the old-school general physical planners, who always emphasized the general public interest—even when they not infrequently acted in the interest of only some classes of the whole population.

Planning, like many another profession, has become technically more sophisticated in recent years. Planners today employ systems analysis, modelling, benefit-cost analysis, cost-effectiveness analysis, and others, in a way that was totally foreign to the profession a decade or more ago. As in other professions, new techniques are adopted by the leaders and the experimentally minded long before they become standard in the profession. Planning, again like other professions, has come to use electronic data processing—for tabulation of data, for calculation of interrelationships among data variables, and for mapping of data—in ways that also were unknown only a few years ago. A notable development has been the establishment of planning consulting firms, some of considerable size and high skill, which undertake planning studies for units of government as well as for private clients. In all of these and in other ways the planning profession is changing; but, as in other professions, the weight of past tradition as well as the skills of older men trained in an earlier day tend to limit the rate of change.

The Legal Basis of Planning and Land Use Control in the Two Countries

Against this historical background, one can now better appreciate the essential difference between the planning and control systems in Britain and the United States. We have already noted one basic distinction: In Britain, planning and control are inevitably and inexorably associated by law in the same institution with a statutory responsibility to administer control in accordance with the plan; in America, the control system may be—and often in practice is—divorced from the plan-making system, where such exists. The historical roots of this distinction have also been noted: The United States acquired its system of land use controls, or zoning, through a crucial court decision of 1926 that asserted the right of local authorities to make regulations in the general public interest without the interjection of new legislation; the British acquired their comprehensive system of controls only as the result of a complex piece of new legislation—the Town and Country Planning Act of 1947. Though people calling themselves planners, and the American Institute of Planners itself, already existed in the United States in 1926, and although several city plans, some rather elaborate, had been made by that date, in the United States the system of land use control largely preceded the system of planning; similarly, though both planners and a planning institute existed in Britain in 1947, there both effective planning and effective planning control were created as parts of a combined system in the act of that year.

These different origins are reflected in the legal basis of control over land use in the two countries since World War II. At first sight, and in strictly formal terms, these public controls in the United States and Great Britain could not be more different. They represent, apparently, both different kinds of control and different degrees of control. The American system relies on *police power*—an American term, unknown in common usage in Britain—which describes:

> . . . the general residual power of government to pass laws in the interests of the general public health, safety, and welfare.[1]

This system, by its nature, tends not to rely on the power of eminent domain, or compulsory purchase. It involves no principle of compensation for loss of rights to develop land in a particular way. The British system, in contrast, relies on a formal and quite drastic limitation of traditional property rights. In effect, it involves the nationalization of those rights apart from the right to occupy the land in its existing state. In its pure and original form, as embodied in the 1947 Act, it logically involved also the loss of all benefit from the development of the land:

> . . . after July 1, 1948, ownership of land, generally speaking, carries with it no more than a bare right to go on using it for its existing purposes. The owner has no right to develop it, that is to say, he has no right to build upon it and no *right* even to change its use, and if he sells it he can (in theory, at least) expect to get only its existing use value because, whatever development value the land had is now expropriated by the State. The new Act does not nationalise the land; what it does is to nationalise the development value in land.[2]

In fact, as we shall see, this pure system has been drastically modified; though nationalization of development rights is a historic and legal fact, since 1953 the situation has been that if an owner received development permission he could also enjoy the benefits, while if he was denied, in general it was assumed that his proposed development was contrary to the public interest. It is this logic that has justified the continued support for the system from both parties. Nevertheless, it is plain that the British system involves a much greater degree of interference with previously existing property rights than the American one. Because of this, it has to make specific provision to compensate for loss of these rights. And—at least in its original pure form as embodied in the 1947 Act—it achieved the feat in theory of putting the power of eminent domain on the same basis, in terms of compensation, as a normal private sale.

[1] John Delafons, *Land Use Controls in the United States*, 2nd edition (Cambridge, Mass.: Joint Center for Urban Studies, 1969), p. 14.
[2] Desmond Heap, *An Outline of the New Planning Law* (London: Sweet and Maxwell, 1949), p. 12. The emphasis is in the original.

THE 1947 SYSTEM OF CONTROL IN BRITAIN—AND ITS MODIFICATION

Because the system created by Britain in 1947 has unique features and because it is a complex system whose complexities have increased with subsequent amendments, its formal structure needs to be described in some detail. First, in this section we shall look at the "pure" 1947 system; second, at the subsequent changes embodied in the British planning law as it stands at the beginning of the 1970s, in the two Town and Country Planning Acts of 1962 and 1968.[3]

The 1947 Act contained three main features, which were closely and logically interlinked.[4] First, it scrapped the previous system of planning, which had been created by various acts ranging from 1909 to 1932 and which in many ways resembled the American system with its reliance on zoning regulations made by a myriad of small local authorities. In its place, it provided that henceforth planning control should be administered by the largest units of local government then available—the County Councils, numbering about eighty, and the large cities (County Boroughs in England and Wales or Large Burghs in Scotland), numbering about ninety in all.[5] Each of these was to produce, within a fixed time limit of three years from July 1948, a Development Plan based on a survey of its area. The plan was to cover a twenty-year period and its content and form were specifically spelled out in the act: It should indicate the manner in which the land in the area was to be used, including the crucial point of whether development was to be allowed or not; it should set out the stages by which it was to be carried out; and it would generally consist of a written statement of proposals plus a map, with other materials as were appropriate. It might define the sites of proposed roads, buildings, airfields, parks, or other developments, and allocate areas for agricultural, residential, or industrial purposes. The plan must be revised, with a new survey, every five years. Both the original plan, and all subsequent revisions, must be submitted to the Minister, who might accept or reject them; he had the right, which in the event was invariably exercised, to make modifications. There was an elaborate procedure for allowing the public to object to the Minister about the content of the plan. If there were objections—and there invariably have been— the Minister might order a public inquiry by one of his inspectors before a decision. But the final decision is his, and it is taken administratively, not judicially or quasi-judicially. This gives the Minister great freedom of action, and it is a fundamental departure from the American tradition of reliance on the courts as final arbiter. Once the Minister has decided, that is the end of the matter: the plan has legal status.

Secondly, the act established a system of development control operated by these same local authorities, which are logically known as local planning authorities.[6]

---

[3] The 1947 Act was repealed in 1962 when those parts of it that were still valid were embodied in the act of that year, which was a consolidating act.

[4] This account relies on the standard source: Desmond Heap, *Encyclopedia of Planning Law and Practice* (London: Sweet and Maxwell, 1959–), vol. I.

[5] These figures relate to Great Britain. At all times since 1947, planning legislation for Scotland has been separate but essentially parallel to the English law.

[6] From what has been written above, it will be clear that not all local authorities are local planning authorities. Up to the local government reform, to be implemented in 1974, there has

It prohibited, with certain defined exceptions, the carrying out of any form of development without the consent of the local planning authority. "Development" is thus a critical word in the British planning vocabulary, and the act spent a great deal of legal verbiage in defining it closely. But essentially, it consists of either the carrying out of operations—building, engineering, mining or otherwise—in, on, over, or under land, or the making of any material change in the use of buildings or land. Thus a central feature of the 1947 system is that the owner no longer has an automatic right to do what he likes with his land. If he wishes to carry out any operation on it that constitutes a development in law, he cannot do so without first *obtaining planning permission*—a phrase that has now become part of everyday language and experience in Britain. If he is refused, he has the right of appeal to the Minister, who may appoint one of his inspectors to hold an inquiry before giving a decision. But again, that is final: though there is a right of appeal to courts on a point of law or defect in procedure, this could not usually reverse the planning decision itself.

Were some lawless person then to proceed with building construction without having obtained planning permission, or in defiance of its denial, he would be promptly taken into court; and, upon a finding by the court of his violation, the buildings he had begun would be demolished, by him or by local authorities at his expense. In perhaps no other aspect of suburban growth and land conversion is the contrast sharper between British and American systems; in Britain, the planning authorities mean what they say, and they have both the legal and the political power to back up their decisions; in the United States, various devices are frequently found to thwart the decisions of the planning and zoning organizations— their pronouncements are often but the beginning, with the final result quite different.

These first two features of the 1947 Act have survived, with modifications, up to the early 1970s; the most important of these modifications, which concern the form of the development plan, are described later. But the third essential feature of the act has been considerably modified and in some respects expunged. This is the nationalization of development *values*, which in the 1947 Act was a logical consequence of the nationalization of development rights. Since development rights had a quite tangible value attaching to them in many cases, the government in 1947 took the view that the owners of those rights should be compensated on a once-for-all basis for the loss of that value. (There was a close analogy here with the compensation paid, at the same time, to the stockholders of the nationalized coal mines, railways, and utility companies.) A careful estimate was made of the value of all development value claims in the country, scaled down to allow for the double counting that must arise from the phenomenon of floating value.[7] It came to £300 mil-

---

been two-tier government outside the cities. Normally the upper-tier (county) authorities have been the planning authorities here. But there are elaborate arrangements for delegation of certain development control powers to larger local (non-planning) authorities, some of which may be claimed by right.

[7] "Floating value" is the phenomenon whereby potential development value "floats" over a number of competing sites all of which are, to all intents and purposes, identical. Not all will be developed; but all the owners have an equal right to believe that theirs is the plot to which the development value will attach itself.

lion. Consequently the act provided that a fund of this size should be established, out of which claimants should be paid (after their claims had been adjudicated) at a specified future date. Once the principle of State expropriation of development rights (with just compensation) had been embodied in the law, there was no logical or moral justification for landowners to receive further profit from the development of their land. So the act provided that in future, in all cases where development permission was granted by a local planning authority, a Development Charge be paid to a State agency, the Central Land Board. This was to represent the development value, i.e., the rise in value that was attributable to the prospect of development. Later, in regulations made under the act, the charge was fixed with equal logic at 100 percent of the difference in value. In other words, the landowner was to get absolutely nothing out of the fact that he could develop his land. He could still enjoy any rise in the value of the land in its existing use, even when this arose from general community influences—for instance, if he owned a house in an area where a new highway enhanced accessibility. But where the rise in value arose from the grant of development permission, that logically belonged to the State.[8]

The logic of this solution extended further, to the difficult problem of valuation in cases of exercise of the right of eminent domain (compulsory purchase) by public authorities for such varied purposes as highway construction, school building, or the creation of a new town. Here, ever since the first recorded case in English law in the year 1427, the problem had been that the public agency might fail to recoup values it had been instrumental in creating. The 1947 solution cut the Gordian knot by providing that in these cases, the public authority should pay merely the existing use value, without any development value attached. Thus, for the owner of land, the result was the same whether he sold land, with development permission attached, to a private buyer, or sold without development permission, or had his land compulsorily purchased. In all three cases, he would receive merely the existing use value of the land. This was important, because at the same time the act gave local authorities of all kinds—not just local planning authorities— wider powers of compulsory purchase. Under the act, for instance, they were encouraged to declare Comprehensive Development Areas for large-scale urban renewal. Had they been compelled to pay full market value for the land, the cost would have been very heavy. The logic of the 1947 Act ensured that they could buy at existing use value, but that this would not leave the owner of the land any worse off than if he had made a willing sale.

This was the logic in theory. Unfortunately, in practice it did not work out so tidily. The problem was that the system required the land market to work, but gave it no incentive to do so on the supply side. By 1950 and early 1951, it was clear that the effect of the financial provisions of the act had been to distort the land market. Some land, it seems, was being withheld from the market in the expectation that the government would have to give way and change the regulation to give landowners a share of development value. Other land was changing hands at in-

---

[8] Strictly speaking, the theory of the act was that the State expropriated development rights and values, compensating for their loss; and then delegated the power of development control in perpetuity to the local planning authorities, with residual rights of intervention.

flated values: buyers were apparently willing to pay extra for it by giving the owner the full development value as well as paying the Development Charge to the Central Land Board.[9] These distortions greatly alarmed the professional associations concerned with land management, who expressed their reservations strongly to the government. When the Conservatives were returned to power at the 1951 election, they used such doubts as justification for a fundamental set of changes in the operation of the financial provisions of the act.

These changes, between 1953 and 1959, were the first major modifications of the 1947 system. In effect, they removed a large part of the financial provisions, and in the process destroyed the logical consistency of the act as a whole. First, in an Act of 1953, Development Charge was abolished, and the once-for-all payment of the £300 million compensation fund (which was due in 1954) was postponed. Then, in 1954, a second act specified that the compensation fund was to be paid out not all at once, but only if and when the owner was prevented from reaping the development value either by a refusal (or limitation) of development permission, or by compulsory acquisition at existing use value, which amounted to the same thing. Lastly, in 1959, a third modificatory act removed an important anomaly created by the abolition of Development Charge. Between 1953 and 1959, an owner who got planning permission could again enjoy all the resulting development value, while the owner whose land was compulsorily purchased got only existing use value. This anomaly was widely attacked as inequitable, notably by the influential Franks Committee report on Tribunals, in 1957. So in the 1959 Act, the government returned to market value as the basis for compulsory purchase. This removed one anomaly. But it left a larger anomaly: that while the whole basis of the 1947 Act continued to be the nationalization of development rights (and compensation was payable in respect of their loss), the community was no longer to gain from the resulting development values. Not only was this illogical; it meant that the community was positively penalized when it purchased land for purposes like schools, hospitals, or roads.

Meanwhile, the passage of the three acts coincided with the beginning of a boom in construction and in land values during the later 1950s. By 1962 and 1963 this was already resulting in serious inflation of land prices for residential construction, above all around London. This was one justification for yet another attack on the problem, and (in effect) another modification to the operation of the 1947 system. Returned to power in 1964, the Labour government in 1965 proposed, and in 1967 passed, an act establishing a Land Commission. In some respects this was a return to the recommendations of the Uthwatt Committee of 1942, which had been passed over by the government in 1947 when they had introduced their Development Charge solution. Under the Uthwatt solution, development rights on all undeveloped land would have been nationalized; owners would have been compensated for their loss (as under the 1947 solution), but would have continued in occupation. However, when the land was actually needed for development, a Central Planning Agency would actually buy it, subsequently leasing or selling it to developers;

[9] Charles M. Haar, *Land Planning Law in a Free Society* (Cambridge, Mass.: Harvard University Press, 1951), p. 162.

logically, it would buy at existing use value and sell at development value, thus gaining the difference for the community. Furthermore, all land (whether developed or not) was to pay a 75 percent "betterment levy" on any increases in the value of the site alone, based on a periodic revaluation. (This value, it should be noted, might contain more than "development value" as defined in 1947; the committee argued that it was impossible conceptually to separate out the different elements in the increase of land value.) The Labour government in 1947 had rejected this as too radical; and the Labour government in 1967 did likewise, though in opposition it had commended the original Uthwatt proposal.

Instead, in the 1967 Act the Land Commission was to buy land as required. It could buy land voluntarily without restriction, but it could use compulsory purchase only for certain defined purposes, which in the early years of the act's operation were to be very specifically defined: the most important was to ensure the early development or redevelopment of the land. The effect, over time, would have been a process of creeping land nationalization not different from the original Uthwatt solution, but slower and (as was apparently hoped) not so ideologically explosive. The 1967 Act also returned to the Uthwatt idea of the general betterment levy. It was, however, to apply only to certain defined transactions and actions that enabled an increase in development value to be realized, not to be a tax on general value increases as had been suggested in 1942; in this respect, it was more like the 1947 Development Charge than the Uthwatt proposal. And it was fixed at a much more modest rate than either of these: 40 percent rising to 45, then 50 percent, and possibly even higher in time, as compared with the 75 percent suggested by Uthwatt and the 100 percent charge in the Act of 1947.

The net effect of the Land Commission Act would almost certainly have been fairly modest. One element, the Betterment Levy, was in effect a capital gains tax on land at a rather higher rate than general capital gains tax; it could and perhaps should have been collected as a tax by the Treasury rather than by the Land Commission, the real job of which was to deal in land. And given all the restrictions on operation in the early years, the commission could have built up its land bank only slowly. One estimate was that by 1980 it might have acquired about 5 percent of the developed acreage of Britain and well under 1 percent of the total acreage.[10] Furthermore, the act was highly pragmatic in character. It simply tried to introduce some specific measures to deal with known anomalies and deficiencies in the existing land development situation of the mid-1960s. It in no way returned to the logic of the 1947 Act or to the even more ruthless logic of the 1942 Uthwatt proposals. In particular, it continued to rely on the normal operations of the land market, inspired by profit; it merely sought to intervene in them. It neither removed the profit altogether from the development business, as the 1947 Act had tried to do, nor abolished the market in developable land altogether, as the Uthwatt recommendations had sought to do. Despite this, it was strongly criticized by Conservative party spokesmen from the start; and it was little surprise, though a disappointment to some, that immediately on return to office in summer 1970 the Conservative government took steps to wind up the commission. The position with regard to

[10] Wyndham Thomas, "Land Planning and Development Values in Postwar Britain," in *Trends* (American Society of Planning Officials) no. 1 (1967), p. 9.

the financial provisions of the 1947 Act, therefore, is that in 1971 Britain was back to the position of 1959,[11] save that land sales had been made subject to capital gains tax.

The foregoing discussion demonstrates how far the market in Britain for urban land, or for potential urban land, departs from a purely competitive economic model. The supply of land and the demand for it are both greatly affected by governmental actions; moreover, the expectations of future governmental actions play a major role in the market at any date. The market for urban land and for land to be converted to urban uses thus includes a large element of political thought and action; this is not to deny the power of economic forces, but such forces operate within a political framework. If one decries the effect of rising land prices on the urban structure, as we do in this book, one cannot blame the result upon some impersonal market but rather must regard it, at least in part, as the result of political decisions.

One other major change has been made in the 1947 system of planning; it is of quite a different order, and it is not a matter of party political controversy. By the mid-1960s, it had become clear to those intimately involved with it that the 1947 system of plan making had shown serious deficiencies in dealing with some of the major planning problems then apparent. In particular, the system was too slow and too inflexible. The plans set out detailed proposals that were often rendered obsolete long before they could be carried through. Because of the detail, the Ministry officials took so long to consider and approve them that in many cases they were again quite out of date by the time approval was forthcoming. Consequently, an Act of 1968 provided that in future, development plans would take a new form. Local authorities would first prepare Structure Plans; these would be statements of general policy, showing trends and the broad patterns of future development. They would mainly consist of a written statement but with appropriate diagrams; they would not spell out proposals in detail, but they must indicate any necessary action areas, i.e., areas selected for comprehensive development in accordance with a detailed local plan to be prepared later. There is the same elaborate procedure for objections to the Minister as under the old system, with even more stringent conditions intended to ensure that the planning authority advertises the existence and content of the plan to the public. Under an act passed by Parliament in 1971, however, the right of objectors to make their case at an inquiry into a structure plan was virtually removed; the Minister in effect will select the groups he thinks ought to be heard. Again, the Minister has the last word in approving, rejecting, or modifying the plan.

For the public, though, there is a difference. By its nature, the Structure Plan will deal with principles and broad trends, not with detailed proposals. It will not contain much that ordinary persons would recognize as a plan. (This was one justification for the 1971 modification outlined above.) The detailed proposals, which will interest them, will come only later, in the so-called Local Plans (including action area plans) which are prepared within the framework of the Structure Plan. And these will not involve the local authority in direct contact with the Minister; objec-

[11] For accounts of the Land Commission see ibid., and Desmond Heap, *Introducing the Land Commission Act* (London: Sweet and Maxwell, 1967).

tions go to the local planning authority, and the decision whether or not to hold an inquiry is in principle theirs. But the Minister has a reserve power: he must be sent the Local Plan for information, and he has the right to intervene and say that the plan shall not have effect until he has approved it. And just as under the old system, the Minister will have power to "call in" and determine the verdict on a plan himself. So essentially, the new Local Plan system is a device for taking much of the detailed work off the backs of central government officials, while leaving them the reserve power of intervention in difficult or controversial cases.

The central point about the 1968 reforms—which have been introduced in stages across the country starting in 1969, 1970, and 1971—is that they change the detailed form and content of the plan. They do not change the essential basis of the 1947 system, as subsequently modified. The 1971 consolidating Town and Country Planning Act in effect combines the 1962 Act, which in essence is the 1947 Act with subsequent modifications, and the 1968 Act. The central feature of postwar British planning—the nationalization of development rights and their vesting in the local planning authorities—remains intact, and seems certain to be a long-enduring feature of British life. It is this feature that, at any rate formally, provides such a sharp contrast to the American system.

There is yet another characteristic of the British system of control that provides a sharp contrast to the American scene. It is not strictly a control over land use, though it has direct and immediate implications for it. Since the passage of the Distribution of Industry Act in 1945, the British government has had the power to regulate the establishment of new factory buildings, or the extension of existing ones, anywhere in Britain. An industrialist wishing to build must apply to the Department of Trade and Industry (formerly the Board of Trade) for an Industrial Development Certificate. The official can grant or refuse the certificate; there is no compensation procedure and no right of appeal. The precise details of operation have varied from time to time and so has the toughness with which the controls have been operated; these details need not concern us here. But broadly, the controls have been used to steer industry away from the more prosperous urban areas, such as London and Birmingham, and toward the Development Areas[12] where a whole host of positive incentives are in operation. It is estimated that between 1945 and 1970 about one million jobs were created in the Development Areas by these means. Since 1965, under the Control of Office and Industrial Development Act of that year, new office developments have also been subject to control under a similar procedure: an intending developer must obtain an Office Development Permit. This system has been subject to changes in detailed operation, but its broad effect again has been to steer new development away from central and inner London. Both the IDC and ODP procedures are linked to the local land use control system, for without possession of the appropriate central government permission, planning consent cannot be granted.

[12] The definition of Development Areas has changed since they were introduced in the Distribution of Industry Act of 1945. In 1972 they included a number of areas in the peripheral western and northern parts of Britain: parts of southwest England (Devon and Cornwall), most of Wales, Merseyside, England north of a line from Lancaster to Scarborough, Scotland, except Edinburgh. Northern Ireland offers a separate but similar set of incentives.

The Formal Structure of the American System

The formal structure of the American system of land use controls differs from the British system because of (1) the difference in history of land use controls, discussed above, and (2) the different distribution of legal and political powers among the various levels of government. Underlying these are differences in philosophy or objective, to which we shall return later. Under the American system of government, land use planning and control are dominantly the domain of local government (cities and counties) under powers delegated by the states. There have been few federal laws relating to land use (except management of federally owned lands) until recently. In the years since World War II, some federal subsidies have been available to state and local government for land planning and land acquisition, but federal controls over land use, or federal legal standards for local land use control, have been lacking. Although local governments have exercised their control over land use under legal and political powers granted by the states, the latter have given little if any supervision to local government in the application of those powers.

As a result, there has been and is great variability among local governments in land use planning and control. Some largely rural counties may do none; others may engage in limited planning and control; and still others—most larger cities— are likely to have relatively developed planning staffs and relatively developed land use controls. Some measure of commonality of approach has been gained as units of local government, and more especially their planning staffs, have learned from each other. But it has been the courts, particularly in their review of zoning appeals, which have been responsible for such uniformity as does exist. But, even here, variability is more notable than is conformity.[13]

Land use planning, zoning, and other land use controls are changing in the United States; they are different in 1972 compared with 1962, and they are likely to be different again in 1982. The federal government is beginning to play a larger role, not only in subsidies to encourage and guide state and local government, but in direct federal participation in land planning. For some years proposals have been made for a National Land Use Planning Act; the bill which passed the Senate in 1972 provided a system of federal grants to states for their land use planning and for greater direct federal participation in land planning. Even prior to this, there had been some stirrings among the states for state activities in land planning.[14] With very few exceptions, however, there is no formal process of land planning review from one level of government to another, such as obtains in Britain.

The high variability of American land use planning is to be seen not only in the detail and skill of such planning, which ranges from simplistic to highly sophisticated, but in the role that it plays in the local community. At one extreme, the land use plan (adopted formally by whatever procedures the local government has speci-

---

[13] Richard F. Babcock, *The Zoning Game—Municipal Practices and Policies* (Madison: University of Wisconsin Press, 1966).

[14] Fred Bosselman and David Callies, *The Quiet Revolution in Land Use Control*, report prepared for the U.S. Council on Environmental Quality (Washington: U.S. Government Printing Office, December 1971).

fied) is the basis on which all land use zoning is enacted, on which public works of all kinds (sewers, roads, schools, etc.) are constructed; and it is a major guide to many private investment decisions. At the other extreme, the land use plan seems to affect public and private actions very little. And, of course, there are all kinds of intermediate situations.

Regardless of the effectiveness of American land use plans prepared by local governments, their basic objectives differ from those of the British land use planning system, which are to preserve open land, preserve agriculture, and contain urban growth. To achieve these objectives the British have been willing to control the location of industrial development and provide a complex system of incentives for industry, householders, and local government. Land use planning and control in the United States are intended to guide development, which is not merely accepted but sought. Development may be guided for efficiency of the economy and for convenience of the public, but rarely will there be significant effort to stop it altogether. There is a deep-seated belief that all land should be used for its highest and best use. Reservation of land for public uses, such as parks or water supply, will typically be defended as the best use of the land; even reservation of wilderness areas from commercial use will be defended on the same ground. Environmental, ecological, and aesthetic considerations in land use have come much to the fore in the United States in the 1960s and may be expected to become more important in the 1970s. But, even here, the argument is more likely to revolve around where and how economic development should proceed, not whether it should proceed at all.

When it comes to control over private land use, local governments in the United States have several legal and administrative tools—all rather weaker in application than in theory. Zoning powers are the cornerstone of such land use control, as planning permission is the cornerstone of the British system. But formally separated as it is from the planning system, zoning is more restricted in its effects and is a more negative system of land use control. As later illustrations will show, a land use ordinance will specify what land uses are permitted (and may also attach many restrictions, such as building setbacks or heights) to these uses. The zoning ordinances may be detailed or general; they may apply to large areas or to small ones. Zoning cannot stop development altogether in order to preserve land in its undeveloped state. Zoning authorities lack the legal power to do this, for the courts have insisted that the landowner be left with some economically feasible use of his land. But the dividing line is a fine one between land use control in the general public interest and land use control that deprive the owner of the right to any economic use—and therein has lain the basis for many a court suit over zoning. Zoning provides little positive incentive to use the land in the way sought by the planning and zoning authorities; initiative lies in the hands of the private developer, and he may prefer to go elsewhere or not develop at all.

Land zoning may be changed by the zoning authority, on its own initiative or at the request of a landowner or developer. Rezoning is typically "upward"—i.e., toward more intensive land uses. Legally, a zoning board may "down zone"—i.e., limit land use to a less intensive purpose than was previously possible. If the landowner can prove that he has made investments rendered useless or partly so by the down-zoning, he can sue the zoning authority and perhaps recover damages.

Only in this case does American zoning include compensation. Compensation would not be granted for denial of development rights that had never been approved for the land, no matter how much the landowner may have expected them.

Another tool of American land use control is used in the subdivision of larger tracts into lots, including the layout of streets, and their offering for sale. While the effects of subdivision control on the ultimate shape and form of the community may be considerable, this form of control has not often been used as a device consciously to affect the amount or timing of land use or development. The subdivision requirements may make development costly and hence inhibit it; but unreasonable requirements would probably be challenged in court. Like zoning, subdivision control is more negative than positive in its effects.

Public health measures are another American tool of land use control, or at least a potential one. For instance, sources of water supply must often meet standards of public health authorities. So must sewage disposal methods. Had public health authorities in the United States adopted a stricter standard of sewage disposal— one that subsequent history has shown to be fully warranted in many cases—a great many of the more distantly scattered suburban residential subdivisions utilizing septic tanks could never have been developed.

Yet another largely potential developmental control lies in the use of building codes. These, established by most larger units of local government, specify building methods. Many of them have been criticized as unnecessarily restrictive, causing higher construction costs, which in turn help to exclude low-income families. But building codes also have been too permissive. Where they could have required special building methods in areas subject to floods, earthquakes, and tornadoes, they usually have not exerted this form of land use control.

Finally, all levels of government in the United States may acquire, own, and manage public land for many purposes, including parks. Where land is thought to have some special value that justifies withholding it from private development, the American practice is to acquire it by public or semi-public bodies rather than seek to reserve it by zoning or other control measures, as would be done in Britain. Location of public open spaces can do much to affect the value of neighboring private development, and thus to guide its location and timing.

The legal problems of public control over private land use in the United States are difficult but not insoluble. The basic problem, however, is political. What does the community seek for itself? How highly does it value some pattern of land use? What is it prepared to forgo or incur to attain that objective? The discussions and arguments over the tools of land use control (such as zoning) have more often confused than clarified the issues. Where there is general agreement over public goals for land use in the United States, the legal machinery to attain those goals exists or can readily be fashioned. Those who would profit by abrogation of the land use plan, where one exists, are more likely to couch their arguments in terms of opposition to the allegedly unfair regulations than they are to basic goals, but it is the goals that are really being opposed.

As noted, there is a deep-seated American belief in economic development in general, and in land development in particular. Zoning is used as a device to guide development, not to stop it. Zoning is a device for protecting the value of the development by ensuring that other incompatible uses will not threaten it. It is essentially a device for protecting private property, as Delafons emphasizes in quoting a New Jersey Supreme Court judgment:

> . . . The real object . . . of promoting the general welfare by zoning ordinances is to protect the private use and enjoyment of property, and to promote the welfare of the individual property owner. In other words, promoting the general welfare is a means of protecting private property.[15]

In this connection, it is useful in the United States to distinguish between situations where most land is already used for some urban purpose (as in older residential and commercial districts) and situations where previously undeveloped land is being brought into some form of urban land use. The former situation will attract widespread public support for rather restrictive land use zoning: there are property values and social objectives to be protected and defended; even the most politically conservative elements of the community will support effective land use zoning; a public hearing on a rezoning application is likely to draw a crowd of vociferous objectors to change—as much, or more, opposition as support. In a developing suburb, in contrast, the most vocal and economically powerful elements in the community fight land use control: they want to develop where, when, and as there is money to be made from development, and they want nothing to stand in their way; and there is no effective local group to oppose them politically. Thus, in the United States land use zoning can be both an effective tool to protect values of developed property and an inadequate tool to guide land use change.

FORMAL STRUCTURES COMPARED

To a large extent, plans and planning procedures in the two countries have a family resemblance. This is inevitably so, since planning by now is a well-developed discipline with generally recognized techniques. In each country the city or metropolitan plan is likely to contain similar information and similar analyses. It will have statistical and other information about past trends in population, employment, manufacturing output (perhaps), income (again perhaps), and transportation, with some projections or forecasts for each of these items. There will almost certainly be a map or maps of the present structure of activities or land uses, and of the projected or proposed future structure, though these may vary considerably as to detail from plan to plan, from country to country, and even from time to time in the same country. Thus, in Britain, the 1968 Planning Act laid down that, in future, general structure plans should not contain land use detail, merely broad diagrammatic plans of urban or regional objectives.

The plan is also likely to contain a statement of policy objectives dealing with specific policy areas, with some account of the ways these objectives are to be achieved. It will conclude with a statement (spelled out in more or less detail with the aid of statements and maps) of the planned distribution of activities and land

---

[15] Delafons, *Land Use Controls . . .* , p. 33.

uses at some stated future date or dates. Commonly, too, there will be some hierarchy of plans, whether provided by the same planning office or by different offices at different scales or levels: a broad regional plan will provide the framework for subsequent more detailed local plans. In that case, the general regional plan usually will be especially concerned with social and economic forces and will be prepared by planners trained in the social sciences, while the more detailed plans will be especially concerned with physical design and will tend to be prepared by planners trained in civic design.

In general, plans in Britain since the 1947 Act have been more standardized than the corresponding plans in the United States. Regulations laid down by the central government department (the Ministry of Town and Country Planning in 1947, subsequently the Ministry of Housing and Local Government, and then from 1970 the Department of the Environment) have been made under the act, and have specified not merely the procedure for submitting plans and for revising them, but also the form of the plans, in considerable detail; the notation to be used on the maps, for instance, was standardized. This reflects the fact that there is a much greater degree of centralized monitoring and approval under the British system than under the American. Clearly, all plans prepared by professional planning staffs —the general or comprehensive planners described above—must be approved by some body, generally a political one but perhaps also some more elevated bureaucracy, before having official force. The critical distinction is whether the plan needs approval by some external governmental body, or not.

In the United States a citizen planning board usually exists; its members are likely to have been appointed by the chief elected official of the city (mayor) rather than elected. Boards differ greatly in their dedication and competence. At best, the planning board reviews the planning effort during its progress, making its contribution to the content and direction of the plan as the latter moves along, so that the plan, when finally completed, is likely to be approved with little difficulty. Sometimes, however, planning boards will have made little input into a plan during its preparation by the professional planning staff; hence the board must review the plan at its completion, adopting or modifying it as the board thinks best. In some cities and states a public hearing is required before the plan can be finally adopted; in others such a hearing is likely but not obligatory. Planning board approval is a necessary but not final step in official adoption of a city or metropolitan plan; the elected governing board (by whatever name it is called) must also approve the plan. This may be more or less pro forma if the planning board is strong and has done its work well, or it may constitute a wholly new review, from which the plan emerges with major modifications. In the end a plan may be approved, or it may be rejected and the planning staff instructed to come up with a different plan.

In the United States no formal review and adoption of city and metropolitan plans is usually required by any unit of government except the city, metropolitan council, or county involved. With perhaps one or two exceptions, state governments do not review and formally approve such plans, nor do federal agencies unless the city or other unit of local government subsequently seeks a loan or grant of funds for some purpose related to the plan. Even then, the review by the federal agency may be limited to those parts of the plan that involve the specific function (highways, sewers, etc.) for which funds are sought.

In Britain the situation has been otherwise. The local authority plan (and subsequent amendments to it) would in effect have to surmount several hurdles. It would first have to be approved by that authority's planning committee—a body usually consisting of elected local politicians, but sometimes containing some co-opted members with an interest in planning, such as the representative from the local voluntary civic association, if any. It would then need to be approved by the full Council, though in many cases this would be a formality after the planning committee had given the plan its blessing. Then it would be submitted to the relevant Minister for planning (in London or Cardiff or Edinburgh) for approval, and published as such. Members of the public would be given a time period to state objections, as a result of which the Minister might declare an administrative (not judicial) public inquiry to be held by one of his own inspectors; such inquiries have been almost invariable for all development plans and revisions of them, as well as for most amendments. Eventually, after studying the inspector's recommendations, the Minister would give his own decision, which would be final; he might approve the plan unchanged, or with such amendments as he chose to make, which would then be binding on the local planning authority. In Britain, therefore, the degree of centralized control is quite considerable; and up to the 1968 Act it applied to every piece of the plan, including the smallest amendment to it. It was primarily because of the delays thus arising, indeed, that the 1968 Act was passed. Since then, the specific approval of the Minister has been needed only for the so-called structure plan—the general plan setting forth the framework for the more detailed local plans—and its subsequent revisions. But the Minister has the reserve power to order an inquiry for any of these local plans, though the clear intention is that normally he will not need to exercise it.

As noted earlier in this chapter, in Britain plan making and development control are inseparably linked—control must be exercised in accordance with the plan—whereas in the United States planning and zoning are two separate steps. Zoning ordinances and maps are prepared separately; they may or may not be based upon the plan. Zoning ordinances describe areas to which certain zoning classifications apply. Typically, ordinances specify the kinds of land uses, the required building setbacks from the street, the required side and back yard (garden) requirements, height limits, floor area ratios, and other requirements or conditions. But there are many instances in which zoning actions are taken without *any* plan as a basis or guide, and still more cases when specific zoning action is taken contrary to the plan. In the detailed studies in the United States that underlie this book, several cases of this kind were found and studied.[16]

The planning staff and board may also be the zoning staff and board; this would seem to be the situation in more than two-thirds of the units of local government;[17]

---

[16] Marion Clawson, *Suburban Land Conversion in the United States—An Economic and Governmental Process* (Baltimore: Johns Hopkins University Press, for Resources for the Future, 1971).

[17] Allen Manvel, *Local Land and Building Regulation—How Many Agencies? What Practice? How Much Personnel?*, Research Report No. 6, National Commission on Urban Problems (Washington: U.S. Government Printing Office, 1968).

but there may be separate boards and staffs, which may or may not cooperate closely with one another. In any case, the plan as such has no legal power over any private developer until it has been translated into a zoning ordinance—and there is many a slip 'twixt cup and the lip. There have been many cases in which courts have refused to uphold zoning ordinances that attempted to incorporate plans by reference; the specific land descriptions must be written into the zoning ordinance.

Where the zoning action in the United States is taken by a special zoning board, or by the planning board that is also the zoning board, appeals from the board's action may normally be taken to the general governing body of the unit of local government, and in some cases or on some grounds to courts as well. When requests for zoning modification are heard, citizen groups and others, in addition to the applicant, may present statements of fact or opinions about the desirability of the action sought. Zoning is far more a political than a legal process; legal circumstances may limit what can be done, or legal irregularities may provide a basis of appeal to the courts; but, in the last analysis, the judgment to grant or to refuse a zoning action or a zoning appeal is a political action. Once taken, a zoning action can be reversed only with difficulty. A landowner or a developer may seek to have a tract of land zoned for more intensive residential development, or for commercial instead of residential use; if the zoning or rezoning is granted, it can be repealed by the same body, but the owner is entitled to damages if he can show that he has made investments predicated upon the zoning. More important than this legal limitation is the political one: the zoning having been granted, it takes relatively great political power to undo it. This is where the landowner and/or developer is in a much stronger strategic position than the general public; the latter may successfully oppose rezoning of a tract a dozen times, as it is brought up time and again, yet if it fails once, the landowner wins. Moreover, typically, the developer is not bound by the statements he makes in support of rezoning. He may paint a picture of a beautiful development he plans to make, but what he basically seeks is rezoning from R-5 (large lot residential) to R-1 (small lot residential) or to C-2 (moderately intensive commercial), and once the rezoning is approved he can ignore his promises—and often has.

Zoning in the United States is often a rather complex process, with a jargon and procedures all its own—easily enough understood by the insiders and practitioners, but often baffling to outsiders. At the end of 1971 in Montgomery County, Maryland, a suburban county bordering Washington, D.C., there were twenty-six different kinds of zones defined in the zoning ordinance, as follows:

Thirteen residential zones: R-A, agricultural residential; RA-C, agricultural residential cluster; R-E, residential estate; R-R, rural residential; R-150, a form of restricted residential; R-90, one-family detached restricted; R-60, one-family detached; R-40, one-family semi-detached and two-family detached; R-T, town house; R-30, multiple-family low density; R-20, multiple-family medium density; R-10, multiple-family high density; and R-H, multiple-family high-rise planned residential.

Seven commercial zones: C-O, commercial-office building; C-P, commercial office park; C-1, local commercial; C-2, general commercial; C-T, commercial transition; C-3, highway commercial, and C-I, country inn.

Three industrial zones: I-1, light industrial; I-2, heavy industrial; and I-3, industrial park.

Three zones of mixed uses: P-R-C, planned retirement community; R-C-B-D, multiple family, central business district residential; and P-N, planned neighborhood zone.

These zones differ, to greater or lesser degree, in the specific land uses permitted, in the exceptions to those uses granted by the County Council under special circumstances, in the building setbacks required, in the requirements for front, side, and back yards, in the building heights permitted, and in other ways. In the C-2 zone (a general commercial zone), for instance, a wide variety of commercial uses is recognized in the ordinance, as well as any multiple-family dwellings provided for in the R-30 zone. In addition, the County Council may authorize other commercial uses as special exceptions.

Once zoned in a particular category, a developer can ordinarily develop the property as he chooses, subject to the conditions in the zoning classification. He must have a building permit, which must conform to the zoning classification, but the building permit is ordinarily allowed as a matter of right if this compliance with zoning is clear. The builder chooses the actual use of the land, subject to the zoning ordinance; and, where many different uses are permitted, as in the example above, the planning office has little control over the specific land uses made.

For some zones in Montgomery County—notably the P-R-C, R-C-B-D, and P-N zones listed above—the developer is given considerable latitude to propose land uses and development programs. In return, he is required to submit his proposals to site plan review as a condition of obtaining a building permit. The Planning Board may refuse him a permit, even though he meets the apparent conditions of the zone, if they do not approve his site plan. In this case, the procedure approaches that typical in Britain, where site plan conformity to plans is required. However, this procedure is relatively uncommon in the United States, and indeed is just being developed in Montgomery County. It is likely to be put to court test, on the grounds of arbitrariness and unreasonableness if none other, before it is fully accepted and widely used.

In Britain, the 1947 Act (and its subsequent amendments and reformulations) gives a clear right of appeal to developers against the exercise of development control, just as it does against the original formulation of the development plan. Thus, a citizen could object against the plan on the ground that it zones his particular property as greenbelt land rather than residential land; he could, even after his objection was rejected and the plan approved, then apply for planning permission on that land, and when rejected by the planning authority then appeal past them to the Minister. But here, just as in the procedure for objections against the development plan, the appeal system is not judicial but quasi-judicial. The appellant has no automatic right of redress to a court hearing; he can only hope that the Minister will decide that the case is of sufficient public interest to hold a full public inquiry. Very many such inquiries have been held, in fact, on appeals against planning refusals when the applications were clearly contraventions of the plan; and while the Minister and his inspector normally uphold the planning authority in these cases, in about one case in ten they allow the appeal. The authority may refuse permission for the building of a house in a village, on the ground that the policy is to restrict the growth of that village; the Minister may allow an appeal on the ground that the particular site is of no value and that the development merely fills a gap in the existing pattern of development in the village.

But the city or metropolitan plan should be of use in guiding actions of its government, aside from the control it may or may not exert on private developers and landowners. The extension of public services of all kinds should be in conformity with the general plan: highways, roads, streets, parking areas, and other transportation should be based upon the plan; so should water lines and sewer lines, both in their location and in their capacity; so should schools, and parks, and the host of other public services.

Sometimes, indeed, this objective has been achieved in American cities, but far more commonly it has not been. It is in this area, in the United States, that the relationship between the general physical planner and the limited function planner is critical. If the latter—who may well be called an engineer rather than a planner —has his own ideas about where the new throughway or sewer line should go and about how big it should be, and if he is able to persuade the general governing board of his ideas, then the general plan is modified or perhaps thrown out. One could argue that the responsibility of the general governing body is to be consistent —not to approve general plans it had no intention of implementing and not to take specific actions contradictory to the general plans it had approved. But, in fact, general governing bodies have often taken such inconsistent or contradictory actions. Sometimes they have seemed unaware of what they were doing—the implications of the general plan for specific actions simply were not perceived. More often, they would defend their actions by saying that each case had "to stand on its own merits," without ever defining a "merit." One could, of course, logically defend a general plan as a general guide to action, recognizing that modest deviations and adjustments would be proper to meet specific local situations, but frequently the degree of deviation from the adopted general plan had been so great as to largely destroy the latter. In some cases, it would appear that local governing boards were responding to pressures of different electorates when their specific actions conflicted with the general plan they had approved. The general plan had attracted one electorate and the process of plan approval had attracted one kind of political support; with approval, that electorate went to sleep, and its support died down. Then, specific zoning actions could be taken or specific public works adopted to please a quite different group of the electorate; and if this was done relatively quietly and on a modest scale, it would arouse too little opposition from the supporters of the general plan to cause any real difficulty.

In Britain, at a formal level, all this should be avoidable; the process laid down in the 1947 Act (modified somewhat in the 1968 Act) specified that the development plan—and each subsequent revision of it—show all proposals of different public authorities, including other agencies or departments within the local authority itself. Thus potential conflicts, both between departments of the authority itself and between that authority and other agencies, should be avoided. In the county boroughs and in the counties, the local authority is simultaneously the statutory planning authority and the education authority, the highway authority and the main drainage authority. The county boroughs, too, are also housing authorities. However, this ignores the fact that in county boroughs especially, the planning office may be a junior partner without effective funds: the highway engineer and the housing manager are much older established and manage large capital funds, which may give them predominant weight in the planning decision-making process.

Furthermore, neither county borough nor county is the authority for hospitals (which are controlled by quite separate executive authorities, responsible to a central government department) or for the most important major highways in the counties, or for the provision of public services like gas or electricity, or even in many cases for water supply. In fact, until the government announced a change in 1971, government departments and so-called statutory undertakers (public utility corporations) had been specifically exempted from the need to obtain planning permission for their developments, though they must inform the planning authority of their proposals. In some cases—as for instance in the celebrated case of the Knightsbridge Barracks, a skyscraper structure overlooking Hyde Park in London —a government department went ahead and built, in the teeth of opposition from the local planners and indeed from the vocal public. An exception to this rule is the construction of major highways (trunk roads), where the Minister must call a public inquiry if an objection is raised by a local authority (and many do so if there is a sufficient volume of objection from the general public), but can afterwards overrule the recommendation of the inspector if he so decides, just as in any other case. In a number of cases, in fact, local planning authorities have found themselves making formal objections to the routes of new highways through their areas; but normally, the engineers of the central government Department of the Environment maintain sufficiently close contact with local highway engineers to avoid this open conflict.

In both Britain and the United States proposed new highways are one of the most fertile sources of planning conflict, especially where they penetrate into urban areas. But in Britain during the 1960s and early 1970s it appeared that much of the potential conflict within governments was in effect being internalized, hidden from public view by the tendency to integrate transportation and general planning within the same agency. The largest local planning authority in the country, the Greater London Council, integrated its Department of Transportation and Department of Planning as early as 1969; the central government followed in October 1970, when it integrated its planning ministry (the Ministry of Housing and Local Government) and its Ministry of Transport into a single giant Department of the Environment.

In each country, with limited exceptions, the plans developed and approved by the general governing body of a unit of local government are effective only within the limits of that unit of local government. That is, the city makes a land use plan for the area within its boundaries, not for land adjoining or surrounding it. In some limited cases in the United States cities do have some zoning power beyond their boundaries, where it can be shown that projected developments outside the boundary would have serious effect within the boundary.

British cities have the power, under the 1952 Town Development Act, to locate their public housing in other local government units beyond their boundaries, even many miles away—but only by agreement with that other unit of government, which must see some advantage in it. In practice, many cities have found it difficult to reach such agreements on a scale sufficient to meet their housing needs; they may in addition have been unwilling to export their populations, so that they have been compelled or have chosen to solve their problems by action within their own restricted boundaries. Considering the arbitrary nature of most present city or metropolitan boundaries, most of which were established many years ago when the situation was different, this limitation on the power of the city is great. The British county boroughs, for instance, were created by an Act of 1888; though most of them have been able to make boundary extensions since then, including some major ones in the interwar period, they have come up against increasing resistance from surrounding county authorities wishing to preserve themselves against the threat of urban encroachment.

In the United States cities have expanded, but the process of boundary extensions is so fraught with difficulties and is so irregular, both temporally and for various cities, that it has not been a practical means of coping with the problem. The legal city no longer conforms to the physical, still less to the economic or social city, so that the legal city is forced to act in ways that would not be rational if only the problems of the urban areas could be attacked as a whole.

The dream of the pioneer thinkers and writers on planning—men like Howard, Geddes, or Mumford—was that rational planning was necessarily region-wide, embracing the whole area within which the urban economy or urban society had its impact. But in practice this idea of city region planning has remained almost everywhere an unrealized aspiration. The only way of realizing it would be through a quite radical transformation of local government, which would be based on the principle of metropolitan or city region government. This is a solution much discussed in both countries since World War II, and in 1969 such a solution was actually recommended for Britain by the official Royal Commissions on Local Government in England and in Scotland. The reform of local government proposed for England and Wales, which seems certain to be carried through by 1974, does partially recognize the metropolitan principle. But around the largest urban agglomerations, where planning problems and conflicts are most acute, it leaves the fast-growing suburbs under county, not metropolitan government. And elsewhere, though it unites cities and their surrounding counties into new units of government with overall plan-making powers, it reserves other important powers—including control over development—to local county districts, which in many cases will continue to represent the rural interests. In accepting this compromise, the government in Britain—just like the state governments in the United States when they take no action whatsoever—essentially is responding to political pressures and popular ideologies that are either anti-city, or deeply rooted in an agrarian past, or both.

The Values of the British System

This last point helps to illustrate the important rule that a formal description of each system, though essential to its understanding, is not enough. In addition one should understand the values which support the system and which, in turn, the system reinforces, and comprehend the political power, or powers, that the system represents. Many descriptions of the planning system, because they are written by planners or by people sympathetic to the ideology of planners, miss this point. Perhaps more important than any specific skill or technique that he possesses is the fact that the professional planner in any country is likely to be instilled with a sense of commitment to a general public good. He thus places great emphasis on comprehensiveness of planning, on consideration of economic and social trends, and on general public welfare. His language is likely to contain many references to "sound principles of civic design," "wise land use," "balanced development," and the like—although many of these may be notable for their lack of precision or exact definition. Implicit in all these statements is the conviction—amounting to an ideology—that the public good exists and that it can be identified.

Such an attitude is useful and even essential for a professional who must spend his career serving political masters; it gives him a certain moral strength in negotiating with them, and perhaps it imparts a certain consistency to the plans, which they would otherwise lack. But it does tend toward the belief that all conflicts between groups and individuals will disappear, given sufficient goodwill and professional objectivity. In other words, it specifically ignores political realities of conflicts of interest and objectives. The danger of this is that language relating to the general public interest may be used to mask sectional private interests. Many an American plan has had as a basic objective the preservation of the social character of the community—in itself not an objectionable goal but one which, further extended, could mean the exclusion of racial, ethnic, or lower-income groups who are rejected as part of the future community. Such an objective would rarely be stated, and the mechanisms for its achievement would most likely be defended on quite different grounds. Similarly, British county plans may argue against future urban growth on the grounds of preserving the agricultural land, whereas the real objective is to avoid an influx of low-income urbanites who may disrupt the social pattern and inflict heavy education or social welfare bills upon the rural community.

It is particularly important, then, to go behind the formal statements in the plans, and to look at the values they serve and reinforce.

The British system has sought to achieve some specific objectives, among the most important being: containment of urban areas, especially large ones; protection of agricultural land and other open countryside of special value (e.g., for recreation, scientific research, or conservation); and creation of self-contained and socially balanced communities. Underlying the objectives has been a set of values, some fairly explicit and understood, some less immediately evident. One of the most important is the control of the pace and direction of economic, social, and physical change. Change as such is not opposed; rather, there is an attempt to organize and control it so as to maintain continuity and stability in society. Another aim has been to avoid public diseconomies in the use of resources, or, as the econo-mists would call them, external costs that could be avoided by conscious planning.

Yet another goal of the system has been a preference for a certain physical quality of urban life, expressed by compactness, smallness, neatness, tidiness, and what is described as a human scale. This leads to preference for small towns as opposed to big cities, for high-density over low-density residential development, and for an urban structure that stresses local movements and relationships on foot rather than wider contacts by car. Lastly, there is a decided feeling for the con-servation of what is best from the past, whether in the towns or in the countryside, and a suspicion of large-scale, rapid development save where the existing environ-ment is held to be beyond redemption. In particular, there is a deep-set feeling that professional planners are exercising a sort of stewardship of the land, which is held to be a unique natural resource to be preserved from one generation to the next.

In many ways, and without using the word in any party political sense, these values are deeply conservative. The basic one—control of change—really under-lies the others, which are expressions of it. The maintenance of small towns, where social relationships are simpler and more easily comprehended, and the steward-ship of the countryside are essentially values dating from the agrarian past and perhaps reflect a deep repugnance for the effects of the Industrial Revolution. Such a set of values is far from unique to Britain; it has been a recurrent theme of American political and social thought. What is distinctive about the British system of 1947 is that a powerful and effective administrative machine and a basic change in property law made it possible for the values to be realized.

The character of the system thus created was, and is, a fundamentally elitist one. It gave guardianship of the values of society to professional planners, who were to be finally accountable to a democratic process, but were to be given a very large degree of freedom in their day-to-day decisions. It thus assumed that planners could be like Solomon, exercising disinterested guidance in the interests of the whole community and reconciling any conflicts of interest. This concept of the higher public interest riding above sectional interests is central to the concept of the British planning system. As in so many other aspects of British life, the system is politically unitary in character, relying on the judgment and incorruptibility of the informed bureaucrat. The public interest, thus defined, was seen in 1947 in terms of a coalition of men of good sense and good will. On the one hand, there was the rural interest, concerned above all with the containment and control of change in the countryside. And on the other, there was what we can call the urban planning interest, concerned with the creation of model communities each of which would avoid the mistakes of earlier unplanned urban growth. In 1947, given the idealism attending the successful end to a popular war, such a coalition seemed natural and workable.

The difficulty was that it contained potential conflicts of sectional interest. The rural interests were by no means identical with, or even reconcilable with, the interests of the new community builders. Given these conflicts, they might have been resolved by a strong central planning authority that would maintain the guardianship of the public interest. And such an authority seems to have been in the mind of the pioneers who created the 1947 system—men like Osborn, Abercrombie, or Reith. But the Labour government, in drafting the 1947 Act, drew back from such a radical conception. It gave the planning powers to the larger local authorities, maintaining only reserve powers at the center in the Minister's right to approve plans and to hear appeals. This balance of power might have worked in a static or slow-moving society where there was plenty of time to absorb the implications of change. But British society since 1947 has been far from slow-moving. The problem was compounded in turn by failure to reform the local government system, though such a reform was actively contemplated at the time the 1947 Act was passed. As a result, planning powers were effectively divided between urban authorities (the county boroughs) and rural authorities (the counties). And since in many cases urban growth had already lapped beyond city boundaries at the time the act was passed, this meant in effect that the planning of urban growth in Britain was given to rural authorities, which politically were almost bound to be opposed to it.

To an American, this opposition will not appear self-evident. But in the English counties the preservation of a way of life seemed to rank even then far above the claims of economic growth. These counties in many cases were controlled by their more prosperous residents, to whom the countryside was a place of consumption rather than a place of production. Even those concerned productively in the countryside—the farmers—might well place the preservation of their traditional way of life above the economic gains they might obtain from selling their land to the developer. Thus it was that a system designed for the control of change in the public interest became, in many cases, a system for the restriction of change in favor of sectional interests. Above all, it has preserved the status quo, or something near to it, for existing residents and for those who represent their interests politically. It has not necessarily been disagreeable to the professionals who serve the system in the rural counties, who have been able to achieve many of their formal objectives—such as containment and protection—all the more effectively. What it seems to have done, in too many cases, is to divorce these formal or physical objectives, and their means of realization, from the more general public interest of the wider society, including the residents of the cities. It was partly to escape from this limitation and to return to more general objectives, indeed, that the 1968 Planning Act was passed and the reform of local government was embarked upon.

The Values of the American System

The American system of land use control, in contrast, is quite specifically and openly concerned with the defense of private interests—a point made by a senior British civil servant:

> . . . we have persistently averted our eyes from the fact that the "public interest" which we believe planning serves is sometimes a quite narrow private interest. The American system makes much more explicit the motives which underlie disputes about land use.[18]

[18] Delafons, *Land Use Controls* . . . , p. 113.

American local politics tend to follow a model, called by Meyerson and Banfield *utilitarian*, whereby local interests and pressure groups organize and express their objectives quite freely and openly to obtain their objectives. The British system, in this terminology, conforms much more to the contrasted *unitary* model, in which decisions are taken centrally according to some supposed concept of the general public interest. Meyerson and Banfield conclude, and Delafons may be tentatively agreeing, that a unitary model is more favorable to upper middle-class groups who know how to manipulate a centralized power structure; the utilitarian model, in contrast, is more populist and thereby, perhaps, more democratic.

Whatever the case, it is a historical fact that zoning was originally introduced for specifically restrictive purposes, to protect the private property of a local group against speculative developments and unwanted newcomers.[19] Its first recorded use —against Chinese laundries in California—had specific undertones of racial segregation. When, therefore, the St. Louis suburb of Black Jack (Missouri) rezoned in 1970 to prevent construction of moderate-income housing for black families, it was acting strictly in accordance with one original purpose of the system.

As in Britain, so in the United States there is a certain consistency between the governmental machinery and the values it is intended to embody and reinforce. In the United States there has always been a positive attitude toward growth and development in general. The land speculator has been not merely tolerated but admired. New activity and business are ordinarily welcomed in a community. In recent years, partly influenced by the conservation movement, there has been some weakening of support for development, or at least some doubt about its universally experienced virtues; but this has not yet gone far toward affecting land use decisions at the local grass-roots level.

In thus stressing the common American attitude toward land as one of development, commercialism, and exploitation, we do not suggest that different attitudes have not been held. There has always been something of a "land ethic" adhered to by many farmers and forest owners among other people; some have regarded the land as possessing more than a capital value. Many immigrants were attracted by the idea of landownership for use; many homesteaders of the public lands and many purchasers of homes regarded their land as a personal and social base as well as an economic one. Nevertheless, the dominant attitude toward land throughout American history has been one of growth or development. Similarly, not all Britishers have held the land mystique described earlier in this chapter; indeed, some have been as interested in turning a fast pound as any American interested in a fast dollar. But the dominant attitudes in the two countries have been different.

In spite of important exceptions, most Americans seem to have little instinctive feeling for the preservation either of open land as such or of agricultural land. This is in sharp contrast to the British attitude, and it results from different historical experience. First, while British people see agriculture as a force that saved them from blockade in World War II, Americans see an industry that has produced enormous quantities of unwanted surplus crops. The underlying attitude is

19 Ibid., pp. 19–20, 29.

that the increasing productivity of industry will bring forth all the production needed, without any worry about land supply and real cost reduction. With defined exceptions, such as the California orange groves or certain market garden (truck farming) areas, this may be objectively true for American and British farming alike. But we are concerned here not so much with objective truth as with the subjective emotional attitude.

Second, there is still (despite a recent weakening of faith) a basic belief in the supreme virtue of free enterprise and in the importance of not fettering it by a host of controls. Put more formally, the belief seems to be that negative economic spillovers may be a price worth paying for the productivity of the system. Any controls that are imposed should be designed to allow the system to work more effectively, not to restrict it.

Third, this attitude goes with a certain mistrust of political processes, at any rate at the local level. There is a widespread underlying belief that politicians are possibly corrupt and officials weak or powerless. In other words, no one is seen as guardian of the general public interest—except the courts, which occupy a far more important place in the American system of land use controls than in the British. This attitude, in turn, is related to the extraordinary degree of fragmentation of local government in the American system; hence most local units can only be viewed as the guardians of strictly local interests.

These underlying features mean that, as compared with the British system, the whole process of decision making is much more dispersed, and is seen as such.

No single person can take into account all the factors that are involved, nor bear all the costs, nor realize all the gains. The task, the responsibility, and the gains are shared. . . . actions are often nullified, in part or in whole, by other actions. Opportunities are missed because no one is in a position to capitalize on them.[20]

In the land development process of the United States, the multiplicity of different agents is bewildering to anyone coming from a more centralized system. There are developers—themselves a fairly complex group, to be distinguished from the land-owners on one side, and the builders (of various sizes and types) on the other. There are government agencies—federal, state, possibly regional, and a variety of different local government agencies—that may well work in different directions for different ends. Agencies may use or fail to use a variety of different tools: the general land use plan, zoning, subdivision control, and the provision of a variety of public services. Any of these agencies may take mutually contradictory decisions, sometimes in quick succession. Then, the various providers of capital and credit—whether to the builder or to the intending home owner—obviously play a critical role. Finally, the home buyer or apartment renter is highly influential: he is final consumer of the product and the consumer is still king, albeit a limited monarch.[21]

The overall conclusion, from a detailed study of the urban development process in three areas of the Northeastern Urban Complex, is just how confused and con-

[20] Clawson, *Suburban Land Conversion* . . . , p. 75.
[21] Ibid., p. 74.

fusing the whole system is in practice. What is lacking, as compared with the situation in a typical European country, is any sense of a central design. Even where an area had some sort of a planning organization—so-called—that organization did not really make overall plans that became the major basis for public and private action. Neither paper plans, nor even zoning ordinances, had any finality; they were broken with impunity.

> In the suburban development process with its numerous actors, there was nothing remotely resembling the architect with his blueprint for the building or the conductor with his score for the orchestra. Each actor "did his thing," taking the existence and the actions of the other actors as part of the environment within which his decision making operated.[22]

*   *   *   *

In assessing the achievements and limitations of the American and the British systems of planning and control, then, it is particularly important to bear all these different underlying objectives and values in mind. Before a valid comparison can be made, we should ask two related questions. The first is: How far has each system been *effective* in realizing the values and objectives it served, and how far have *side effects* occurred that were unwanted and unforeseen by those who administered the machinery? The second question is: What elements of each system might be borrowed by the other to help meet these deficiencies, and if so, what changes might be needed to meet the rather different circumstances in the other country? We will try to answer the first of these questions for the British system, and then for the American. The second we will reserve for the final chapter of the book.

THE ACHIEVEMENTS AND LIMITATIONS OF THE BRITISH SYSTEM

In trying to pass a judgment on the British system, we have to bear in mind that the system changed its character substantially during the postwar period; a number of things happened to change the 1947 prescription. The planned developments—the new towns and expanded towns—together provided only a small fraction of all new housing built in Britain, instead of a large majority. Between 1958 and 1969 a majority of all new housing every year in Britain was produced once again by private speculative builders for sale, as had been the case between the two World Wars. The decisions to build or not to build these houses were taken as the result of a complex set of interactions between different agents: local authority planners, developers, builders, landowners, potential buyers, and credit companies. In this respect, the system became more like that in the United States. But there was one critical difference from the old system and from the American system: land development rights remained nationalized, and finally, at least in formal terms, the professional planner had power in theory to say what should be developed, where, and when.

[22] Ibid., p. 260.

The most important result has been that this power has been used to contain the growth of urban areas. Greenbelts have been drawn around the conurbations and the larger freestanding cities. Thus, valuable agricultural land and scenic areas have been preserved—something that only the nationalization of development rights made possible. But often greenbelts have been made and maintained for neither of these uses; they have been justified on the basis that continued suburban growth ought to be stopped. Two results have almost inevitably followed. One is that the density of new development has been increased. This partly results from deliberate policy and partly from the land shortage consequent on the containment policy—which will form the subject of separate comments below. The other is that new development has been diverted elsewhere, beyond the greenbelt, into additions to smaller towns or villages. The process of suburbanization, in other words, has been transferred from the urban periphery to the countryside at the fringe of the metropolitan area, or beyond.

But—and this is the next important result—the process is still one of suburbanization. The process of creating independent, self-contained and balanced communities, which loomed so large in the original postwar program, catered for only a very small part of the total new housing development that actually took place. So the bulk of the housing, during the late 1950s and throughout the 1960s, has been built by the private developer for sale on mortgage, just as in the United States. It has been accompanied by schools, shops, and necessary services, through a combination of efforts by the professional planners—both the land use planners and the planners of special functions such as schools—and private commercial agencies. But it has not been accompanied by the provision of basic jobs. The process of urban containment has actually intensified the decentralization of residential population from the core cities to the suburbs of British metropolitan areas, since it has put a greater distance between the city and the average suburban development. But though there has been faster growth of jobs in the suburban ring than in the core—and, in many areas during the 1960s, an actual decline in core employment—the whole process of decentralization of jobs has been more tardy and more limited than the outward push of people and homes. Many new jobs have been created in the cities. The paradoxical result is that the British postwar planning system, one of the basic objectives of which was to reduce commuting distances, times, and costs, has actually increased them as compared with the interwar situation.

One last main result, also, was quite unintended by the architects of the 1947 system. With the financial provisions of that system dismantled in the fifties, speculation in land for development once again became profitable. With rapidly rising population after 1955 and even more rapid formation of new households, coupled with a general and accelerating process of inflation typical of the postwar period almost throughout the western world, property ownership became a splendid investment and a hedge against inflation. But this in turn increased the speculative pressure on land. Even if there had been no effective planning controls, doubtless these influences would have caused the price of land to ratchet upwards in Britain, as it did in the United States and many other countries. But by identifying the land that could be developed and making it fairly certain that other tracts would not be developed, the controls increased the pressure by channelling it. The gap between land without planning permission, and land with it, tended constantly to increase. Because of this, the price of land to the builder tended to increase. As he was experiencing pressures on other costs—albeit less seriously—at the same time, the builder was virtually forced to reduce the land content of his housing package if he was to continue to sell in the same bracket of the market as before. Some seem to have given up the attempt and to have concentrated only on higher-priced housing where the cost of land, in relation to the total package, matters less. (Others may have left the British market altogether, concentrating on retirement or vacation homes abroad.) But yet others, seeking to cope, progressively reduced both the size of the plot on which they built, and the quantity and quality of interior fittings. Unlike the local authority builders of public housing, they were under no obligation to produce dwellings of a fixed standard, save the general demand to meet the quality standards of the National House Builders' Guarantee Registration scheme. And in general, they found local authority professional planners sympathetic to their efforts to increase densities and save land.

The local authorities in the urban areas, who have been building between 40 and 50 percent of all new housing during the 1960s, have faced a slightly different but equally difficult problem as the result of containment policies on the part of the neighboring counties. Though, under the 1952 Town Development Act, in some cases they have been able to conclude agreements with nearby local authorities in the counties—and sometimes with more distant ones—in many other cases they have failed. In any case, they have often been less than enthusiastic about such agreements because they felt they had a responsibility to house their own people, especially where these people were displaced by slum clearance, and because they feared the loss of property tax (rateable value) that would result. So they have tended to prefer to build within their own boundaries, even where this meant progressively higher densities and the substitution of multistory apartment blocks for single-family houses. Because play space near the dwelling was lacking, these blocks were deservedly unpopular with families having small children; yet they continued to attract differentially high central government subsidies throughout most of the 1960s, and big city authorities responded to the inducement. Whereas a full three-fourths of all local authority dwellings completed between 1945 and 1960 were single-family homes; in the early 1960s this proportion fell to just over one-half, and then in the late 1960s to under one-half.

The private builder, faced with land shortage in the counties and consequent rising land costs, responded differently—though equally perversely. He did not switch from single-family home construction to apartment construction, as many developers did during the 1960s in the United States. In contrast to the public sector, during this decade apartments constituted less than 10 percent of the private sector output of housing in England and Wales. In the upper part of the housing market, where the land price was a sufficiently small part of the final sales price, the developer could easily carry the cost, and some probably switched their main efforts into this price bracket. But those developers whose programs had traditionally concentrated at the lower end of the price range were faced with a peculiarly acute problem, to which they responded by restricting the space standards and the interior facilities of the houses they built. Evidence for this is provided by several cases in the developer survey conducted as part of the PEP study;[23] it received indirect support from the figures of new mortgaged houses published by the Nationwide Building Society. True, this evidence does show a very slight increase in space standards during the mid-1960s; bigger houses (more than 1,250 square feet) marginally increased as a share of all new mortgaged housing between 1962 and 1970, from 5.3 percent to 7.5 percent of all housing; while the smallest size group of all (less than 750 square feet) fell sharply from 26.6 to 15.9 percent. But the group of relatively small dwellings, with between 750 and 1,000 square feet, actually increased from 53.5 to 61.0 percent; while the group of slightly larger dwellings remained almost constant at around 14.6–15.8 percent. Eighty-one percent of all dwellings in 1962, and 77 percent in 1970, were still less than 1,000 square feet in size. Though overall this represents a modest net improvement, it is a surprisingly small one in view of the rapidly rising affluence of this period; and it undoubtedly conceals many actual reductions in size within this group. The most striking point is that new mortgaged homes in 1970 were consistently smaller than the total of mortgaged new and old homes. In other words, it seems that over a longer period the average size of the new British private-sector home has been falling; it was probably less in 1970 than it had been in the interwar period, when such a large proportion of the older housing stock had been built. This in turn helps explain another surprising Nationwide Building Society statistic: that the prices of the old homes bought on mortgage are almost identical with those of the new ones. Part of the explanation here may well be that old homes are more accessible to urban jobs and services—a product of the tardy decentralization of such functions in Britain's metropolitan areas. But a large part of the explanation must be that despite higher maintenance costs and perhaps lack of some modern fittings, these older homes are notably more spacious.

It is true that from 1931 to 1961 British Census data show a remarkably sharp fall in standards of crowding, as measured by average persons per room; and since then, the Nationwide figures show a steady increase in the average number of rooms in new houses. But two comments need to be made. The first is that a greater number of rooms can go together with the same or less overall space, as the Nationwide figures show. The second is that the Census figures mainly reflect the rapid rate of household formation among young adults and old people; household size has fallen while dwelling size has remained rather stable, or has even fallen. Two separate studies, one by Ray Thomas as part of the PEP project, the other by the government Building Research Station, confirm this. Ray Thomas concludes that the most crowded households were about as badly off, relative to the average, in 1961 as they were in 1931. Certainly, these studies strengthen rather than weaken the central conclusion: in a period of unprecedented mass affluence, when possessions of all kinds have grown in volume as never before, it is anomalous that the average new house for the growing family with children is probably no larger than the houses built for families with the more modest material possessions of the 1930s. It seems that these houses will be increasingly inadequate for the needs of their occupiers. First, they will not provide enough privacy for

[23] See p. v.

separate functions—boisterous children's play and quiet adult reading, a teenage party and younger children's sleep—to happen simultaneously. Second, the family that can afford a growing volume of material possessions typical of the late twentieth century—such as more than one car, perhaps a trailer and a boat, camping equipment, hi-fi, TV sets, bulky gardening equipment, tools for hobbies—finds it more difficult to discover a house and garden (yard) large enough to accommodate such possessions. Compared with the older more spacious housing, they may soon become substandard.

One justification for them might be that they represent a conscious trade-off for better accessibility to jobs and other urban services. But much of this housing is in suburbs remote from these opportunities. It might be argued that these residents have traded off everything else for easy access to countryside. But they were never explicitly given the choice. Had they been, it seems unlikely that they would have accepted it.

Thus there have been losers as a result of the operation of the controls. Many new suburban buyers have obtained smaller, less well-equipped housing, on smaller plots than suburban buyers had been able to obtain in the 1930s. Almost certainly, this would not have occurred if controls had been absent. In general, this has affected most seriously the lower, marginal end of the owner-occupier market, where the buyers are just able to afford the cheapest house available. These houses will be difficult to convert as space standards rise, and to that extent they will be a permanent resource cost to the community. But, beyond that, the system has failed to provide housing at any price for a much wider group that cannot afford even the minimal standard of owner-occupied housing. These are the households that, in many cases, are trapped in poor rented accommodations in the cities. Just as in the United States, this is the group that has most conspicuously failed to gain from the postwar development of suburbia.

On the other hand, there have been gainers—and also those who have neither gained nor lost much. The true gainers are the existing rural residents who have preserved a way of life they hold dear. If for many people regulation of social and physical change is an important value, at any rate in their immediate residential neighborhood, then the British planning system has achieved this at least as effectively as the American system of zoning and other controls, and possibly more so. But it so happens that in both countries the people who have mainly benefited are those toward the top end of the income scale—just as many of those who have gained nothing are toward the bottom end. In between is a mass of new buyers of houses above the marginal level who have probably not gained or lost very much. At most, they are probably occupying rather smaller houses, on smaller lots, than would otherwise have been the case.

There is, however, one important difference between the two countries. In Britain the public sector has provided about one-half of all new homes built since World War II. On the whole, it has provided rented housing for those in greatest housing need, irrespective of ability to pay. This has not always been perfect: substantial numbers of poor tenants are found in substandard privately rented homes, as noted in chapter 4, while—as we shall see in chapter 6—the new towns have failed to contribute much to the housing needs of the poor. Furthermore, much of the municipal housing has been crowded at relatively high densities into city redevelopment areas, as a direct result of urban containment policies pursued by the rural counties. Nevertheless, the public program has made an appreciable contribution to the housing of lower-income groups, and has maintained high standards of planning and construction—often higher, indeed, than at the bottom of the private-sector price range.

In terms of the wider public interest, it is difficult to draw a conclusion. Containment has almost certainly avoided the heavy public costs of scatteration. Shorter, more intensively used main services for water, utilities, and sewerage have lowered unit costs. Furthermore, since the likely pattern of development has been fixed by the planning process, there are fewer unexpected costs arising from unforeseen changes. Similarly, higher densities reduce the length of the average journey to work or to shop—though the preservation of open countryside is likely to negate this completely. More importantly, they may make it easier to support a public transport system (or at least, one that requires less in subsidy) as car ownership rises. If it is determined as public policy that the system must be maintained for those who will continue to depend on it, then any reduction in unit cost of operation in this way should be counted a public benefit.

Most fundamentally but least capable of calculation, the operation of the entire planning and control system has involved some direct economic losses. New factories have been refused permission to locate in certain areas, so that entrepreneurs have continued to operate inefficiently in old, congested, badly laid out city plants; some may even have moved operations abroad. Planning has worked to restrict the development of out-of-town shopping centers, drive-in banks, and the other paraphernalia of a suburban motorized society; as a result, with the rise of car ownership, there has been serious and mounting congestion in the older central city shopping centers, with a call for massive redevelopment to deal with the problem. The economic cost of this congestion, again, is difficult to calculate. Both work journeys and shopping journeys have been lengthened by the trends in population and employment, which planning policies have encouraged; this again involved economic costs. The operation of the entire system has involved the use of human and other resources, which might have been used in more directly productive pursuits.

All these effects must be regarded as trade-offs against the qualities the system has preserved: a traditional landscape and a way of life. It should be stressed that though in part they were consciously willed and planned, in part they were incidental and unexpected by-products. The original plans, produced by the county planning offices soon after 1947, were based on serious underestimates of future population and economic activity; the same was true in the United States, but in Britain it was more serious because elaborate policies of control were based on the projections and could not easily be modified. The policies, based on the comfortable assumption that change was slow and controllable and that rural arcadia could be preserved, seemed sensible enough at the time; but afterwards they were in increasing discord with the facts. An important by-product was that the estimates of planned overspill were wrong. These estimates, representing the residue requiring to be rehoused outside the city boundaries, were based on the assumption that slum areas would be redeveloped at lower densities and that the city would be contained by greenbelts and other devices, which in turn was based on the assumption that natural growth within the city would be low and that migration into it for work could be restrained by industrial location policies. Both assumptions proved to be wrong, and it was particularly ironic that the cities started on their extensive slum clearance programs in 1955, just as the birthrate began to turn unexpectedly upward again.

Partly, however, the policies were conscious. Local planning authorities were consciously enjoined by the central Ministry in London to create greenbelts so as to restrict the growth of the biggest cities and conurbations, and official pronouncements stressed that the principal function of the greenbelt was purely restrictive—not necessarily to provide fine countryside or open air recreation. Similarly, there was a deliberate drive by the Ministry to drive up residential densities in areas of single-family houses in the interests of saving agricultural land—even though research in agricultural economics had already clearly shown that the value of such saved land for agriculture was extremely modest. Later, indeed, while densities were rising in response to the Ministry's advice, further results of the research showed clearly that the nation did not require the land at all in order to maintain a rapidly rising agricultural output. But nevertheless, densities continued to remain high.

The Achievements and Limitations of the American System

We need to start by stressing the distinction we have made more than once: that in the American system, planning and land use control are frequently divorced. City planning in the United States may have had impressive intellectual support, not only from professional planners themselves but from businessmen who saw the efficiency and economy that could be attained by coordination of public programs. It has also had some political leverage from federal government funds. But by and large, as compared with Europe in general and Britain in particular, one outstanding fact about planning in the United States is that it has generally had a weak local political base. Thus, many groups within the city might regard a city planning organization as a generally "good thing," and encouragement from the federal government to city planning would thus find a local receptivity. But, when the inevitable crunch came, when a plan prevented public or private action wanted by an influential figure or group (and unless a plan sooner or later prevents something from being done that otherwise would be done, the plan is innocuous to the point of impotence), the planning organization usually had little political muscle. As Banfield has said, city planning lacked political sex appeal. There have been exceptions, of course; and some city planners have been effective local politicians. But vague lip service to planning or support of planning as a means of getting a federal grant is far different from willingness to adhere to a plan, even an officially adopted one, in the scheduling of public improvements or in the zoning of private land.

City and metropolitan planning organizations in the United States have produced many plans in the past twenty-five years. Particularly notable is the work of the Regional Plan Association in New York and the Delaware Valley Regional Planning Commission. The plans prepared in the many cities and metropolitan regions of the United States have varied in detail and sophistication; many have been professionally and technically outstanding. One should not underestimate their value and their effect; even when not directly implemented, they may still have had a substantial indirect effect upon the thinking of public officials and private businessmen.

But the plain fact is that most of the plans developed by U.S. city planning organizations have had limited effect: implementation has not lived up to the promise of the plan. As a result, a great deal of city planning in the United States has been wasted professional effort. The reason for this seems to lie centrally in the fact that there is no automatic link in the United States, as there is in Britain, between the making of a plan and its subsequent implementation. Effective planning seems minimally to demand two things, both of which have normally been lacking in the United States. The first of these is *positive* power of the planning office— that is, the agency that makes the general comprehensive plan—over the disposition and the programming of new public investment in infrastructure such as highways, sewers, mass transit, or schools. This has been lacking because of the fragmented structure of local government and of decision making about public investment generally, with its multiplicity of special purpose, ad hoc authorities, each with its own limited function planners. It has been compounded by the fact that in many cases, even within the city or county, the planning agency is only one element in a complex set of political powers, and that consequently it may not get approval of the plans it makes; even if it does, it will have no guarantee that the plan will later be adhered to.

The second necessary element is *negative* power to stop developments—principally, though not exclusively, in the private sector—that contradict the plan. This too has been lacking because there has been no automatic connection between the plan-making agency and the agency of land use control. Though in many cases a zoning board would in practice take the plan as the general framework for its decisions, and though planners might be members of this board, there has been no guarantee that zoning provisions would be in accord with the plan, if a plan existed. Thus there has been no firm basis for the land use control decisions that were made. And given the opportunity, and even the financial incentive, for landowners and developers to seek zoning not in accordance with the plan, this could lead to the total destruction of the plan in practice. Once again, the diversity of the decision-making process, with no one agency given complete control, produces a situation that seems almost anarchic to Europeans.

They, accustomed to a very different order of things, might conclude that the system is completely ineffectual, but this would be a mistake. American urban and suburban land use plans do have an effect; some public improvements and some private actions are based on them. The estimates of future economic growth, which such plans typically include, often provide a basis for private investment. Even though land can be rezoned on application and when the economic demand is strong enough, this takes time, involves costs, and the outcome is not fully certain; hence it may be easier, cheaper, and quicker to buy land zoned for the use desired. In the United States, as indeed in Britain, planners may appear to use delay as a tactic. Unable to oppose a land rezoning in an outright struggle, they may wear out the applicant or lead him to take action elsewhere more nearly in conformity with the plan. Moreover, federal and state grants for open space, sewer systems, and other purposes are often based on land use plans. Thus, one may be critical of the effectiveness of typical American urban and suburban land use plans, but it would be a mistake to conclude that they are useless. In fact, looking at the history of development since World War II, it can be seen to have produced some strong advantages.

First, it has been a process of great vitality. The postwar period in the United States has been a period of great economic growth and change, particularly in the amount of migration—migration from rural areas and small towns to larger urban areas, and, within those urban areas, from central cities to suburbs, involving not only people and homes but industry and trade. Millions of homes and hundreds of shopping centers have been built. The process, despite the apparent confusion, has harnessed the energies of many different private persons and agencies and many public agencies. Whatever reservations one may have about the result, one cannot deny that the sheer scale of the achievement reflects an enormous vitality, which the system did not thwart and may even have encouraged.

Second, the system has produced a lot of rather good housing and a lot of rather pleasant neighborhoods. It has become the fashion to deride the quality of life lived in these areas. But millions of families have found comfortable housing— some even rather gracious—with modern conveniences and gadgets, and served reasonably well by schools, churches, shops, and other community services. For the most part, these areas were developed specifically to serve the needs of young families with children. In this purpose there is no clear or definite evidence that the suburbs failed. On the contrary, it could be argued that, for those who had the fortune to live in them, these suburbs did as well or better than any comparable development elsewhere in the world.

Third, though dispersed decision making inevitably leads to some inconsistent results, with one part of the process working against other parts, it may nevertheless avoid massive errors. For each group, seeking its own advantage, will be quick to capitalize on the errors of others. A central planning agency might produce a far better coordinated plan, but it might go astray far more massively.

Having said this, it must be allowed that even in terms of the system's own values and objectives it has resulted in some quite concrete disadvantages, which do not seem to have been to anyone's good—certainly not to the good of the wider community.

The first of these disadvantages is that the costs of the operation have been too high for the results. The suburban land conversion process has left a lot of land simply unused, standing in and among the areas of new development. Though low density on the individual plot (in the form of big lots, and/or low floorspace-to-plot ratio) may well have benefits as well as costs for the suburban home owner, this process of leapfrogging or scatteration brings only costs. Firm figures are hard to come by, but our calculations indicate that direct public costs (for highways, sewers, water supply, parks, and some other services) may come to $150 per family per year.[24] This figure excludes direct or indirect private costs, such as the cost of commuting by auto with only one rider per vehicle, or the increased costs of a far-flung road network. Nor does it include the costs of the other forms of low density just mentioned. Considering that there may be 10 million suburban households bearing at least this figure as an annual cost, it seems that the costs of sprawl are significant even in an age of affluence.

The second point is that suburban sprawl has been wasteful of land: land is simply taken out of any productive use—agriculture, forestry, or any other primary use—but is not then developed. Much land within so-called "urbanized areas," as defined by the Bureau of the Census, is simply idle or vacant. While such land might be permanently reserved as parks or open space, it is of little use for this purpose unless a definite decision is made about its future. Some of this land may sooner or later be drawn into urban use through infilling. But this is a slow process and in any case may not reduce the public costs referred to above: if facilities such as sewers are built with capacity to take later infilling, there is a cost of idle capacity; if they are built to the right original scale but then need to be expanded, economies of scale are lost.

A third criticism is more tendentious, but has been widely voiced: it is the aesthetics of suburbia, particularly the element of idle land. What seems undeniable is that in all too many cases, the land developed for suburbia is denuded of all vegetation during the house-building process, after which the new owner struggles for years to grow lawn, shrubs, and trees. Since he shows by his actions that he wants his house surrounded by rich and mature vegetation, it seems clear that its removal is a definite cost to him, extending over years and even decades.

The fourth criticism is the most serious. It is that whatever the deficiencies and the achievements of postwar American suburbia, it has not produced housing for a full half of the population: its costs have been too great. Clearly, much of the responsibility for this must lie with housing policies, but land planning (or the lack of it) has made important contributions. Often, suburban local governments have deliberately arranged that the costs of new suburban housing should be beyond the reach of middle- and lower-income groups. But in any event, imperfections in the suburban land market plus other factors have led to land costs per dwelling unit that were high and rising; housing construction costs have reflected labor costs and have also risen with per capita incomes. So long, therefore, as there is a fraction of the population with incomes less than half median income, then there is likely to be a similar fraction that cannot afford to buy new houses. But the effects are great: urban populations are being increasingly stratified by race, occupation, and income, creating or exacerbating severe social stresses and strains. And even if the suburban land conversion process cannot bear the whole blame for this, it must bear a part.

This, in turn, is associated with a fifth criticism: the great activity associated with suburban land development stands in marked contrast to the limited progress in rebuilding or restoring the housing in older, outworn areas, especially those

[24] Clawson, *Suburban Land Conversion . . .* , pp. 149–59.

areas occupied by lower-income groups. Again, land use planning is not wholly but partially responsible. The simple reason is that while money could be made in developing new suburban housing, paradoxically money could also be made in keeping older housing, especially apartments, unimproved and harvesting tax depreciation allowances.

Sixth, the whole process seems to have been costly not only of land and public services, but of scarce manpower and entrepreneurial talent. The rewards of thwarting plans and controls have often been greater than those of conforming to them, and this has directed a lot of misplaced talent and energy into the thwarting process. Perhaps this is an inevitable feature of any modern state with a system of bureaucratic controls; it is a complaint heard often in the social democracies of Western Europe, as in the East European countries. What is remarkable about the American system is that the positive achievements of control seem to have been small in relation to the costs.

Lastly, it has been difficult to take actions in a coordinated way on a metropolitan scale to deal with problems such as air pollution or transportation planning. This is not a direct result of the suburbanization process itself, but it is a result of the fragmented system of government, which was an essential part of the dispersed decision-making process we have described.

Not all these deficiencies, it will be clear, arose from accident. Some were desired, if not explicitly voiced, by some people. But, for the most part, they must be regarded as unintentional results of the operation of the system, and most result directly from two features of the system: the extreme dispersal of the power to take decisions among many individuals and groups, so that there is no single person or organization in reasonably effective control; and the relatively weak nature of the legal tools available to influence the pattern of land use, in particular the lack of effective power to say *which* tracts of land shall be developed *when*.

Although the American system of land use planning and control has several weaknesses, the remedy does not lie in its abandonment. The system is too deeply embedded in current urban development practice and potentially too powerful and too useful to be abandoned. Modifications, large and small, are possible, and these are discussed in later chapters.

A Provisional Conclusion: The Two Systems Compared

The conclusions that follow are frankly interpretative. In the nature of the case, they cannot be supported by detailed statistical justification. But they do stem from our detailed consideration in the two studies cited in the Preface and from the knowledge we have gained in the course of their preparation.

Despite the apparent dissimilarities between the two systems, in some important respects they seem to have produced results that are alike, though it must be stressed that these similarities in part reflect deep social and economic forces that would operate whatever the system of planning and control. Both have resulted in extensive suburban growth through interaction among many different agents or actors. Both have acted to preserve the rights of existing residents. Both have failed to prevent ratcheting land prices that have particularly penalized poorer members of the community, many of whom have failed to join the privileged owner-occupier class and remain trapped in poor rented accommodation in the central cities. But in Britain the existence of a large program of subsidized public-sector house building for rent has ameliorated the position of this group far more effectively than in the United States. Both involve increasing separation of home and work. Both, however, have quite specific features—strengths as well as weaknesses. In each case, the strengths of the system seem to have been intended and well understood and appreciated, both in the country concerned and by repute in the other. The weaknesses partly arose by accident rather than design; they seem to have been all too little understood by many informed people at home, still less on the other side of the Atlantic.

In the United States, planning and development control have never had a very exalted reputation; planning has never promised much and it has not delivered very much, but the gap between promise and achievement may not be much wider than for the more prestigious British system. The intellectual ancestry and foundations of city planning for the United States are much less impressive than for Britain; its public and official acceptance has been much less; its output, in terms of plans, has been technically good if not outstanding. Its effects have been modest, largely because plans have not been followed. The system of zoning has worked in a rather loose and malleable way; it has probably produced a higher level of environment, especially in residential suburbs, than would have been available without it (though in its absence, perhaps other private systems of control might have taken its place). Overall, the system produced impressive results in the postwar period, both in the quantity of suburban development and in quality— a fact that is too often ignored on both sides of the Atlantic. The criticisms to be laid against it are that too often it produced a chaotic pattern of development of benefit to no one, and that this inflicted direct economic costs on the people involved. But some of this may be regarded as the price to be paid for the dynamism and vitality of the whole system.

In Britain, the system had a more auspicious beginning after World War II, with a coherent philosophy of planning embodied in major legislation, which created strong and effective planning and control machinery. This machinery has been altered in various respects subsequently, including some major changes in the financial provisions; but its main features have survived. It seems to have been effective, as promised, in achieving its objectives; but in the process there have been unforeseen side effects due to a failure to estimate the extent of the demographic, economic, and social changes that had to be accommodated. More important is the fact that though it purported to serve the general public interest, in practice the main effect of the system has been to benefit certain groups and penalize others. City and county planning, as now practiced in Britain, has benefited rural residents and those who try to retain an old style of English country living. True, by effectively preserving land of really high landscape quality, it has created values—at least potentially—for the whole community, including the deprived, but to achieve this it need not necessarily have had the negative scale effects that are observable. The most important of these is that planning has unnecessarily confined the city, forcing a dense pattern of residential living both within the city and in the new suburbs outside it: a style of housing that a large part of the population might not have chosen if meaningful choices had been open to them. In total, it has produced a pattern of urban and suburban living that may well be unacceptable and unworkable in another generation. In other words, it has failed seriously to consider the balance of advantage of different groups: urbanites and new suburbanites versus old ruralites, and the present generation versus the next. Planning, in practice and effectualness, seems to have gone astray from the goals and objectives its intellectual ancestors had in mind a generation before.

To the American planner, or businessman, or intellectual, who is only casually confronted with the attractive aspects of British city planning (such as the new towns or the more attractive urban high-density housing developments) the system seems effective in the sense that, unlike the frequent experience in America, plans are typically put into action. On this point there is general agreement, whether one regards the results of British planning as greatly superior to or less successful than those obtained in America. What is all too little realized in either country is that both British and American planning have been seriously defective, albeit in slightly different ways.

It may be helpful to end this comparison of the two systems by summarizing what we see as their most serious shortcomings up to the end of 1971. We recognize that planning leaders in both countries are aware of some of these deficiencies and are seeking to remedy them, and that in Britain the 1968 Act provides a new structure of plan making that may achieve this.

1. Planning for a city, metropolis, or county is typically a plan for a specified future date, for which population, employment, transportation, land use, and other aspects are estimated. These future situations have been wrongly estimated, with serious results in the case of British planning. But our criticism is directed to more than the inevitable errors of forecasting. The basic weakness in planning for a future date with its built-in specifications lies in the failure to give sufficient consideration to *process*. How does the area concerned, and its people, proceed from here to there? And, perhaps more important, what happens *after* the planning date? Some plans read almost as though there were no future after the plan is set in motion—not "after me, the deluge," but "after our plan date, time stands still forever." A whole range of facts on population, employment, income, transportation, land use, and other matters is presented as applying to the present and to the target future date; intermediate steps are missing. No process is outlined for moving from one situation to another, and no consideration is given to future change after the target date. To understand how poorly the process of change is incorporated into urban planning and development, one has only to observe the turmoil that can arise over a proposal to rezone some tract of land in an American city. Planners frequently say that planning is a process; but when, given the funds, they make new plans, each is geared to a different target date, and each starts from a different present, and there is still little concern with process. Yet it can be argued that process of change, which is constantly operative, is far more important than target of change, which is, and must always be, indefinite as to form or time.

2. City planning as practiced in both countries gives inadequate consideration to costs, benefits, and alternatives. A single plan is put up by the planners, and official and public approval are sought on the assertion of the planners that this is the most logical and most desirable way for the city (or metropolis) to grow. The plan may include some estimates of cost (estimates that frequently prove to be too low), but it will rarely if ever include rigorous estimate of the benefits or values it proposes to create. There may be general terms, such as "more orderly traffic patterns," "better land use patterns," and the like, but no monetary or other quantitative values are assigned. Only rarely will alternatives be mentioned, and almost never will they be developed. Only a well-informed citizen could know that the plan proposed is one of several possible alternatives open to consideration if he objects to the end results of the one proposed. True, in both countries some of the subregional planning exercises of the late 1960s newly stressed evaluation of alternative strategies and public participation at various stages of the planning process, from goal formulation to evaluation. But by the end of the decade far too great a gap still remained between best practice and usual practice. For many years in the United States the plans of highway and water engineers have included some analysis of costs and benefits, but not usually information on alternative ways of development. Provoked by economists, engineers in these fields are only now beginning to present competent analyses of costs and benefits and also alternative development programs. City planners are even further behind in this type of social analysis.

3. City planners in both countries base their work on professional standards; this is necessary and desirable, but the professional standards are vague, often meaningless to those who are not members of the fraternity, and often lacking logical or empirical foundation. "Wise land use" is basic to all city planning; but what is wise in a specific situation? Separation of incompatible land uses is another cliché; but what uses are incompatible, how far must they be separated, and what costs does separation impose on the people concerned? Preservation of the character of a residential area is another broad goal; but what values attach to diversity? There is more than a suspicion that the standards of the planning profession are the standards of the upper middle class in their respective countries; that the planners, unconsciously or deliberately, seek to impose these standards on a larger and more diverse population. Does "greenbelt" have the same meaning to lower-income workmen as it does to higher-income salaried men or to men living from capital income? The divergence of interest in planning and zoning, between middle- to upper-income suburban whites and lower-income, central-city blacks in the typical American big city has been noted. The planning process in each country typically ignores this divergence. Not only is there an untested assumption that everyone is better off by a plan which asserts that the totality of the plan is better than the totality of no-plan, but the whole problem is ignored, at least publicly and in the printed plan.

4. The relationships between the planners and the electorate they purport to serve are deficient. Typically, planners consult the general public, its leaders, and its elected representatives only after a plan has been prepared; approval is sought, but suggestions for change are deftly brushed aside. To some extent, this arises

out of an elitist approach and philosophy: technical or professional planners know far better what is best than can a relatively uninformed citizenry. But in part it arises because the planners' education has not fitted them for cooperative work with the citizenry, who should be their clientele. We fully appreciate that meaningful consultation and cooperation with the public during the planning process would be difficult: much of the affected public prefers to sleep and to criticize only too late; the crackpots (and it seems to be a law of life that every body of men and women includes some crackpot fringe) would tend to monopolize the time of planners; and some members of the public would quickly move to take personal financial advantage of what they learned from discussions with planners. But the present typical process leaves the planners with weak public support. When their plans are attacked, as they almost surely will be if they have any real content, the planner must fight the battle against the critic with few allies. If one's objective is preparation and publication of neat plans that will impress one's professional colleagues, then the present process has many advantages; if one's objective is to have plans carried out, then a much more intensive program of working with the citizenry during the planning process may not be inefficient.

5. Finally, the physical, or general-purpose, planners frequently are unable to bring about the coordination of the various specialized programs of government—transportation, sewerage, water supply, schools, parks, and others. Programs in these fields are usually developed by limited function planners within the respective agencies. These specialized governmental programs may operate at cross-purposes with one another, or in conflict with the general, or comprehensive, plan. Though the physical planner emphasizes the comprehensiveness of his approach and the need to coordinate special programs, in fact he is frequently unable to deliver such coordination. It may well be argued that the fault lies not with the planner, but with the general governing body under whom both specialized programs and general physical planning are, at least theoretically, directed. But it can be said that the assertions and perspectives of the general physical planners have not been made effective in practice, and that their philosophy of coordination has not been sold adequately to the general governing bodies.

In making these comments about city planning in both countries, we are aware that differences exist between countries and among cities and other areas in each country. Cooperation with the citizenry during the planning process, for example, ranges from nonexistent to reasonably close in each country. Exceptions to generalizations always exist; but, in our judgment, the foregoing criticisms apply to city planning across the board in each country—we have not picked out the exceptional cases as a basis for our comments.

chapter 6

New towns

West or east of the Atlantic, almost every book or article dealing with urban development turns to the subject of new towns. The claim is constantly made that the new towns are Britain's outstanding contribution to the theory and practice of twentieth century town planning. They are said to have provided a civilized, humane environment for hundreds of thousands of people, superior to the standards of ordinary suburbia, at far lower cost than any conceivable alternative solution. They are alleged to have provided a way whereby Britain has avoided the so-called excesses of American postwar suburban growth. They are canvassed, in the United States, as a relevant answer to American urban problems. Experimental American new towns, such as Reston in Virginia, Columbia in Maryland, and Irvine in California, are asserted to be the first tentative steps towards a general policy of new towns for America.

The purpose of this chapter is to look as dispassionately as possible at these claims. For obvious reasons, we shall concentrate particularly on the British new towns, looking at their basic objectives and their particular place within general urban planning policies; at the realization of these objectives in terms of size, location, and function; and at the system of administration and finance common to all the new towns. We shall consider particularly whether, or how far, the new towns have achieved some of the basic social and economic objectives that were put forward by those who campaigned for them and that provided an important part of the justification for the whole program after World War II. Lastly, we shall ask how far the experience of new town building in Britain is applicable to the somewhat different American urban situation of the 1970s.

To do this, it is first necessary to define the term *new town* rather precisely. The term is slightly ambiguous even in Britain; but as between Britain and the United States, a wealth of misunderstanding is possible. Most observers would presumably agree that if a new town is anything, it must be a town and it must be new. That implies some minimum size: the development at New Ash Green in Kent some twenty miles from London, for instance, a private enterprise venture for 7,000 new families, was described by its promoters as a new village, not a new town. It implies, too, that the development is basically the creation of a new urban community, even if it swallows up certain preexisting settlements on the site. We shall see later in this chapter, in fact, that several British new towns started with appreciable existing population and urban development, and that some of those started in the 1960s are attached to major towns or cities. Urban character and newness are therefore necessary conditions, but in the British use of the term *new town* they are not themselves sufficient.

The British new town, in fact, is narrowly and precisely defined. It is a town built under the provisions of the 1946 New Towns Act by a Development Corporation after designation by the relevant Minister—formerly the Minister of Housing and Local Government, since 1970 the Secretary of State for the Environment—with direct Treasury finance. It is invariably built to perform specific planning functions, of which by far the most common have been the reception of overspill population from large urban agglomerations whose growth is being restrained by planning policies, and the promotion of economic and social development in problem areas of declining or stagnant industry. It contains a substantial proportion—in the past a great majority, in the future, according to planning targets, about one-half—of public housing for rent, built by the Development Corporation with the aid of central government public housing subsidies. It is planned to be reasonably self-contained, so that it grows through a carefully phased program of attracting industry and other employment in step with population; this is achieved by a variety of inducements, including the deliberate provision of housing for workers in industries that locate in the town. It is supposed also to be socially balanced, in the sense that it contains a mixture of different occupational, social, and age groups. It is built, in other words, to fulfill specific social purposes, which were first set out by the pamphleteer and reformer Ebenezer Howard in his book *Tomorrow*—later renamed *Garden Cities of Tomorrow*—in 1898. The new town, in British parlance, is essentially an alternative term for a garden city. But it is important that both terms are used in a precise, technical sense.

At the beginning of 1971 there were twenty-eight such towns in Britain: twenty-one in England, two in Wales, and five in Scotland. Excluding a few recent projects,[1] these towns housed some 1,415,000 people, representing an addition of almost 700,000 to the 718,000 who had been living in them at the dates of their respective designations. Counting original and additional populations together, about one in every sixty Britons lived in a new town at this date, exactly a quarter century after the passage of the New Towns Act. The towns contained over 182,000 new houses, over 35 million square feet of new factory space, over 350 new schools with over 150,000 places, and over 4 million square feet of office space—an impressive achievement for a nation whose financial resources have been almost constantly strained since World War II. Furthermore, these totals exclude a variety of other

---

[1] These were four in number, attached to existing towns with considerable existing populations (Northampton, Peterborough, Warrington, and Central Lancashire); to include them would distort the overall picture.

planned communities, which do not happen to be new towns in the strict technical sense. Under the 1952 Town Development Act, for example, a large number of existing towns have been expanded by agreement between "exporting" authorities in the great urban agglomerations, and "importing" authorities, with central government assistance for major capital works like sewerage and roads. Although many of these have been small-scale schemes for a few hundred or a few thousand families, some—such as the agreements made by London with Basingstoke and Andover in Hampshire and with Swindon in Wiltshire—have been major schemes fully resembling new town developments. Under the same act, the Northumberland County Council has built two communities just on the edge of the Tyneside conurbation in northern England—North Killingworth and Cramlington—which are new towns in title and in function, though they do not satisfy the strict criteria outlined above. But having noted the exceptions and anomalies, it will be easiest to restrict our attention in the remainder of this chapter to the new towns in the strict sense.

All these towns were deliberately created for a purpose, by decision of the central government, after careful consideration of the planning problems of the region in which they were located. Most, though not all, were located as a result of regional studies or strategies or plans, which recommended them some time in advance of their actual designation by the Minister. The act of designation—often after a public inquiry by an independent inspector, who hears objections and reports with recommendations to the Minister—fixes the site of the new town, which is liable to progressive compulsory purchase (eminent domain) as the land is needed for building. It also allows the Minister to appoint a Development Corporation to act as overall authority for building the town; this corporation, consisting of a chairman and part-time members, then appoints the general manager or chief permanent executive and subsequently (directly or indirectly) the staff responsible for planning and building the town. The Development Corporation is a peculiarly British administrative device, reminiscent in many ways of the nationalized industry boards, which manage the state-run airlines, railways, coal mines and public utilities of gas and electricity, or the British Broadcasting Corporation. It is a public corporation appointed directly by the relevant Minister, and responsible to Parliament through an annual report, but deliberately shielded from public interference and scrutiny in its day-to-day dealings, so as to give it a measure of independence similar to that enjoyed by a private firm. There have been objections, particularly in relation to new towns, that the device is undemocratic. But to this, the answer is that so big a construction job could not be left to a local authority—or, at any rate, to the rather small local authority that is likely to be responsible for the area when the town is first designated. It needs above all managerial expertise, which the Development Corporation is supposed to provide.

The financial basis of the new towns is quite specific and is laid down by the act. The Development Corporations may borrow money from the central government, to tide them over the difficult period until the returns flow back, but may borrow from no one else. (Partnerships with private enterprise on town center and other schemes are possible, however, and may allow a Development Corporation partly to circumvent this provision legally.) Much of the development in the town—in particular, shops and offices and factories—is eventually very profitable to the community. But about half the investment in the average town, and about 70 percent of that by the Development Corporation, is in houses; and here the corporation merely aims to break even, drawing the same subsidies on construction from the central government as are payable to local authorities for their public housing schemes. The corporation has the power to buy land compulsorily within its designated area as and when it needs it, though in most cases the owner can also compel the corporation to buy when he requires; the compensation is based on a complex formula, which is well above agricultural value but is below the speculative development value, and which is supposed to exclude the value created by the existence of the town. Major capital development projects have to be separately submitted by the corporation to the Minister for his approval as part of the Ministry's total investment budget for that year. The accounts of each new town are submitted annually to the Minister and are open to scrutiny by the Public Accounts Committee of Parliament.

Just as the administrative and financial structure of the new towns is special, so is their general purpose. This purpose stems directly from the tireless efforts of the propagandists of the Garden City movement, banded together in the Town and Country Planning Association, a body founded by Sir Ebenezer Howard to campaign for the ideas set out in his book. Essentially, Howard's argument must be seen in its historical context. At the time he wrote, slum housing, overcrowding, poor working conditions, pollution, high rents, and difficult travel were all too apparent. So also was the rapid migration from the countryside into the cities, brought about by the competition of cheap foreign foodstuffs and the resultant conversion of British farming into labor-saving lines of production; to the average worker at that time, the countryside offered neither economic nor social opportunity. Howard argued that the problems of town and country could be solved by the creation of an entirely new type of community, town-country or garden city. A public or charitable private body would buy agricultural land cheaply at some distance from the city; factories and their workers would simultaneously move out from the city to the new site. Thus a new community would be created with good housing, pleasant working conditions, no travel problems and a lack of pollution. This would allow the growth of the city to be stemmed; further growth would be diverted progressively into new garden cities, and as each reached some maximum size (set by the requirement that each citizen should be able easily to walk into open countryside) its growth in turn would cease as a new city was started up nearby. To guarantee this, the land bought for each city would include generous allowance for a greenbelt around it, which would house farming, waste disposal, and institutions needing a rural setting. But the separate garden cities thus created would not be entirely self-contained; though each would provide work and social opportunities for most needs of its citizens, they would be interconnected by a frequent and rapid mass transportation system, thus providing a city region offering wider opportunities, or, in Howard's graphic phrase, a *Social City*.

The Chronology of New Town Building

It is important to realize that the new towns built in Britain since World War II share this common basis in Howard's philosophy. They are intended to be largely self-contained, socially balanced communities combining home and work, which will provide for surplus populations from the conurbations and cities, and will thus serve the purpose of containing urban growth. In their location—particularly their relationship to the great conurbations—in their size, and in their character, they have tried to put Howard's essential ideas into practice. But in the process the ideas have been modified somewhat.

The new towns built since World War II fall, on a chronological basis, into two well-defined groups. The first, often known as the *Mark One* new towns, comprise fourteen towns—twelve in England and Wales and two in Scotland—all designated in a short burst of activity between 1946 and 1950. And with one exception, this group may be divided into two subgroups according to the purpose of designation. The larger group consists of towns created to serve the specific purpose of Ebenezer Howard: to provide for the orderly decentralization of population and jobs from the great urban agglomerations. In England all the eight new towns designated during this time around London had this purpose; so did the town of East Kilbride in Scotland, near Glasgow. But East Kilbride also served a second purpose: to aid regional development policies in an area that had suffered particularly from economic decline between the two wars. Glenrothes, the second Scottish new town of the Mark One period, also fell into the Development Area category; so did Newton Aycliffe and Peterlee in County Durham (North East England) and Cwmbran in Monmouthshire. Of this group, Newton Aycliffe and Cwmbran were built around existing industrial estates, while both Peterlee and Glenrothes were to assist in the redeployment of coal miners. Finally among the Mark One towns, Corby in Northamptonshire was an anomaly. Situated in the East Midlands, a region lacking the problems either of the conurbations or the development areas, it was set up to provide housing and communal services for a large steelworks built just before the Second World War (figure 26).

The second group marks a significant break. Between 1950 and 1961 only one new town—Cumbernauld in Central Scotland, designated to provide for Glasgow overspill and help promote a Development Area—was started in Britain. The Conservative government tried to put the emphasis on town development schemes under the 1952 Act, and even announced in 1957 that no more new towns would be started. But this policy had to be reversed after 1961, when it became clear that this program was not solving problems of overspill from the conurbations quickly enough. Thirteen more new towns were designated between Skelmersdale (1961) and Central Lancashire (1970). With a specific exception—Newtown, a small development announced in 1967 to help solve the problems of the thinly populated hill area of Mid-Wales—all were intended to solve the specific overspill problems of the major conurbations. Three further new towns were announced for London, two of them attached to the existing cities of Northampton and Peterborough, two towns were announced for the West Midlands, two for Merseyside, and two for the Greater Manchester area; there was one designation for the

KEY:

◆ New towns

○ Other major cities

SCOTLAND

Glenrothes ◆

Cumbernauld ◆

○ Edinburgh

Glasgow ○ ◆ Livingston

◆ East Kilbride

Irvine ◆

Newcastle ○

Washington ◆

Peterlee ◆

Newton Aycliffe ◆

York ○

Central Lancashire ◆

○ Leeds

Skelmersdale ◆

Liverpool ○ ○ Manchester

◆ Warrington

Runcorn ◆

○ Sheffield

○ Nottingham

Telford ◆

ENGLAND

Newtown ◆

Leicester ○

◆ Peterborough

Birmingham ○

◆ Corby

◆ Northampton

Redditch ◆

◆ Milton Keynes

Stevenage ◆ ◆ Welwyn

Hatfield

Cwmbran ◆

Hemel Hempstead ◆ ◆ Harlow

Cardiff ○

◆ Basildon

LONDON ○

Bristol ○   Bracknell ◆

WALES

◆ Crawley

Southampton ○   Brighton ○

Plymouth

0   50   100   150 KILOMETERS

0   50   100 MILES

FIGURE 26. Between the end of World War II and 1971, twenty-eight new towns were built in Britain.

Tyneside area, and two further towns in Central Scotland to provide for Glasgow overspill. These last three towns, in addition, served the purpose of promoting regional development in North East England and in Central Scotland, respectively. So did the two Merseyside towns, since throughout the period since World War

II the Merseyside area has been judged to be in need of special government assistance.

Thus, of the twenty-eight towns started in Britain since World War II, no less than twenty-three have served wholly or partly for the reception of conurbation overspill—eighteen in England and five in Scotland. (Eight of these—three in England and by definition all five in Scotland—also promoted regional development.) Two towns in England and two in Wales served regional development without a specific overspill function. And lastly there was the anomalous case of the steelworks town of Corby. The full list of towns is set out in table 25.

The clear distinction between the two groups in this table—the Mark One new towns of 1946–50 (together with Cumbernauld), and the Mark Two new towns of 1961–70—is particularly important when considering their location and size. Of those Mark One new towns designated for overspill purposes, the eight London new towns were all between twenty-one and thirty-two miles from London, which was about as near as they could be considering the radius of the conurbation (twelve–fifteen miles) and the width of the planned greenbelt (five–ten miles); while next to the compact Clydeside conurbation, East Kilbride was also close to the center of Glasgow (nine miles). Some of the Mark Two new towns built to deal with the overspill problems of the provincial conurbations, too, were close to their parent conurbations: Redditch was fourteen miles from Birmingham, Skelmersdale twelve and Runcorn fourteen miles from Liverpool, Washington only eight miles from Newcastle. But some of these were decidedly more distant: Telford is thirty-four miles from Birmingham, Central Lancashire thirty miles from Manchester, Livingston and Irvine twenty-six miles from Glasgow. And the three Mark Two new towns designed for London overspill were all deliberately sited at greater distances from the conurbation, so as to try to guarantee that they will not become commuter towns: Milton Keynes is forty-nine miles, Northampton sixty-six miles and Peterborough no less than eighty-one miles from London.[2]

This distinction between the two groups is even more important, though, when considering their size. The pioneers of the new-town movement had recommended rather small garden cities: Howard, in a diagram, had suggested units of 32,000—though, an important modification often missed by later observers, these were to be grouped into multicentered units of 250,000 or even more—while the official Reith Committee on New Towns in 1945 and 1946 had suggested a range between 30,000 and 50,000, with some latitude above and below. In fact the Mark One towns were remarkably faithful to the Reith recommendations: all save two had target populations between 25,000 and 60,000. This uniformity concealed some variations in the amount of growth that was entailed, for while most of the sites had only villages or small market towns with 5,000 or 10,000 people, four—Hemel Hempstead, Welwyn Garden City, Basildon, and Corby—already had substantial urban development with between 15,000 and 25,000 people on the site. What is most notable, perhaps, is that very few of the sites were wholly without some existing village or town.

[2] Soon after designation, the element of planned London overspill in the growth of these towns was seriously diminished.

TABLE 25

New Towns in Britain, January 1971

	Date of designation	Original population	Target population (all populations in 1,000s)		Distance from conurbation or city center (miles)
			Original	Revised	
CONURBATION OVERSPILL TOWNS					
GREATER LONDON					
Stevenage	1946	7	60	105	32
Crawley	1947	9	50	80	31
Hemel Hempstead	1947	21	80	–	25
Harlow	1947	4	60	90	25
Hatfield	1948	8	29	–	21
Welwyn Garden City	1948	18	36	50	23
Basildon	1949	25	50	133	29
Bracknell	1949	5	25	61	30
Milton Keynes	1967	40	250	–	49
Peterborough	1967	84	190	–	81
Northampton	1968	131	300	–	66
BIRMINGHAM (WEST MIDLANDS)					
Telford (Dawley)	1963	70	90	220	34
Redditch	1964	32	90	–	14
LIVERPOOL (MERSEYSIDE)					
Skelmersdale[1]	1961	8	80	–	12
Runcorn[1]	1964	28	100	–	14
MANCHESTER (SOUTH EAST LANCASHIRE/NORTH EAST CHESHIRE)					
Warrington	1968	122	200	–	18
Central Lancashire	1970	240	430	–	30
NEWCASTLE UPON TYNE (TYNESIDE)					
Washington[1]	1964	20	80	–	8
GLASGOW (CENTRAL CLYDESIDE)					
East Kilbride[1]	1947	2	45	100	9
Glenrothes[1,2]	1948	1	32	95	58
Cumbernauld[1]	1955	3	70	–	14
Livingston[1]	1962	2	100	–	26
Irvine[1]	1966	36	116	–	26
DEVELOPMENT AREA TOWNS					
Newton Aycliffe	1947	0	10	45	–
Peterlee	1948	200	30	–	–
Cwmbran	1949	12	55	–	–
Newtown	1967	6	11	–	–
OTHER TOWNS					
Corby	1950	16	40	80	–
Total (28)		1,210	2,709	3,270[3]	

Sources: F. J. Osborn and Arnold Whittick, *The New Towns: The Answer to Megalopolis,* 2nd ed. (London: Leonard Hill, 1969); Frank Schaffer, *The New Town Story* (London: Macgibbon & Kee, 1970); *Town and Country Planning,* January 1971; and gazeteers.

[1] Also served development area purposes, and receives development area aid.

[2] Not originally designated for Glasgow overspill purposes but received this function after failure of original purpose (development of new coal mine in Fife coalfield).

[3] Including original targets for towns where these were not revised.

However, the formula for the new towns of the 1960s provides much greater variation and experiment. Several, built for overspill from the provincial conurbations, followed the traditional formula but with modest increases in the planned targets, to between 80,000 and 100,000. This reflected a fairly general belief among new town planners, by this time, that a town of this size was needed to provide adequate levels of shopping and other urban services; it corresponds to a well-established level in the British central-place hierarchy, as established by a number of studies, and several of the older new towns had their original targets raised to about this level at the same time, as table 25 shows. But Northampton and Peterborough for London overspill, plus Warrington for Greater Manchester overspill, use a quite new formula: expansion of an existing large town (Peterborough 84,000, Northampton 131,000, Warrington 122,000) by a factor of about two, to levels of 190,000, 300,000, and 200,000 respectively. Milton Keynes, also designated for London overspill, uses a slightly different formula: the creation of a big new city for a quarter of a million people, in an area where previously there were three small towns and a number of rural villages. Lastly, an even more radical departure from traditional norms is presented by the Central Lancashire new city, which will be created in a large, already highly urbanized linear region containing several towns and an existing population of 240,000, to be expanded rapidly to a target of 430,000. Thus, during the 1960s the concept of a modest-sized new town of 50,000–60,000 has been inflated and altered into various new forms: a new town added to an old town, and even the creation of a planned city region for nearly half a million people. But this last, it is important to bear in mind, is not far removed from the essential idea of the Social City, first enunciated by Ebenezer Howard in a forgotten diagram[3] in his book of 1898.

Most new towns, having been built either for overspill or regional development purposes or both, fit within clear regional strategies. Thus the original eight London new towns were an integral and important part of Abercrombie's 1944 *Greater London Plan*[4] for the decentralization of people and jobs from London; the more recent and more distant new towns of South East England were designed to fit the prescription for longer-distance overspill beyond the limits of London's commuting field, contained in the *South East Study* of 1964;[5] Washington in County Durham is a direct outcome of a regional strategy for North East England.[6] Most new towns in England, whether in development areas or more prosperous regions, form part of plans to move people and employment from the older, more congested inner rings of the major cities and conurbations—again in accordance with Howard's original thesis of 1898.

[3] This is one of the mysteries of planning history. The original colored diagram, which showed Howard's full conception of Social City, was not reproduced when the book was republished in 1901; and subsequent editions of the book, also, have failed to include it. Belatedly, however, F. J. Osborn has drawn attention to this in his "The History of Howard's Social Cities," *Town and Country Planning*, 39 (December 1971), pp. 539–45.

[4] Patrick Abercrombie, *Greater London Plan, 1944* (London: His Majesty's Stationery Office, 1945).

[5] U.K., Ministry of Housing and Local Government, *The South East Study, 1961–1981* (London: Her Majesty's Stationery Office, 1964).

[6] U.K., *The North-East: A Programme for Regional Development and Growth* (London: Her Majesty's Stationery Office, 1963).

THE IDEA OF SELF-CONTAINMENT

Whether at the level of the individual garden city or at the higher level of Social City, there is no doubt that the idea of self-containment has been central to the whole philosophy of the garden city–new town movement from the original publication of Howard's book down to the 1970s. New towns are specifically designed not to be commuter settlements for neighboring urban areas; they are planned settlements, in which the growth of residential population is carefully geared to the provision of new jobs. One important reason for increasing the size of new towns in the 1960s, indeed, has been the argument that with increasing sophistication of skills, a far greater range of job opportunities is needed than in the past. And it may even be allowed (Howard, in writing about Social City, seems specifically to have been thinking of the possibility) that some workers will need to go, or will wish to go, farther afield in the pursuit of the particular job they want. But it seems generally to have been agreed that if the new town were properly planned, only a minority would find themselves in this position. New towns are supposed to be an alternative to suburbia, not a superior form of it. In the words of the Reith Committee in their 1946 report, they are to be "self-contained and balanced communities for working and living."

The ideal of self-containment, in fact, implies the other element in the equation: social balance. A fully developed town, providing an adequate range of services for its inhabitants, will necessarily include not merely factories but also shops, schools and colleges, hospital and clinic facilities, offices and research establishments, sections of local and central government departments. If therefore the town is to be reasonably self-contained, it must provide the homes for the people who perform these jobs. Thus it will come to house a wide cross-section of the population: not merely factory workers but white-collar office workers, managers and professionals. And this, in turn, would bring further benefits to the town: not merely the economic strength that will arise from the presence of higher-income groups, but also a rich social mix that would avoid the formation of one-class communities. The experience of the interwar years, where vast municipal housing projects had been created on the periphery of British cities for displaced slum dwellers without any admixture of other groups, was very much in the minds of the Reith Committee and of the new-town propagandists as an example to avoid.

In fact, British new-town planners have been in a strong position to ensure a high degree of self-containment. For obvious reasons firms have been anxious to establish plants in the new towns. Around London it was easier to obtain government permission to establish new plants in the new towns than elsewhere outside the Development Areas; there were generous incentives, including provision of land or even a general-purpose factory, and the provision of housing for the workers was an important attraction in itself. Workers migrating with the factory would get housing priority in the new town. But, in addition, the new towns have tried to relieve the conurbation housing problems through the Industrial Selection Scheme. People on the London housing lists, for instance, who were willing to move to a new town were kept on a special employment register. New-town firms looking for workers could go to these registers, find suitable workers, and houses were then made available. Thus, with rare exceptions, the only way to get a rented house in a new town is to have a job there first. Though the firm is free to employ whom it likes and the worker, once he has the house, is free to get a job anywhere—inside the town or outside it—in practice there is a fairly close connection between the possession of a job in the town and the possession of a house in it.

It might be thought that even if this principle worked at first, after a time it would break down. Some workers in the town might decide that they preferred to live outside it. Wives, sons, daughters might seek jobs unavailable in the town— an important factor if the employment structure happened to be biased against factory industry when a second generation was seeking white-collar jobs. As car ownership rises, workers will tend to seek a wider range of job opportunities be- cause they can easily commute. But to counteract these trends, as long as the town is growing the new arrivals will tend to contribute to self-containment. So there is a tug-of-war, the results of which can be gauged by looking at commuting patterns.

Ray Thomas made this analysis as a part of the PEP study of urban growth in England (mentioned in the Preface to this book). For it, he developed a special terminology. Journeys within any local authority area were known as *local jour- neys*. Journeys crossing local authority boundaries—the sum of those in and out— were known as *crossing journeys*. And the ratio of local to crossing journeys was known as the *independence index*. Thomas's analysis shows that for six of the eight London new towns where data were available this index actually increased between 1951 and 1966. In some ways this is not surprising. At the beginning of this period the new towns, as such, hardly existed, and job opportunities for the local population were very likely to be found in nearby local authorities rather than in the particular local authority itself. But as the town grew, it could provide more local job opportunities. It is significant that by 1966, the largest new towns tended to be the most self-contained; and there, insofar as there was a movement across local authority boundaries, it tended to be an *inward* movement resulting from an employment surplus in the new town. One of the main reasons for the relative independence of the new towns is that they tended to employ a large proportion of their adult female populations. Women tend to be less mobile than men, for obvious reasons; and if we consider only the male populations, then the new towns were becoming slightly less self-contained during the period 1951–66. But this is not surprising: the new towns of the London area, which Ray Thomas studied in detail, lie in a part of England with rapidly increasing job opportunities and rising mobility. The relevant comparison is between the new towns and other parts of the so-called Outer Metropolitan Area around London.

Such a comparison produces startlingly impressive results, as figures 27 and 28 show. There are no towns within thirty-five miles of London, and with popula- tions of less than 150,000, that are as self-contained as the four big new towns of Harlow, Stevenage, Hemel Hempstead and Crawley. Only a small number of other towns are as self-contained as Basildon, Bracknell, or Welwyn Garden City. The only new town comparable with other towns in the Outer Metropolitan Area is Hatfield, which is the nearest to London and happens to have a big concentration of employment in the aircraft industry, drawing workers from outside. This picture may change somewhat over time: as the older new towns mature, further building by the local authority or by private builders is not likely to respect home–work links as faithfully as the original building program of the Development Corporation. But it seems likely that the new towns will always remain distinctively more self-contained than the average town in the South East.

Social Balance in the British New Towns

So it seems fair to say that the new towns have achieved one of the objectives that were set for them: economic self-containment. But as to the other main objective, social balance, the record is not so clear. It is difficult to find a good yardstick for comparison. The entire population of Britain includes rural workers who are not relevant for comparative purposes, while Greater London has a somewhat specialized economic and social structure. But taking both comparisons into account, it seems clear that in general the new towns have big surpluses of high-income manual workers and well-marked deficits in the low-income group "Other Manual Workers" (figure 29). This is because the sort of growth industry that has been attracted to the London new towns typically has high proportions of skilled and

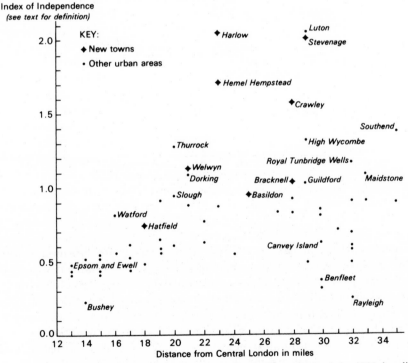

FIGURE 27. Indices of commuting independence in South East England in 1966 by distance from Central London. (The distance of an area from Central London is taken as the airline distance from Charing Cross to the approximate center of the area in a whole number of miles.)

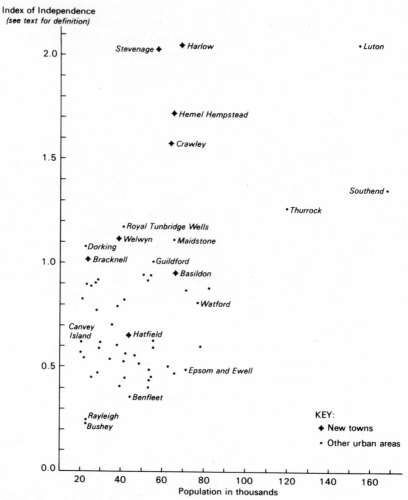

Index of Independence
(see text for definition)

FIGURE 28. Indices of commuting independence for towns within thirty-five miles of London in 1966, by size.

professional workers; it has not offered many openings for low-income workers. And the employee selection process may have helped: firms in the new towns, able to offer housing as well as a job as an incentive, have been able to take their pick of better-qualified workers. Perhaps most important of all, the excess of high-skill workers may be due to the fact that the new towns contain a rather young work-force, which may tend to be more skilled than an older group of workers.

For five of the eight London new towns, Ray Thomas was able to take the analysis further, and compare the skills of residents with the available job opportunities (figure 30). The analysis shows that in general there are more white-collar jobs in the new towns than there are white-collar residents, so that there is a net inflow of these workers into the new towns every weekday morning. This may well arise from choice: white-collar workers, both senior and junior, may prefer to live outside the town. Numbers of higher-income manual workers, on the other hand, are very well balanced: there are about as many jobs of this sort, demanding some measure of skill, as there are workers to fill them. But lastly and perhaps most significantly, there are more low-income, unskilled or semiskilled jobs in the new towns than there are low-income, unskilled or semiskilled residents to fill them. The deficit of workers in these categories amounted to no less than 2,000 in the five towns analyzed. It seems unlikely, on the face of it, that low-income workers would have been reluctant to live in the new towns if they could; the more likely explanation is that the Industrial Selection Scheme discriminated against them, coupled with the fact that a low-income worker might not be able to afford the rent of a new Development Corporation house. By definition, in the early days the new towns did not have a pool of older housing available at low rents. To have overcome this would have demanded a deliberately discriminatory policy on rents, in favor of low-income workers; and this the new towns did not at first seem to have been willing to undertake, though by the late 1960s they all were operating such policies.

It seems then that the new towns around London have been very successful in being self-contained and less successful in being socially balanced communities. They are the only English new towns built for overspill purposes that are old

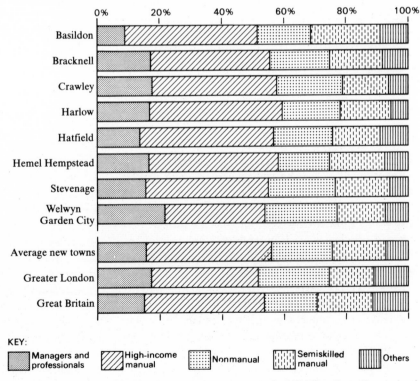

FIGURE 29. The social composition of London's new towns in 1966, based on the proportion of adult males by socioeconomic group.

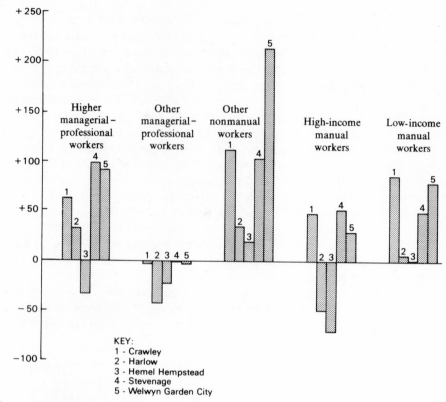

FIGURE 30. Employment surpluses and deficits in five new towns in 1966, analyzed by socio-economic group.

enough, in 1973, to be analyzed in this way. The other new towns of the Mark One generation, built for other purposes (mainly in development areas), also seem to have been successful in bringing about a balance between population and employment, and in becoming economically self-contained. But they tend, like the London new towns, to have a conspicuously lower proportion of low-income group populations than their immediately surrounding areas. Once again, it appears that the most striking apparent deficiency of new-towns policy in Britain has been this failure to provide for the needs of low-income groups.

The broad conclusion of Ray Thomas's analysis, therefore, is that the contribution new towns have made to a solution of the housing problem in Britain has been a rather specialized one. They tended above all to help young couples wanting a home. They have helped people who probably, between the two world wars, would have started married life (and perhaps would have continued) in privately rented accommodation of rather low quality. Since 1945, with the contraction of the privately rented sector, there have been few available homes in this category; and if these couples had not gone to a new town, most of them would doubtless have struggled to become owner-occupiers or would have joined the long waiting lists for council housing within the conurbations. What the new towns had not done after twenty-five years, was substantially to help the old or the poor or the colored.

One incidental result, as table 26 illustrates, is that the new towns are socially imbalanced not merely in terms of occupations, but also in terms of age groups. They contain surpluses of children and their young adult parents, deficits of young people, older adults, and the old. But it should be said that they are almost certainly less imbalanced, in terms of age of social groups, than typical new suburban areas nearby.

Other factors, it is true, may have contributed to this imbalance. In particular, rent control—total or partial—in the conurbations may have given little incentive to tenants to search for better housing in a new town. But the policy of the new town Development Corporations, under which the craftsman and the unskilled laborer both got the same housing with the same amount of subsidy, did not help. Not until the late 1960s were there any substantial differences in new town rents, related to income.

In defense of the new towns, it must be said that the first job was to be successful, which meant attracting industry and building good housing. To have provided more housing for the poor would have meant either building lower-cost housing—and thus, possibly, attracting the charge of exporting slums to the countryside—or demanding more money in subsidy from the government, which might well have meant less for important capital investments. The new towns decided, at least initially, to go all out for growth and success. So the problems of the urban poor were left to be solved largely by the local authorities in the conurbations and cities, if they were solved at all.

Latterly there have been some signs that the emphasis is changing. One of the Mark Two London new towns of the 1960s, Peterborough, timed the start of its construction program to coincide with a series of "London Weeks," in which an intensive publicity campaign was beamed in turn at one inner London borough after another, beginning in the spring of 1971 with Lambeth and Haringey. Another, Milton Keynes, has gone on record in its social plan that it will attract a due share of low-income residents. It is too early yet to judge what success these efforts have had.

TABLE 26

AGE STRUCTURES IN EIGHT SELECTED NEW TOWNS AND IN
ENGLAND AND WALES, 1966

	8 new towns[1] (unweighted average)	England and Wales	Deviation of new towns from national average
Children (0–14)	32.2%	23.0%	+9.2%
Young People (15–24)	13.9	14.5	−0.6
Young Adults (25–44)	30.8	24.8	+6.0
Older Adults (45–64)	17.5	25.1	−7.6
Pensioners (65+)	5.6	12.6	−7.0
	100.0	100.0	0.0

Source: Frank Schaffer, *The New Town Story* (London: Macgibbon & Kee, 1970), p. 171, based on Census, 1966.
[1] Bracknell, Crawley, Harlow, Hemel Hempstead, Corby, Aycliffe, Peterlee, and Skelmersdale.

Financing the New Towns

The Development Corporations, which build the new towns, have to rely for all their capital on loans from the central government Treasury, which must be repaid with interest over a sixty-year period; the money to meet these repayments must by definition come from the rents—residential, industrial, and commercial—paid by those who work or live in the town. In this sense, it is true that the cost of building the town is actually paid by those who live or work there. Of course, if there were a deficit the taxpayer would be forced to meet it; but in the much more likely event of a surplus, this reverts to the central government purse and thus to the benefit of the general taxpayer. Subsidies on public rented housing are paid to the Development Corporations as they would be to local authorities elsewhere; and similarly subsidies for new school or highway construction are paid to the local authority concerned, just as they would be anywhere else. But it can reasonably be argued that if these subsidies were not paid in the new towns, they would have to be paid somewhere else anyway; and that the cost to the public purse of providing these services is probably at least as low as, and often lower than, in congested urban locations.

In fact, all the new towns rely almost completely on their industry and commerce for any profit they may deliver back to the central government; housing, which represents about 70 percent of the typical development corporation investment (and about 50 percent of the total new town investment, including other public sector and also private investment), is expected merely to break even in financial terms. It is therefore of critical importance to the new towns that they attract industry and commerce; and attempts by government to restrict the amount of development of this sort have met with resistance from the Development Corporations, who do not want to see this activity pass to private enterprise, though they are willing to go into partnership with it. The different records of new towns in the various regions amply illustrate the importance of the industrial and commercial element: whereas some of the new towns around London started showing a surplus on general revenue account after eight or ten years because they proved magnets to private firms, new towns of the same age elsewhere have found it much more difficult to reach a point of profitability. However, with a sixty-year repayment period there is little danger that any new town will fail to repay its own costs. And the element of capital appreciation has been considerable in the inflationary conditions prevailing since World War II.

The Significance of the New-Towns Program

There seems to be little doubt, from the pronouncements made in the period 1945–50, that the pioneers of the postwar British planning system—men like Abercrombie and Reith and Osborn—intended that in postwar Britain there would be a major shift in the nature of the housing program. Whereas in the interwar years the private speculative builder had been responsible for the great majority of new development, thenceforth planned communities were to make up by far the greater part of the housing output. In Abercrombie's Greater London Plan of 1944, for instance, out of a total of 1,270,000 people to be housed as overspill outside the conurbation, only 214,000 would be housed outside planned communities. Of the remainder, some 383,000 would move in planned migration programs to the new towns and another 19,000 would move there spontaneously. Over 500,000, in addition, would go to planned expansions of existing towns at up to 100 miles from London. Though new towns as such would take only about one-third of the planned overspill, new towns and town expansions together would make up by far the largest part of the total. Accordingly, the New Towns Act of 1946 provided for the first and the Town Development Act of 1952 for the second.

As has been shown, however, the postwar reality in Britain has been very different. In fact, over the whole of the period 1945–70, public housing contributed about 54 percent and private housing about 46 percent of the total housing stock built in England and Wales. But of the total, the new-town Development Corporations provided only about 2.8 percent and the expanding towns program (under the 1952 Act) only 1.1 percent. Even this achievement is far from negligible: the new-town corporations provided 182,000 dwellings, sufficient for a total of about 550,000 people, and the expanded towns provided 68,000 dwellings with a capacity for about 200,000 more. But a total of 750,000 new residents in public housing in planned communities is a small proportion of the people who have been housed in the 6½ million new dwellings built in England and Wales during this quarter century —a total of people which must amount to close on 20 million if not more.[6] Around Greater London, for instance, though the new towns and expanded towns programs were carried out substantially as Abercrombie intended, the rapid population growth means that a majority of the new population—rather than a small minority, as in the 1944 Plan—was housed by the private builder.

Even if the new towns program had fully achieved its objectives, then it achieved them for a small minority of the people. This was a long way from the intention of those who saw the garden city as a new settlement form, replacing the suburban growth that British planners had so disliked in the 1930s. The suburban growth has continued to take place, though it has been contained by development control policies.

New Towns for the United States?

The United States does not have, and never has had, new towns in the British sense of that term. The British new town, as noted in this chapter, has to be both a town and new, but also must be largely self-contained economically, and socially balanced. Developed by government corporations, the new towns have been financially successful, but their first objectives were to achieve certain desired population distributions. Simply listing these basic characteristics makes it clear that nothing that has happened in the past or is developing today in the United States conforms to this model.

---

[6] It is impossible to calculate these figures exactly because they depend on average household size, which was falling systematically.

As a new country, the United States has seen the creation of literally thousands of "new towns" over the past 200 years or so—fair-sized cities have grown up in two generations or less, where for centuries only forest or prairie had existed. Many of these new towns were developed on townsites established by the federal government, on the then public domain. All of them have benefited from government actions, notably the development of transportation—railroads, highways, airlines. But these towns have been private in their entrepreneurship and their capital, and in their profits and losses. The U.S. government has indeed built some small towns of its own, under special conditions—Norris, Tennessee, in the TVA country; Boulder City, Nevada, near Hoover Dam; Grand Coulee, Washington, near the Coulee Dam; at various military installations, and perhaps others. In the New Deal period, some new "Greenbelt" towns were built with major federal subsidy. When the pragmatic circumstances of a particular situation seemed to require it, the federal government in the United States has thus stepped into the town-building process—but not on the terms or scale of the British new towns. Clarence Stein and others proposed "new towns" for the United States, much as Ebenezer Howard had for Britain, and one (Radburn, New Jersey) was built, but the idea did not catch on.

In recent years there has been much talk of new towns under construction in the United States: Columbia and Reston in the general Washington, D.C. area; Foster City, Irvine, Valencia, and Westlake Village in California; Levittown on Long Island; Park Forest in Illinois; New Orleans East in Louisiana; and Clear Lake City in Texas are most often mentioned. But, save for their location at some distance from existing metropolitan areas and their planned considerable size, these towns have little in common with the British new towns. The American communities are created by private enterprise. As yet, and probably when fully developed, they are neither self-contained nor socially balanced; they tend principally, and almost exclusively in some cases, to consist of homes for sale in the upper-income brackets; and since industry, if it comes at all, comes to them of its own accord, these new towns produce considerable numbers of long-distance commuters back into the inner or suburban parts of the metropolitan areas. They contain no public housing and so they receive no public housing subsidy. Their land holding and servicing costs in the early days have been great, and have had to be borne by their promoters with only limited government financial guarantees under the 1968 Housing Act. Under that act, ten "new towns" (Jonathan, Minnesota; St. Charles, Maryland; Park Forest South, Illinois; Flower Mound New Town, Texas; Maumelle, Arkansas; Cedar-Riverside, Minnesota; Riverton, New York; San Antonio Ranch, Texas; The Woodlands, Texas; and Gananda, New York) had received federal financial guarantees totaling $226 million by late spring 1972. New York State, under its Urban Development Corporation, has announced its approval of three "new towns" (Amherst, Lysander, and Welfare Island) for development. Other states are considering legislation to promote new towns. Singly or in combination, some very large private firms are proposing, with or without federal financial help, to build "new towns." These and other efforts are likely to produce a great deal of new housing and some new suburban communities, some of them perhaps quite distinguished. But none will be new towns in the British sense of the term.

Why have no new towns of the British type been built in the United States to date? Dissatisfactions with American urban development and with the resulting national pattern of population distribution have simply not been sufficiently great or widespread to demand governmental action. Faith in the ability of private enterprise to build good homes and communities has been very strong. There has been extensive philosophical opposition to government action of the kind and scale required to build new towns of the British type.

But there are signs of change. A rising volume of criticism directed at the privately built suburbs, and above all at the population concentrations in the metropolitan areas, led to the passage of the Housing and Urban Development Act of 1970. This act makes a very modest, even timid, step toward the evolution of a national policy of settlement pattern. Title VII, which deals with new towns, was forced upon a reluctant Republican President by liberal Democratic forces in the Congress; but its substantive provisions are weak and its financial provisions still weaker. Some modest funds will be available to help develop new towns, but these may or may not approximate the British model.

As Eichler and Kaplan, the chroniclers of American planned communities, put it:

> A new town is an attempt to break the pattern of urban growth, and at the same time to shift development to different places and to control it. A new community is a way of ordering the business of land development at the fringe of American metropolitan areas.[7]

The true comparison should be between the British new town and the postwar American suburb, when judging forms of development for meeting the housing and planning problems of American society during the later 1960s and early 1970s.[8] These problems have been much discussed, but it is important to be specific about them here, because they cover a wide range of characteristics upon which not all observers may agree.

Basically, they fall into two groups: problems of the central city, and problems of the suburbs. The problems of the central city include:

—the continued existence of large areas of substandard housing, obsolescent and poorly equipped with the facilities widely regarded as normal and necessary in American society today;

—the general decline in the quality of the urban environment in these areas, resulting from physical decay, pollution, and traffic congestion;

—the relative, and in some cases the absolute, decline of the central city as manufacturing, commerce, and services grow rapidly in the suburbs;

---

[7] Edward P. Eichler and Marshall Kaplan, *The Community Builders* (Berkeley and Los Angeles: University of California Press, 1967), p. 24.

[8] In the chapter presenting our conclusions, we make another comparison between American and British suburbs, both of which have handled the great majority of urban growth since World War II.

—the consequent growing lack of local job opportunities for central city residents, with the necessity to travel increasingly long distances to them if they can be found at all;

—the inability to find homes nearer to these job opportunities because of racial or economic exclusion from suburban residential areas, except perhaps the innermost, oldest suburban areas on the fringes of the central cities;

—the growing inability of the central city administrations to fund their escalating public programs, as social needs of all kinds increase and as their tax base is eroded by the flight of the urban economy and the wealthier residents to the suburbs;

—consequently a vicious circle of growing poverty, growing urban bankruptcy, and growing income segregation which also means racial and social segregation.

The problems of the suburbs, according to the many critiques, are different but just as real. They include the following:

—the poor aesthetic quality of much of the suburban environment: uniformity, unimaginative housing design, bulldozing of trees and the natural environment generally, ugly wirespaces, advertising, and freeways;

—the lack of local accessibility to employment and service opportunities (stores, schools, professional and other services), with the necessity to travel long distances to obtain these opportunities;

—the lack of effective mass transportation, mainly brought about by the prevailing uniform low densities, with the almost total dependence on the private automobile, and the resulting deprivation of non-car–owning (or non-car–using) groups, such as children, old people, and wives whose husbands drive the sole family car to work;

—the high costs of servicing (electricity, gas, phones, piped water, main sewerage if available at all) because of the low density and scattered nature of the development;

—the fragmented local government pattern in many areas, with the multiplication of ad hoc agencies, leading to inadequate powers to control and guide development;

—the massive consumption of land, which may be of unique quality in some cases: for instance, the orange groves of Southern California;

—the homogeneity of life styles and the lack of cultural foci such as the central city used to provide, leading progressively to cultural dissatisfaction and even revolt among certain sections of the urban population—especially the young.[9]

To these criticisms of the central cities and of the suburbs has been added, in increasing volume in recent years, further criticism that the continued growth of metropolitan areas and the continued stagnation or decline of nonmetropolitan areas is producing a national pattern of population distribution which is, in some sense, socially undesirable. Those who make the latter criticism often make much of the fact that 80 percent or some other large proportion of the national popula-

[9] Many of these criticisms are set out in a well-known commentary: Donald Canty, ed., *The New City* (New York: Praeger, 1969), pp. 18–32.

tion is concentrated on 1 to 2 percent of the total land area—as if these statistics in themselves were adequate proof of a socially undesirable situation. But these same critics often cite the ills of the large city, described above, and also the decay of the small towns and rural communities.

New towns on the British model—so the argument runs—would help solve many of these problems.[10] For the deprived central city resident, they would provide a prospect of decent housing in a high-quality environment outside the city, with easy access to local employment. For many suburbanites, they would provide an aesthetically superior alternative with good access to jobs and services, a choice between use of the auto and mass transit, lower servicing costs, and a rich diversity of life styles and cultural provision. And the new town, of human size, would provide a better alternative than the big metropolis for the young people desirous of a more exciting life than the small towns and rural areas offer. By locating the new towns around the country, with some in relatively empty areas, the argument runs, further gains in terms of desired population pattern would be achieved.

The formula, according to the new-town advocates, would be to borrow from British experience:

> Making new communities part of a national urban growth strategy requires stronger public incentives to see that they are built when and how they will be needed. Private enterprise can—and should—be heavily involved in the building process, but public policy should influence decisions about location of new communities—and require that they accommodate a significant share of the poor and minorities whose main recourse now is the inner-city. New communities also need to be larger in size and numbers to make a noticeable difference in the way growth occurs. They need to be new cities, with the scale and diversity that implies, rather than new towns. This means public investment—money that can be returned (with profit) and reused, as Britain's experience shows, but enough money to get the city-building process started.[11]

In judging this argument, it is necessary to recall what British new towns actually achieved in approximately the quarter-century from 1946 to 1971, and anticipate what they might achieve in the 1970s and 1980s. The British new towns have been fairly good at achieving certain of their objectives, less good at others. They have moved industry and people out in step; thus they have achieved a higher degree of self-sufficiency, or self-containment, in provision of local employment than is typical for other towns of equivalent size and in equivalent locations. For many hundreds of thousands of people they have provided modest but well-built houses, with basic amenities, in a high-quality urban environment, at fairly low cost. They have probably provided some sense of community. Up to the early 1970s, they seem to have been reasonably successful in offering a choice between congestion-free use of the car and availability of mass transportation. They will almost certainly represent an extremely profitable long-term investment for the community. They have not, however, achieved true social balance. While some groups—particularly

---

[10] Advisory Commission on Intergovernmental Relations, *Urban and Rural America: Policies for Future Growth* (Washington: U.S. Government Printing Office), 1968.
[11] Canty, *The New City*, p. 115.

the skilled blue-collar worker—are overrepresented, other groups—above all the poorly paid unskilled and semiskilled manual worker groups, but also the highly paid professional and managerial group—are underrepresented. And while the absence of the second may be attributed to choice, the absence of the first definitely can not. Though public housing—by far the most common type of housing in the new towns so far—has been subsidized by the central government, the subsidy does not seem to have been sufficient to attract low-income residents in large numbers from the cities. There is, however, some promise that this will be rectified—at least by some new towns—during the 1970s.

By the late 1960s, the scale of planned overspill from several of the major agglomerations was decreasing quite sharply, as the waiting list for municipal housing there fell; more and more families, who would previously have rented public sector housing, were preferring the advantages of owner-occupation. This alone might cause the new towns to seek more actively for lower-income residents; it has been underlined by the 1972 Housing Finance Act, which relates rents of public sector housing to cost of construction and need, and will make this new-town housing (built economically on low-cost land) relatively attractive to low-income groups in comparison with more expensive municipal housing in the conurbations.

It is also essential to point out that British new towns have made only a very limited contribution to the goal of population distribution or redistribution. The effect of new towns in this regard will obviously depend upon the scale of their building. The additional population in twenty-three new towns of England and Wales, above that which was there when they were established as new towns, was less than 1 percent of the national population in 1971. And, as earlier noted, the new-town corporations built less than 3 percent of the national total new housing units over the period 1946–70. Thus, the new-town program was probably dwarfed, as far as population distribution is concerned, by the industrial and other location programs. In the United States, if one would seek to modify patterns of population distribution to a significant degree, the scale of new-town building would have to be far larger, because the patterns of population change take place on a larger national scale.

This record suggests an obvious comparison. The British new towns have provided better housing conditions for a particular socioeconomic group. In the same period, from 1945 onwards, the main thrust of American public programs—such as those of the Federal Housing Administration and the Veterans Administration— seems to have been to provide improved housing conditions for exactly the same group: the skilled blue-collar workers and the less skilled white-collar workers. It is the means to the end that have differed. Whereas the British provided public housing with direct subsidy for rent in the new towns, the American program provided suburban housing for sale. But for the future, as the British new-towns program shifts a planned 50:50 mix between public and private housing, with an extended mortgage program (the Option Mortgage scheme) for lower-income families who do not get significant tax relief from existing programs, the difference between the two methods will surely grow less. What will remain is the emphasis in the British program on self-containment, with provision of housing close to industrial employment opportunities; the greater degree of social mix (if indeed this is eventually achieved); the mix of public and private transportation opportunities; the different form of development, with higher densities and more clustering; the greater sense of community; the better aesthetic quality of the design; and the public ownership of the land.

Some of these differences, it must be said, contain a large element of subjective judgment. Urban planners, both in Britain and the United States, seem to prefer cluster housing—with groups of medium-density structures (twelve to twenty houses per net acre) separated by big areas of public open space—to the American suburban formula, which gives each detached house a surrounding substantial piece of private space, at between one and twelve houses per acre. Eichler and Kaplan[12] point out that up to 1967 cluster housing had been notably unsuccessful in open market sales in new American communities, while the renters in British new towns really have no choice to express a preference. However, cluster housing has subsequently sold well at Columbia and elsewhere. Again, urban planners seem to prefer the planned shopping centers they find in new communities in Europe, like Stevenage in England or Farsta in Sweden, to the typical American suburban center. But in many design elements—the use of pedestrian malls, the generous parking space—the two are remarkably similar. Perhaps the chief distinctive feature of the European model is the ready availability of public transportation. But it must be remembered that in the early 1970s most European urban areas have a lower level of car ownership than American suburbs. The true comparison will come only in the 1980s, when European levels of ownership begin to catch up. Already, in the early 1970s, there are indications that rising car ownership may make mass transportation difficult to operate viably, as has been the case for many years in the United States.

Some of the elements of difference, such as aesthetic and cultural qualities, are even more troublesome to resolve objectively. They raise questions of different national taste, the wisdom of allowing free consumer choice versus the attempt deliberately to impose standards through conscious design, and the impact of factors such as education and national cultural patterns. It is certainly difficult to obtain any objective measure, for instance, of whether the American suburb or the English new town produces richer cultural activity per inhabitant. Even if such a measure were available it might not be very significant, because of the basic difficulty of comparing two populations with different standards of material wealth, educational level, and cultural tradition.

The one difference possible to measure objectively and quantitatively is the self-containment of the new town. Certainly, by any available measure, the new town brings its working inhabitants closer to their work, on average, than the American suburb. But it is necessary to make some reservations. First, to some extent this results simply from the lower residential density of the suburb; it represents a trade-off between accessibility and space, which is fairly familiar to all students of urban affairs. Second, the meaningful comparison is not so much in terms of mileage distances, but in terms of money and time costs of commuting. The Ameri-

[12] *The Community Builders.*

can suburbanite, who characteristically travels by car using an elaborate (and expensive) highway system, may travel several times faster than his counterpart in a British new town who uses the bus—though his money costs are undeniably greater. Third, to the extent that the American pattern involves very long commuter journeys—over forty-five minutes each day each way, for instance—this may to some extent be a temporary phenomenon of the development of suburbia: there may be a time lag of several years between the outward movement of people and the outward movement of industry, whereas the new-town building process achieves both simultaneously. And fourth, to tie up the preceding arguments, the only fair comparison is in terms of preferences. The American commuter may be willing to trade off high commuting costs—in money and to some degree in time— up to a certain point, in order to obtain the sort of environment, social and physical, that he wants.

Some writers, including the sociologist Herbert Gans,[13] indicate that up to a certain commuting distance the suburbanite may be remarkably indifferent to variations in journey length: he decides that he is willing to travel up to a certain distance, say forty-five minutes each way, and then seeks the best possible environment available at the price he can afford. It was recognition of this fact, early in the postwar era, that caused Levitt to start building his developments farther away from the central city than had previously been thought viable: Levitt reckoned that people would travel further in search of space and a good environment at a lower price. Latterly, as Eichler and Kaplan point out, the developers of new communities have taken the argument a step further: they are building expensive homes at considerably greater distances from the centers of the metropolitan areas, on the argument that the propensity to travel in search of good environment is greater than has been supposed. Probably no definite satisfactory verdict can be reached on this point. The evidence does suggest that there is no mystical virtue in self-containment in itself, divorced from people's own preference patterns. Still, there is a case for giving people the choice.

The crucial element in the argument for new towns in America is probably different. It is argued that only a conscious publicly sponsored effort to create new communities will break the vicious circle of poverty, lack of opportunity, and bankruptcy in the central cities. There is a widespread and growing belief in the United States that this situation can be changed only by a deliberate policy of rapid dispersion of the concentrations of poverty. After an extensive analysis of this and other urban problems, for instance, the Committee on Urban Growth Policy recommended a national policy, with federal government funding, for the creation of 100 new communities averaging 100,000 people each and 10 each of at least 1 million, which:

> . . . should result in socially and economically adjusted communities. Special account should be taken of the needs of low and moderate income families. Special opportunities should be provided to afford gainful, varied and satisfying employment to such families. They should not, however, be induced to

[13] Herbert J. Gans, *The Levittowners: Ways of Life and Politics in a New Suburban City* (New York: Pantheon, 1967), p. 222.

migrate to new towns without the assistance of having there employment, adequate housing, recreation, and like facilities.[14]

The conclusion from the British new towns experience is that if this were to be achieved, it would require a quite deliberate effort which has not yet been made. However, it is important to distinguish here between income mix—to which also social mix approximates—and racial mix. New towns in America might well be successful in attracting skilled and semiskilled blacks of above average or average income, who were anxious to leave the central city ghetto areas. In that way, they would make available superior central city housing for lower-income groups. This filtering process could be frustrated by further inmigration from rural areas into the central cities, causing further pressure on available housing resources and rapid deterioration of the housing stock. But there is some fairly strong evidence that by the late 1960s the pace of this migration was slowing down. If this is true, and if the great wave of rapid migration from the south and the Appalachians is nearly over, then the early 1970s would be the best possible time for a policy of selective settlement of middle-income black families in new planned communities outside the existing metropolitan areas. But, it should be noticed, this will only intensify the low-income character of the central city populations and further exacerbate the revenue problems of the city administrations. And it would do nothing to remove, rather it would increase, the growing distance between the unskilled labor force able and willing to fill service job opportunities, and the growing volume of those job opportunities outside the central city.

The last distinctive point about the new-towns solution is that, under it, values revert to the community. And the evidence is clear that in Britain new towns represent a good bargain. Typically, they start to yield a profit to the community after only about twelve years of life. Over a long term, the gains should be very considerable. The net income may be used for various purposes according to the practices and preferences of the community concerned; in Britain, because of a long-standing Treasury prejudice against "earmarked" moneys being used by public agencies, they are returned to the general Treasury pool. But they could well be used to finance a larger-scale attack on the problems of the central cities. Under this prescription a number of new towns would be financed and built by a common Development Corporation which could also have responsibility for urban renewal in the central city. At first, outside help from federal or state governments would certainly be necessary to meet the heavy initial costs of getting the new towns started. But after a few years the return flow could be considerable.

But, paradoxically, it is this very prospect of public profit that will be a major political objection to the development of new towns on a significant scale in the United States: if there is profit to be made, let it go to private enterprise. The fact that new towns, thus far at least, have neither made a profit for private builders nor seemed attractive as a source of profits, would not fully meet this type of objection. Purchase of land at nodal points on the Interstate Highway system or near stations on new subway systems would also prove highly profitable to the

[14] Canty, *The New City*, p. 173.

public agencies; but, with limited exceptions, it has been opposed successfully for the very reason that it did have profit opportunities.

With all these reservations, there still seems a strong case for developing new-town programs for some of the larger American metropolitan areas. For the community as a whole they should be no more expensive than any other form of urban development planned to achieve the same purposes, and they would be cheaper than high-density renewal;[15] moreover, in time they would yield considerable community benefits. They might well be less self-contained than their British equivalents, but if they attracted industry in step with population, they could at least offer their residents a choice of jobs near at hand. They might well be built at lower densities than British new towns, reflecting a tradition of more generous space consumption than in Britain; but by building a variety of housing types experimentally, at different densities and associated with different degrees of accessibility to mass transportation systems, they could again offer a choice that in many suburbs has been lacking. They would almost certainly not in themselves solve the complex problems of the central cities, and above all the problems of the low-income residents there; but they might help indirectly—through the promotion of a filtering process in housing and through the return, in time, of profits—to aid the central cities.

If a program of new towns is desirable, the question then is whether it is feasible. The British new-towns program essentially rests on two foundations of public policy (as well as upon mass programs of subsidized public housing and public ownership of land, each of which would present problems for American policy). One of these would not be too difficult to replicate in the United States: a semi-autonomous public corporation, with direct finance from central (i.e., federal or state) government. Because of the problems of the central cities, there might be a case for associating them closely with the corporation, perhaps through the right to nominate a number of the members. The other is essentially more difficult: it is the power to attract industry to the new towns through a battery of negative and positive devices. Though the British new-town corporations are able to offer important incentives to industry in the form of rentable land or ready-built factory floorspace, it is doubtful whether these would prove so attractive in themselves if it were not for the powerful controls on new factory location, or on factory extension, in the form of the Industrial Development Certificate procedure. Essentially, many firms have come to the new towns around London from the capital,

---

[15] In Britain, the Town and Country Planning Association has produced evidence, which has not been refuted though it has been challenged in detail, that to provide new-town housing is considerably cheaper, in terms of capital and subsidies, to the public purse than to provide the same amount of housing in the form of high-density urban renewal schemes. Thus if 1,000 families are to be rehoused in an urban area, it would have cost £1,165,000 ($3,262,000) more to house them all in 12-story apartment blocks in the city than to house only half in this way and to house the other half in a new town. (These values refer to the year 1958.) Cf. F. J. Osborn and Arnold Whittick, *The New Towns: Answer to Megalopolis* (New York: McGraw Hill, 1963), p. 99. Since then P. A. Stone has calculated that dwellings in high blocks are 35–45 percent more expensive than houses in London, 60–70 percent more in provincial Britain. An increase in the proportion of high blocks from the present 10 percent to 30 percent would raise the entire community's housing costs by about 10 percent. P. A. Stone, *Urban Development in Britain: Standards, Costs and Resources 1964–2004*, vol. I, *Population Trends and Housing* (Cambridge, England: University Press, 1970), p. 97.

because they have been refused permission to set up a new branch or to build an extension in London itself. The same applies to those new towns in the Development Areas, which can offer even more substantial inducements to firms unable to expand in London or the southeast part of England. It seems inconceivable that in the immediate future the United States could bring itself to impose such controls on industrial location; such a notion would be totally out of character with the traditions of the nation. Therefore, the only way to achieve the desired diversion of industry would be through positive inducements. Here, though, American new towns would be aided by one obvious feature: the tendency for industry to move outwards in any event, under the pressure of economic forces. It would merely be necessary to use positive inducements to attract a proportion of this movement into the new towns, so as to provide for the matching of employment growth and house building that would be central to the whole operation.

In thus advancing the positive case for new-town development in the United States, it is necessary to keep a perspective. At the largest imaginable scale of new-town building in the United States, only a small part of the total increase in national population could be cared for in this way. Most of the population increase in the United States over the next two or three decades will live in suburbs—the older city centers are nearly full, the nonmetropolitan areas seem to face stagnation or at least absence of growth, and the net increase will be located primarily in the suburbs. The scale of new-town building suggested by the Committee on Urban Growth Policy (100 new communities of 100,000 each and 10 of 1 million each) might indeed accommodate all the increase in national population, but a program of this scale seems highly unlikely.

If suburbs are to be the future home of most of the increased population, then programs to improve their quality and efficiency must remain high on the priority list.

chapter 7

Urbanization and the
natural environment

The urbanization processes of the United States and Britain, and the planning and control systems that have guided and regulated them, have often paid little explicit attention to the natural environment; when they have, policies have often been superficial and misguided. To show why this has been so, we need first to make a systematic analysis of environmental problems and impacts, and then to see how urban growth processes have entered into them.

NATURE OF URBAN-ENVIRONMENTAL RELATIONS

The impact of urban development upon the natural environment may be divided into direct or primary impacts and indirect or secondary ones. Although these are not separated by a clean, sharp line, there are major differences, and it is helpful to consider them separately.

The direct impact involves land use changes, when the land is converted from some rural use to some urban one. Of course, the terms *rural* and *urban* are increasingly ambiguous, as urban impacts on the countryside grow in range and intensity; but here we are referring to urban land uses in the fairly narrow sense. Direct impacts, in this sense, mean the physical growth of the metropolitan area, in terms of factories and offices, schools, colleges and hospitals, retail stores and other services, residential areas, and transportation lines. Among these different land uses, the residential element is dominant, particularly when associated local streets and schools and services are taken into account; and though there is some ambiguity still in drawing the limit of permanent new residential settlement, nevertheless in most cases it can be done without too much difficulty. Urbanization in this sense has very definite impacts on the environment. Often the vegetation is cleared, leaving the land bare for some months during the building process; buildings are erected and streets are paved, creating impervious surfaces from which runoff is 100 percent and immediate, rather than partial and delayed; earth is often moved, in a modification of the micro-relief (hills cut down, low places filled, etc.); and generally the natural environment of the land is materially modified. This is often fairly obvious, especially during the development process itself. While some of this modification affects other land, as when soil washed off exposed surfaces is deposited elsewhere, much of this impact is on the land surface concerned.

The indirect or secondary effects of urbanization on the environment are more diverse and less obvious, more likely to involve other areas and other people in addition to the particular tract of land, and usually more serious in their long-term effects. Indeed, in any economically advanced and technologically sophisticated country, so diverse and widespread are these impacts that it is difficult to draw any limits to them; they are inseparable from the general effects of technology. People make journeys to work, or in the course of their work, by car; thus they deposit pollution in the air, make demands on natural resources of steel and rubber and other raw materials, and increase the demand on land for road space. They fly to meetings in distant cities, leaving in the upper air jet contrails that obscure the sunlight below and may change the air's constitution permanently; they also impose noise shadows on people living under approach and take-off paths; the planes themselves and their airports make further immense demands on natural materials. Urban families, in their apparently insatiable demands for food and raw materials, may encourage over-exploitation of plant or animal species, even leading to depletion or extinction of some species. These demands may also lead to the development of fertilizers or pesticides which, applied to foodstuffs, may have unpredictable effects on the human organism. Rising levels of material consumption, in turn, produce increasing quantities of waste matter—solid, liquid, and gaseous—posing immense and widespread problems of disposal; in the air or in the water, they may sometimes cause damage to life. All these impacts are important to most urban men and women, and some may literally be vital; but many are difficult to trace.

Within the limits of this book we cannot deal with all the indirect effects of affluence and high technology that are invariably associated with urban growth in Britain and the United States; our examination of environmental impacts must focus on urban growth and on attempts to plan and control that growth. Within this framework, it is possible to surmise that the most important types of indirect impact will be these:

1. *The indirect effects of urban growth on development of the land*, development being defined as any change in land use requiring a change in the landscape, of a duration long enough for any one generation to regard it as permanent. This includes provision of urban services involving development of rural land: e.g., power stations, power lines, reservoirs, airports, interurban highways, mines and quarries providing raw materials (such as bricks or gravel) specifically for urban development, together with a wide variety of recreational developments such as ski resorts, marinas, second homes, and campsites. Many if not all of these man-made features make a considerable impact on the rural landscape, and considerable controversy may attend their siting and design. But not all these aspects can be discussed here, and we shall need to concentrate on those cases where the form of the urban development affects the nature of the environmental problem; where,

in other words, it might be possible to reduce or even remove environmental impacts by careful planning of urban areas.

2. Pollution of air and water, including pollution of the air by noise. Here again we shall need to concentrate specifically on the effects of different urban forms on the phenomena.

3. Production of urban wastes—solid, liquid, and gaseous—and the problems of their disposal in the rural areas outside. Here again we shall need to focus on the question: how far are the dimensions of the problem affected by different forms of urban growth?

Under each of these headings, clearly, the first question we shall need to ask is: How do different patterns of urban growth affect the nature and intensity of environmental impacts? Do these impacts vary substantially according to whether development is high or low density, scattered or concentrated, in planned self-contained communities or in suburbs with few jobs?

Secondly, having isolated the impacts that do vary in this way, we should ask: How are they to be measured? Are there comparable indices of impact in terms of human welfare? Can one realistically quantify different types of impact for the purpose of making decisions about controlling them? Can one, for instance, measure the importance of loss of wildlife as against water pollution as against noise impacts? And how far have decision takers actually used such an approach; what in fact have been the criteria used to reach policy decisions in this field?

Thirdly, we shall need to ask: Assuming that decisions are made, on whatever criteria, to take public action to prohibit or regulate or compensate for these impacts, what sorts of action are open to the policy maker? And what sorts have in fact been used by policy makers in the recent past in the United States and in Britain?

A fourth and final question is: How are the different programs of control or compensation related to each other? Are they part of an integrated program, in which decisions are taken on roughly consistent criteria across the whole field, or are they compartmentalized? How far is integration feasible in principle? And how far has it been achieved in practice?

Environmental Hazards in Britain and in the United States

In order to compare the environmental problems created by urbanization and suburbanization in the two countries, one must first consider briefly the nature of the environmental hazards in each. Basically, the United States faces a more difficult environmental problem than does Britain.

Provision of the many goods and services of modern living in a reasonably affluent society necessarily involves impacts on the areas of origin of the necessary raw materials. The metals going into a modern automobile, refrigerator, television set or any other household appliance must come from somewhere; so must the coal, oil, gas, or other fuel needed to operate many of these devices of modern living, either directly as fuel or indirectly as electricity derived from the fuel. Mines, whether open-cut or underground, necessarily leave scars, as do the means of conveying the raw materials to the centers of consumption—rail lines, electric power lines, and others. All this is relatively well understood, though many urban dwellers ignore or are unconscious of these environmental impacts because they lie somewhere else.

But less frequently understood is the fact that all these raw materials that enter into modern living (which is also dominantly urban living) must be disposed of, somewhere, in some way. When one flushes the toilet or gets rid of a worn-out refrigerator, or when a derelict auto is abandoned on the street (as increasingly happens in both the United States and Britain today), the "residual" of the consumption process does not neatly disappear. On the contrary, it continues to exist; nothing is ever really destroyed—it is simply changed in form. This is the law of the conservation of matter, discovered and proclaimed by scientists many decades ago, but commonly ignored on the urban scene of today. All the water, fuel, food, building materials, and other raw materials flowing into a great metropolis such as London or New York must flow out again (barring relatively modest changes in inventory); they may go out as pollutants to the air or to the water, or they may be buried as solid wastes. But they do not go away. The waste disposal problem can get as sticky as that faced by the Australian primitive who tries to throw away his used boomerang; the trash (rubbish) one hopes is gone forever, simply because the trashman (dustman) took it away, has a way of turning up again.

What can be done about these modern problems of "residuals," "wastes," "pollution," or whatever one chooses to call them? First of all, the production-consumption-disposal process must be looked at as an entirety, not as three separate processes. Too often manufacturers, marketers, and even economists have looked only at production; when a product has been sold to a consumer, interest has ended. Secondly, as one looks at this whole process, maintenance (or, in some cases, improvement) of the environment is likely to mean changes in each part. For example, ideally, manufacturers will no longer make only what sells best, without concern for how it serves the consumer or for how it can be disposed of when no longer useful; and consumers will no longer demand everything they want, without concern for its environmental effects. Substantial changes in production methods, marketing methods, and consumption patterns may all be necessary. Thirdly, because the residuals can be disposed of in various ways—to the air, water, or land—there are trade-offs, as when stack gases from an electric generating station are scrubbed and the particulate matter is dumped in streams, or when waste is burned to avoid landfill problems but at the cost of air pollution. Because of these trade-offs, it is misleading to consider singly air pollution problems, or water pollution problems, or landfill problems. There is a problem of residuals management, a major aspect of which is, or should be, recycling to recover the greatest possible (economic) amount of the original raw materials. All of this concerns more than the city; it concerns the totality of a modern economy and society. But because that society and economy is becoming increasingly an urban one, the overlap between environmental problems and urban problems is large.

The climate of the two countries we are comparing greatly affects their environmental problems. Americans visiting Britain are impressed by the rolling green countryside, unscarred by erosion or by exposures of raw earth, and with streams unladen with sediments from erosion; and the conclusion is often drawn that the

British take better care of their land because they love it more. Perhaps they do, but the climate makes their job easier. Rainfall in Britain is less than most Americans would estimate as they look at the ubiquitous green grass and trees. All of Britain lies north of the most northerly point in the forty-eight conterminous states; it is thus cooler and evaporation and transpiration are lower. An annual rainfall of 22–35 inches, which typifies much of urban Britain, is appreciably less than the 30–50 inches typifying the eastern half of the United States. Still more important, in terms of soil erosion hazard, is the fact that British rainfall typically comes down at a much gentler rate. With a lower rate of rainfall and a cooler climate, vegetation (especially grasses) grows more densely and covers a larger proportion of the total land surface in much of Britain; soil is less exposed to erosion. The closest comparable situation in the forty-eight conterminous states is to be found in northern Wisconsin, where one rarely sees an eroding soil surface. In the Northeastern Urban Complex, which we have considered in some detail in this book, the soil erosion hazard is much greater, resulting in many bare and severely eroding surfaces around most cities of the region.

Accompanying these differences in rainfall patterns are further differences in the nature of the flood and stream siltation problems of the two countries. If a flood is defined as a stream overtopping its normal banks, then floods may occur anywhere, because the cutting of the channel and the defining of the normal banks is partly a function of the average rainfall. Where the rainfall is erratic but sometimes violent, floods are more common and more devastating than where rains are more dependable and more gentle, because stream flow peaks are so much higher in relation to average stream flows. Severe floods occur in desert areas of the western United States; the stream bed is dust-dry 360 days of the year, but carries a raging torrent for several days as severe storms sweep the watershed; the peak flow may last only a matter of hours or even minutes. With variations in flow, differences in sediment content occur; where rainfall is slow enough to permit much of it to infiltrate the soil, and where vegetation leads to slow runoff, the waters are likely to be clear, even in flood. Where precipitation is highly variable and heavy when it does fall, soil movement is almost inevitable—though man's activities have often greatly accelerated it—and the waters, especially in time of flood, are brown and dirty.

Under these differing natural conditions in the two countries, the problems of flood plain use also differ. Since 1936, the United States has put into effect major programs of flood protection, and up to 1966 some $7,000 million had been spent for flood protection. In spite of this expenditure, and to some degree because of it, the flood risk of the nation increased over these years. People expanded onto the flood plains with dwellings, industrial plants, commercial establishments, and other activities, faster than flood protection could be extended. Almost every American city has a major problem of flood plain management, growing largely out of the expansion of its urban area. In Britain, this problem is less troublesome. British rivers have a more even regime; in their lower courses, where they approach urban areas, they do so in wide flood plains, which since early times have been generally avoided for building. The biggest flood dangers to these lowland cities come from a combination of high river levels and tide surges in the North Sea, which caused extensive rural flooding in eastern England in 1953 and which, as announced in 1970, have justified the construction of a £5 million flood barrier for the Thames below London.

The two countries differ also in the role which "natural" vegetation plays. When in the seventeenth century European colonists began settling what is now the United States, the vegetation along the Atlantic Seaboard had been little influenced by man. Apart from small clearings, where Indians practiced agriculture, nearly all of the region was covered with dense forests. Further west, extensive prairies were a product of the Indians' use of fire to control the vegetation. In the 300 or more years since those early colonial settlements, most of the forests have been cut and recut; most of the land not used regularly for crops has grown back into trees—some of them species quite different from the original ones. Today, in the Northeastern Urban Complex and throughout much of the eastern half of the United States, land abandoned from other uses tends to grow a cover, first of shrubs, then of trees, often with a more or less predictable cycle of tree species. "Forest" is thus a common, almost ubiquitous condition; but "forestry" as a purposeful economic enterprise is much less common. Many tracts of "woods" grow largely unattended; when some trees reach merchantable size, they may be cut. Thus, the suburban real estate developer often faces a tree growth on the raw land he intends to use for housing. More often than not, in the interests of economy he bulldozes the trees and shrubs, leaving the land bare; and later the new home buyers painfully and slowly grow new trees, grass, shrubs, and flowers.

In Britain, much of what appears to the casual eye as "natural" vegetation is very much a man-made landscape. The so-called "natural" vegetation may have been removed centuries or even millenia ago; in southern England, for instance, much of the chalklands were probably deforested in prehistoric times, while the heavier, low-lying claylands were cleared by Anglo-Saxon invaders between the sixth and the eighth centuries. The present-day trees and hedges—where these have not been grubbed up by post-1945 farmers in the name of mechanization and efficiency—were planted by eighteenth century gentlemen farmers after the enclosure of the big medieval open fields at that time. Only in a few parts of the country, where enclosure came earlier and took place direct from the waste— as in Devon and Cornwall—is the man-made landscape of earlier date. But, of course, the fact that a landscape is largely man-made, rather than natural in its origins, does not deny its beauty or the case for preserving it. The typical English landscape of rectangular hedged fields and frequent coppice timber, which was a planned landscape of two centuries ago, is now the image of the country in the tourist posters. Sometimes those conservationists who object to the new open-field landscape of eastern England are startled to be reminded that it is a return to the landscape of the Middle Ages.

So far as air pollution is concerned, the conditions that generate it are common to all large, modern cities. On the whole, as emissions from open fires have decreased with effective smoke control and with the development of central heating, emissions from automobiles have increased. Over and around each major urban area there exists an airshed (American term), capable of receiving and dissipating pollutants—a capacity which depends in part upon prevailing wind movements.

In some parts of the United States, notably in the western Mountain and Pacific states, a particularly difficult combination of geologic relief and climate prevails: the cities are ringed or bordered by mountains that interfere with air movements; at the same time they are subject to long periods when still, anticyclonic air persists. Inversions grow up, whereby an upper cooler layer prevents the dissipation of the rising warmer air with its burden of pollution; thus smog builds up and remains, flowing to and fro across the city without escaping, just as water-borne pollution ebbs and flows in the estuarial part of a stream. Inversion fogs are common in other parts of the world: London, which stands in a shallow but well-defined basin, became notorious for them in the age of Dickens, when the smoke from millions of domestic coal fires became trapped on still November nights. But since the 1950s, as London has enforced strict air pollution controls and as the private automobile replaces the private hearth as the chief source of pollution, Los Angeles has taken over from London the unenviable title of the world's smoggiest city— at least by repute.[1]

COMPETITION FOR LAND AND OTHER NATURAL RESOURCES

The city, as a collection of persons and as a locale for economic activity, competes with other groups of persons and other economic activities for the use of various kinds of natural resources.

First of all, urban expansion is likely to take place at the cost of agriculture. The same natural conditions of modest slopes, medium-textured soils, good surface and internal soil drainage, and others favor both crop farming and urban land use. Moreover, the better soils near cities are likely to be used for intensive agriculture, especially market gardens and fruit production; the nearby urban market has often stimulated this type of agricultural production. The permanent loss of good farmland as it is covered with buildings and streets has been disturbing to many.

Concern over urban encroachment upon good farming lands provided much of the steam behind Britain's planning program. The experience in two world wars, within easy memory of persons living through both and with their attendant disruption in the supply of agricultural commodities, was a further disturbing factor. The value of agriculture, as a means both of preserving the highly desired appearance of rural Britain and of rendering the country less vulnerable to interruptions in supply of commodities, was considered to be very great indeed. This has been reflected in county planning of the past quarter century, in which the impact of proposed urban expansion upon agricultural land use has often been a major consideration.

During the 1930s, before present planning controls were imposed in Britain, the conversion of farmland to urban uses rose to as much as 60,000 acres annually.

[1] The two types of "smog" are, however, so dissimilar that it may not be helpful to give them the same name—especially as few victims of the one have experienced the other. Both are characteristically yellow and rasping. But the London "pea-souper"—the last example of which occurred, probably for all time, in 1952—was thick, with virtually zero visibility; Los Angeles smog is a much thinner, orange-yellow veil over the sun.

Land was comparatively cheap, and many homes were built with relatively generous gardens (lots). Since World War II, land conversion from farming to urban
uses has declined to the order of 36,000 acres annually, and this in spite of a
higher rate of growth of urban population.

The British concern with the loss of agricultural land to urban uses seems to an
American almost an obsession. It clearly is not guided by economic considerations
alone; those defending continued agricultural use of land reject the notion that
its market price, even when supplemented by calculations of indirect values, is a
suitable test. The overriding concern with area has tended to block out the other
dimension of agricultural production—output per acre. Crop yields and livestock
output per animal have been rising in Britain, as in every other economically advanced country. Moreover, concern over land use has obscured the fact that imports of agricultural commodities, which represent a cost to Britain, are nevertheless an income to the exporting countries—an income that may be basic to their
purchase of industrial goods manufactured in Britain for export.

The total area of urban land in England and Wales is estimated as 2 million
acres in 1900 and as 4.4 million in 1970. A fairly generous allowance for population growth and a somewhat more generous allowance than exists today for urban
land area in relation to urban population yields an estimate of total urban land in
the year 2000 of 6 million acres; even a very generous allowance for increased
urban land area would require only 7 million acres.[2] While this is 18 percent of
the total land area of 37 million acres, it is still obviously a minor part of the
total land area. With the agricultural trends now probable, Britain would be more
nearly self-sufficient in agricultural commodities in 2000 than she now is, even
with this loss of agricultural land.

In the United States agriculturists, planners, and the general public have expressed some concern over the loss of farmland as the cities have expanded, but
none of the few attempts to preserve the farmland has been noticeably successful,
for several reasons. First, in the United States a great deal of land is *not* in
farms and *not* in cities. In the Northeastern Urban Complex, for instance, 21
percent of the total land area in 1960 was in some form of urban use (by relatively
generous definition), 35 percent was in farms (much of which was rough pasture
or forested), and 44 percent was "not" land—that is, it was in neither farms nor
cities. Mostly it had tree cover, but rarely was in purposefully managed forests;
usually it was owned by individuals for speculative, recreational, or personal reasons, but was not used intensively. In this connection, it should be borne in mind
again that the Northeastern Urban Complex and Megalopolis England are approximately the same size and have approximately the same total populations. While
the situation in the Northeast may be somewhat extreme, even for the United
States, idle land near large cities is a very common feature of the American
scene.

In the United States, agriculture has become specialized over the decades, reflecting the twin influences of market demand and physical production possibilities.
Production of fruits and vegetables for the large urban markets is mostly in

[2] Robin H. Best, "The Future Urban Acreage," *Town and Country Planning*, vol. 32 (1964),
table 1, p. 352.

specialized areas of Florida, Texas, Arizona, and California, rather than near the large cities of the Northeastern Urban Complex. Agriculture in the latter area has tended to specialize in the production of fresh milk and, to a lesser extent in recent years, of poultry and eggs. Total agricultural output in the Northeastern Urban Complex has held up remarkably well; value of output rose from 1940 to 1959, but proportionately less than for the United States as a whole.

As was pointed out in chapter 3, a distinctive difference between England and Wales (Megalopolis England) and the northeastern United States (the Northeastern Urban Complex) is the greater importance of agriculture in the British area. The agricultural plant is much larger in Britain. Nevertheless, its capacity to feed the national population is less than that of U.S. agriculture as a whole to feed its national population. Agricultural output in Britain has varied greatly over the decades, partly because foreign trade policies have at times permitted imports of low-cost agricultural products and at other times have stimulated intense domestic expansion during wartime blockades. The Agricultural Revolution, whereby much more output than in the past is obtained from a given area of land, has transformed British agriculture as much as it has American agriculture. Since World War II, national policy has been directed toward keeping agricultural output high—not at wartime levels, but far above prewar levels. Since the mid-1950s, agricultural output in Britain has risen by nearly 40 percent, whereas in the United States the rise has been about 25 percent.

In both countries competition exists between uses of land for urban development and for mineral production; and urban growth in itself stimulates mineral exploitation. Sand, gravel, clay, and building stone—all heavy building materials—cannot economically be transported far. Consequently, sand and gravel deposits, or stone which can be converted into sand and gravel, often from wet diggings, are developed near all large cities, and their exploitation creates problems for the city dwellers in terms not only of ruined landscape and noisy operations, but also of actual danger to the unwary. However, good city planning requires that good sand and gravel deposits be reserved for extraction of these minerals, rather than be built on for residential or other purposes. The excavated areas, after they have been worked out and abandoned, might be used for deposit of solid urban wastes— landfill in U.S. terms, tipping areas in English terminology; but the coordination of extraction and of fill has thus far been largely unattainable. In some cases, more common in the United States than in Britain so far, the large excavated areas have been converted into artificial lakes as a central feature of parks.

The economic development of both countries, which has been associated in time and in function with urban growth, has also led to large-scale development of other minerals. Industry requires iron, steel, coal, and many other minerals, and their extraction from the earth results in large heaps of wastes—dumps, in U.S. terms, slag heaps or spoil heaps in English terms. These and the excavations, if the mineral is extracted from surface workings, form derelict areas—unsightly, barren, and sometimes dangerous. While they are sometimes remote from the cities themselves—and hence tend to be ignored by many city residents and perhaps by city planners—these derelict areas are scars resulting from a city's industrial development.

The city and its associated economic growth have required substantial amounts of energy. In each country the consumption of energy from all sources has risen steadily, at a rate of perhaps 10 percent annually—at least, at a rate several times the annual rate of growth of population. The Industrial Revolution of Britain was fueled by coal, and coal and its derivatives have been critical to U.S. industrial growth. In the past two or three decades, petroleum, including natural gas, has surpassed coal in terms of total energy supplied, but coal remains a major source of power. Britain's most important coal field in production—the Yorkshire, Derbyshire, and Nottingham field—lies wholly within Megalopolis England, whereas in the United States the coal fields usually lie outside the most heavily urbanized areas. In both countries, sources of petroleum are located beyond the major urban areas—indeed, to a large extent in foreign countries. In each country, electric power is produced at hydro installations as far as this is possible; but hydro power is a minor source of energy in the United States as a whole and especially so in the Northeastern Urban Complex, and it is not a major source of power in Britain, being virtually restricted to the Scottish Highlands. In each country, atomic energy installations are playing an increasing role in the production of electric energy; but some of the easy optimism of a few years ago, as to the ready development of cheap electric energy from atomic sources, has evaporated in the light of cold experience. While in Britain the average cost of producing atomic power fell by 60 percent in just over a decade, its production is neither easy nor cheap, though it will undoubtedly play a larger and larger role in the future.

In each country, a number of factors dictate location of power plants. They must be reasonably near their consumer markets because of high transmission costs. If coal fired, they should be located near the source of coal; if oil or gas fired, they should be near ports where petroleum is imported or —although this is less vital— near gas fields; if atomic powered, they should be located away from large population centers and near large supplies of cooling water. In all these cases, major transmission lines to city power consumption centers are necessary; and these invariably are a blot upon the landscape they traverse. If the modern urban lifestyle is to be supported and continued, large amounts of power are necessary. It may well be argued that national policy will require a curbing of past rates of growth in power consumption, but some continued growth seems inescapable. In both the United States and Britain the energy problem as a whole, and the electric energy problem in particular, is very similar. Some impact upon the environment is unavoidable; the practical planning problem arises from attempts to minimize this impact.

The modern city requires a lot of water for many varied purposes. The consumption of water per capita has risen in most cities over the past several decades, in part because water is so cheap to the consumer. In the United States the average price of potable water delivered to the consumer is in the general magnitude of 40 cents per 1,000 gallons. Even though people drink only a minute fraction of it, this water is available in any quantity for any purpose within the capacity of the consumer's delivery system and at any time-demand schedule he chooses. In the typical American city one can have 1,000 gallons of potable water delivered in the home for about the same price paid for one gallon of gasoline (petrol) at the service station. Experience in the United States has demonstrated that when water is metered, so that users pay in proportion to the amounts used, consumption falls markedly; and the one example of a metered scheme in Britain—in the small resort town of Malvern—shows the same result. (It is expected that in Britain meter charges for water will be generally introduced during the 1970s as a result of a reorganization of water supply in 1974.) If water were several times as costly as it now is, undoubtedly many ways would be found to reduce per capita consumption without severe impairment of living standards.

In each country some decades ago, urban water supplies could usually be obtained from a stream or a lake or groundwater source nearby the city. But as the cities have grown, water has had to be brought in from more distant sources: New York City has reached into the Catskills, Boston into western Massachusetts, Liverpool and Birmingham into Mid-Wales, Manchester into the Lake District. These sources have always lain outside the legal and political boundaries of the cities concerned, and the areas of origin have been less than enthusiastic about yielding their water to the distant city. In many cases, a storage reservoir in the watershed or river basin has taken land out of other uses and often has robbed the surrounding area of its beauty. Sometimes use of the watershed or river basin has been severely limited because of possible pollution of the water. An especially contentious issue has arisen over the possibility of recreational use of many reservoirs. In this matter urban water supply personnel and public health people have resisted use of the water bodies for recreation, while park and recreation people as well as the general public have sought their use for this purpose. Practice has been highly inconsistent in the United States. Some cities have permitted a rather wide range of water reservoir uses, although many have forbidden direct personal water-contact sports; other cities have been adamant in their refusal to allow any recreation on their reservoirs or in their catchment areas. In Britain, too, past policies have been invariably restrictive: fishing might be allowed under license, but boating was forbidden and even lakeside picnicking was discouraged. Latterly, under pressure from recreational interests and with new abstraction and treatment methods—particularly the development of upland reservoirs for purely regulatory purposes, with abstraction downstream—a much more liberal policy has been evident.

All of these more or less direct conflicts in use of land and other natural resources, between the city and other users and other areas, will probably increase in severity. The actual areas involved are often not large compared with total land area within Megalopolis England or the Northeastern Urban Complex. But the areas concerned are often strategically located, or have uses that have been entrenched and resist change, or otherwise lead to sharp struggles over resource use.

Some Effects of Urban Patterns on the Environment

In chapters 3 and 4 we found some important differences in the ways British and American urban areas had developed since World War II; in chapter 5 we found some reasons for those differences, in the very different mechanisms that had operated to control the direct impacts of urbanization on the natural environment. But some of these differences also have important influences on the more indirect impacts discussed at the beginning of this chapter.

Some impacts, it is true, seem to be virtually independent of urban patterns; they are a function of the size of the urban population, its level of material affluence, and the physical geography of the country concerned. Population size and per capita income, in combination, will determine the consumption of many public goods such as water and open space for recreation; in turn, they will fix the level of disposal of wastes resulting from those consumption patterns—solid, liquid, and airborne.

In the case of Britain, water demand rose between 2 and 3.5 percent a year between 1945 and 1970, and it is expected to continue to increase at about 3 percent per year to 2000, thus doubling the demand in the last thirty years of the century and approximately doubling the amount of liquid waste. The volume of solid house refuse per person per week doubled between 1936 and 1970, and is expected nearly to double again by 1980, though its density will fall so that its total weight will rise only slightly. The construction industry's demand for sand and gravel is predicted to double between the early 1960s and the late 1970s. Electricity demand doubles approximately every ten years, and with it the demand for cooling water and the production of solid waste in the form of pulverized fuel ash. The number of private automobiles doubled between 1962 and 1970 and is expected to treble between 1962 and 1980, bringing between one-third and two-thirds of the entire population into zones seriously affected by vehicle noise and greatly increasing the amount of air pollution. Outdoor activities needing substantial amounts of space on land, water, or in the air—such as golf, sailing and subaquatic sports, and gliding—are showing growth rates well in excess of population or earnings.

The way these demands are met will depend largely on the fixed geographical distribution of resources. Unless the costs of desalination are greatly reduced—as they may well be by the 1990s[3]—or unless expensive new reservoirs are developed on a large scale at estuarine sites such as the Wash, the Dee, Morecambe Bay, or the Solway Firth, then rising water demands will have to be met mainly from upland reservoirs, since the possibilities of increased use of lowland river water are limited and so are the resources left in the ground. Though the costs of atomic energy have dropped dramatically in relation to conventional thermal production, giving greater freedom for power station location along Britain's long coastline, the location of thermal stations is still closely constrained by the costs of transporting coal to them, and of transmitting power to major urban areas. Liquid wastes will need to be emptied into rivers or the sea; most solid wastes will probably continue to be tipped onto nearby land, because this is currently by far the cheapest way of getting rid of them; most recreational demands will continue to be heavily concentrated on the areas within one or two hours' weekend drive from major concentrations of population, while most distant areas will remain largely unused except for brief summer or winter vacation periods.

---

[3] An experimental desalination plant was announced in 1971 for Ipswich, an eastern English town just outside Megalopolis, with an acute water supply problem due to reservoir delays. One main purpose of the experiment was to determine costs, but they were expected to be perhaps twice those of conventional supplies. The plan was in fact abandoned in 1972.

Many of these impacts, then, will be unaffected by the different spatial forms urbanization may take. High density versus low density, concentration versus scatter, will not notably affect the demand for power or water or the production of solid or liquid wastes; nor, in most cases, will it affect the ways these demands are met. Nevertheless, there are some important ways in which different urban patterns may affect both the impacts and the ways in which these impacts are handled.

The density of new residential areas is a particularly important variable here. We have seen earlier that, typically, many postwar suburban tracts in the United States have been built at net densities that are very low by conventional European standards—four, or even two or one houses per residential acre. In contrast, British densities of new single-family suburban housing have been high—twelve or even fourteen to the acre. Whatever the density, residents in these new areas will expect to be supplied with basic services such as electricity, running water, telephone and mail service; and they will expect to get these services on a postage-stamp basis that is independent of the cost of producing them. But in some cases this simple equivalence breaks down. Virtually all British postwar suburban housing has been supplied with main drainage; in fact, 96 percent of all homes in England and Wales, urban and rural, are connected to sewerage systems. In contrast, a high proportion of new postwar American suburban housing has been served by septic tank systems. Both these patterns have presented serious, though different, problems. In Britain, planning authorities in practice would not release land for housing development until it was properly sewered; but programs of investment in new sewerage systems were delayed by cuts in central government expenditure; by timid and piecemeal planning on the part of the sewerage planning authorities, who in the counties were the second-tier local authorities, not the county making the development plan; and by understandable reluctance on the part of local authorities to incur expenditure on behalf of people who were, by definition, not yet voters. In practice, too, the existence of sewerage systems (coupled with the lack of sewered land elsewhere) was an important factor in driving up the densities of new development. In the United States, in contrast, the widespread reliance on septic tanks—coupled with a wish on the part of some authorities to limit the costs of new suburban growth—led to extremely low-density zoning; in order to maintain public health standards, no higher density could be permitted. So in practice, the problem of waste disposal has produced contrasted patterns of urban development; but these forms have, in turn, encouraged continued reliance on the same techniques.

The same effect is seen for solid waste collection and disposal. If settlement densities fall very low, public collection becomes economically difficult and there is a tendency to use incineration, which may be a cause of air pollution. On the other hand, residents may clear their own solid waste, which is likely to lead to uncontrolled dumping rather than the controlled forms responsible for 90 percent of British solid trash and garbage collection.

Though both British and American suburbanites rely heavily on automobile transportation, with 70 or 80 percent of work journeys commonly made in this way, there are important differences, especially in the ownership and use of second cars. In 1966 only about 6 percent of British families owned two or more cars as compared with 29 percent of American families; both these proportions are of course higher in the suburban areas, which form the main focus of this book, but in general the higher-density British suburb has a better developed public transport system, usually by bus. Probably, therefore, there are differences in the amount of air pollution from car exhausts in the two countries, though these do not seem to have been systematically measured.

Noise pollution is almost certainly many times lower in the average American than in the average British suburb. This is not merely due to the lower density, which means that—despite the higher car ownership—there are many fewer cars per square mile. It is also paradoxically due to the great size of the average American car and the correspondingly powerful engine: typically, the American family car has an engine between two and four times bigger than the corresponding European, so that in acceleration there is far less work involved. On the other hand, the fuel consumption of the typical American car is about double the fuel use of its European counterpart and its emission of wastes into the atmosphere is correspondingly greater. (Recent legislation in the United States is designed to greatly reduce exhaust gas emission, and Britain has gone some way in the same direction.) To some extent, these characteristics of the American car reflect the needs of the American suburbanite: average commuter distances are longer, middle-class families have typically been larger than in Britain. Coupled with the low costs of indigenous fuel and the lack of parking difficulties common to old city centers, these facts have naturally engendered the big car.

It might be thought that the low-density American suburb, with its generous private open space for family play and hobbies, would reduce the demands for outdoor recreation outside the home. But as far as can be established in international comparative studies, there is no evidence of this: American households show a much greater rate of participation in most active forms of outdoor recreation outside the home altogether, reflecting the combined operation of such factors as higher incomes, higher personal mobility, and higher educational levels. Moreover, within the United States, suburbanites as a whole are more active in outdoor recreation than are either central city or rural people. Probably both Britain and the United States show a lower propensity to second-home ownership than a country like Sweden, where a high level of affluence is accompanied by a tradition of high-density inner city apartment living. But here comparable statistics are lacking and inferences are dangerous: there is a marked trend in the early 1970s toward speculation in recreational real estate within easy weekend driving time of America's East Coast cities, which may lead to a rapid expansion in second-home ownership. Yet in turn, this may well be an adaptation to the high proportion of new suburban building in the 1960s, which took the form of apartments—a phenomenon not so far paralleled in England.

Not merely the density of the development at the local scale, but its general space relationships at the macro scale, may have important environmental impacts. As shown in chapter 3, Megalopolis England and the Northeastern Urban Complex share the characteristic that they are highly urbanized and densely populated; the spheres of influence of their major cities, in terms of commuter or service areas, extend outwards to touch each other, often enveloping the more limited catchment areas of the smaller cities. Nevertheless, the general overall population density is much higher in the English case: a similar population is crowded onto a much smaller area. As a result, commuter and service fields tend to be smaller; there is much less intervening space between one city and another. Many of the problems of competition for space in the rural hinterland—for uses like water, solid waste disposal, recreation, wildlife preservation or agriculture—are correspondingly more acute in Megalopolis England. Even the so-called remote areas of declining population, which are identified in chapter 4, are under heavy urban pressure for water supply or for recreation. Mid-Wales, one of the largest areas of persistent population loss in England and Wales, has long been a source of water supply for both Birmingham and Liverpool, which are less than 100 miles away. The Lake District National Park is less than two hours' driving time from Manchester, or three from Birmingham since the opening of the M6 motorway;[4] the Snowdonia National Park is only an hour from the Merseyside conurbation; the Peak Park is less than that from either Manchester or Sheffield. No American national park—not even Shenandoah—comes under the same urban pressures as the Peak.

This, in turn, reflects the fact that Britain suffers from a smaller-scale but quite extreme version of the problem identified by the Outdoor Recreation Review Commission for the United States: the supply of outdoor recreation land does not correspond geographically with the demand for it. Much of the really fine highland landscape, together with much of the coast and much of the good fishing rivers—together with all the skiing terrain—is in Central and Northern Scotland, which is minimally about 250 miles and maximally as much as 600 miles from the major urban centers of Megalopolis England. The national parks accessible to the urban populations for short weekend trips are relatively small and very intensively used; by definition, it would be impossible to find there anything like the U.S. wilderness areas, which are outside the range of a normal day's walk from the outside accessible world.

The close proximity of urban areas creates particular problems in dealing with air or water pollution. Heavily polluted air from one city may be blown by prevailing winds over the area of another, which may have been far more assiduous in its own air control programs; 30 percent of British drinking water comes from rivers receiving effluent and, typically, water on an average lowland river may be recycled two or three times in less than 100 miles, so that, for instance, London drinking water has already been used twice—by Oxford and by Reading. Since many large cities tend to be located on the downstream stretches of their rivers, this creates particular problems where there has been uncontrolled discharge of effluents from upstream industrial areas—as along the Tame-Trent system in Midland England.

The close juxtaposition of cities produces similar problems in the winning and working-up of building materials. London depends for much of its bricks upon the great brickfields of the Oxford and Kimmeridge Clay sixty and seventy miles to the north. But these great scars on the landscape, and the noxious air pollution

[4] The prefix M (Motorway) in Britain has the same signification as I (Interstate) in the United States.

that accompanies brick baking, impinge uncomfortably close on the new towns of Milton Keynes and Peterborough. Gravel working, which accounts for one-third of all the land used for quarrying in England and Wales, involves the creation of water-filled holes that can be reclaimed only when suitable urban solid waste is available for the purpose; latterly, inspired by examples such as the Huron-Clinton metropolitan parks in Detroit, there has been increasing interest in the large-scale recreational use of such pits.

The cities of Megalopolis England, like those of the Northeastern Urban Complex, have a markedly linear disposition along a principal axis. This is probably efficient in terms of economic organization, since it permits the creation of high-capacity transportation and communications systems at low unit costs, but it may create serious environmental problems where a heavy concentration of highways, railroads, high-tension lines, and airlanes cross areas of high scenic potential or recreational importance. The Chiltern Hills north of London, an officially designated Area of Outstanding Natural Beauty of great importance in serving London's recreational needs, were the center of several major controversies in the 1960s concerning the location of superhighways or power lines. Similar controversies have broken out in other areas of sensitive chalk downland between the major urban centers: the building of the M4 London–Bristol motorway was delayed for years by a controversy over its siting through the Thames Valley and Chiltern Hills, while a high-tension line across the South Downs south of London was also bitterly fought. Rerouting of a motorway may cost up to £1 million a mile in capital costs plus extra running costs for all time subsequently; while the average cost of burying a power line is some twenty times that of a conventional overhead line.

Both Megalopolis England and the Northeastern Urban Complex abut on the coast; and most of the major cities in both areas are within about one hour's access of it. This leads to conflicting pressures: for urban development, for recreation, for power stations (particularly the nuclear variety), and for waste disposal. In several of the counties of Megalopolis England, more than one-half the total coastline is already lost to urban development; stringent steps are now being taken to conserve the rest, but until a series of conferences called by the National Parks Commission in 1967–69, the need for a concerted policy among the various planning authorities does not seem to have been generally realized. Fortunately, in major resorts such as Blackpool, Brighton, or Bournemouth, a very large part of the coastal urban development is devoted in part to providing mass recreation facilities for the casual day or weekend visitor. In the Northeastern Urban Complex, Atlantic City and Ocean City perform the same function. Increasingly, however, mass car ownership is distributing the pressures more widely; the traditional pattern of holiday is changing as people tour from one spot to another, never staying in one place for long; and the accommodation of caravans (trailers) has become a major problem even in quite remote stretches of seashore, such as Pembrokeshire or Cornwall. (Curiously, it was a loophole in the elaborate 1947 system of planning control that had allowed caravans to be sited in any existing campground, without contest, and that had allowed many operators to evade the planning controls in practice; this was sealed only by a special act of Parliament in 1960.)

Local authorities on the coast, principally though not exclusively tourist resorts, are responsible for the situation of many of the 6 million of the British population whose sewage was still, in 1970, being deposited in the sea—generally with minimal treatment or no treatment at all. The resulting condition of the sea at some major resorts, an official report of 1970 concluded, was "aesthetically revolting" even if not outright dangerous to health.

Both Megalopolis England and the Northeastern Urban Complex contain substantial areas scarred by the evidence of past industrialism: the Black Country between Birmingham, Wolverhampton, and Walsall in England, the Scranton–Wilkes Barre anthracite field of eastern Pennsylvania. These areas pose both problems and opportunities. The amount of such land is not absolutely large, but it is significant in relation to the total size of the two complexes: an estimated quarter of a million acres out of 37 million acres in England and Wales, for instance. Furthermore, it is constantly being added to every year by open-cut mining, quarrying, new spoil heaps and other activities. It represents a unique chance for imaginative redevelopment, whether for recreation or urban use; but, especially in relation to the last, it poses considerable technical problems. Two English new towns, Peterlee in County Durham and Telford in Shropshire, have been located on areas of derelict land; both have faced considerable problems of urban design due to the limited load-bearing capacity of the bedrock, which has resulted in higher costs of development.

Special Problems of Outdoor Recreation

The problems of outdoor recreation have arisen concurrently with, and partly as a result of, the rise of cities. In a largely agrarian society, which nearly always means a relatively low-income one, the mass of the people get little recreation, whether indoors or outdoors, and what they do get is likely to be of rather simple types and close to home. In the United States today, in spite of the general urban standards and values of the farm and rural population, farmers and other rural people seem to participate much less in outdoor recreation than do urban people. We say "seem," because the available data are not as precise and reliable as one would wish. The question may well be raised: Do rural people have less need for outdoor recreation because they live and work closer to the open country? Or do they have less taste for it because they are surrounded by the outdoors in their daily lives? Or do they simply have less income, making it less easy to engage in outdoor recreation? We do know that city people, the world around, engage increasingly in outdoor recreation as income and leisure rise and as transportation facilities improve.

As factory and mine employment grew in the late eighteenth and throughout the nineteenth centuries in Britain, and somewhat later in the United States, ordinary workmen and their families were increasingly cut off from the countryside. Their hours of work were long—often all days of the week, and long hours per day; their incomes were low, and any time taken for recreation would have been without pay; and the means of transport were poor, so that travel was expensive, slow, and uncomfortable. The earliest outlets for recreation were city parks—Hyde Park in London in 1635, Vauxhall Gardens in London in 1661, Stanley Park in Liverpool in 1870, Central Park in New York in 1856, and many others. City parks were often provided rather grudgingly by city governments, yet there was a substantial rise of city parks in each country in the latter half of the nineteenth century and in the first decades of the twentieth century. In the United States, park acreage in the larger cities during this general period expanded at least as fast as did the populations of those cities.

During the nineteenth century the habit of vacationing became fairly widespread in Britain and to a lesser degree in the United States. While it was confined mostly to the well-to-do, it created a definite pattern of activity. The seashore was the prime area for Britain, while in the United States lakes and mountains were also popular areas. In Britain, the railways were a particularly important factor, especially from the middle of the nineteenth century. In the United States, electric trolley lines often reached into the nearby countryside in the early twentieth century, and many people took advantage of them for a day in the country. But it was the rise of the private automobile which really triggered the rise of massive outdoor recreation characterizing each country today—between the two world wars in the United States, after the second in Britain. Overall, car ownership levels in Britain have lagged twenty-five years behind the United States, with corresponding effects on outdoor recreation patterns. The automobiles needed roads, and road building was a major form of economic activity from 1920 onward. But ordinary working people began to get more leisure as well—shorter typical working hours per day, longer paid vacations (earlier in Britain than in the United States, but nearly universal in each country today). During the Great Depression of the 1930s (and sometimes earlier), the typical work week shortened to five instead of six or seven days, thus permitting a day of leisure activity, which often took the form of a day in the country. And all this was accompanied by rising average real incomes, thus permitting expenditures specifically for outdoor recreation.

All these factors, and others, have a demonstrable effect on recreation patterns. British work shows clearly that the higher the income level, the occupational class, and the educational status of the person or family, the greater the number of different recreational activities that are pursued, particularly those of an active nature; and it is clear that these people are constituting, and will constitute, an increasing proportion of the entire population. Car ownership is linked with these factors; higher-income groups (who happen often to be higher occupational and educational groups) tend to exhibit higher rates of car ownership, and this itself encourages participation in many types of recreation, especially through the stimulation of awareness of new types of activity. The important point here is that the effect of these factors is far from uniform for different types of outdoor recreation. Cycling and team games are pursued almost as easily by those with low incomes, and can be provided within urban areas; camping, sea sailing and golf, which tend to be pursued by the higher-income groups, are rural or at any rate suburban activities. Of those activities expected to increase most rapidly in the future, only one, athletics, can be described as fundamentally an urban activity, and one, golf, as suburban or exurban; others (motoring, mountaineering, skiing, camping, horseback riding, fishing, water sports, and nature study) are all mainly rural. The most explosive rates of growth have been, and are likely to be, in water-based sports, which make some of the most specialized demands on the use of land.

In order that people may partake of outdoor recreation, there must be suitable areas of land and water. There are many types of outdoor recreation areas in each country, often known by a variety of names that sometimes have no real significance. But it is useful in considering the problems of urban growth to group outdoor recreation areas into three general categories dependent primarily upon when and how they can be used. There are nearby parks and playfields, primarily for use during daily leisure or for simple weekend activity. (These have been called "user-oriented.")[5] A playing field for small children must usually be within a half-mile of where they live; some other kinds of areas can be farther, but all must be within a fairly close radius. The tracts of land can be, and often are, small —a few acres or less; and the physical requirements of the land are not too exacting. Location is the dominant characteristic of this kind of recreation area. Then there are areas suitable for day-long or weekend outings (termed "intermediate areas").[6] Distance is still important; in Britain in 1965 the average one-way distance for half-day trips was twenty-nine miles; for all-day trips, fifty miles. A more important dimension is travel time. Most such areas should be within an hour's travel time (one way) and few will be used where one-way travel time exceeds two hours. As highway transportation improves, the actual distances can increase considerably within these time limits. This type of outdoor recreation activity should ordinarily be located on the most attractive sites within the distance range. Water bodies are especially prized; tracts should individually be larger, often some hundreds of acres; and mass outdoor recreation, with a variety of specific activities, can well be encouraged. The third major type of outdoor recreation area is that suitable for vacation (the "resource-based" area).[7] Because it is a vacation or holiday area, more time can be spent in travel; sometimes, in fact, the travel itself becomes a major part of the recreation. In the United States, some visitors to national parks will have travelled 2,000 miles or more one way on a trip of which the visit to the national park is a part, but often only one part, of a long vacation. The dominant characteristic of this type of outdoor recreation area is its natural features—seashore, lake, mountains, etc. Individually, the tracts should be relatively large; some U.S. national parks exceed a million acres.

An important point is that two of these three categories demand recreation areas within close and easy reach of people's homes. The second type, which is exceptionally important as car ownership rises in Britain and has long been important in the United States, puts immense strain on natural resources, such as national and state parks or stretches of unspoilt coast within driving distance of an hour or two. In Britain these pressures are even more acute than in the eastern United States since the population density is so high and the individual major urban areas impinge on each other so sharply.

[5] Marion Clawson and Jack L. Knetsch, *Economics of Outdoor Recreation* (Baltimore: The Johns Hopkins Press for Resources for the Future, 1966).
[6] Ibid.
[7] Ibid.

In the United States there has been a gradual development of outdoor recreation areas (under various names) for nearly a hundred years. This development has proceeded from two origins and, to a degree, in two streams. There has been the city park–city playground development, proceeding from an interest in urban people, especially those of lower income, and their need for recreational activity; and there have been natural resource areas, mostly publicly owned, whose managers saw outdoor recreation as one of the uses of their land. Although the city parks and playgrounds have often been deficient in the lower-income parts of cities, they have nevertheless sought to serve all urban classes. The men and women working in this activity are likely to have been trained in physical education. While city parks require land, and land closely related to their potential users, yet facilities of all kinds and trained leadership have been at least as important as land areas.

In the early 1970s the mythical average American spent about one day in outdoor recreation at a unit of the national park system, about one day in a national forest, about a day-and-a-half at a federal reservoir, about two days at a state park, and made some six or more visits to a city or county park—a total of roughly a dozen visits to some publicly owned area. Considering that perhaps as many as half of all the people in the United States, because of age, poor health, poverty, or disinterest, failed to visit such areas, the average number of visits by those who went is much higher than this. Far more impressive is the fact that total visits to these areas have been mounting at an annual rate of about 8 to 10 percent. The available statistical record for the national parks stretches back to around 1910. It shows that since then, with intervals due to wartime conditions, use has increased at this rate—the same rate as has been in evidence for increasing visits to all publicly owned areas. Statistically, a uniform rate of increase leads to nonsensical figures in time; but so far there has been no clear slowing down in the rate of increase. This is mass outdoor recreation, modern American style.

For various reasons, the development of outdoor recreation in Britain has been slower, but one can logically argue that it has begun a process similar to that of the United States—with a lag of perhaps twenty years due largely to the slower growth of private car ownership. Partly because it is a relatively small island, the coast has always played a dominant role in British holiday making. For many years railroads have run excursion trains to the coastal resorts. These have a special characteristic: they cater to urban people, who take their vacations in an essentially urban environment, albeit by the sea. This type of recreation is dominantly privately run, and the facilities of these resorts are mostly privately owned. But at the same time numerous forms of outdoor recreation have developed locally at city parks, playing fields, and swimming pools. And it should not be overlooked that from time immemorial Britain has been laced with rural footpaths—rights-of-way on which hiking has been common in a way that is just beginning to develop in the United States.

For long, many people who were concerned for the protection of the British countryside and for its development in the interests of public enjoyment had sought the establishment of national parks; this was accomplished by the National Parks and Access to the Countryside Act of 1949. But the National Parks thus created differ in several important respects from the U.S. National Parks. The pioneers who had campaigned for them in Britain wanted something much closer to the American concept: a national system, nationally administered, and managed according to a philosophy of development for the healthy enjoyment and open-air recreation of the whole nation. This would involve extensive capital spending and land acquisition; an official report in 1947 suggested that one-tenth of the land in the parks would be publicly owned within ten years. Instead, the 1949 Act gave the management of the parks to committees of the local authorities concerned, with a minority of outside membership. Where parks ran across local authority boundaries, as in the Lake District or the Peak District, provision was made for joint boards. The land in the parks remains almost all privately owned, and, in fact, provides homes for some 260,000 people—a striking contrast to the American situation, where most of the parks are deliberately left almost unpopulated.

While the local planning committees can act to prevent incompatible developments within the parks, they are limited by lack of funds in the programs they can carry out. Central grants are available but have hardly been taken up; the expenditure of most parks authorities has been negligible. Simply, local authorities have been reluctant to spend money from local rates: better facilities would surely attract more visitors, and most local voters do not want them. The National Parks, in fact, have provided extreme examples of the sort of negative, restrictive planning policies that have too often obtained in rural England since 1947—a far cry from what the pioneers who established the system intended.

The National Parks Commission, set up under the 1949 Act to coordinate the program on a purely advisory basis, was also given other responsibilities—particularly, the establishment of long-distance footpaths (trails) on the model of the American Appalachian Trail. But here, too, progress has been disappointingly slow—again, due to the reluctance of local authorities to spend money or to assert their legal rights. Five of the trails had been opened in 1972, after more than twenty years' work. But others were still incomplete nearly two decades after they had been first approved.

Britain has not yet developed mass outdoor recreation areas on the scale found in the United States. Some reservoirs developed for other purposes, such as water supply or hydroelectric power, play a role in Britain similar to that served by some reservoirs in the United States. Additionally, many private houses and their country parks are open for public recreation, often through the mechanism of the National Trust (a voluntary body using charitable funds to subsidize house owners who open their property to the public) or by private individuals on their own account. Some of the larger of these estates, such as the Duke of Bedford's Woburn Park or the Earl of Montagu's Beaulieu Abbey, had become major mass recreation areas by 1970, and were still developing and diversifying. But elsewhere, especially near the urban areas, progress was slow; the greenbelts, established by county planning authorities in the 1950s at the behest of the then Ministry of Housing and Local Government, were used as negative devices to contain urban growth rather than as positive areas for development of outdoor recreation. By 1968, increasing concern over the need for outdoor recreation areas reasonably accessible to urban people had led to the passage of the Countryside Act. This renamed the National Parks Commission as the Countryside Commission and greatly broadened its power. The purpose was to establish, over a period of years, a system of out-door recreation areas near to major urban centers—the Country Parks—which would act as "honeypots" drawing large crowds of weekend visitors, relieving pressures on the more distant National Parks. Funds available to the commission for all purposes, including National Parks, are still extremely limited—£1.4 million in 1971–72, equal to little more than the construction cost of two miles of rural motorway—and the progress will be slow until much more is available. And the commission remains a fundamentally advisory body. The real powers to initiate schemes, whether in the National Parks or for the establishment of new Country Parks, remain with the local authorities, and a proposal to give the National Parks a special status under a reformed system of local government was dropped by the incoming Conservative government in 1971. Meanwhile some county authorities and private bodies, at least, had shown themselves enthusiastic about the possibilities of the Countryside Act: by September 1972, seventy-nine Country Parks had been designated and approved for aid by the commission.

In recent years in the United States, popular interest has centered on the wilderness areas. Aldo Leopold, who originated the idea of specially reserved wilderness areas, defined them as areas so large that it required two days' travel by horseback to reach their center from a peripheral access point. The Forest Service for long restricted this classification to areas of 100,000 or more acres, lacking in access roads but generally with trails for foot or horse travel. With passage of the Wilderness Act in 1964, some areas have been formally designated as wilderness by a rather complicated process which involves both the Executive agencies and the Congress, and additional areas have been proposed. The size restrictions have been materially relaxed, so that some areas as small as 5,000 acres have been so designated; the emphasis remains on limited access and preservation in as near pristine condition as possible. Most commercial activities are excluded, although grazing by domestic livestock is permitted; in practice, most wilderness areas have very limited low-value grazing, in part because of their remoteness. The greatest threat to wilderness areas in the United States today is their lovers, who "love them to death" by visiting them in such numbers as to make retention of their desired condition very difficult. Several million people in the United States, who rarely if ever have visited a wilderness area and who have no expectations of visiting them, hold a powerful sentiment in favor of their reservation. Obviously, wilderness areas are easier to establish in a large country with much unpopulated back country than they are in a smaller and more densely settled country; however, at least one wilderness area has been established in the Northeastern Urban Complex—the Great Swamp in New Jersey. In Britain no such area has been designated; and it would be difficult to imagine one outside the Scottish Highlands, where large areas have reverted to wilderness.

The long recreation trip is much less common in Britain than in the United States. A much larger proportion of British than of Americans go abroad, primarily to the Continent and especially to the Mediterranean, though in *absolute* numbers, many West European countries receive more American than British visitors. This is a function of the small size of Britain: a trip of equivalent length to that taken by an American is more likely to cross international frontiers. Many of the tourists fly, since the journey to the Mediterranean coasts averages 1,000–1,200 miles and the European equivalent of the American Interstate Highway system will not be complete until the mid-1970s. A trip of this length by car, pulling one's own caravan (trailer) behind—so common a sight in the United States—is not yet common in Europe, though it is growing in popularity. As the European high-speed highway system is completed, and particularly if or when the tunnel under the Channel is constructed, an enormous boost would be given to this type of long-distance recreation travel; the entire European continent would then be open to the British in the same way that the entire sweep of the United States is now open to Americans for vacation travel in their own cars. Then, to an even greater extent than at present, Britain would export many of its environmental planning problems to other countries—some of them less well placed, administratively and financially, to deal with them.

The years since World War II have produced a remarkable number of gadgets for outdoor recreation. This development is more marked in the United States than in Britain, where some of these trends are yet to emerge. Gadgets in turn present problems of urban space needs. Boats have been made of new, light materials requiring less maintenance, and capable of being pulled on special trailers behind ordinary cars. Thus the boat owner can enjoy different waters at a considerable distance from his home. At the same time, new boat motors—especially high-powered outboard motors of lower cost per horsepower than in the past—enable boats to go much faster. And this has opened up water skiing as a popular pastime. For land use, trail bikes have been developed, which enable one to ride over trails or across open land previously accessible only on foot or on animal back. Motorcycle riding has developed into a mass activity, taking thousands of persons to locations previously largely inaccessible. Snowmobiling has brought many people into rural areas in the wintertime. There is an enormous range of camping equipment, ranging from simple (but often expensive) light tents that may be carried on the back, to larger and heavier tents for auto camping, to light auto trailers with fold-up tents, to trailers (caravans) of all sizes and weights and degrees of luxury, to campers (really small houses on pickup trucks), to motor homes (rather large houses built on truck chassis). And numerous kinds of special clothing, special foods (e.g., freeze-dry light-weight foods for backpacking), and other equipment have been developed and popularized. In all this, the U.S. experience is far ahead of the British, but may well portend the direction that British outdoor recreation activity will take over the next few decades.

This development of recreation gadgetry has one aspect of special importance for a consideration of urban growth—all the gadgets must be stored somewhere, and this takes space. Boats may be kept in rivers or lakes or at the seaside, though many owners prefer to keep them at home. Campers and motor homes are so large that they may have to be stored at a storage yard if they cannot be kept at home. But most of the outdoor recreation gear must be stored at home; and where can this be done, if the house and surrounding area are too small?

In both Britain and the United States the provision of outdoor recreation areas and their management is the responsibility of government at different levels and of several agencies at each level. In the United States there are several federal agencies—Bureau of Outdoor Recreation, National Park Service, Forest Service, Corps of Engineers, Bureau of Land Management, Tennessee Valley Authority, Fish and Wildlife Service, and other resource-managing agencies, as well as the Soil Conservation Service, the Farmers Home Administration, the Public Health Service, the Coast Guard, and others which perform technical advisory or regulatory functions. Each state has a state parks agency (sometimes called by a slightly different name), and some have several similar agencies, as well as forestry services, game management agencies, public health agencies, and others, which perform various functions in the park and recreation field. Most cities of any reasonable size have a city park department and usually a city recreation department as well, besides various other agencies that perform functions related to parks and recreation. Counties, special districts of all kinds, and various quasi-governmental organizations also provide parks, direct recreational activities or provide some special services. In addition, there are extensive transfers of funds between units or levels of government such as federal grants-in-aid to states and cities and state grants to cities. Still further, there is a host of private nonprofit organizations providing recreational opportunities to their members or to special groups. All in all, it is a complex and frequently confusing assemblage of agencies and organizations, each with its special interests, special rules, and usually with its own bureaucracy.

The situation in Britain is not quite so confused, but complex enough. At the national level there is the Countryside Commission, whose task it is to recommend the establishment of National Parks, to promote the negotiation of agreements on public trails, and to develop national plans for parks and recreation; the Nature Conservancy is a government agency (an organization of the same name in the United States is a private organization), whose task has been to select, reserve, and manage National Nature Reserves of unusual beauty or scientific value (some 124 in 1968), to promote research on the same, and to provide educational services for the public about such areas; the Forestry Commission managed over a million acres of forested areas which were used for outdoor recreation by three-fourths of a million people in 1968; the British Waterways Board has managed a network of canals for cruising and other recreational purposes; and the former Ministry of Public Buildings and Works, now part of the Department of the Environment, is responsible for a large number and variety of historic buildings and sites of all kinds. There is also the National Trust, the voluntary body mentioned earlier in this chapter. The Sports Council has an advisory role in stimulating and aiding the provision of sports areas in various parts of the country. At the county and city level, local authorities are engaged individually (or jointly in the case of the Peak and Lake District parks) in the management of National Parks and in proposals for setting up and managing Country Parks and Picnic Sites.

Overall, the verdict in Britain must be that the administrative apparatus has not been well geared to the needs of a largely urban population seeking extended opportunities for outdoor recreation. Countryside planning, which has been left in the hands of the rural planning authorities, has been negatively successful in conserving the natural beauty—above all, the picturesque quality of the British landscape, with its characteristic imagery admired by foreign visitors and local residents alike—and prohibiting alien development. It has not been so successful in making the sort of positive provision that the pioneers of National Parks imagined. The National Parks Commission, and its successor, the Countryside Commission, have done the best they can with an extremely circumscribed role. Other bodies with a stronger positive role and an independent budget—such as the Nature Conservancy or the Forestry Commission—have played an incidental role in developing the public's enjoyment of the countryside, but their main roles have been quite properly elsewhere. Perhaps the most positive role has been played by the former Ministry of Public Buildings and Works (see above), in whose custody many unique cultural and historic sites have been acquired and maintained for the enjoyment and instruction of the public. But with the possible exception of the last, none of these agencies has been empowered with the responsibility to provide for the growth of outdoor recreation that has been unleashed by the onset of mass mobility. Furthermore, the work of the different agencies is inadequately coordinated at the center. The Countryside Commission reports to the Department of the Environment, and the former Public Buildings and Works Ministry is part of that agency, but the Nature Conservancy and the Sports Council report to the Department of Education and Science, while the Forestry Commission reports to the Ministry of Agriculture, Fisheries and Food.[8] There would seem to be a strong case for many of these activities to be transferred to a single semi-autonomous national heritage commission, with adequate funding, responsible to the Secretary of State (Minister) for the Environment.

The major factors underlying the fast rise in demand for outdoor recreation have been increasing population, rising real incomes per capita, increased leisure, and improved transportation. In both Britain and the United States all these factors continue to trend upward, though not necessarily at the same rates. Areas suitable for outdoor recreation are becoming accessible to larger numbers of people, thereby putting pressure of heavy use on many areas hitherto protected by their remoteness. Neither country will restrict its outdoor recreation to its own land, but recreation beyond its own borders is likely to be especially important for Britain; increasingly, all of Europe will be visited, as will more remote areas of the world. Competition between outdoor recreation and other uses of land and water resources will continue to increase; the problems of coping with crowds of visitors at popular areas will grow in severity. As recreational activity mounts, the questions of who pays for the areas required and how payment is to be collected will grow in importance. Thus far, much—perhaps most—outdoor recreation on public areas has been provided without specific charge to the user; the costs are met out of taxes. But the trend, at least in the United States, is toward making the user pay more of the costs through charges levied at the site and for each use; it is argued that the family that can afford to travel to a park, especially a relatively distant one, can afford to pay a reasonable fee for the services the park will provide.

[8] Under new arrangements announced in summer 1972, the conservancy management functions of the Nature Conservancy will fall under the Department of the Environment.

Responsibility for Environmental Controls

As one recalls earlier chapters, it is apparent that maintenance of the environment in the large was not the direct responsibility of any government agency or person among the numerous actors involved in the urbanization and suburbanization processes. The indirect or secondary effects of urbanization were unrealized for a long time, and those who foresaw a problem often felt, with some accuracy, that doing something about it was not their particular responsibility. As a result, the pollution, transportation, and other undesirable aspects of growing and spreading cities were all too often ignored or deplored, but not counteracted. And if action was taken, it was often fragmented and ill coordinated.

When it comes to the more obvious environmental impacts of urbanization upon the natural environment, more agencies have been directly concerned and have attempted to cope with them. In both countries planning organizations have typically considered the impacts on the land of proposed urban developments. In Britain these have been more clearly kept in mind and have entered more directly into planning decisions than in the United States; and in Britain the planning agencies have been in a much stronger position to enforce their decisions. We have seen how this concern for the land has been effectuated in practice in Britain. In the United States planners have had more limited concern with the direct impacts of urbanization on the environment and have had weaker powers of enforcement. But public health authorities could (but often did not) prohibit the building of septic tanks in unsuitable soils, thus preventing the construction of dwellings until sewer connections were available. Subdivision controls have often limited the layout of streets, including grades and curves. But private developers have typically cleared sites of all vegetation, allowing heavy movement of soil materials into streams, without effective control.

In a great many situations in each country conflict has arisen between environmental preservation and economic development. The opening or operation of an open-pit mine, with its attendant deep scars and piles of overburden, or the construction of an electric power line from generating plant to urban load center, with its attendant conspicuous towers and lines, or any one of several other types of economic development has inevitably had adverse environmental consequences. Those consequences could often be reduced by careful planning, but not eliminated.

In this contest between development and environment the spokesmen for environment were usually few; until recently, this has been particularly marked in the United States. In Britain some voices have always been raised publicly for environmental protection, although often they were few and unsuccessful. In the United States, until a decade or so ago, little if any public protest was likely to be made about an economic development that provided jobs and income, regardless of its adverse environmental effect. It once was said that there was nothing so beautiful as a smokestack belching black smoke, for that meant jobs. As they used to say in the north of England, "Where there's muck, there's money." But this simple equation has lost much of its validity in the twentieth century, as the scarred places of the industrial revolution—South Wales or West Virginia, West Hartlepool or Scranton—also became areas of declining industry and high unemployment. What did remain true was that such areas were generally more eager to obtain new industry without any arguments; Interstate Highways were built more easily in the Appalachians, motorways in County Durham,[9] than in San Francisco or London. And such areas often lacked the will, or the imagination, or simply the funds to clean up their past industrial scars quickly. As one British Member of Parliament put it after the collapse of a coal tip (slack heap) onto a school in South Wales, claiming the lives of many children: "Let us suppose that such a monstrous mountain had been built above Hampstead or Eton, where the children of the men of power and wealth are at school. . . ." It is especially in the affluent urban areas, where, ironically, the case of new power stations or highways is strongest, that these developments are now opposed on the grounds of environmental impact. In the Northeastern Urban Complex, the building of power plants was delayed by opposition so often that the area experienced power brownouts in the early 1970s. In Britain, rejection of reservoir plans after fierce controversy similarly threatens severe water shortages in several cities; while the important M4 London–Bristol–South Wales motorway was held up for ten years by repeated objections to successive lines of route.[10]

What seems to have been lacking in both countries is a consistent framework for analysis and decision taking. But it must be said in the administrator's defense that until very recently he had very little academic help in thinking about the problem. It is only since the late 1950s, for instance, that economists have been making serious recreational studies. Their interest in other aspects of environmental management is even more recent. Decisions therefore have had to be taken in a theoretical vacuum; they were ad hoc and unrelated.

The theoretical approach that now exists has been provided by economists. They describe environmental impacts as spillovers and externalities. The first term refers to the fact that the environmental impact is usually incidental to the main aim pursued by the agent: no one wills the creation of air or water pollution, or soil erosion, and even though the builder consciously develops land for profit, the effect of his development on the total landscape is commonly an unintended spillover. The second term refers to the fact that the impact, whether troublesome or beneficial, is commonly visited upon a person or group other than or in addition to the person or group that creates it. Such effect is outside the usual market mechanism.

This second point is worth further discussion. Externalities by definition affect other people. They may do so either at the time they are created or later; either directly, by action on the scene, or indirectly, through environmental processes; they affect groups of varying sizes, which may or may not include the perpetrator. Thus noise pollution is visited directly on its victims; the perpetrator is likely to be affected, but to a smaller degree than most of the victims. Land development has

---

[9] It should in fairness be noted that the Durham motorway was the pioneer example in Britain of "corridor" treatment of a new highway, with systematic reclamation and landscaping of the whole area within view of the road.

[10] A BBC television program on this last controversy concluded that the line finally selected was probably the least offensive environmentally; thus, by a series of successive approximations, the right solution had been reached. But meanwhile, the costs of inaction—in congestion and in accidents—had been monumental.

a long-delayed impact, stretching often over generations. Air pollution will be experienced immediately, but its effect on organisms is long-term and insidious; the perpetrator need not, but is likely to be, among those affected. Thus, in many cases of externalities the problem is that a whole group creates the problem, and all suffer; its members lack effective controls to discipline each other.

What complicates discussion of the issue is the fact that any given social or technological development is likely to have more than one environmental impact. Thus the social and technological development, *reliance on automobile transportation*, has at least these main aspects: use of scarce, perhaps irreplaceable, resources; use of land; air and noise pollution. The social development, *growth of outdoor recreation* (with the parallel technological development, *use of powered aids to recreation*) has, inter alia, these aspects: use of resources, especially land; air pollution; water pollution; and noise pollution. Many urban planning decisions must deal with the policies to be adopted towards these developments—for instance, which sorts of outdoor recreation should be encouraged, which restricted, and where; or the extent to which mass transit should be developed as an alternative to the private automobile in any given urban area. It will be necessary, therefore, to take all the impacts as fully as possible into account before a rational decision can be made.

Provided that externalities can be identified and then quantified in whatever form, appropriate policies can be devised to reduce them, or at least to regulate them. Ideally, the economist would like a quantification in terms of resource costs, expressed in money terms; but in many cases this is very difficult to calculate. Cost-benefit analysis depends on finding some proxy for market prices; and if this is completely lacking, as here it may well be, there is no way to proceed. In that case, the much cruder decision may be made that the scale of the problem is big enough (in some physical sense) to justify control or regulation. This suggests that there are two broad approaches to corrective policies: pricing or control.

A pricing policy could be adopted by a public agency (or imposed on a private agency) to take account of the externalities. The "noise pollution tax," suggested for jet airplane travel, is an example. Raising the costs of driving in cities to such a level that the urban fabric could be reconstructed to adequate environmental standards so as to accommodate the car, as suggested in Britain's Buchanan report,[11] is another. There are, notoriously, great practical difficulties in using pricing policies for such purposes. They include the difficulty of quantifying the effect in money terms; the difficulty of collecting the tax and of identifying and compensating the victims; and the danger that the tax may be passed on into the general wage and price system. Such a tax might also be regressive in its distributional effects. Because of these difficulties, there are few examples of the pricing solution to environmental externalities in practice. Admission fees to American National Parks are a possible exception.

Regulation or outright prohibition has therefore been by far the commoner solution to problems of spillover. Nearly all the cases considered in this chapter, in both countries, have been dealt with in this way. But there are practical difficulties

---

[11] *Traffic in Towns* (London: Her Majesty's Stationery Office, 1963).

even here. Regulation is usually by nature complex; it is slow and costly to enforce properly. The effects may be regressive, in that some of the costs may be borne by the poor; this is especially true if the system of control involves more expensive forms of treatment, the costs of which are not wholly subsidized by the public purse. There may be a price to pay in economic inefficiency (though this may depend on the scope of the efficiency criterion used). These difficulties apply with equal force to a special case of the regulatory solution: segregation, as employed in zoning or land use planning. Segregation may well be regressive, in that the poor suffer the spillovers while the rich enjoy a higher standard of living (as occurred in the nineteenth century answer to smoke control: the rich lived upwind and the poor lived downwind). And, on occasion, it may be totally impractical: it is impossible, for instance, to segregate the waters of Lake Erie into clean and dirty parts.

This discussion suggests that in devising a policy for dealing with environmental externalities, several different effects of the policy measures must be kept in mind. They include the effect on economic efficiency—with particular attention to the difficulty of defining it; the effect on extending the freedom of consumer choice through the provision of "psychic goods" that cannot be sold in the marketplace; the effect on the distribution of income, arising from the fact that the incidence of costs and benefits may be very different for the rich and the poor (psychic goods have a high income elasticity of demand, so that they may be worth more to the rich); and time effects, affecting the trade-off between one generation and another, which may be very important where the environmental effects extend over a long period. All these complexities make it difficult indeed to devise rational and consistent policies.

The vast majority of the environmental policies in Britain have been regulatory in character, with an emphasis on persuasion and cooperation rather then on legal penalties. There is an extraordinary variety of them; a 1971 supplement to the *Journal of the Town Planning Institute* shows no less than fifty-five separate Acts of Parliament on the matter, ranging in date from 1875 to 1970. They give regulatory powers to a bewildering variety of Ministers of the Crown, local authorities (in various capacities), and ad hoc official bodies such as the Countryside Commission, the Forestry Commission, the Natural Environment Research Council, the River Authorities, and the Water Resources Board. They also give some more positive powers to some of these authorities to initiate schemes such as National Parks, Country Parks, or National Nature Reserves.

The areas of control are similarly wide-ranging and complex. There is, first, control over pollution of various sorts. In Britain air pollution is governed by various acts, ranging from the Alkali Act of 1906 to the Clean Air acts of 1956 and 1968; it is controlled by stringent regulation, either by central government officials (the Alkali inspectors) or local authorities with central monitoring. Control has been quite effective within a short time, leading to a dramatic improvement of air quality in London (which by 1970 was enjoying the same quantity of bright sunshine as the surrounding countryside) and some other major cities, although black spots remain in heavy industrial areas. The costs have been borne mainly through central government payments for conversions of fuel systems, so that the system has been reasonably progressive. Water pollution control has been scattered and less effective; it has been performed by ad hoc statutory undertakers (the river authorities), which have existed only since an Act of 1963, and whose responsibilities in the field of water quality are somewhat obscure; the costs are borne mainly through the local property tax (rating) system, so that the system is reasonably though not entirely progressive in its effects on distribution of income. Control of noise pollution, being relatively recent, is hardly effective as yet, though it may prove more effective in the later 1970s. It works mainly by regulation of manufacturers' designs, partly through controls on use (e.g., bans on heavy trucks in certain areas of cities, or on night flights from airports). Until recently, little account has been taken of this latter problem in land use planning—a neglect that has led, for instance, to badly sited airports near major cities.

Controls over rural developments, such as mineral-working or recreational schemes, have been part of the land use planning system. The powers have been comprehensive and effective, with a major loophole concerning the statutory undertakers, such as electricity boards, which have considerable freedom in theory to avoid the controls altogether but in practice are limited by public opinion. The controls seldom seem to have been based, in practice, on a coherent set of criteria. Specific natural resources, such as wildlife or forests, have been conserved and even fostered by special-purpose agencies such as the Forestry Commission or the Nature Conservancy. The powers have been used with varying assurance, depending on the status of the agency and in particular on its financial independence. But, in general, those authorities able to carry out developments directly with central government funds (such as the Forestry Commission or Nature Conservancy) have been in a much stronger position than those exercising a merely advisory function to local or other authorities (such as the Countryside Commission or the Water Resources Board).

In the United States, where there have been far fewer direct controls over environmental matters than in Britain, the approach has been more through research, technical advisory services, and financial grants. For instance, the Soil Conservation Service and other agricultural agencies have provided technical services and some grants to landowners, especially farmers, to reduce soil erosion; the Corps of Engineers and other agencies have built flood protection works, thus enabling some land to be used more intensively than otherwise would be possible; the Corps and the Public Health Service have exerted some very limited controls over water pollution; grants to acquire land for park and open space use have been available from the federal government to states, and from them to cities and counties; and so on. In the individual states limited controls have been exercised by public health agencies and others.

The facts that such controls have not been effective, that environmental degradation has reached serious or alarming stages in many areas, and that there is now greatly heightened public environmental concern, have led to some new and stronger approaches to environmental problems in the United States. The National Environmental Policy Act of 1969 established the Council on Environmental Quality as a general watchdog agency. It is to study and report on environmental problems and to propose federal actions to deal with them. One major feature of the act is the requirement that every federal agency file an environmental impact statement for virtually every project having, or likely to have, an environmental impact. This latter activity was greatly strengthened by passage of the Environmental Quality Improvement Act of 1970. The council has had its problems in getting federal agencies to file meaningful impact statements, including analyses of ways in which impact can be reduced or alternatives found; but great progress has been made. A monthly report, abstracting these impact statements, is published by the council, thus enabling interested citizens to protest proposed projects by the various agencies. Impact statements are also required from state and local governments, if federal funds are used, thus greatly broadening the scope of the acts.

In 1970 a considerable number of previously separate federal agencies were brought into a new Environmental Protection Agency, and programs for control of water and air pollution and of solid waste management were transferred to this agency. It also was given responsibility for controlling use of pesticides and other chemicals that might have adverse environmental effects. The agency has promulgated various standards for control of pollutants, and has issued orders to cities and to private firms to cease certain polluting actions or to clean up certain undesirable situations. While this agency is new, some of its constituent parts are relatively old. While it has important new legislation, it also has some old laws to enforce—one of these, enacted in 1899, gives considerable control over the dumping of wastes into navigable waters, but has never been effectively enforced. While the agency faces many difficult technical and administrative problems, its greatest problems lie in the political and public relations arenas. Can it adopt and enforce tough standards that the President, Congress, and the general public will support? Only time can tell, but the 1970s have started with far more enforcement authority and enthusiasm than have previously been available.

A number of states have enacted, or are seriously considering enacting, stronger measures to control pollution and other threats to the environment. In some ways the problems faced by a state in enforcing effective environmental controls are more difficult than those of the federal government, for it is quite possible that a firm will move, or threaten to move, to another state in order to avoid complying with strict environmental measures.

One attack upon environmental problems that has arisen in the United States in the 1960s has no counterpart, thus far, in Britain. This is the citizen suit to enforce compliance with laws or to prevent public actions which, it is argued, are not in compliance with the law or are not in the general public interest. Such suits may be brought by a few individuals; more commonly, they are brought by a citizen organization. A new feature of this line of attack is the liberal attitude the courts have been taking toward allowing such groups to represent larger but unnamed groups with similar interests; the interest of the suing persons may be modest, but it is the class action which gives their efforts significant weight. Various federal, state, and local agencies have at least temporarily been stopped from carrying out proposed programs by this means. Perhaps more important than the actual suits brought has been the threat that they could be brought; this has made all public agencies more cautious and more careful.

It is extremely difficult to draw any general conclusions from such a complex picture; there must be many qualifications and exceptions. But common to much of the picture are these features:

First, many controlling functions are performed by statutory authorities with specific remit to perform that control either as a central duty or as a necessary or desirable by-product of some other duty (for instance, water purity as a by-product of water supply). This is logical, because the exercise of these functions demands considerable specialized expertise. Many of these authorities have a geographically limited and defined area; but it is difficult neatly to dovetail these different geographical areas, so that a number of functions could be made responsible to the same local government authority. For example, water resource management is in the hands of river basin authorities, but local authorities are responsible for solid waste collection and disposal. Who, then, in a reformed local government system, should be responsible for sewage disposal? Or to take another example: recreational planning is closely related to tourism; the regional tourist boards reflect the main concentrations of tourists and may not easily fit local government boundaries; regional sports councils have different boundaries again; local authorities have the statutory remit to carry out land use planning. Which, then, is the logical organization for recreational planning? Examples like these suggest that even comprehensive local government reform, intended to be carried through in Britain between 1972 and 1974, will provide no easy solution to this problem.

Second, central government responsibilities are equally confused. Many control functions and some initiatory functions are closely linked with—in fact, are by-products of—different areas of technical expertise. For instance, in Britain the after-treatment of mineral workings is closely related to the responsibilities of the Ministry of Power (now part of the Department of Trade and Industry); the work of the Nature Conservancy is related to the Natural Environment Research Council and thus to the Department of Education and Science; the control of water quality, and so of effluent discharge, must be related to the responsibilities of the River Authorities and the Water Resources Board, and thus to the Department of the Environment. But these close relationships pose two problems. One is that in many cases control over the actions of some agent is closely related to promotion of the activities of that agent. The Minister for Power has a general responsibility to see that the Central Electricity Generating Board produces sufficient power for national needs; if he must simultaneously limit its freedom to establish new power stations on environmental grounds, he may suffer a conflict of loyalties. The other problem is that in very many cases the work of these agencies has more than one face. Is the Nature Conservancy mainly concerned with research (its educational face) or conservation (its planning face)? Its responsibility to the Department of Education and Science indicates the first; but does this tend to downgrade the importance of the conservation work? (Evidently, the British government held this view when it was decided in summer 1972 to split the two functions, placing conservation research under the aegis of the Natural Environment Research Council reporting to the Secretary of State for Education and Science, and placing management of nature reserves in the hands of a new Nature Conservancy Council responsible to the Secretary of State for the Environment.) Again, is National Parks policy principally a matter of catering for tourist demands—in which case it would properly be a responsibility of the Secretary of State for Trade and Industry? Or is it one of promoting wise land use planning and the conservation of resources—in which case the Secretary for the Environment should carry the responsibility? Or is National Parks policy to be seen as part of a general program for the creative enjoyment of leisure—in which case it might be associated with museums and theaters as a responsibility of the Secretary for Education and Science? In point of fact, the second of these three alternatives has been chosen; but a strong case could be made for either of the others.

Deeper than these organizational questions lies a third criticism, of a conceptual nature: that fundamental, comparable, consistent criteria for decision making in this whole field have been lacking. This is simply a reflection of the lack of work in the field, to which we referred earlier. Policy on conservation seems to have been arrived at by a process of disjointed incrementalism. In particular, isolated political impulses or chance events seem to have been unduly responsible for many of the more important advances in environmental policy. It is an open secret in Britain that the creation of the Nature Conservancy, and its privileged position with regard to direct central government funding, resulted from the persuasiveness of Max Nicholson as a senior civil servant in the time of the 1945–50 Labour government. The Clean Air Act of 1956, which has been so remarkably effective within such a short time in producing a dramatic improvement in air quality in Britain's major cities, was a direct result of the recommendations of the 1954 Beaver Committee report, which in turn resulted from panic action by the government after the 1952 killer London fog. Very probably, it is because no such catastrophe occurred to British water supplies that action on water pollution control came much later—partly, perhaps, because of the general emphasis on conservation during 1970 and 1971, which seems to have been a direct importation from the United States fostered largely by the press. Nevertheless, this more recent action may well bring results.

In any event, the government seized the opportunity given by the general reorganization of local government to decide that from April 1974—when the new local government structure will become operative—the whole management of water supply and of liquid waste disposal should be taken out of the new structure and put into the hands of strong ad hoc regional authorities, each based on a river basin. Thus, from 1974 the management of the entire hydrological cycle on land will be discharged by a single authority within each major area of the country— a highly desirable step in a small and highly urbanized country, where problems of urban water supply and urban waste disposal are so intimately connected. But, even here, some contrary considerations emerged; the proposal abolishes the British Waterways Board, bringing the canals under the Regional Water Authorities, yet by definition these canals form a network running across river basin boundaries. Water recreational interests therefore expressed concern at the proposals, so that finally the government had to agree to retain the Waterways Board.

Not only do the different agencies work separately, pursuing their own ends and coordinated only through fairly loose ad hoc committees. There is also an almost total lack of overall criteria for determining priorities or relating programs to objectives. How should the Natural Environment Research Council determine the relative expenditure on conservation versus research, or the work of the Nature Conservancy versus that of the Antarctic Survey? At a higher level, what determines the conservation expenditures of the council versus the spending programs of the Countryside Commission? How are expenditures on water pollution control related to those on air pollution control? In a different area—that of land use planning itself—how does the development control machine weigh up the competing claims of conservation of nature, the need for outdoor recreation, the urban demand for water, and the claims for preserving agriculture in an area like a national park? Is it feasible to arrive at some common economic yardstick of measurement, which would show the comparative "return" to the community of these different functions in different locations? If the answer is *no* (and certainly, in respect of most of these functions, it is *no* at present), then what cruder substitutes are available?

Lastly, the fundamental criticism of all is that in most cases these questions do not even seem to have been asked. After the great controversy over the siting of London's third airport—where an elaborate cost-benefit analysis was used to support one choice on the part of a Commission of Inquiry, which was afterwards overruled on planning grounds—the criticism was raised that economic analysis may be positively perverse in appearing to give clear-cut, quantified answers to questions where the basic variables are very often open to considerable doubt. The counter-defense of the commission's work was that however much disagreement there may be about the individual items that enter into the analysis, it still provides an orderly framework for a logical and disciplined discussion; in particular, it permits a much more constructive debate about how much value the community places on certain qualities of life, such as freedom from noise versus easy accessibility to work. At present, in most of the policy areas discussed in this chapter, no such rational discussion is possible. The community as a whole simply does not know why it is doing what it is doing.

This has some pernicious consequences. The case for any one policy or one program tends to be argued in terms of absolute imperative—the air *must* be cleaned up, this program *must* be funded—instead of the language of rational priorities. And there is a failure to relate the different programs to the central touchstone of human welfare. Difficult as it may be to trace the effect on human well-being of the preservation of a tree or an animal species, or the cleaning up of a river so that fish may again live in it, or the preservation of a remote area as wilderness, that is no excuse for the failure to try.

chapter 8

Summary, appraisal, and outlook

The urban planning systems of Britain and the United States, each in its own way, have produced inconsistent and perverse results. The British system has been more successful than the American in enforcing public policies; but since these policies have often been ill-grounded and ill-related to the facts of the situation, like the looser American system it has produced an urban structure few among the public can be said to have chosen and few would want if they were given the choice.

To justify this conclusion we shall summarize a few of the major points from previous chapters; we shall also offer an appraisal—necessarily somewhat subjective, as every appraisal must be—and speculate a little about the forces that will shape the form of the future city. Throughout this chapter, the main conclusions are deliberately set out starkly, without detailed support or justification. They rest on the analyses in earlier chapters and on the general understanding we have developed in the course of the comprehensive studies mentioned in the Preface and on which this book is based.

SIMILARITIES BETWEEN BRITAIN AND THE UNITED STATES

There are many similarities in the urban situation of Britain and the United States. When comparisons are made on a national basis, some of these are obscured, but when the northeastern region of the United States, equal in area to England and Wales, is compared with the latter, as was done in chapter 3, the similarities become more evident. In each country, population, employment, and income have grown, particularly since the close of World War II; and because each country is now dominantly urban by residence of its people, this growth has been largely urban growth. The rate of growth has differed somewhat between the two countries, as it has between the more comparable areas that have been studied in each;

it has also differed somewhat between years. Nevertheless, growth—not stability—has been a dominant fact in each country in the past, and seems likely to continue as a dominant force in the future.

Partly as a result of this general growth, but partly in addition to it, the cities or urban-like areas have been spreading outward, absorbing more land. This is a process of expansion, or of suburbanization. Although territorially confined in Britain by its urban planning system, nevertheless suburbanization has proceeded there; it is more a suburbanization of residence, employment, and function, than it is of physical sprawl as in the United States. In both countries there is some flight from the older and less attractive residential city centers; in the United States this has been exacerbated by the racial changes taking place in the city core. The older city centers are being rebuilt slowly, though somewhat more rapidly in Britain than in the United States. When rebuilding does occur, it is likely to displace some former residents and to aim at lower overall densities. In the United States, it replaces lower-income residents by higher-income newcomers; in Britain, public housing programs reduce this probability.

Growth being the dominant fact about urban centers in each country, one might logically expect that city planning in each would focus on the growth process: how change does occur and how its course might be altered to produce some socially more desirable result. Curiously, city planning in each country—more so in Britain, perhaps, but in the United States also—has been static in its approach. The present situation is typically inventoried: a picture of a desired or a possible future situation is drawn, and attention focuses on that future situation, not upon the processes of getting from here to there, much less upon the processes by which the city's life will go forward after that planned date. For a time after World War II, British city planning was beguiled by the possibility of a stationary population, and growth was denied or ignored. The United States was not quite so convinced that a stationary population was about to happen, yet the rates of growth were frequently misjudged—estimates were too low while rate of population growth was increasing, and then were too high as the rate of growth slacked off. Leaders in the planning field are aware of this deficiency and efforts are being made to change it, but the weight of planning practice still justifies this judgment.

Each country has adopted governmental programs to affect, if not to control, the amount, form, shape, and direction of urban growth. Neither country has been willing to let a "free" market operate without direction and control. Indeed, one powerful political support for the more restrictive British urban planning was dissatisfaction with what the relatively unfettered private market was producing during the 1930s. The two countries have differed in the precise nature of their urban planning and urban controls; neither has adopted controls totally consistent with their objectives or fully effective in their achievement. In each country, city planning and government controls over urban development are so firmly entrenched, we judge, that they will never be abandoned or repudiated. The real issues are: How far, and in what ways, should they, or might they, be modified?

In each country there is a multiplicity of public and private decision makers. These include elected public officials, nonelected officials, private firms and public bodies engaged in one or more specialized tasks in actual city building, private landowners, prospective home buyers, and many others. The precise roles of each differ between the countries, and in different situations in each country. By and large, the city planner plays a larger and more powerful role in Britain than his counterpart does in the United States, where the private interests are often more powerful. But, contrary to a widely held impression in the United States, in Britain the private builder in a normal year constructs well over half of the new dwellings.

While the British planner is more nearly in control of the final result of city building than is any other actor on either the British or the American scene, even his powers and his freedom of action are guided and controlled by other forces, including notably the attitudes and convictions of the electorate and its elected representatives in his area of operation. City building is notably an enterprise of interrelations among and within groups.

One could go on, noting other similarities (including that of a superficially common language!), but the differences require attention also.

BRITISH CITY PLANNING

Compared with American city planning, British city planning has as one dominant characteristic a philosophy or a theory of what the ideal urban structure should be. Based on the pioneering work of Ebenezer Howard, British city planning seeks to control the size and to some extent the internal structure of the larger cities, in terms both of population and employment and of physical extent, and to promote the development of certain types and sizes of smaller cities in relatively well-defined locations with respect to these large cities. Differences of opinion have existed among planners and among political leaders, as well as among the general public. Yet, to an American, the most impressive aspect of British city planning has been this dominance of a relatively consistent theory or conception of the ideal city structure.

This view was not politically positive until after World War II. Then, the combination of vocal intellectualism, postwar idealism, and concern over the loss of agricultural land during the relatively uncontrolled urban development of the 1930s, combined to achieve passage of several notable laws, the most important of which was the Town and Country Planning Act of 1947. From an objective view, it was a curious combination of political forces: idealists, intellectuals, rural fundamentalists, and others. Although the act was passed, it did not include all aspects of the intellectual concepts of Howard and others, and, as has become apparent over the years, there was far from full understanding or agreement concerning those parts that would have severely limited the financial gains of land owners. While city planning as a whole, and much of its specifics, have not been partisan political issues in Britain, the matter of control over land prices, or the public capture of the land values created by urban planning, has been very much a partisan political issue. Labour has tried, ineffectually, to control land prices or at least to capture for the public part or all of the increases in price due to public action; the Conservatives have repealed or nullified such efforts, when in power.

British city planning has clearly controlled the physical spread of cities. The greenbelt around London is obvious to the casual traveller, and around some other large cities there are physically similar areas, though not always so designated. Urban growth is neat and tidy in its extensions, with none of the sprawl and disorder so characteristic of the American suburb. Clearly, land has been used more intensively and more fully, with little or none idle; and the many public services (such as sewers, water supply, transport, and others), whose costs depend upon areal extent and distance as much as upon numbers of customers, can be provided more efficiently than under conditions of sprawl. To some, these achievements alone are so worthwhile that nothing else matters; we, too, consider them achievements, but ones to be reckoned against the less evident costs. This control over the physical extension of the city has not prevented a less obvious suburbanization; people have moved their residences outside the central city, to some satellite city, while their jobs have more frequently remained in the older city. Decentralization of residence has proceeded much more rapidly than decentralization of employment—indeed, in many instances, especially up to the mid-1960s, employment was centralizing both absolutely and relatively. As a result, journeys to work have increased, as home and job have been increasingly separated; the older city centers are becoming more and more congested as car ownership rises, and the problem can be met only by drastic urban surgery. Efforts to control industrial employment are beginning to be effective in some older cities, and efforts to control office employment may be coming to be effective for London.

British city planning, combined with other public and private programs, has produced a good deal of housing since World War II—not at a rate higher than the more nearly private market produced during the 1930s, nor at a rate adequate to replace all the substandard housing, yet at a considerable rate. To an American, the outstanding aspect of postwar housing has been the remarkably high densities at which it has been built—three to six or more times the number of houses per acre than what is considered moderate density in the United States. The higher density has been achieved mostly by crowding houses closely together rather than by going upward. In part, high densities have been urged because of a desire to conserve agricultural land, especially land of the most productive kinds. Concern over agricultural land conservation may by some be regarded as an obsession. Advocates reject market values or economic tests as criteria; they ignore the growing agricultural output per acre; and they can think only of the two periods in a lifetime when England suffered partial blockade of imported foods. But the higher residential densities have grown out of other, largely unintended, forces and situations. Planning powers have been given to rural areas (counties) and to cities (county boroughs); the former had the land, but did not want the urban people because they wished to preserve their rural life-style; the latter had the people who must be housed, but often had limited land area. The solution for public and private builders alike has been to crowd more residential units onto a given area of land.

This trend, which would have been powerful enough in any case, has been greatly reinforced by the rapid rise in land prices—a rise at least double the rate of the rise in the United States, which seems rapid enough to those observing it. Planning, by designating enough land barely to meet the calculated "need"—and this typically underestimated—gave a powerful monopsonistic power to the owners of such land. They could, and did, demand and get very high prices for land with planning permission. One adjustment to these rapidly rising land prices was to reduce the amount of land per dwelling unit. "Two up and two down" housing—very small and cramped quarters on plots of land not much more than double the size of the small house—became one answer, much used by private builders of modestly priced houses for sale. High-rise apartment blocks were the typical response of the municipal housing departments in the cities. Such high-density housing makes scant allowance for a single automobile per family, virtually none for second and possibly third cars, and none for caravans (trailers), boats, and other recreational gear demanded by some families as their real incomes rise.

It is doubtful if many British householders would deliberately choose the kind of high-density housing that has been built, were the range of choice wider. Some planners may like it; the high densities do economize on the provision of some public services, and it is at least arguable that they facilitate community social relationships. But house buyers have had little choice; the financial rewards of house purchase were too great to be resisted, and a new house, even a grossly inadequate one, might be better than any alternative. The risk is grave, however, that this housing will be socially obsolete long before it is physically obsolete. In this way, crowded British housing may turn out to be the counterpart of American public housing in large cities, where inadequate design, faulty construction, and intense crowding have led to virtually uninhabitable structures when more than half of the planned life still remained to be amortized.

British planning has been notably successful in its preservation of the rural countryside. Not only has the physical sprawl, characteristic of the American suburban scene, been kept out of rural areas, but the intrusion of city people has been made difficult and that of city industry even more so. The kind of rural scene and rural life dominant in an earlier generation has been preserved remarkably intact. The people who have benefited in their daily lives are small in number, but they have been influential. The visual results are impressive and pleasing; it is only when one looks more closely at the social results that doubts and criticisms arise.

One aspect of rural countryside preservation is particularly intriguing to an American. Owners of the rural land have generally been willing to forgo speculative gains from a rise in its price, such as has occurred for many miles around American cities. The price of land with planning permission has indeed risen greatly, but the price of land without planning permission, and unlikely to get it, has risen relatively little.[1] While some political and other pressures have been exerted to extract planning permission for more land, many owners of rural land seem to have accepted a loss of speculative gain in land prices as a necessary and reasonable price to pay to preserve a way of life.

The obverse of this is the congestion generated by British planning policies. People are congested inside their new suburban homes and on the minute lots that surround them; they are congested in the high-rise municipal housing schemes in the cities; they are congested on the highways, due to the relatively high density

[1] A rapid rise in the price of rural land without planning permission occurred in 1972. The causes were obscure, though doubtless they were related to the prevailing general inflation.

of much development and separation of one small town from another. Above all, many suffer the effects of congestion in city and town centers. Instead of decentralizing into suburban locations that would comfortably accommodate the private car, employment and retailing have continued to expand in ancient urban cores ill-adapted to the rising flood of traffic. No planner could have defended as a policy the production of mass congestion; it just happened, through failure to predict basic trends like the rise in car ownership, plus the fatal alliance in practice between city authorities determined to preserve their tax base and county authorities determined to preserve their land and their way of life.

U.S. City Planning and City Building

In the United States no philosophy of city planning and city structure has been dominant, as it has been in Britain. Although the United States has had its outstanding city planners, none has had the impact on public policy that Howard imprinted on Britain. Numerous concepts have been proposed of how the ideal American city should look, or how the ideal city building process should be formed, but none of these has achieved the acceptance of a philosophy or an ideal of city structure, as did the 1947 Town and Country Planning Act in Britain. In light of the experience since 1947, it could well be argued that acceptance of the ideals of the 1947 Act was less than complete in Britain; party reversals of control over land prices and divergence in interest between the counties and the boroughs are evidence of far from full national agreement. But some elements of a philosophy or a theory have been politically dominant since 1947. Nothing like this has existed in the United States; there have been too many theories of ideal urban form and growth for any one to have become national policy.

Partly because of this, city planning and city planners in the United States have never had the intellectual, economic, political, and practical force their counterparts have had in Britain. Plans have indeed been made for most large American cities or metropolitan areas; they have rarely been widely understood or supported by the electorate at large. The plans have had some effect—it is a mistake to think they have been useless or impotent—but their effect has been moderate. They have frequently served to guide some private and public actions but, when faced with strong opposition from a group or a powerful individual whose ends would have been thwarted by the plan, they have not had the public support necessary to ensure conformance with the plan. There is widespread endorsement of city planning in the United States, but only as long as planners and public officials do not insist upon compliance with the plan. Development and growth psychology is still dominant in the United States, in spite of recent concern for the ultimate results of uncontrolled growth.

In the United States the making of city plans is divorced from any attempt to implement them; their implementation is influenced primarily by zoning, and to a lesser extent by subdivision control, building codes, scheduling of public works, and other measures that in some degree limit or influence actual city development. Zoning may be undertaken prior to or in the absence of a plan, or in disregard of the plan, or in opposition to it—and all this typically without apology or explanation by the public officials concerned. Indeed, many will argue that there should be no relation between planning and zoning. Such an argument often derives from the fact that these people want the planning to be as ineffectual, private, and inconspicuous as possible, so that it can be challenged by none, yet be effective if it should guarantee the ends they seek. In the United States frank political pressure is more commonly and openly used, and is vastly more effective in the making of city plans, in the initial zoning, and in the rezoning, than is the case in Britain. Some leaders in planning and in government recognize this situation and seek to change it; but prevailing practice still conforms to this model.

U.S. city building reflects this lack of consensus of desired city form and this lack of power in the city planning process. The number of major actors in the decision-making process is much greater than in Britain; more of them have real power than in Britain. The land speculator, the developer, and the builder can and do innovate, often without regard to plans and zoning ordinances and sometimes in (successful) efforts to destroy them. The unit of suburban residential growth is the subdivision—an area ranging upward from a few acres to several hundred—which one developer and usually one builder seek to develop more or less as a unit, especially in terms of its neighborhood characteristics and of marketing its houses. Subdivisions frequently are not contiguous to existing subdivisions; they may be separated by a mile or more in some cases. Neither developer nor house buyer suffers direct cost by such discontiguity; in spite of higher costs, public services are typically priced on a postage-stamp basis—no higher in the distant than in the adjacent subdivision. Given the nature of the suburban land market, where the landowners often have quite different expectations of future rises in land prices and different holding costs, and have different abilities to hold out for the large but distant gain, the discontiguous sprawl that typifies most American suburbs is a natural result.

But it is a mistake to stress the shortcomings of this suburbanization process without recognizing that it has some strengths too. It is a process of great vitality. Millions of homes and thousands of shopping districts have been built through the efforts of large numbers of diverse actors. Many of the suburban neighborhoods have been quite pleasant, with comfortable, even excellent, housing; and, while there may have been notable lack of coordination of all parts of this development, the diversity of decision making has prevented massive errors too. But it is equally true that this process of American suburb building has had serious weaknesses. It has cost too much for what it has produced; substantial savings could have been achieved. It has all too frequently been unaesthetic and monotonous. And, above all, it has met the needs of only an upper-income fraction of the population. Also it has been wasteful of land, though this perhaps could be tolerated if its results were better.

Just as the dominant American impression of contemporary Britain is one of urban and suburban congestion, so the dominant British impression of contemporary North America is one of suburban sprawl—albeit coupled with high densities and vertical extensions in the urban cores. One does not use the word sprawl in a pejorative way: sprawl, in the form of low-density suburban expansion over vast areas, is simply a statistical and visual fact. At every price bracket, new sub-urban houses are much larger than their new British equivalents; they stand on lots typically three or six times as large; they are more lavishly equipped with special-function rooms and with storage space. The new suburbs are equipped with roadspace designed to deal with nearly universal ownership of large cars; crossing through large segments of the suburbs, four-lane highways are standard and six-lane highways are common. Above all, their workplaces and shopping patterns reflect total reliance on the private automobile: the smallest local shopping center must provide spaces for several hundred parked cars, the largest for up to 10,000 at one time. Since land is cheap and costs must be kept low, invariably this is all on the ground. As a result, any typical commercial use of land consists of a building isolated in a vast sea of parking space. When to these features are added some of the incidental but invariable features of the American landscape—the huge illu-minated signs competing desperately to get their messages home, the extraordinary wilderness of overhead wirescape, and the tracts of land that appear to be utterly abandoned—the result to a European eye is alien, often alarming, and not infre-quently offensive. Many Americans, indeed, profess the same reactions. But it is important to distinguish the central fact of spread and sprawl from some of the more garish manifestations. Unlikely as it might seem to many Americans, the former could exist quite well without the latter. To a large degree, suburban sprawl has been necessary to accommodate the American suburban way of life; had it been limited, the way of life would necessarily have changed also; but there is little evidence that the bulk of people are dissatisfied with this way of life.

Efficiency Versus Equity or Welfare

Most analysis and discussion about urban growth in Britain and in the United States have focused on its efficiency or lack of it—the costs, the values, and the relation between them. This is indeed highly important; national income is not unlimited in either country, and neither can well afford to waste effort if some other form of city structure would have been more efficient. But this is far from the whole of the story. Who has gained, and who has lost, either absolutely or relatively, by the city-building process? This aspect of urban growth and develop-ment has received much less attention; many people have preferred to ignore it.

In each country the higher-income end of the income spectrum has gained con-siderably; there have been numerous financial advantages to the family able to buy a home—not the least of which has been the hedge it has afforded against continued inflation. In Britain the residents of small villages and rural areas have been protected against change in their way of life. In the United States many land speculators, developers, and builders have achieved substantial financial gains. By and large, these appear to have been the principal gainers from the process of urban planning and growth as it has actually operated over the past quarter century in each country.

People at the lower end of the income spectrum have lost most, at least relatively and sometimes absolutely—and this "end" is not a tiny fraction but perhaps half of all families. Lacking savings for a down-payment on a house and/or lacking sufficient income to meet monthly house payments, they have been unable to purchase a house. Not only have they lost the opportunity for financial gain, but they have been condemned to renting older residential units, some of which range downward to slums. Britain's public housing program—far bigger than in the United States—has for many at least met the basic necessities of shelter and sometimes, in the case of the new towns and several expanded towns, provided a high level of environment. But it has surely been less desirable than owning a new home, if a different policy had permitted lower-income groups to share the advantages of owner occupation. Besides which, public housing has all too often been unavailable to families who needed it. Millions of families in each country have been housed in old, seriously rundown, miserable housing, often apartments, for which they paid a great deal considering how little they really got. Moreover, many residents of such areas have suffered severely from another aspect of the urbanization process: their jobs have moved to the suburbs, where they could not find housing at prices they could afford, and to which public transport was deficient.

In part, public programs have been responsible for this situation, by encouraging the private automobile for upper-income classes and in the process destroying the economic base of public transportation. This process has been more pronounced in the United States than in Britain; but there are distinct signs in the early 1970s that the same process might also be in train there. In the United States the sprawling suburbs are obvious to any observer, however casual; in Britain all seems neat and tidy, because physical sprawl has been prevented by planning; but functional suburbanization has gone on, producing as much and perhaps more separation of home and work place as in the United States.

In both countries the divergence of interest and rewards has followed lines of economic or income classes—the relatively well-to-do against the poor. In the United States the economic division is often accompanied by a racial division. Some, but far from all, low-income people who can afford to live only in older, decadent housing are black or belong to one or another ethnic minority. Though Britain has experienced severe racial problems in recent years, its racial problem is on a very much smaller scale than that of the United States. But both countries have a problem of the continued existence of substantial low-income groups—white as well as black.

MIGHT IT HAVE BEEN DIFFERENT?

Might the course of urban growth and development in Britain or in the United States have been different over this past quarter century? In one sense, there is little to be gained from a game of "might have been." But in another sense there may be merit in briefly contemplating the differences that might have been; at least the exercise forces one to evaluate the actual experience and to calculate what factors have been basic and what effect a different set of basic forces might have had.

It is not impossible, we think, to set forth some conditions or circumstances that would have led to a notably different pattern of urban growth and development over these years. Some of them follow; some are suggested in rather more detail in chapter 9. Presumably, one would seek to find arrangements that would have removed or lessened the deficiencies of the urban growth process as it has actually worked, without at the same time losing any or many of the advantages it has shown. Since the dominant deficiency of the actual urban growth process has been its inability to provide satisfactory housing for the lower half (or more) of the income range, correction of this deficiency must stand at the top of any list of "might have beens." In Britain, a reduction in journeys to work, or a bringing of home and work place closer together, must also stand high on such a list. Though the data picture is blurred for the United States, a similar improvement probably must stand about as high there. For Britain, a reduction in the extraordinarily high densities of suburban residential development, where today houses are crowded on tiny plots of land in what are likely to be the suburban slums of the 1990s, would surely rank high on an improvement list. In the United States, a reduction if not abolition of the land-wasting urban sprawl, with its accompanying high real costs of public services of all kinds, must also stand high on the list. One could go on, but these seem to be at least the major deficiencies one would wish to cure, could he relive the past twenty-five or so years.

These various measures of improvement have one common thread: they would require a different land policy and different controls over land use than have existed during this period. One basic change would have been to limit private control over developable suburban land, particularly to restrict the opportunity for private profit from a rise in land prices. If housing is ever to be built for people of less than average income, then it must be on land priced relatively low —not only because savings in lower land price contribute directly to a lower final cost, but also because land cost must be held to an acceptable proportion of the final price of house and lot. In actuality, government action in both countries has been exactly opposite. Land for suburban growth has been made artificially scarce by planning controls in Britain and by land zoning in the United States, and the landowner or speculator has been aided in various effective ways in his understandable desire to push his land price upward.

Oddly, either less intervention or more might have been preferable; what was not satisfactory was the halfway house. A totally unfettered competitive market for land would surely not have shown such advances in land prices. To the extent that land use planning reduced the supply of land available for building—as it surely did in Britain and probably did in the United States—then it pushed up the price of such land. Effective control over land use and over land prices would have been basic to a more generous use of land in the British suburbs and towns, and to a more rational and efficient use of land in U.S. suburbs. Again, many of the actual governmental programs operated in the opposite direction. Given the uncontrolled and mounting land prices, and given the reluctance to exercise control over units of local government, which successfully sought their own advantage though at the general public expense, the high densities in Britain and the sprawl in America made a kind of sense—but of a kind that a drunken man finds in continuing to drink so that he may be spared the pain of sobering up. If home and work place were to be brought closer to reduce journeys to work in general, and especially to make them easier for those who could not afford private cars, then, again, a different form of land use controls would have been necessary.

To some greater control over private land, particularly over its prices, would have been added some greater central government control over small units of local government. No country can have a coherent national land policy, or a coherent urban growth policy, that allows minuscule units of local government—small fractions of the total of any metropolitan area—to take independent action nullifying or perverting the results of governmental action at other levels. In Britain the persistent tendency to draw the boundary of planning jurisdictions at approximately the edge of the heavily developed cities was especially pernicious: it gave one unit of local government the responsibility for planning for people but denied it land, while it gave another the needed land area without any responsibility to care for the people. The situation in the United States has been more haphazard— less intentionally perverse, but perverse for all of that. As long as suburbs may, de facto, keep themselves lily-white for upper-income families, while forcing the central cities to cope on a shrinking revenue base with the problems of low-income and racial minority groups, one can scarcely be surprised that the deficiencies of the urban growth process continue.

The new towns in Britain were an imaginative move away from some of these problems. Possibly they would have been sufficient, or at least more nearly so, had the expected condition of a nearly stationary population actually resulted. As it was, their effect, though on the plus side, was small; unless their number could have been much greater, or their average size greater, or both, they could not have been a significant answer to the urban problems as we have described them. In the United States, in spite of talk, no new towns exist on the British model, and one can scarcely conceive of their being built at a rate capable of affecting urban growth and development more than marginally.

One might summarize all this still further by saying that in each country a sufficiently powerful coalition of political forces combined to modify a free market in land, but lacked either the vision or the courage or the capacity to carry their goals into realistic practice. Land use controls were instituted in each country; Britain had a curious dance into and out of control over land prices; each sought, in its own way, to influence locations of both jobs and homes; but the results have been far from fully satisfactory in each country, in large part because the tools provided were inadequate for the job to be done. If one seeks a different outcome from that which an uncontrolled market will produce, then one must be prepared, psychologically and politically, to modify that uncontrolled market in sufficient degree and in sufficient direction to accomplish what one seeks.

This brings us to the nub of the "might have beens." Accepting that, at least in retrospect, one can devise or propose a system of land use and other governmental policies capable of producing a more desirable urban growth pattern, could the necessary steps have been taken, given the political realities of the times in each country? This is, at least for us, a very difficult question for which we have no confident answer. One has to be somewhat pessimistic; the need for stronger measures was not clearly perceived or not generally accepted. In Britain, the proposals in the various Royal Commissions and official committee reports were seriously watered down in the 1947 Planning Act, and some of these were abandoned within six years. In the United States, there has never been a truly serious move to control or restrict prices of private land in suburban zones, and it is greatly to be doubted if one could have been adopted. In each country the dedicated professional planners sought utopia in their own way, each relying on his own presumed special competence but without any real evidence that his approach to Heaven would really get him there.

In the absence of an intellectual recognition of the need for a different approach than was actually taken, one cannot be sure that the necessary political will would not have been forthcoming. Possibly it might have been, in Britain, for the end of World War II brought into being an immensely powerful popular demand for major improvements in the social structure and in life in all its aspects; possibly better tools for urban planning and growth could have been forged, had there been a better recognition of their necessity. In the United States, even up to today, one must be more hesitant; today there is increasing clamor that further growth of the really big cities and further decline of the small cities, towns, and remote countryside are not in the national interest. But this disquiet with what the existing system is producing has not brought a real consensus about what should take its place, or a real understanding of the costs involved, or a real commitment to assume those costs.

Thus, one is tempted to conclude that, given the circumstances of the times, nothing really better could have been put into operation in this past quarter century; if we are now dissatisfied with the results, at least in part, then we must accept them as part of the price we have paid for our unwillingness to do better. Even if such pessimism is warranted for the past, does it extend equally to the future?

One is tempted to ask: Which country did worse—Britain with a rather elaborate system of urban planning, which has produced results different from those its sponsors intended, or the United States, where city planning never really promised much, and never delivered much? An impossible question, but an intriguing one; the answer will depend on the values of the observer. If his philosophy puts a high value on giving a large section of the population the material goods they want through market mechanisms, then he must conclude that American suburbia, for all its inefficiency and its occasional ugliness, is greatly superior to the cramped and costly British equivalent. If his philosophy puts a greater value on protection by society of its land and the natural resources that go with it, he will probably elect the British system of effective land use planning. These different value systems have, in fact, been deeply instilled in the policies the two nations have pursued. The American policy has been more populist, the British policy more elitist; the American results have the virtues and vices of a society that respects the preferences of the common man (as expressed through the power of his dollar in the marketplace); conversely, the British results have the benefits and drawbacks deriving from a more aristocratic, paternalistic view of the relationship between the State and the public.

In raising this question, one must recognize that there have been refreshing exceptions to the prevailing mediocrity in both countries: the great majority of all development in the British new towns; some of the better large-scale American private housing developments, in particular the new communities; urban conservation in some British small towns, and the splendid work of the U.S. National Park Service; urban renewal in the centers of a few major British cities, and one or two of the finer out-of-town shopping centers in the United States; many miles of sensitively designed and landscaped new highways in both countries, almost making up for earlier disasters.

The Urban World of the Future

As noted in the Preface, the purpose of this book is to present, in as comprehensive a way as is possible in a book of moderate length, a view of the processes of suburban and urban growth in Britain and in the United States. As such, the emphasis is on the past and the present—how these processes have worked and now work. Neither this book nor the more detailed studies on which it rests includes a formal and detailed projection of the future. Nevertheless, any review of past and present inevitably has implications for the future. Therefore, we shall try to outline what we see as the likely trends and forces in society and in social attitudes that will shape the future urban world. The analysis in this section is neither detailed nor statistical; the time period is a generation or more into the future.

We are unable to conceive of any pattern of human settlement, for a generation at least, which does not involve as much or more emphasis on the city, or on a city-like grouping of people, as exists today in each country. Estimates of future "urbanization" are likely to get entangled in definitions of "city" and similar terms. But the trend toward people living in relatively close proximity to others, at densities in the range of five to ten or more thousands of people per square mile, has been very powerful over the past, and we judge is likely to continue strongly. This will not preclude substantial numbers of people living at some distance from such population centers and commuting to work and to shop and for play. It is likely to include central cities, satellite cities, new towns of considerable independence but linked to central cities, and many other aspects of the present urban scene. Perhaps more meaningfully, we reject any idea that population concentrations will disappear or dwindle greatly in numbers, size, and importance. There are serious problems of the future for the older city centers, and we do not suggest that all presently decadent urban areas will be restored to activity. But we do think that the urban grouping of population is permanent, at least from the perspective of public policy for the next generation; the city is here, will remain, and we must learn to control its form to our ends. Moreover, though some new towns may be built in each country, we judge that the majority of the increase in population will have to be housed in suburbs to existing cities—that is, areas physically adjacent to the city, many of whose inhabitants find employment or urban services in the city. It is for this reason that we believe an understanding of the suburbanization process to be vital.

We think it highly probable that population will continue to increase in each country, not only for the next generation—the present age structure virtually guarantees that—but for a generation or more further into the future. Population projections have been notoriously inaccurate in the past, in large part because man's reproductive processes have been so unpredictably variable. But, for our present purpose, a quantitative and hopefully accurate population projection is not necessary; it is enough to say that urban planning and urban programs for several decades must expect to cope with somewhat more people than at present.

We also think it highly probable that real income per person will continue to rise. There may well be question as to the rate of that rise, and as to the composition of the output, and as to the impact upon the natural environment, but we think the scientific, technological, economic, business, and psychological pressures for growth are too strong to be countered easily, even were there general agreement on an economic no-growth policy—which there certainly is not in either country today. Indeed, we would reject an objective of no-growth. One can be concerned with the kind of life that is being created, and with the impact that economic growth of the present style is having on the natural environment, and yet see that no-growth would create more problems than it would solve. As long as substantial segments of the total population live under conditions that most people would regard as unsatisfactory, then more real output is necessary, although not sufficient alone—unless we are willing to consider income redistribution on a truly massive scale, which would be politically infeasible. Amelioration of unsatisfactory environmental conditions will itself require investment and effort, which will be easier to manage if total economic output is growing. Economic growth in the long run rests upon greater productivity per worker, and we see no virtue in striving to prevent either reduction in effort for given output or increased output per unit of effort.

As a concomitant to increased population and increased output, there will be some increase in employment—at least, in numbers of persons working, although possibly hours worked per worker may decline so that total hours of labor may rise only slowly or perhaps not at all. Productive and constructive employment does more for most persons than merely provide income; at its best, it also provides basic satisfactions of achievement and purpose.

We think it probable that the recent trends toward more single-person households, and toward more than one living space per household, will continue. Young and older people alike will increasingly live in their own one-person households; this is both an expression of the times and a reflection of increased income. But many families or individuals will have a second, and some perhaps a third, or even a fourth home—for different seasons, for different purposes, in different locations. A downtown urban home for living while working, a suburban home for its spaciousness and privacy and for weekends, a mountain home for summer vacations, a beach home for winter vacations; housing standards or luxury now available only to the very rich may become available to a vastly larger fraction of the total population. If this seems utopian today, the reader should contemplate the consequences of a doubling of real per capita income—which means a much more rapid rise in disposable income; he should also reflect that a generation ago a forecast of one car per household, let alone the two or more which is becoming common today, would have seemed equally utopian.

Rising incomes per capita will surely express themselves in rapidly rising production of material goods and services for private consumption. Admittedly, there may be a strong move to divert a greater proportion of rising living standards into the production of public goods and services of all kinds. This may partly arise from a call for redistribution of income, both internally within the affluent developed nations, and above all internationally; but partly the motive will be simply that these public goods are demanded by an affluent population. Since Galbraith first painted his picture of the American middle-class consumer, surrounded by private luxuries and by public squalor, an increasing consciousness has come into being in the United States that many desirable things, ranging from clean air to unpolluted rivers to unravaged landscapes, require public action and public expenditure. We should expect that realization to grow stronger. Nevertheless, experience in all advanced countries since World War II shows that the amount of marginal income taken in taxation can only vary within limits, short of some revolution which would impose a different system of government. We should therefore presume that private disposable income and expenditure on income-elastic goods and services, such as durable consumables and tourism, will increase in relation to GNP almost as rapidly in the future as in the past.

In concluding thus, we are aware that many people take a different view. They see a new consciousness among the young: a rejection of the prevalent western ethic of material advancement and a return to a simpler life-style with greater leisure and, above all, more contemplation. We do not deny that this style may appeal to large numbers of people: for many during a short period of their lives, and for a few during their whole lives. But we doubt whether it will have more than a marginal effect on total consumption patterns. Even in affluent North America and Western Europe, it is obvious that the great majority of people still regard the standard of living and the cost of living as the overwhelmingly most important political problem. And even among the young it is significant to notice that the consumer society continues to make headway; even the simple life, it seems, demands regular jet flights from one part of the world to another, not to mention hi-fi apparatus, a camera and a few other necessary impedimenta. The great bulk of society, we can safely assume, will not be following the latter-day Thoreaus back to Walden Pond.

All of these trends must mean that the demands on land will be greater in scale and variety than in the past. More people will be split up into more households, occupying more homes on average. These homes will contain many more material goods, and their inhabitants will have much more elaborate notions of privacy and separation at certain times. The types of home they occupy will be more varied, ranging from the traditional main family home to the weekday city apartment, the weekend cottage (or two), the motel, the resort center, the country club, the trailer or the tent. Any given number of people will demand a much greater total number of bedspaces and living spaces in the future than now. And more of them will be travelling greater distances between these various locations, making extra demands on highways, airports, and railroad lines. True, there may be countervailing trends: people may rent and share equipment more than now, travel may be faster and in bigger units so that it occupies less space per mile travelled. (The Jumbo Jet is a major antidote to the threat of more and bigger airports.) But the broad trend is unmistakable.

The demands on land we have just been discussing are essentially private ones. But, as we earlier suggested, at the same time there will be increasingly strong popular demands for preservation of land, landscape, and natural resources for public enjoyment. The resulting pressures on land are certain to be acute in every advanced country. But whether we label them private or public, the resulting land uses will satisfy the needs of largely urban population; we do not see how the most stringent controls over land use could avoid conversion of some land— probably a good deal of it—from rural to urban uses. But we would hope that the problems of urban land use could be looked at rather differently in the future than they have been in the past. There has been too great a tendency to look at urban and recreational uses of land as somehow unproductive, even parasitic, although necessary. Agricultural fundamentalism has been much stronger in Britain than in the United States: the passionate desire to retain the rural countryside just as it was—and the strategic political position of these fundamentalists—has dominated urban planning and urban growth more than any other single factor. We suggest that the time has come for a drastically different approach—a recognition that land used for urban purposes is fully as productive of things people want as is agricultural land; a recognition that agricultural output can increase even if its land area shrinks; a recognition that future wars, if they come and if man survives, will not drag on more than a few days or involve blockades; and a recognition that Britain must live by international trade, part of which might well be in agricultural commodities. Future British cities could well be built on a very different system of land use. But the American wasteful use of suburban land and the needlessly costly public services it creates are equally unsuited to the future. One would hope that suburban land use in the future could be brought more into line with the economic and cultural possibilities.

All of the foregoing aspects of future urban life are part of a changing urban life-style. As more people become better educated, as real incomes rise, as meaningful leisure and means to enjoy it increase, the whole pattern of life will surely change. One can read about life in British manufacturing cities a century ago—miserable hovels, no sanitary facilities, filth in the streets, no medical programs for working-men, rampant ill-health and disease, no retirement programs for old age, and often no hope of improvement for the average man; and one can contrast this situation with the present, and see immense progress in terms of living conditions for the average man. Or one can read of the American frontier of a century ago, with its crudity, lack of culture, and bad physical living conditions; and one can contrast this with living in typical American suburbs today; again we can note immense progress in the condition of the average man. But there is little reason to think that dramatic changes are all in the past, any more than there can be complacency with conditions that are unnecessarily bad by the standards of today, though good by the standards of a century ago. We judge that men of higher, average, and lower incomes are each, in their own ways, moving to new consumption patterns, new ways of life—and that the city must be modified and transformed to meet these demands of the future.

One urban issue totally unresolved today is that of the city form versus the automobile. The older cities, built before the day of the car, do not adapt easily to it. Most obvious in Western Europe, but visible also in some older cities of North America, are the results: congestion on the one hand, expensive and drastic urban surgery on the other. Newer cities, such as the planned creations of Britain or Scandinavia or the spontaneous growths of the American West—Los Angeles, Phoenix, Las Vegas—reflect the influence of the car to a much greater degree; but they, too, show features of the older urban form. There is a tendency in popular discussion, and even among planners, to treat this issue far too simply, as if all cities were alike: cars must be banned, public transport must be supported at all costs. Closer analysis shows that the situation is more complex. The traditional city is incompatible with really free use of the car; but even there, the suburban areas permit a remarkable degree of reliance upon it. Newer cities show a surprisingly high capacity to absorb mass automobile use; yet even there, a substantial part of the population has no access to a car much of the time, and because of the pattern of the city it may have no adequate public transportation and no capacity to serve the needs of pedestrians. Some planners in Britain and elsewhere believe that the circle can be squared: that with sufficient attention to densities and groupings of activities, it is possible to design a low-density suburban form that supports free use of the private car and also an adequate, frequent, and cheap mass transit service. But there is no practical working proof of this yet; and some experts are beginning to think that a time will come when the whole population will come to depend on private transport in some way or another. Others see a possible revulsion against the use of the car, though for this there is little physical evidence; yet others foresee the development of a hybrid type of vehicle, which will give the flexibility of the private car and the compactness and efficiency of the public transport system.

It seems clear to us that cities will indeed change over the decades ahead—change in physical form, but even more in function and in operation. Whatever the forms of transportation, the workers and residents of cities in the future will have far more flexibility of movement even than at present, and will demand far more in terms of gracious living. This is abundantly clear already if one looks at the progress of the great bulk of the population in the two nations since the 1930s, or if one compares the greater material affluence of the average American today with that of his British counterpart. But as we have tried to stress, it would be a great mistake to see this progress merely in terms of private consumption. Though the British sacrificed equity and even perhaps economic growth in their determination to conserve and improve the natural environment, it may well be that in this regard they grasped a mood that swept their country thirty years before it swept the United States. We should expect that in the future both countries will present the same central problem: the desire on the part of the mass of the population both to eat their cake and have it, in terms of a high level of private space consumption together with strong public controls over the quality of the environment.

These probable trends in the city of the future raise important issues of public policy; trends are not inevitable, but choices are possible. The issues must be resolved by political processes. To this, we turn in chapter 9.

chapter 9

Lessons to be learned

As one contemplates the experience with urban growth and development in Britain and in the United States over the past twenty-five years, what lessons does that experience seem to offer for the future? In particular, how far does experience in the other country offer some guides to future policy?

Obviously, these are not simple questions to answer. Even were the past experience wholly known and understood—and the more one studies it and accumulates knowledge about it, the more one realizes that understanding is limited—there would still be difficult problems in trying to distill that experience into "lessons." Such a distillation is necessarily a somewhat subjective one; other persons, looking at the same record, might well draw different conclusions. Nevertheless, we offer for the reader some of our thoughts on the subject, as we review and contemplate this experience.

THE NEED FOR EXPLICIT GOALS

First of all, the goals, objectives, and purposes of urban planning and urban land use control should be more explicitly articulated than they have been in the two countries in the past quarter century. The goals and objectives of the British Town and Country Planning Act of 1947 may have been clearly formulated in the minds of its proponents, although one may express doubts even here; but those goals and objectives seem not to have been so clearly understood and supported by the electorate at large. Substantial changes in the original concept were made, even in the act itself; in turn, the financial keystone of the whole structure was drastically modified by Parliament about six years later; in operation, the act has gone far astray from the original objectives—and all this, apparently, without any really effective voices being raised to point out what was going on. In the United States the situation has been far worse. National legislation and local ordinances have been enacted the goals and purposes of which must have been most imperfectly understood. The record shows much action that can charitably be described as inconsistent, but to which little objection was raised on this account.

A suggestion that goals and purposes of legislation and of governmental programs be explicitly articulated may seem a little like a recommendation in favor of virtue and against sin—and to some extent it is. Legislation is frequently passed in each country precisely because it is vague, so that different persons and groups may support it in the hope that it means what they want it to mean; and programs are frequently established vaguely by legislation, only to be worked out explicitly in practice, sometimes in directions unforeseen or even opposed at the time of the legislation. But legislation based on vagueness has its dangers; unless or until the resultant program develops some real popular support, it is fragile and in danger of repeal or perversion.

Each country has clearly, and we think finally, turned its back upon a totally free market in suburban land, in urban growth, and in related aspects of the growing modern metropolis. But neither country has clearly established what it wishes to accomplish with the land use and other controls that have modified the free market for land. Until there can be greater agreement on goals and objectives, operating governmental programs will inevitably lack clear guidance.

One important need is that such goals and objectives should be set out clearly in terms of human welfare. This sounds elementary, almost obvious; but it is remarkable to notice how often it has been ignored in the past. Where objectives have been voiced, they tend to have been presented as absolute moral imperatives, almost entirely unrelated to any discussion of the aspirations and needs of the mass of the people. In Britain it was assumed that agricultural land *must* be saved at all cost; that life in large cities was *necessarily* bad; that densities *should* be raised. Occasionally in the mass of documents, as in the writings of Howard or in the Barlow report, one finds an attempt at reasoned justification for these precepts. Most of the time they seem simply to have been accepted as revealed truth. In the United States there seems to have been a similar avoidance of discussion of basic issues, though it came about in a different way. The private market provided what it thought Americans wanted, and they in turn appeared to approve of it by buying it. But for much of the time there was no alternative to the standard low-density, single-family housing that the speculative builders provided. Significantly, when these same builders went into other sorts of housing—suburban apartment blocks, or town houses built in clusters—quite large sections of the public revealed that they approved of these types also. What was lacking in both countries was a meaningful public discussion about the life-styles different people might want to lead, and about how these would best be served in terms of a choice of different physical designs. In both countries the public were simply fobbed off with the familiar; they could hardly be expected to guess that anything different was possible and might serve their needs better.

A New Stress on Equity

This in turn relates to a second point: that the distributional or equity or welfare aspects of urban land use planning and of urban development should be frankly faced. These aspects have had far less attention than have the efficiency aspects. Most debate and discussion have been in terms of the costs of alternative ways of city growth; but all policies and programs have differential effects upon different groups within the whole population. At the very least, it seems to us, the probable nature of such effects should be studied and estimated before legislation is passed or before governmental programs are implemented.

It is absurd to ignore the fact that some groups or some individuals gain from any program of land use control, while other groups or individuals lose from the same program. No effective program can be wholly neutral in its income-distribution effects; indeed, one purpose of programs may be to achieve a degree of income redistribution. What are the probable income-redistribution effects of a proposed legislation or program? Do we really want those effects? If we want something else, are we prepared to modify the program to achieve a desired end? Are we willing to offset one set of undesired effects by a program in a different field, which will leave the injured persons no worse off?

We have noted that suburbanization, as it has actually worked in practice in each country, has worked to the advantage of the upper-income groups and to the disadvantage of the lower-income groups. In this sense, it has been regressive; its benefits have accrued to higher-income persons, its real costs have fallen most heavily on lower-income persons. Possibly this type of regressive result was actually sought in each country. We doubt it; there is nothing in the available record that suggests such regression was desired and intended. But there is precious little in the record to show that the regressive results of land planning and land use controls were understood, much less that they were effectively opposed on this ground of regressivity. The containment of city spread in Britain may have greatly benefitted those who wished to preserve the countryside as it was; but it cost the lower-income classes dearly as housing costs rose beyond their ability to buy new houses, and it cost the middle-income classes as they were forced to accept higher densities and smaller lots than they—or at least many of them—would have chosen. Such a program obviously has support from its beneficiaries, and in Britain they seem to have been in politically strategic positions. But does the substantial class, which is not greatly affected personally by this program, realize its consequences and approve them? In the United States, the lack of effective control over suburban land use and the several public measures aiding land speculators have obviously benefitted this class, at the expense of the same groups that have lost in Britain. Again, does the mass of people, many not directly affected either way by these programs, realize what is happening and approve of it? Perhaps no one can be expected to carry a fight for the interest of the poor—and they seem unable to do it effectively for themselves—but we think the intellectual community has more responsibility to point out clearly what is happening than seems to have been acknowledged.

THE CONTROL OF LAND PRICES

The means adopted to control suburban land use or to control the spread of cities should be appropriate and adequate to the goals. We think relatively little is accomplished, and much harm may be done, by promulgation of high-sounding goals, which cannot be translated into action because the necessary tools are lacking. Yet, as we look at the record, that seems to have been done repeatedly in each country.

Land use planning and permission to develop in Britain does not always ensure that development actually takes place exactly as planned; even more, when it does do so there is no control over the costs of the land to the developer or of the consequences of the rising costs that may ensue. Planning that limits land supply, without attempting to control land prices, gives a substantial degree of monopsony power to the landowner; he can simply sit back and wait for developers to meet his terms, reasonably secure that the government has created an effective monopoly for him. The situation is not quite so bad in the United States, simply because land use planning and land zoning are so much more ineffective; but even here there is some degree of monopoly power conferred by public action. The consequences in both countries have been steeply rising land prices—almost certainly more rapidly rising than would have been the case in a completely free land market; the consequences of rising land prices have been higher costs of finished houses— higher not only by the amount of the increased land price, but higher also because the larger size and more luxurious nature of the house has resulted in higher costs also, in order that the land cost will not seem an unreasonably high proportion of the price of the finished house. In Britain, rising land costs have been a powerful factor inducing building at very high densities—densities which in another generation will make the houses functionally obsolete long before they are physically obsolete.

We cannot see any real change in urban and suburban land conversion, from rural to urban uses, that will be significantly different from the past, unless or until some real control is exercised over raw land prices. This control might take various forms: direct government purchase at prices only modestly above alternative use values (with later resale or long-term lease to developers), retention of a private market but some form of restriction on mark-up above previously paid prices, etc. Or it might take the form of reduced income tax incentive, or of increased local taxes on land withheld from development. The U.S. real estate tax on idle suburban land generally does not conform to the law, being far lower than it should be; but in Britain there is no tax (rate) on unimproved land, so that even the mild pressures of the United States are lacking. Each country, if it chooses, can continue to treat owners of developable suburban land with tenderness, helping them by government action to obtain large gains in increased land value, which they could never win in a free market; but neither country can expect to have moderately priced new housing on reasonable-size lots as long as it continues to treat landowners so tenderly.

THE ROLE OF LOCAL GOVERNMENT

Each country has entrusted land use planning and control to local units of government with demonstrated incapacity to use such power in a national interest. In Britain, the rural counties and the cities each have had the power to make land use plans and to give or to refuse planning permission. The cities have had the people but little undeveloped land; the counties have had ample land but, in many cases, have had an antipathy to urban growth, whether residential or industrial, and have fenced the cities in. Although the plans of each have been subject to review and approval by the Ministry, often after change, the Ministry has not generally seen fit to impose a land use plan appropriate to the entire metropolitan area. The results have been pernicious and contrary to all good concepts of humane land use planning: congestion of commercial land uses and of traffic in the old city centers, often coupled with drastic and insensitive urban surgery; high-density urban renewal involving the use of high-rise blocks by the city housing administrations; crowded suburbs of homes that are functionally obsolescent almost the day they are finished. In the United States, satellite cities and towns and largely rural counties have often had the planning and zoning power; typically only small parts of their respective metropolitan complexes, they have acted in their own narrow interests, without regard for the effect of their actions upon the entire metropolitan situation. Their plans and actions have not been subject to review or control by any metropolitan, state, or federal agency, except to the very limited extent that was involved in state or federal grants.

There is only one way to end such a situation: to bring about a fundamental reform of local government on the basis of the metropolitan or city region principle, or alternatively to transfer planning and land use control powers to higher-level regional units of government. There is nothing to be gained by broad statements of national or regional urban growth policy so long as their implementation can be, and is, effectively blocked by small units of government. Here, indeed, is a classic case of the means being inadequate to the ends.

Britain in 1974 will implement a fundamental reform of local government. The details vary somewhat from Scotland to England and Wales, but over most of England and Wales the result will be to create big units for plan-making purposes, based as far as possible on the historic counties but combining cities and the surrounding rural countryside. This will be a considerable advance, but it is subject to two limitations. First it does not apply to the major urban agglomerations, where some of the biggest problems of land use planning arise; there, the metropolitan counties will still be faced by rural counties intent on guarding their interests. And second, in both types of county planning will be a divided responsibility; while structure plans will be made by the county authority, most local plans and all development control will be in the hands of local districts who may appoint their own planning staff. It would be premature to pass judgment on the reform until it has been in operation a few years, but there is a real danger that the new system will reproduce many of the worst vices of the old. In the United States, on the other hand, despite much fierce debate the prospects for local government reform seem as far away as ever. And even the so-called experiments in metropolitan government, as in the Minneapolis–St. Paul area, really represent loose coalitions of existing local governments that could collapse in the first serious storm.

In both countries the pressures for fundamental reform are potentially strong. Basically, the older cities are under increasing strain as their higher-income residents, and even their tax-producing commercial activities, move out to the suburbs.

They face increasing costs of providing welfare services, but find a decreasing tax base to fund them. This has been particularly evident in the United States for some years; it is now being recognized as a danger in Britain also. Migration to suburbs robs the inner city of potential social and political leadership; in the United States this is evident for black and white populations alike. It is clear that in both countries maintenance of the status quo helps the areas outside the city—the suburbs in the American case, the rural areas in the British—to conserve their way of life against the threat of a mass incursion of lower-income residents. In effect, these people are walled up within the city either in high-density public housing schemes or in shabby privately rented apartments. The fact that in Britain the public sector provides more of this urban housing, and that it is often of higher quality than its American equivalent, or that in the United States many of the city residents are black while in Britain most are white, does not alter the basic similarity between the two situations. Oddly, urban interests in both countries seem to have been relatively weak in pressing their case on politicians at the national level; but surely, as the common interest is better identified, this situation will rapidly change during the 1970s.

Even if such a reform were forthcoming, but still more if it were not, there is a strong case for the creation of what can be called semi-autonomous public corporations in the field of development and conservation. In different ways, the experience of both countries shows that such entities can be highly effective in varied roles ranging from the development of new communities to the preservation of fine landscapes or national monuments. It shows, too, that varying degrees of autonomy seem to produce good results: the former Ministry of Public Buildings and Works in Britain was a civil service department; the National Park Service of the U.S. Department of the Interior is an agency; the New Town Development Corporations and the Commission for the New Towns in England have a greater degree of autonomy resembling that of the boards of Britain's nationalized industries. In their different ways, they demonstrate the wisdom of Lord Reith, who in his 1945 committee report on the establishment of Britain's new towns, stated that to obtain strong positive action in new development it is desirable to sacrifice local democracy somewhat for a time. Put simply, a local democratic body is not an appropriate agency for creating a new town or a national park, any more than it would be for running an airline or a steel works. This does not mean that all democratic responsibility or control is abandoned; it does mean that the executive agency has to be given a good deal of day-to-day freedom to get on with its job. The traditional New Town Development Corporation may not be the only means of achieving what is needed; an agency based on local authority, with day-to-day freedom of operation, may prove a viable alternative.

Such an agency, working closely in cooperation with private enterprise, could play a particularly important role in developing new urban areas at the fringes of the existing metropolitan areas. We do not envisage these as fully self-contained new towns; but neither would they be mere residential suburbs. The new zones would, in fact, contain several different types of settlement as they developed, ranging from more or less pure suburbs to quite well-developed satellite towns with their own industry and commerce. They would also contain substantial areas of land preserved as open space for the enjoyment of the entire metropolitan area: a system of regional parks. The corporations building such new planned agglomerations would buy the land well in advance at fairly low prices. They might operate discreetly in the open market, but they would have to be given powers of eminent domain to ensure that they could buy at a fair price. Otherwise, they would undoubtedly find themselves paying speculative values that their existence had brought about—a paradoxical result that has always proved to be problematic in the establishment of new communities. This idea—of a public corporation establishing a whole regional complex of cities and towns, set against a background of open public parkland—was, in fact, the original vision of Ebenezer Howard and of his followers Raymond Unwin and Barry Parker. But, nowhere in the world has it been carried through as they imagined it. We believe that both nations could profitably return to these men's ideas.

An Optimal Rate of Urban Change

Review of the processes of urban growth and development in the United States and in Britain over the past twenty-five years confirms one's intuition that there is an optimum rate of social and economic change, one neither "too fast" nor "too slow," difficult though it may be to agree on what that optimum rate is. Cities of both countries, and indeed of the whole world, have been, are, and will be changing under the impact of various demographic, technological, economic, and social forces. As they grow larger in numbers of people, the cities must change, including change in parts of the city that do not increase in population. As transportation and other technologies change, the relation of one part of the city to another, or the functions of each part, must change also. As average real incomes per capita grow, people will demand many services and will engage in many activities not readily available to people whose real incomes were lower. And it seems fairly clear that many social forces, including different human goals and objectives, exert an influence on city form and functioning. So, whether one wishes it or not, cities must and will change in numerous ways.

But a modern city has an enormous built-in rigidity toward change. There are great investments in relatively long-lived structures, whose usefulness will continue for years or decades. And the incremental process of city building and rebuilding means that new structures are greatly influenced in location, size, and function by the existing structures, which are a major part of the economic and social environment for the new ones. On the purely physical side, the continued existence of a city in its present form is reinforced by a vast investment in facilities placed underground—electric power lines, water and sewer lines, telephone lines, and others, all basic to the functioning of a modern city but normally concealed from view. And the spatial layout of the city into blocks and lots may be equally influential. One need only recall how most cities rebuild on past lines after a disaster which, by destroying extensive areas, could theoretically offer an opportunity for reshaping the city's spatial layout. Inherited structure, sometimes reaching back many centuries, provides an enormous resistance to change.

But social and institutional resistance to change is probably even stronger. A city is a collection of people who have complex social and economic interrelationships. Each person lives by providing goods or services for others, each is dependent upon others for his social life in its broadest dimensions. The web of interpersonal relationships may individually be weak and fragile, but collectively it is enormously strong. Though these relationships are in constant process of change, at any time they can become a powerful force resisting change, especially change of large, unexpected, and undesired form.

Urban planning, with its planning permission in Britain and its land use zoning in the United States, seeks to reduce the rate of change in established urban areas; one of the common objectives of a land use plan is to "preserve the character" of an established residential district, for instance. And these tools have been fairly successful in attaining this objective. In the United States, where land use zoning and rezoning is so politically sensitive and vulnerable, the political pressures against change can often be more powerful than those pushing for change. One could make a good case that this resistance to change of established areas is sometimes not in the general public interest, however that might be defined. For instance, the obstacles to rebuilding decayed older-city residential areas are often great; the respect for or obeisance to private property rights prevents effective change. Without, at this moment, either endorsing the wisdom of the city stability or condemning it, we can assert that land use planning and associated measures, as actually found in each country, are powerful forces tending to slow down change in urban structure and function.

In Britain land use planning is equally a force against change in the growing edge of cities—the suburbs. While land use plans and planning permission do provide for additional areas of land, additional houses or other dwelling units, and for additional shops and industry, they clearly restrict the opportunities for such new growth below what a freely functioning competitive market would provide. The areas are restricted and specifically located; the densities of residential development are spelled out in detail, or are greatly influenced by land prices and land availability or both. In establishing some areas for development, others are restrained from development, and this is perhaps an equally important consequence of urban planning—that the rural countryside is preserved as it was and as many of its residents want it to be. Again, without at this point expressing a judgment as to the social wisdom of British land use planning, one can confidently assert that its major effect has been to reduce the rate of change in urban growth and development; indeed, although not expressed in these terms, that was one of its purposes.

In the United States land use planning and associated measures have had vastly less effect upon the location, nature, structure, and functioning of the new suburbs. While some efforts have been made to plan suburban growth, they have not often been carried into effect. Indeed, one of the dominant characteristics of the American land use planning system is that its unintended effects have been quantitatively more important than its intended effects. For instance, there is nothing in the record to indicate that the suburban sprawl, so ubiquitous and dominant, was intended by any land planning legislation. Yet, given the nature of the suburban land

market, including the proclivity of government to deal tenderly with land speculators, and given the nature of the public services built and the system for their
repayment, one can expect nothing else than the kind of sprawl one sees. While
land conversion and associated changes are facilitated under the American system
of suburban land use planning and control, these have also had a type of political
and social momentum that has made their guidance difficult.

To an American, the overwhelming desire of the British to preserve their agricultural land—to protect it against urban encroachment—seems an aggravated
instance of resistance to change. Although Britain has a highly productive agriculture, it has long since ceased to be an agricultural country. Although its agriculture
is producing more output from the same area of land or even from a shrinking
land base, the nation is dependent on foreign sources for much of its food, and
always will be. Its imports of agricultural products may be basic to its export of
industrial products. Although twice in the lifetime of older persons the country
has experienced serious food blockades in time of war, it is doubtful that any
future war will involve similar blockades. This method of waging war, if we must
have war, may be as obsolete for the future as is the cavalry charge or the long-
bow. Land has many functions in the modern age besides the production of food;
urban development, recreation, and other nonfood-producing uses may be as economic as food production. A generous, instead of niggardly, provision of land for
urban growth in Britain would still involve only a small fraction of the total land
area for one or two generations ahead. It would not drastically alter the population-
food balances, and it would greatly improve the quality of the country's cities and
suburbs. It is hard to imagine a more extreme case of land planning based on the
past, and intended to prevent change as far as possible, than the British reverence
for unspoiled rural areas.

In both countries land planning and associated measures have not evolved to
simplify and make easy the changes in land use that do occur. One need only read
the details of the long and often acrimonious struggles of some large British cities
to obtain land in a rural county to construct housing for their overspill populations.
Or one need only follow an American proposal to rezone land within a city or in
a growing suburb when there is both strong support and strong opposition. In
both cases it is clearly seen how slowly, creakily, and uncertainly the whole process
works. One is reminded of the ancient cars in the early days of mass motoring,
when to shift gears was always a sporting proposition (sometimes you made it,
sometimes you didn't, rarely smoothly, and sometimes you yanked out the clutch
or the rearend or broke an axle) and compare them with modern automobiles with
their smooth-flowing automatic transmissions. One cannot escape the conclusion
that the land use planning process is as antiquated and technically inefficient as
the mechanism of an antiquated car; as with the car, one may be unable to prescribe the engineering specifications of a better system, and yet be convinced that
the existing one is badly designed.

No small part of the land use problem arises from the fact that land use planning, as practiced in each country, is based essentially on a static society. Plans
are developed for a future date, with a specified population, income, employment,
residential density, and other characteristics. Relatively little attention is given to

the process of getting from here to there, and virtually none to what may happen after the planning date. When the plans are revised the process is repeated, with simply new dates and new figures inserted. If land use planning could focus on the processes of change in land use, analyzing the forces for and against change, finding ways in which those forces could be marshalled and weighed, and devising processes of facilitating change, one cannot help but think the contribution of land use planning would be greater than it has been this past quarter century—or than it promises to be in the next period if past processes continue.

The likelihood is that they will change. Many events—in Britain, the new planning system ushered in by the 1968 Act, and the new emphasis on systems approach to plan making and revision—seem to guarantee that in future planning will be more oriented towards processes. The plan-making sequence now stresses urban and regional systems and their interrelationships. The planner seeks to intervene in those processes with a reasonably good advance knowledge of what the total (direct and indirect) effects of his intervention will be. Furthermore, the new system explicitly starts with goals and objectives; it stresses choice among different future alternatives and the rational evaluation of these alternatives. Evidence exists of probable change in the United States also.

In thus becoming more process oriented, planning in both countries could become more efficient. But the intention also is to make it more democratic by introducing a strong element of public participation. The populace is to be asked to "vote," in some way as yet unspecified, for one or other of the alternatives formulated by the professional planners. It is clear that this poses difficulties; the results may be far from what were intended. Our study has demonstrated, and this chapter has emphasized, that there are those among the public who know clearly what they want; they are likely to be the people with something to lose. Those with something to gain, on the other hand, are likely to be vague about what they want. Thus the people in possession always have the stronger hand; and the greater the degree of participation, other things being equal, the greater the danger of a negative approach to planning. Participation could achieve the paradoxical result of being more democratic in a formal sense, and more regressive in its overall welfare impact.

There are ways of correcting this—at least to some degree. With greater education and better mass communication, poorer groups in the population are likely to become more conscious of their rights, and more willing to assert them. Many professionals may be willing to assist them by acting as advocacy planners for a whole or a part of their careers; society in general could recognize this role, and positively support it. A more open style of planning inquiry, in which an independent panel of assessors is deliberately appointed to take a sceptical and critical view of professional plans—as is evidenced in the British 1972 Town and Country Planning Act—may perform something of the same function, in practice. The United States seems to be taking the lead in advocacy planning; Britain is pioneering in the new-style planning inquiry, as exemplified by the Roskill Commission on the third London airport or the Greater London Development Plan inquiry.

For the future, therefore, we hope and expect that planning will become more sophisticated technically and also more controversial. The professionals, rightly, will try to increase their objective knowledge of, and their scientific control over, social and economic processes. But at the same time they will have to recognize that, at bottom, planning is essentially a political process in which groups and individuals campaign and coalesce in defense of their interests. Hopefully, by coming to understand more carefully the nature of the different language people use in arguing about planning—language in which the same word can come to have different meanings for different people—some element of reconciliation and of compromise can be reached. And, by more careful analysis of the impacts of planning decisions on different groups, society can hope to reach some sort of optimal solution—not perhaps that state imagined by Pareto, in which some were better off than before and no one was worse off, but at least a situation where the gains greatly exceed the losses. For gainers and losers from planning decisions there are and will be. Perhaps the chief lesson of this book is that in the past, this fact has not been frankly faced. In the future, it must.

index